ARDENT SPIRITS

Other Books by JOHN KOBLER

Capone: *The Life and World of Al Capone*

ARDENT SPIRITS

SPIRITS

The Rise and Fall of Prohibition

by JOHN KOBLER

London

MICHAEL JOSEPH

Illustrations will be found following pages 98 *and* 258

First published in Great Britain by
Michael Joseph Ltd
52 Bedford Square
London WC1B 3EF
1974

ISBN 0 7181 1252 0

Printed in Great Britain by
Hollen Street Press Ltd at Slough
and bound by Dorstel Press at Harlow, Essex

For Evelyn again and always

All laws which can be broken without any injury to another are counted but a laughing-stock, and are so far from bridling the desires and lusts of men, that on the contrary they stimulate them. For "we are ever eager for forbidden fruit, and desire what is denied." Nor do idle men ever lack ability to elude the laws which are instituted about things, which cannot absolutely be forbidden.

—Baruch de Spinzoa; *Of Aristocracy*

Contents

III. The Noble Experiment 1920–1934

Elegy for Hell's Best Friend

After one year from the ratification of this article the manufacture, sale or transportation of intoxicating liquors within, the importation thereof into, or the exportation thereof from the United States and all territory subject to the jurisdiction thereof for beverage purposes is hereby prohibited.

—The Constitution of the United States of America,
Article XVIII (January 29, 1919)

"IT is here at last—dry America's first birthday," proclaimed the Anti-Saloon League of New York.

The date was January 16, 1920, a Friday.

"At one minute past twelve tomorrow morning a new nation will be born. . . . Tonight John Barleycorn makes his last will and testament. Now for an era of clear thinking and clean living! The Anti-Saloon League wishes every man, woman and child a happy New Dry Year."

As the moment drew near, jubilant temperance leaders gathered in churches and auditoriums from coast to coast to hold watch night services. In San Francisco Miss Christine Tilling, an official of the local Women's Christian Temperance Union, hailed prohibition as "God's present to the nation." In Chicago the "White Ribboners," as the indomitable lady crusaders were popularly known after their insignia, dedicated themselves to drying up the rest of the world. In its invitations to a celebratory gathering at the Hempstead, Long Island, Presbyterian Church the local WCTU exhorted the faithful:

Let the church bells ring and let there be great rejoicing, for an enemy the equal of Prussianism in frightfulness has been over-thrown and victory crowns the efforts of the forces of righteousness. Let us see that no Bolshevistic liquor interests shall ever tear the Eighteenth Amendment from the Constitution of the United States.

The menace of Bolshevism was also preying on the minds of
the Nashville, Tennessee, chapter of the Anti-Saloon League as it
inaugurated a campaign to support enforcement of the new law
with the warning:

> Bolshevism flourishes in wet soil. Failure to enforce Prohibition
> in Russia was followed by Bolshevism.
> Failure to enforce Prohibition HERE will encourage disrespect
> for law and INVITE INDUSTRIAL DISASTER.
> Radical and Bolshevist outbreaks are practically unknown in
> states where Prohibition has been in effect for years. Bolshevism
> lives on booze.

Through the streets of Norfolk, Virginia, 20 pallbearers
escorted a horse-drawn hearse containing an effigy of John
Barleycorn. Behind it walked a masquerader dressed as Satan,
feigning hysterical grief. The cortege entered Billy Sunday's
tabernacle. "Good-bye, John!" roared the evangelist from the
tabernacle door. "You were God's worst enemy. You were hell's
best friend. I hate you with a perfect hatred. I love to hate you,"
and he promised his spellbound congregation of 10,000: "The
reign of tears is over. The slums will soon be a memory. We will
turn our prisons into factories and our jails into storehouses and
corncribs. Men will walk upright now, women will smile and the
children will laugh. Hell will be forever for rent."

The chief architects of prohibition assembled for their watch
night service in Washington's First Congregational Church.
There, toward midnight, William Jennings Bryan, who though
thrice defeated as a Democratic Presidential candidate had
rallied a multitude of voters to the temperance banner with his
flaming oratory ("You shall not bury the Democratic Party in a
drunkard's grave!"), mounted the pulpit, his great bald dome
shining like a beacon light, a smile of righteous triumph
distending his cavernous mouth. "They are dead which sought
the young child's life," the silver tongue declaimed, quoting the
Gospel according to St. Matthew. . . .

His listeners included Wayne B. Wheeler, the Anti-Saloon
League's wily general counsel; Bishop James Cannon, Jr.,
chairman of the Commission on Temperance and Social Service
of the Methodist Episcopal Church, South; Senator Morris
Sheppard of Texas, who introduced the Eighteenth Amendment

in the Capitol; Andrew Joseph Volstead, the tobacco-chewing, shoebrush-mustached Republican Congressman from Yellow Medicine County, Minnesota, who wrote the enforcing National Prohibition Act, commonly called the Volstead Act; Josephus Daniels, Secretary of the Navy and honorary president of the Fifteenth International Congress Against Alcohol. Daniels' major contribution to the cause had been to ban liquor from Navy vessels and Navy yards, as well as all areas under Navy control. Recalling, in this hour of victory, the protests of the wets that such untraditional strictures would ruin the Navy as a fighting force, he remarked: "I have ruined it every year since I have been Secretary of the Navy except during the period in which it was needed to win the war."

Under the Volstead Act "any person who manufactures or sells liquor . . . shall for a first offense be fined no more than $1000 or imprisoned not exceeding six months, and for a second offense shall be fined not less than $200 nor more than $2000 and be imprisoned not less than one month nor more than five years." Secretary Daniels followed Bryan to the pulpit to prophesy: "No man living will ever see a Congress that will lessen the enforcement of that law. The saloon is as dead as slavery!"

An equally radiant optimism sustained the officials charged with enforcement. At the Washington headquarters of the Prohibition Unit, a newly created division of the Bureau of Internal Revenue, Commissioner John F. Kramer—"Honest John" they called him in his native Mansfield, Ohio, where he had been practicing law—vowed: "This law will be obeyed in cities large and small, and in villages, and where it is not obeyed it will be enforced. . . . We shall see to it that [liquor] is not manufactured nor sold nor given away nor hauled in anything on the surface of the earth or under the earth or in the air."

For administrative purposes the country had been divided into ten departments, each headed by an assistant commissioner. In addition, each state had a federal prohibition director with an assistant and a legal adviser. At the lowest echelon, confidently poised for action, stood 1,500 recently invested, gun-toting revenue agents. Immigration and Customs officers plus tens of thousands of state, county and city police completed prohibition's army. "The penalties for violation are so drastic," trumpeted New York's chief revenue agent, Colonel Daniel Porter, "that the

people of New York will not attempt to violate it. There will be
no violations to speak of."

As a service to its readers the New York *Daily News* of January
16 spelled out what they could and could not do under the
Eighteenth Amendment:

> You may drink intoxicating liquor in your own home or in the
> home of a friend when you are a bona fide guest,
>
> You may buy intoxicating liquor on a bona fide medical
> prescription of a doctor. A pint can be bought every ten days.
>
> You may consider any place you live permanently as your
> home. If you have more than one home, you may keep a stock of
> liquor in each.
>
> You may keep liquor in any storage room or club locker,
> provided the storage place is for the exclusive use of yourself,
> family or bona fide friends.
>
> You may get a permit to move liquor when you change your
> residence.
>
> You may manufacture, sell or transport liquor for non-beverage
> or sacramental purposes provided you obtain a Government
> permit.
>
> You cannot carry a pocket flask.
>
> You cannot give away or receive a bottle of liquor as a gift.
>
> You cannot take liquor to hotels or restaurants and drink it in
> the public dining rooms.
>
> You cannot buy or sell formulas or recipes for home-made
> liquors.
>
> You cannot ship liquor for beverage use.
>
> You cannot manufacture anything above one-half of one per
> cent in your home.
>
> You cannot store liquor in any place except your own home.
>
> You cannot display liquor signs or advertisements on your
> premises.
>
> You cannot remove reserve stock from storage.

In the same issue the *Daily News* announced the winner of its
weekly limerick contest, one Fred Wolfe, whose prize entry ran:

> Whenever you go for a trip
> If you want an occasional nip
> You'd best take enough
> Of your own private stuff
> Take my tip, slip a sip in your grip.

A federal judge's last-minute decision sowed panic among the legion of tipplers who had been piling up reserves in warehouses and safe-deposit vaults against the coming of the great drought. Private hoards so stored, the judge ruled, would be liable to seizure after midnight of January 16; home would be the only inviolable depository. All day, all over the country chaos reigned as the frantic hoarders commandeered everything on wheels they could find to convey their liquid treasure from condemned shelters to domestic sanctuary. Booze-laden flivvers, limousines, vans, horse-and-buggies snarled street traffic, while pedestrians struggling with luggage, go-carts, baby carriages and receptacles of every description turned the sidewalks into obstacle courses. In New York's Hotel McAlpin a visitor summoned the public stenographer and dictated his will: "I give and bequeath to my three sons and two daughters equal portions and shares of my valued stock of champagnes, whiskies and cordials now contained in the wine cellar of my country home in York Harbor, Maine."

The liquor dealers, meanwhile, were rushing their stock to railway yards and piers for shipment abroad before the fateful hour struck, but the available freight cars and vessels could handle only a small fraction. The Kentucky distillers, having failed to export 35,000,000 gallons of bourbon, worth about $400,000,000, now stood in peril of losing the lot to the government. (The owners were eventually licensed to dispense it for medicinal purposes.) The Green River Distilling Company of New York had no sooner loaded the last of a $150,000 consignment of whiskey aboard a Hudson River barge than a slab of ice smote the barge and sank it. A salvage crew toiled in vain to raise the precious cargo before midnight, and the government laid claim to every bottle. A disgusted Providence, Rhode Island, brewer offered each of his stockholders two barrels of beer in lieu of a final dividend. Rather than surrender his stock to the government, a brewer in Passaic, New Jersey, threatened to dump it all into the Passaic River. When midnight came, there remained altogether in bonded warehouses close to 70,000,000 gallons of forbidden beverages. A California vintner took such a dark view of the future that he killed himself.

A feeling of unreality gripped the saloon habitués of the big cities. "Christy," a stunned New York bartender named Bleeck asked his Congressman and long-standing customer, Christopher

D. Sullivan, "are they really going to enforce it?" "Yes, I think so," the Congressman replied. "There won't be any more liquor." The city editor of the New York *Herald Tribune*, Stanley Walker, who also frequented the bar, recorded the exchange in his book *The Night Club Era*, noting, "In later years they laughed at the memory of this curiously naïve conversation."

The popular urban pleasure palaces observed the death of the old era with a mixture of resignation, melancholy and forced gaiety. In New York City, where heavy snow was falling and the thermometer read 18°, mock obsequies marked the approach of midnight. That week the metropolis had been denounced in a statement signed by 1,000 upstate ministers as "the center of nullification and seditious activity to prevent the enforcement of the Eighteenth Amendment." Tom Healey, the owner of the Golden Glades Restaurant, a resort renowned for its ice-skating extravaganzas, had a coffin paraded around the dance floor for everybody to throw his last bottle and glass into. Louis Fischer, who ran Reisenweber's café, had sent black-bordered cards to his regular clientele, bidding them to a funeral ball. The ladies who accepted received vanity cases in the shape of coffins. At midnight six waiter-pallbearers carried a real coffin across the room to the strains of Chopin's "Funeral March." The liveliest tune heard in the Hotel Vanderbilt's Della Robbia Room was "Good-by Forever" while the management distributed free champagne. (Elsewhere the price of the last legal drinks soared from a preprohibition 40 to 60 cents to $3.) At the Majestic Hotel the star comedian, Dan Healey, impersonated "Mr. Prohibition," the Tartuffe-like figure created by Rollin Kirby in his antidry cartoons—undertaker's stovepipe hat and black gloves, gimlet nose and cruel mouth. The most elaborate mummery was staged by a visiting Philadelphia publisher, George Sheldon, who took over an entire dining room at the Hotel Park Avenue. His guests, 200 of them, wearing black clothes as instructed, were seated at tables covered, like the walls and candelabra, with black cloth. The tableware had black handles. Napkins and glasses were black. The waiters, all in black, served black caviar. An enormous black coffin full of black bottles occupied the center of the room, and a black-clad band played funeral dirges. Following a midnight toast, the lights went out and spotlights framed a mournful *tableau vivant:* At a rear table two couples poured the last drops from a black bottle into their black glasses, sobbing and dabbing at their eyes.

For liquor lovers thus bereaved a remote solace was suggested when Sir Oliver Joseph Lodge, the British physicist and spiritualist, who had come to the States to lecture on life after death, disclosed a conversation with his late son. The younger Lodge, said his father, had mentioned the existence of strong drink in the great beyond.

Not all imbibers accepted their loss meekly. When a Brooklynite named Kiren Leishin entered his favorite saloon a few minutes after midnight and was refused a drink, he lay about him with a club, inflicting severe damage upon glassware, bottles and the proprietor.

The public libraries of New Haven, Connecticut, and Springfield, Massachusetts, among others, yielding to pressure from local temperance groups, withdrew all literature describing the manufacture of alcohol. But the director of the New York Public Library, Edwin H. Anderson, refused. "I would no more think of forbidding readers to consult such books," he said, "than I would ban books on aviation."

From London one of prohibition's martyrs, the Anti-Saloon Leaguer William Eugene "Pussyfoot" Johnson, sent home an exultant message. The year before, during a debate in London's Essex Hall, he had so enraged a group of university students with his fanaticism that they rioted. In the ensuing fracas he lost an eye. Now he had returned undaunted to London, his first stop on an international temperance tour. "This is a solemn moment for me," said Johnson, "because from this day the flag of my country will no longer float over any brewery or distillery. My flag is clean and from beginning to end our statute books will direct war against this traffic in human misery and debauchery."

Author Harry Golden remembers Gold's dollar-a-bottle sale
 After classes at CCNY, where I was taking night courses, I hurried over to Broadway to watch the excitement. I used to earn a few extra pennies delivering packages for Gold's liquor store, especially at Passover when the demands for sacramental wine were heavy. Gold's was on Forty-second Street and Broadway where the Rialto Theater now stands. The owner, a tall, thin man with a handlebar mustache

and a thick German-Jewish accent, ran a wholesale as well as a retail business. For 10 cents you could also buy a drink at his counter. He stocked some of the choicest stuff in town—Hennessy brandies, French vintage wines, the brands of scotch King George liked. After watching the crowds streaming in and out of places like Reisenweber's cabaret, where Doraldina danced the shimmy and the hula, Shanley's lobster palace and Bustanoby's Café des Beaux Arts, where the bachelor swells took their chorus girl friends—all about to close their doors forever—I decided to see how my old boss was getting along. I found him moving his stock out to the sidewalk, all those wonderful wines and liquors, and selling them at $1 a bottle. Yes, and throwing in an extra bottle if you bought half a dozen. He was that sure the end of drinking in America had come. So was I. So was everybody I knew. (But some of Gold's customers weren't quite so pessimistic. Not many years later I saw a lot of those same bottles selling in fancy speakeasies at $20 and up.)

When I got home that night to our railroad flat on the Lower East Side, I found my father, Leib Goldhirsch, who was a teacher and a Bal Tvilah—an auxiliary cantor at the synagogue—in a mood of sorrowful resignation. He'd always been against prohibition. He saw it as a political game, not a moral reform. Every week as far back as I can remember he'd been buying one bottle of Pennsylvania Rye Whiskey. I can still see the label—WE GUARANTEE THIS WHISKEY HAS BEEN AGED IN WOOD FOR TEN YEARS BEFORE BOTTLING. It cost $1.85. An imperial quart, mind you, not a fifth. Occasionally my father would let me have a sip. We'd finished that week's bottle, and we never expected to see another.

Gordon Brown, retired businessman of Montclair, New Jersey, remembers his last preprohibition drink

It was getting close to the deadline when my mother asked me to run out and buy a bottle of brandy and a bottle of whiskey for medicinal use. And she meant medicinal use, too. We weren't a hard-drinking family. We had no culture of wine or whiskey in our background. My father, a bicycle dealer and later tire manufacturer—as a matter of fact, he imported the first pneumatic tire into America—would serve a little wine when guests came to dinner, and after an evening of whist with her club ladies my mother might offer them each a thimbleful of cherry bounce, a concoction she made herself. She simply added sugar to sour cherries and steeped the cherries in brandy. Then after a month or two she'd pour off the brandy and squeeze the liquid out of the cherries, and so she'd get a brandy with a strong cherry flavor. . . . As a high school student I would keep a case of beer in the cellar for my friends and later a bottle of sauterne.

For me prohibition had already started two years before, in 1917, when it became illegal to serve liquor to soldiers. I was in training camp at Fort Myer, Virginia. My oldest brother, Sandy, came to visit me, and he took me to the Raleigh Hotel in nearby Washington for a drink. We had to have it in his room, and I had to take off my uniform or the waiter wouldn't have served me. We ordered Tom Collinses, and it turned out to be the most memorable drink I ever tasted. The weather was blistering hot as only Washington weather can get. The waiter arrived with these enormous glasses brimming with the Tom Collins ingredients and ice, but no water yet. He poured club soda over the ice, gave it a stir and held the glass up to my face. The bubbles hit my nose. I smelled the gin. It was exquisite.

For the bottles my mother wanted I went to a barrelhouse in Bloomfield where we used to drink beer when I was in high school. It wasn't a saloon. There was no bar to stand at. They'd serve you at a table if you wished, but mainly they dispensed bulk beer, wine and liquor from a long row of barrels on the counter. You brought your own container—a bottle or a bucket. The beer buckets were called growlers, and refilling them was known as rushing the growler.

I brought home mother's medicinal booze—house brands straight from the barrel costing under $2 each—but she never did open them. She hid those two bottles, and my brothers and I, we searched the house years after both our parents died, but we never found them.

Our attitude toward prohibition was fairly typical of the community we lived in. We were thoroughly sold by the Anti-Saloon League and the WCTU. We accepted the notion that liquor was bad for the economy, bad for the country in every way. We were no teetotalers, but we were willing to give up the small amounts of liquor we did enjoy for what we had been told was the common good. You might say we were motivated by a certain idealism.

I. Temperance 1609–1860

1. The True Instaurator

In folly, it causes him to resemble a calf,—in stupidity, an ass,—in roaring, a mad bull,—in quarrelling and fighting, a dog,—in cruelty, a tyger,—in fetor, a skunk,—in filthiness, a hog,—and in obscenity, a he-goat.

—Benjamin Rush, *An Inquiry into the Effects of Ardent Spirits upon the Human Mind and Body*

BENJAMIN RUSH was the young nation's preeminent man of medicine, the "Hippocrates of Pennsylvania," whose opinions carried for many of his countrymen the force of revelation. A graduate of the College of New Jersey (later Princeton) at the age of fifteen, he began his medical studies in Philadelphia, obtained his MD degree from the University of Edinburgh and got his early clinical experience in London and Paris. At twenty-four he was appointed professor of chemistry at the Philadelphia Medical College and, soon after, staff surgeon to the Pennsylvania Hospital. He was a co-founder of Dickinson College, the Philadelphia Dispensary and the College of Physicians. During the Revolution he served first as surgeon general of the Middle Department of the Continental Army, then as the Army's physician general. But Rush's enormous prestige did not stem from his professional distinctions alone. A friend of Benjamin Franklin (who had lent him money to pursue his studies abroad), of John Adams, Thomas Jefferson and George Washington, he had been a member of the Continental Congress and a signer of the Declaration of Independence.

Rush pontificated incessantly in papers and lectures on a diversity of medical, educational and philosophical topics. A good deal of his theories and therapy were at best nonsensical and at worst disastrous, though no more so than those of his colleagues. He may have killed as many patients as he cured by his reliance on bleeding and purgation for fever and violent exercise for tuberculosis. Yet in the dim light in which eighteenth-century medicine had to labor, Rush stood head and shoulders above most of the profession. His view of mental illness, for example, was humane and progressive far beyond the practices then prevalent in the bedlams where inmates were whipped, strapped into straitjackets and abandoned in solitary confinement. Rush suspected what modern psychiatrists know, that emotional states can produce physical disorders and vice versa, and he anticipated psychosomatic medicine.

Born near Philadelphia to a Quaker family, Rush fell early under the influence of Anthony Benezet, a saintly Quaker teacher and reformer of such humility that he implored his disciples not to attempt his biography, but to remember him only as "a Poor Creature," who "through Divine favor was enabled to know it." Passionately opposed to slavery, he founded a school for black children, endowing it with nearly all of his small fortune. Rush later helped to establish the first antislavery society in America.

During his declining years Benezet took up temperance work. Dismayed by the alcoholic excesses of Colonial society, not excepting his Quaker brethren, he published anonymously in 1774 the first American temperance pamphlet. It was entitled *The Mighty Destroyer Displayed, in Some Account of the Dreadful Havock made by the mistaken Use as well as Abuse of Distilled Spirituous Liquors, by a Lover of Mankind.* "An evil so amazingly great," Benezet wrote, "that, did not useful experience too fully prove it, it seems incredible, that any whom it concerns could possibly be so negligent as not to use the utmost endeavors to suppress the destructive MAN-BANE." He advocated "laying such high taxes upon distilled spirituous liquors . . . as will make the drinking of it sufficiently expensive to put it out of the reach of so great a number of insatiable drinkers. . . ."

Seventeen years later Congress did enact an excise liquor law, not as a temperance measure, but to raise desperately needed revenue. A tax of 11 cents a gallon was levied on spirits distilled from imported ingredients such as molasses and 9 cents a gallon on spirits distilled from domestic ingredients such as grain. The burden fell heavily on the farmers of western Pennsylvania, who first manufactured rye whiskey toward the middle of the century and had been developing the industry ever since as the most lucrative way to merchandise grain. Whiskey, in fact, had become their principal source of income. (The New England Puritans began distilling rum from West Indian molasses half a century earlier but produced other profitable articles of commerce. Kentucky corn liquor or bourbon came much later, the first distillery in Bourbon County dating from 1789.) Inflamed by what they considered a violation of states' rights, the Pennsylvanians rebelled. They assaulted the tax collectors, tarred and feathered them and set fire to barns belonging to farmers suspected of informing. The Whiskey Rebellion raged along the Monongahela River for two years, culminating in a meeting of about 7,000 people at Parkinson's Ferry on August 1, 1794, to protest the removal of several moonshiners to Philadelphia for trial. When Pennsylvania's Governor Thomas Mifflin defied an order to call out the state militia, President Washington mustered 15,000 troops from Pennsylvania and three neighboring states. It was the government's first such exercise of its constitutional authority. Led by Colonel Henry "Light-Horse Harry" Lee, the father of Robert E. Lee, the militia swiftly quelled the uprising. The distillers thereafter acknowledged the superior power of the federal government and dutifully paid their liquor taxes, those, that is, who did not "bootleg" the stuff, a term derived from the old smugglers' trick of transporting contraband in receptacles tucked into the tops of their boots.

Benjamin Rush came to share his older friend's concern about intemperance, and as both Army physician and private practitioner he devoted himself to combating the "Man-Bane." In doing so he challenged a tradition deeply cherished by his fellow Americans.

So highly did the colonies prize booze that their statutes regulating its sale spoke of it as "one of the good creatures of God, to be received with thanskgiving." In some communities it was traditional to seal a bottle of whiskey in the cornerstone of a new church or public building. Taverns were not only licensed to sell liquor, but required by law to keep sufficient supplies on tap. Few business transactions were consummated, few births, christenings, graduations, marriages or investitures were celebrated without torrential libations. The patroon De Peysters of the Hudson Valley toasted the appearance of a new infant in heroic drafts of caudle, a hot punch, using a family recipe that called for gallons of madeira. Harvard University operated its own brewery, and commencements grew so riotous that rigid rules had to be imposed to reduce "the Excesses, Immoralities and Disorders." Of Chief Justice John Marshall, his associate on the Supreme Court, Judge Joseph Story, recalled: "The chief was brought up on Federalism and Madeira and he is not the man to outgrow his early prejudices. The best Madeira was that labeled 'The Supreme Court,' as their Honors the Justices used to make a direct importation every year, and sip it as they consulted over the cases before them every day after dinner, when the cloth had been removed." Funerals occasioned marathon drinking bouts. Following the services held for Peter Jacobs Marinus, a prominent New York merchant, twenty-nine gallons of wine and half a vat of beer were consumed. Workmen received part of their pay in rum, and their employers would set aside certain days of the year for total inebriety.

Hard liquor had the endorsement of doctors, who prescribed it for practically every affliction from painful teething in infancy to the aches of old age. According to the medical mythology of the era, rum-and-milk was a boon to pregnant women, as well as nursing mothers. Rum-soaked cherries supposedly prevented colds. The plethora of cure-all tinctures, tonics and elixirs contained mainly alcohol and colored water. A life insurance company increased its premiums by 10 percent for the abstainer, whom it considered "thin and watery, and as mentally cranked, in that he repudiated the good creatures of God as found in alcoholic drinks."

Jacob Carter of Philadelphia, rescued from a "drunkard's grave," remembers his first drink*

[I was] then seven years of age. I had then and still have, a very indulgent father, who, in order to gratify me and tickle my fancy, placed to my mouth that of a demijohn, expecting undoubtedly, that I would merely inhale the fume thereof, and being considerably beyond its equilibrium my mouth (involuntarily it may have been) became filled with the very palatable liquid, which, I have since understood was choice Madeira. One mouthful (believe me when I tell you, that it went beyond the orifice of my face), coupled with my then extreme youth,

* *My Drunken Life, and Original Songs.* 1848.

suffered to place me in that condition, which champagne, brandy, gin, whiskey, &c, &c, have had the credit for the last twenty years of effectually establishing, i.e. a DRUNKARD. . . . I commenced loving my daily glass, my age then twelve years. My parents observing, from time to time, that such was the case, and that those whom I had selected as associates, were far from being morally inclined, resolved to have me removed from the "City of Brotherly Love" (the place of my nativity) to a boarding school under the direction of the religious Society of Friends. . . . Drinking had already awakened in my mind a spirit of adventure, and a recklessness as regards affection for family or home; I therefore cheerfully coincided with my mother, not that I expected or desired to be benefited in a Christian sense. . . . [After many drunken adventures which took him back and forth across the country, he reached New York.] Got on a spree, walked the street two or three nights: went to painting for my board; got drunk, left that, and started down Pearl street, for the purpose of shipping on board a whaler: could not find the office: continued drinking: got a head on me about double the ordinary size: engaged to attend a policy office and drug store, for a New Yorker, got drunk, left him: went to board with a man by the name of K., was taken sick one day, and while lying in bed, saw a large snake and other reptiles under the bed: started up, laid down again, saw the most awful looking characters that any one can imagine. In fact, a person in his right mind cannot imagine any such appearances. Men without noses, some with only one eye and that in the middle of his face; and each and all of them glaring at me. . . . I distinctly recollect chasing them about the room hitting, and apparently dashing to pieces vermin about the walls and floor . . . I ran until I reached the Tombs; entered and called for an officer. K. entered. I told my story: he told his: I was coaxed into a cell down stairs. Having entered, the door was bolted. I immediately saw a scorpion spring towards me from the wall. I screamed, fell and lay there forty-eight hours. I do not mean that I lay still, but that I was out of my mind. I thought I was sentenced to die, for one thing or another, but the judge said I might take my own life if I preferred doing that. I recollect looking for a knife, but could not find one. . . . I was carried to the lunatic asylum; was kept there two weeks, then discharged; went to Boston, from thence to Bangor; thence to Boston, from there to New York, then to Philadelphia, became bloated with rum, and without a place to lay my head; discarded by my relatives, and whilst in this degraded state was picked up drunk by Barney Corse, a Philanthropist,

*and through his interposition and encouragement, I am what I
am.. . . .*

No class imbibed more freely than the clergy. "I could reckon
among my acquaintances forty ministers," wrote the Reverend
Leonard Woods, a professor of theology at Andover Seminary,
"and none of them at a great distance, who were either
drunkards, or so far addicted to drinking, that their reputation
and usefulness were greatly impaired, if not utterly ruined. I
could mention an ordination which took place about twenty
years ago at which I myself was ashamed and grieved to see two
aged ministers literally drunk, and a third indecently excited."

When ministers visited a parish to take part in the religious
services surrounding an ordination, the customary scene of
after-church hospitality was the local tavern. The charges
incurred by such a group of celebrants in Hartford, Connecticut,
ran as follows:

	£	s.	d.
To keeping ministers,			
2 mugs toddy,		2	4
5 segars,		5	10
1 pint wine		3	9
3 Lodgings,		9	
3 Bitters,			9
3 Breakfasts		3	6
15 Boles punch	1	10	
24 dinners	1	16	
11 bottles wine		3	6
5 Mugs flip		5	10
5 Boles punch		6	
3 Boles toddy		3	6

At the ordination of the Reverend Edwin Jackson in Woborn,
Massachusetts, in 1729, the community footed the bill for six and
a half barrels of hard cider, twenty-five gallons of wine, two
gallons of brandy and four gallons of rum.

That austere Boston divine Cotton Mather, despite his lifelong
crusade against intemperance, was not above sanctioning piracy
to secure a cargo of rum. In 1682 he wrote to his friend, "ye Aged
and Beloved Mr. John Higginson":

There is now at sea a ship called the Welcome, which has on board an hundred or more of the heretics and malignants called Quakers, with W. Penn, who is the chief scamp, at the head of them.

The general court has accordingly given secret orders to Master Malachi Muscott, of the brig Porpoise, to waylay the said Welcome, slyly, as near the Cape of Cod as may be, and make captive the said Penn, and his ungodly crew, so that the Lord may be glorified, and not mocked on the soil of this new country with the heathen worship of these people. Much spoil can be made by selling the whole lot to Barbadoes, where slaves fetch good prices in rum and sugar, and we shall not only do the Lord great service by punishing the wicked, but we shall make great good for his ministers and people.

Master Muscott feels hopeful and I will set down the news when the ship comes back.

Yours in ye bowels of Christ,
COTTON MATHER.

The *Porpoise* failed to intercept the *Welcome*, and William Penn proceeded unharmed to the Quaker colony of Pennsylvania, where he built, as an adjunct to his mansion, his own brewery.

For most early Americans, young or old, male or female, the day began with a tumbler full of rum or whiskey taken upon arising as an "eye-opener." They then sat down to a breakfast accompanied by a copious flow of spirits. In the South it might be mint-flavored whiskey or a fruit cordial. In New York the breakfast beverages were likely to include Dutch-brewed beer, genever—Dutch gin, colloquially called strip-and-go-naked and blue ruin or applejack (Jersey lightnin'). In New England hard cider and rum were favored. At 11 A.M. everywhere offices, shops and factories closed while the employees repaired to tavern or pothouse for their " 'leven o'clock bitters," a liquory interlude that was repeated daily at 4 P.M. So faithfully did the inhabitants of Portland, Maine, honor the observance that on the dot of 11 and again at 4 a bell in the town hall tolled. The term "bitters" covered a multitude of potent concoctions, among them toddies, a mixture of rum, sugar and the pulp of roasted apples, drunk hot or cold according to the season; slings or long sups (half spirits, half water, sweetened and spiced); flips, also called tiffs (rum, beer and sugar, to which a burned, bitter flavor was imparted by stirring with a red-hot "flip iron"); meridians (brandy and tea); manathan (beer, rum and sugar); hotchpotch (the same, warmed); sillabub (warm milk, wine and sugar). . . . Rum, whiskey and brandy sluiced down lunch and dinner, and before bedtime prayers a nightcap or two was deemed an indispensable precaution against night chills.

Besides these more or less fixed drinking periods, numerous opportunities for a nip arose in the course of an average day. Shopkeepers would stand a barrel of rum by the entrance and, when customers dropped in to pay a bill or place a large order, urge them to help themselves. Social calls almost always began with a welcoming dram and ended with a stirrup cup.

Though rum and whiskey remained the liquid staples of both rich and poor, the rich householders stocked imported liquor as well, a favorite being arrack, a fiery Far Eastern brandy distilled from palms, and heavy sweet wines like port, malaga, canary and madeira. Prosperous New Yorkers doted on sangaree—red wine, water, lemon juice and nutmeg—while their New England peers were partial to mead and metheglin, distillations of honey and yeast. Where even the standard commercial product proved too costly for a poor man, he devised his own intoxicant from whatever nature's bounty brought to hand. He made peachy and perry, that is, hard cider from peaches and pears; beer from sassafras and pine sap; wine from elderberries, pumpkins, cornstalks, hickory nuts and birch bark.

In 1792 there were 2,579 registered distilleries in the United States, which then had a population slightly above 4,000,000. Production, as reported to tax assessors, totaled 5,200,000 gallons, and consumption, counting imported spirits, came to 11,008,447, or an average of about 2½ gallons for every man, woman and child in the country. Within the next eighteen years the number of distilleries increased to 14,191, and consumption, again taking into account both domestic and foreign spirits, tripled. Yet the population had not even doubled. This brought the per capita consumption to almost 4½ gallons. If, moreover, the probable nondrinkers were omitted and the number of illicit stills estimated, the average annual intake of the actual drinkers appeared vastly greater—at least 12 gallons.

Though temperance leaders have claimed them as spiritual ancestors, the nation's Founding Fathers tended to preach abstemiousness somewhat more than they practiced it. John

Adams, to be sure, was a lifelong foe of the public house, who recalled in his old age:

Fifty-three years ago I was fired with a zeal, amounting to enthusiasm, against ardent spirits, the multiplication of taverns, retailers and dram-shops and tippling-houses. Grieved to the heart to see the number of idlers, thieves, sots and consumptive patients made for the use of physicians in these infamous seminaries, I applied to the court of sessions, procured a committee of inspection and inquiry, reduced the number of licensed houses, &c. But I only acquired the reputation of a hypocrite and an ambitious demagogue by it. The number of licensed houses was soon reinstated, drams, grogs and setting were not diminished, and remain to this day as deplorable as ever.

Adams himself emptied a large tankard of hard cider every morning before breakfast. In 1774, when the Continental Congress was sitting in Philadelphia, he professed to be shocked by the extravagance of the food and liquor provided, but could not resist them. "A mighty feast again," he noted in his journal; "nothing less than the very best of Claret, Madeira, and Burgundy. I drank Madeira at a great rate and found no inconvenience." And not long after: "A most sinful feast again . . . punch, wine, porter, beer, etc."

The Washingtonians, an early nineteenth-century confraternity of teetotalers, so named themselves after George Washington. It was an odd choice of patron hero, considering the first President's marked fondness for a drink. True, in a cautionary note to Thomas Green, a carpenter employed on his Mount Vernon estate, he wrote: "The sure means to avoid evil is—first to refrain from drink which is the source of all evil and the ruin of half the workmen in the country." Yet upon hiring a gardener not long before he had agreed to augment his regular wages by "four dollars at Christmas with which he may be drunk for four days and nights; two dollars at Easter to effect the same purpose; two dollars at Whitsuntide to be drunk for two days; a dram in the morning and a drink of grog at noon."

Even as William Penn owned a brewery in Philadelphia, so Washington installed a distillery at Mount Vernon. In 1766, having decided to send an intractable slave to the West Indies for resale, he instructed the ship's captain to bring back in exchange:

> One hhd of best molasses
> One ditto of best rum

One barrel of lymes, if good and cheap
One pot of tamarinds, containing about 10 lbs.
Two small ditto of mixed sweetmeats, about 5 lbs. each.
And the residue, much or little in good old spirits.

Under a Virginia statute a candidate for public office who
courted the voters' favor by treating them to food or liquor was
disqualified. Nevertheless, when the young Washington stood for
election to the Virginia House of Burgesses, he distributed among
the voters of Frederick County 160 gallons of beer, wine, cider,
punch and rum. After the election, which he won by a majority
of 310 to 15, he wrote to his campaign manager, James Wood: "I
hope no exception was taken to any that voted against me, but
all were alike treated, and all had enough. My only fear is that
you spent with too sparing a hand." During two later Virginia
campaigns, both victorious, he spent 115 pounds regaling the
voters.

In his amusing analysis of Washington's expense account as
Commander in Chief of the Continental Army Marvin Kitman
notes after an entry for September 7, 1775—"To Mr. Sparhawks
. . . Acc . . . £22":

> We might as well discuss General Washington's
> drinking habits, since these trips to stores
> like Mr. Sparhawk's recur so frequently in
> the expense account. . . .
>
> Washington never drank more than a bottle of
> Madeira at night, as all the historians say,
> besides rum, punch and beer. He preferred
> Madeira to all other beverages, as previously
> noted, but he was catholic—not presbyterian,
> episcopalian or hard-shell baptist—in his
> drinking habits. He often drank cider, cham-
> pagne and brandy. . . .
>
> Much of Washington's continuing good cheer
> and famed fortitude during the long years
> of the war, caused to some extent by his overly
> cautious military tactics, may have come
> from the bottle.

During Washington's first three months as President almost a fourth of his entire household expenses, totaling 741 pounds, 9 shillings, went for liquor.

Thomas Jefferson disliked hard liquor. At the end of his second Presidential term he complained:

> The habit of using ardent spirits by men in public office has often produced more injury to the public service, and more trouble to me, than any other circumstance that has occurred in the internal concerns of the country during my administration. And were I to commence my administration again, with the knowledge which from experience I have acquired, the first question that I would ask with regard to every candidate for office should be, "Is he addicted to the use of ardent spirits?"

Jefferson had no aversion to wine, however, and during his two terms he laid by $10,855 worth, personally supervising each selection. One contented guest, the Reverend Manasseh Cutler, reported: "You drink as you please and converse at your ease. . . . We enjoyed ourselves very well," while another guest pronounced Jefferson's champagne (which he served in the amount of one bottle for every three and one-seventh persons) "delicious . . . the best I ever drank."

Another Founding Father whose drinking habits afforded the temperance camp scant comfort was Benjamin Franklin. As an apprentice printer in London, it is true, he was so abstemious (though more from frugality than preference) that his beer-swilling co-workers dubbed him "the Water American." But at home during the Indian wars, commanding fifty Pennsylvania rangers, he rationed to each a daily gill of rum, and when the chaplain complained that they seldom attended prayer meetings, Franklin told him: "It is perhaps below the dignity of your profession to act as steward of the rum; but if you were to deal it out, and only just after prayers, you would have them all about you." The chaplain took this advice. "And never," Franklin observed, "were prayers more generally and more punctually attended."

He himself developed a taste for madeira and rum, and he usually drank a glass or two of punch in the evening. "You will say my *advice* smells of *Madeira*," he wrote to his friend, the English printer William Strahan. "You are right. This foolish letter is mere chitchat *between ourselves* over the *second bottle*." Franklin composed a number of drinking songs:

The Antidiluvians were all very sober,
For they had no Wine and they brewed no October;
All wicked, bad Livers, on Mischief still thinking,
For there can't be good Living where there is not good Drinking,

                                                    Derry down—

'Twas honest old Noah first planted the Vine,
And mended his morals by drinking its Wine;
And thenceforth justly the drinking of Water decry'd
For he knew that all Mankind by drinking it dy'd.

                                                    Derry Down—

From this Piece of History plainly we find
That Water's good neither for Body or Mind;
That Virtue and Safety in Wine-bibbing's found
While all that drink Water deserve to be drown'd.

                                                    Derry Down

So For Safety and Honesty put the Glass round.

Franklin's taproom conviviality moved his friend the Abbé
Guillaume Raynal, a French revolutionary propagandist, to
eulogize him in doggerel:

            Great in politics is he
            At the table gay and free;
            Founding empires, see him quaff
            Gay and grave as a capuchin
            Such is our Benjamin.

In his old age Franklin wrote to the abbé:

My Christian brother, be kind and benevolent like God, and do
not spoil his good work. He made wine to gladden the heart of
men; do not, therefore, when at table you see your neighbor pour
wine into his glass, be eager to mingle water with it. Why would
you drown the *truth*? . . . Do not, then, offer water except to
children; 'tis a mistaken piece of politeness, and often very
inconvenient. I give you this hint as a man of the world; and I will
finish as I began, like a good Christian, in making a religious
observation of high importance, taken from the Holy Scriptures. I
mean that the apostle Paul counselled Timothy very seriously to

put wine into his water for the sake of his health; but that not one
of the apostles or holy fathers ever recommended putting *water to
wine*.

Such prohibitory laws as the colonists enacted were intended
to prevent drunkenness, not to eliminate "the good creature of
God." The earliest attempt at prohibition in the New World was
made by General James Edward Oglethorpe when, in 1733, he
led a band of persecuted British Protestants and debtors to what
became the colony of Georgia. The ship that sailed them across
the Atlantic carried copies of Dr. Stephen Hales' *A Friendly
Admonition to the Drinkers of Brandy*. The second day after landing
Oglethorpe decreed that "the importation of ardent spirits is
illegal" because he feared lest liquor render the colonists
incapable of coping with the rigors ahead. Smugglers from South
Carolina sold them the rum they craved. Nine years later
Parliament rescinded Governor Oglethorpe's statute, and Georgia remained soaking wet for the next 166 years.

In the general view, abstinence as urged by Quaker Benezet
and his followers appeared unnatural, a fantasy of deranged,
bigoted minds. The Virginia Assembly required ministers to
reprove drunkards publicly. Judges who drank to excess during
court hours were fined 500 pounds for the first offense, 1,000
pounds for the second and, for the third, removed from the
bench. The Massachusetts Bay Colony defined excess as "more
than half a pint at one time" and forbade tippling "above ye
space of half an hour." Debauchees persisting in "the swinish sin
of drunkenness" were variously fined, whipped, thrown into
stocks, sentenced to wear a red "D" around their necks.
Connecticut assessed anybody found drunk in a private dwelling
20 shillings and the host, 10 shillings. New Hampshire posted the
names of drunkards. The Plymouth Colony disenfranchised
them. But the sources of liquor remained comparatively free of
restrictions. The only blanket embargo, which all the colonies
eventually imposed, was on the sale of liquor to Indians.

The liquor that the white man introduced to the Indians
proved as deadly as his gunpowder or his diseases. It ruined
whole tribes. Not that intoxicants were totally unknown to the
aborigines of North America before the invader came. Some of
the tribes roving the northeastern forests brewed a relatively mild
beer from both corn and maple sap. For a drink to enliven their

tribal rites the Huron of the Great Lakes devised a peculiarly revolting recipe. They would leave unripe corn to rot for months in a pool of stagnant water, producing a ferment loathsome to taste and smell, but mildly intoxicating. The Carolina Cherokee drank the fermented juices of wild fruits. The Koniaga, an Eskimo tribe inhabiting the otherwise alcohol-free far northwest, favored fermented raspberry and blueberry juice. The only Southwestern aborigines who tended to drink strong liquor to excess occupied what became lower California, Arizona and New Mexico. One of its chief sources was the pitahaya, a giant cactus flourishing on the high tablelands. From the pulp of its fruit the Pima, Maricopa and other redskins obtained a powerful intoxicant and once a year, at harvesttime, would gather for an orgy lasting a week or two. Only a third of the tribe would get drunk at a time, so that the sober two-thirds could protect them from each other's violence or from hostile tribes. In addition to pitahaya, the Southwestern Indians fermented alcoholic beverages from agave, mesquite pods, corn, wild prickly pear, wild grapes, wheat, honey, maguey or aloes (whose fermented juice produced pulque) and mescal (distilled pulque). A bizarre system of sharing their mesquite liquor existed among the Mexican Indians based at the confluence of the Gila and Colorado rivers. After the pods had fermented in a vat of water, they would chew them to extract the liquor, then spit them back into the vat to be rechewed over and over again by their fellow tribesmen.

With rare exceptions, none of these aboriginal intoxicants had a high enough alcoholic content or were in plentiful enough supply to permit general excess. Many tribes, in fact, never fermented a drop. It took the white man's liquor—his rum, whiskey, brandy and gin—to cultivate what appears to have been a latent alcoholic addiction common to the majority of Indians.

The first recorded encounter between an American Indian and European-manufactured liquor occurred in 1609, when Henry Hudson sailed his *Half Moon* into what is now New York Bay and put ashore on an island where some Delaware tribesmen were fishing. As a gesture of goodwill he offered them some brandy. The Delaware, completely ignorant of any fermented beverages, hung back, all but their chief who bravely drained a cup. After a burst of wild hilarity, he fell into a stupor

so profound that his comrades believed him dead. But when he
finally recovered, he described his sensations with such enthusiasm that they all clamored for some of the same. According to
legend, in memory of the ensuing debauch they named the island
Manahachtanienk, meaning in the Delaware tongue "the island
where we all got drunk," which the later colonists corrupted into
Manhattan.*

The seventeenth-century Ottawa chieftain John Le Blanc, or
"White John," as the British colonists called him, who with his
first drink acquired a lifelong passion for alcohol, replied, when
asked what ingredients he thought it contained: "Hearts and
tongues; for when I have drunken plentifully of it, my heart is a
thousand strong, and I can talk, too, with astonishing freedom
and rapidity."

Near its headwaters in Vermont the Connecticut River
plunges through a chasm about 400 yards long. Supposedly, the
only human who ever passed through it alive was an Indian girl.
She had meant to paddle her canoe across the river above the
chasm, but the current swept her off course. As she whirled
toward destruction, she seized a bottle of rum she had brought
along and drained it to the last drop. Her tribesmen managed to
haul her ashore at the far end of the chasm, blind drunk but
unhurt. She had emptied the bottle in the face of death, she
explained when able to talk, because come what may she could
not bear to waste any of the precious liquid.

"If your Excellency still intends to punish the Indians farther
for their barbarities," wrote Henry Gladwin, the British commanding officer at Detroit, to Lord Amherst, the Governor-Gen-
eral of Canada, after the defeat of the Ottawa tribes under Chief
Pontiac, "it may easily be done without expense to the crown by
permitting a free sale of rum which will destroy them more
effectually than fire and sword."

The colonial traders were already so destroying them. Liquor
was their principal medium of barter. The rich fur industry
largely depended on it. "The rum ruins us," one of the chiefs of
the Six Nations, Scarrooysdy, lamented during a treaty palaver
at Carlisle, Pennsylvania, in 1753:

> We beg you would prevent its coming in such quantities, by
> regulating the traders. We never understood the trade was for

---

* Most students of American Indian dialects agree that it means "the high island"—in
the physical, not the euphoric sense.

whiskey. We desire it may be forbidden, and none sold in the Indian country, but that if the Indians will have any, they will go among the inhabitants and deal with them for it. When these whiskey traders come, they bring thirty or forty cags, put them down before us, and make us drink, and get all the skins that should go to pay the debts we have contracted, for goods bought of fair traders, and by these means, we not only ruin ourselves, but them too. These wicked whiskey sellers, when they have once got the Indians in liquor, make them sell their very clothes from their backs. In short, if this practice be continued, we must be inevitably ruined. We most earnestly, therefore, beseech you to remedy it.

In the northeastern wilds the French voyageurs would exchange brandy for beaver pelts and, when the Indian trappers had thoroughly besotted themselves, swindle them out of more goods. The French Jesuit missionaries denounced the traffic and threatened to refuse absolution to those who persisted in it. For decades they threatened in vain.

Not conscience but fear finally led to the enactment of the first prohibition laws, for liquor was turning otherwise tractable Indians into homicidal maniacs. The effect they sought in alcohol was mystical and orgiastic, an illusion of Godlike or demonic omnipotence that made them dangerous to themselves and to others. Typically, upon reaching a trading post, a band of Indian fur trappers would trade part of their catch for clothes, weapons, food staples and a keg of rum. In council they would then decide who could get drunk and who must stay sober to watch over them. The latter hid all the weapons, and the debauch began. As soon as the keg of rum ran dry, the orgiasts would exchange some more of their furs for another keg, and so it went until the last pelt had been exchanged. By then the drunken Indians would be in a state of frothing frenzy, and no matter how hard their sober companions might try to prevent it, almost always there would be a killing or two before morning. Then the survivors, nursing head-shattering hangovers, stripped of all their valuables, would drag themselves off into the forests again in quest of more animals to hunt.

The French Jesuit Pierre Charlevoix, who came to Canada in 1705, wrote: "Husbands, wives, fathers, mothers, brothers and sisters, were frequently seen in the streets of Montreal in a state of intoxication, worrying one another with their teeth like so many enraged wolves." Of the Mohawk Indians, among whom he had lived, a Protestant minister, the Reverend Mr. Andrews, reported: "They grow quite mad, burn their own little huts, murder their wives and children, or one another, so that their wives are forced to hide their guns and hatchets, and themselves too, for fear of mischief."

Even the ablest of the early Indian chieftains found it hard to resist the white man's firewater. The redoubtable Pontiac, who had rallied every tribe between Lake Superior and the lower Mississippi in his campaign to drive out the English, periodically relapsed into drunkenness. "Our people love liquor," he admitted in a tirade against the English liquor traders, "and if we dwelt near your old village of Detroit, our warriors would always be drunk." No sooner had he finished speaking than he ordered a barrel of rum broached to slake his own and his warriors' thirst. For a bribe of rum from an English trader a Kaskaskia tribesman overtook Pontiac in a wood a few years later and split his skull with a hatchet.

Liquor caused some of the bloodiest clashes in colonial annals. The war of 1639 between the Pequod and the Connecticut Colony started when a band of Pequod, murderously drunk on rum sold to them by white traders, sacked a Connecticut settlement. It ended when the colonists destroyed a Pequod village, slaughtering every inhabitant—600 men, women and children.

In 1676 the Rhode Island authorities demanded that the Wampanoag Indians, who had been wrecking taverns in their cups and stealing cattle and crops, disarm. Meeting with the deputy governor and his council, the Wampanoag sachem, Metacomet, whom the English called King Philip, presented a list of his own grievances: Let the tavern keepers stop plying the Indians with drink, then cheating them. Drunk, he added, they became as dangerous to their law-abiding, sober brothers as they did to the whites. The New England slavers had also devised a system for enslaving Indians. They would make them drunk, and when they had committed some violence, as they frequently did, the courts would sentence them to servitude in the West Indies. A hundred such offenders were awaiting transportation, and King Philip included their freedom in his terms of peace. When the council brushed aside his grievances, he stalked out of the room, enraged, and there followed the most destructive war to afflict the New England colony since its founding.

In the four colonies that joined forces—Rhode Island, Connecticut, Plymouth and Massachusetts Bay—more than a tenth of all the whites fighting died, besides their women and children. Thirteen white settlements, comprising 600 dwellings, were razed; cattle by the thousands and an entire year's harvest were lost, leaving the colonies with a debt of hundreds of thousands of pounds. The whites ultimately annihilated the Wampanoag, as well as their allies, the Narragansett. They caught and killed King Philip, quartering his body and hanging the parts from trees. They exposed his head on a pole in Plymouth for almost twenty-five years. They sold his wife and children into slavery. The body of his sister-in-law, Wetamoo, "the Squaw Sachem of Pocasset," drowned while trying to escape the same fate, they also decapitated and paraded her head on a pole through the Bay Colony.

Amid such atrocities there arose a number of sachems and Indian religious prophets who not only renounced all alcoholic beverages, but became temperance preachers, winning many converts among their own people. It was an Algonquin chief who addressed the first recorded temperance meeting held on American soil. The place was Sillery, Canada, in 1648, following the Jesuit-influenced governor's edict of death for traders caught selling liquor to Indians. The Algonquin sachem urged total abstinence upon his tribesmen and swore to turn all drunkards over to the French for drastic punishment. The French prohibition lasted forty-three years until Louis XIV yielded to the arguments of Canada's leading merchants that the Indians were taking their furs to the Dutch for gin or to the British for whiskey and he forbade further interference with the brandy dealers. Ten years later Father Étienne de Carheil reported in a letter to an intendant:

> Our missionaries are reduced to such extremity that we can no longer maintain them against the infinity of disorder, brutality, violence, injustice, impiety, insolence, scorn and insult, that the deplorable and infamous traffic in brandy has spread universally among the Indians of these parts. In the despair in which we are plunged, nothing remains for us but to abandon them to the brandy-sellers as a domain of drunkenness and debauchery. All our Indian villages are so many taverns for drunkenness and Sodoms of iniquity, which we shall be forced to leave to the just wrath and vengeance of God.

Some of the Indian temperance pioneers like Pontiac's inspirer, "the Delaware Prophet" (history knows him by no other name), called for a holy war against the rum traders. Others like the Miami chief Michikinikwa (Little Turtle) journeyed peaceably from colony to colony, pleading with legislators through their interpreters—in Little Turtle's case his son-in-law, William Wells, a white man—to outlaw the traffic in the common interests of whites and redskins.

Puritan Massachusetts, which at first had encouraged the exploitation of the Indian's inability to drink moderately and granted liquor monopolies in Indian country under its control, was the first colony to enact a prohibitory law. "No man," its General Court ruled, "shall sell or give away strong water to an Indian." A decade later the same court rescinded the act in words of hypocritical piety:

> The corte apprehending that it is not fit to deprive the Indians of any lawful comfort which God alloweth to all men by the use of wine, do order that it shall be lawful for such as are or shall be allowed license to retail wines to sell also to Indians so much so as may be fit for their needful use and refreshing.

In 1657 the court readopted the original law and punished violations with a fine of 40 shillings.

Vacillation generally characterized colonial policy on this issue, the legislatures alternating between strictures and permissiveness according to economic conditions and the political pressures of the merchants. But by the late eighteenth century most of the statute books contained clauses excluding the Indian from the liquor market and fixing penalties ranging from fines to imprisonment.

In 1801 Chief Little Turtle, having journeyed on horseback to Baltimore, spoke through his son-in-law at a Quaker meeting. "Brothers," he said, "we want you to send to our great father, the President of the United States, and let him know our deplorable situation, that the bad ones among our white brothers may be stopped from selling whiskey to the Indians. Could you, my brothers, see the evil of this barbarous practice, you would pity the poor Indians."

The Quakers petitioned President Jefferson, who asked Congress to consider appropriate action. Congress responded gingerly on March 30, 1802, with an act authorizing the President "to take such measures from time to time as may appear to him expedient to prevent or restrain the vending or distributing of spirituous liquors among all or any of the said Indian tribes. . . ."

Under Jefferson's instructions Secretary of War Henry Dearborn then issued a general order to military posts, placing Indian country out of bounds for liquor dealers, but mentioning no penalties. Not until Andrew Jackson's second administration in 1834 did the Twenty-third Congress pass the first of a series of stringent laws with penalties of up to two years' imprisonment. In the vast, remote lands covered by these federal laws, enforcement was impossible, and droves of liquor traders continued to operate there with impunity. Such sobriety as the Indians maintained resulted chiefly from the evangelism of the prophets who followed Little Turtle, notably Elkswatawa, twin brother of the Shawnee warrior Tecumseh; Handsome Lake, a visionary who founded a new religious cult; and the Ojibway Kah-ge-gah-bowh, a drunkard's son—all three ex-alcoholics.

For the white antiliquor preachers like Benezet the image of the hell-roaring Indian boozer, which had become a stereotype of temperance homiletics despite the thousands of Indians who no longer touched a drop, served as the horrid example. If liquor could reduce the noble savage to such depths of bestial depravity, what horrors might it not visit upon his hard-drinking white brother? But the preachers attracted few listeners and reformed fewer still. What they needed to give the liquor-loving masses pause was a champion of universal renown, ideally a man of science. Such a champion they found in Benezet's disciple, Dr. Benjamin Rush. In 1785 Rush produced the first widely influential document in temperance history—*An Inquiry into the Effect of Ardent Spirits*. It won him the sobriquet of "the True Instaurator"—that is, inaugurator.

I have classed death among the consequences of hard drinking. But it is not death from the immediate hand of the Deity, nor from any of the instruments of it which were created by him. It is death from SUICIDE. Yes—thou poor degraded creature, who are daily lifting the poisoned bowl to thy lips—cease to avoid the unhallowed ground in which the self-murder is interred, and wonder no longer that the sun should shine, and the rain fall, and the grass look green upon his grave. Thou art perpetrating gradually, by the use of ardent spirits, what he has effected suddenly by opium—or a halter. Considering how many circumstances from surprise, or derangement, may palliate his guilt, or that (unlike yours) it was not preceded and accompanied by any other crime, it is probable his condemnation will be less than your's at the day of judgment.

The *Inquiry* contained Rush's customary admixture of purple rhetoric, sense and nonsense, with nonsense distinctly preponderant. It started off on a note somewhat disappointing to the temperance extremists by exculpating wine as an enemy of man. The doctor even went so far as to prescribe moderate amounts of wine for health and longevity. But even moderate amounts of ardent spirits, he cautioned, could bring moral decay, disease and death. "They dispose to every form of acute disease"—yellow fevers ("Hard drinkers seldom escape, and rarely recover from them"), obstruction of the liver, jaundice, dropsy of the belly, limbs and every body cavity, consumption, diabetes, rashes, flatulence ("Dr. Haller relates the case of a notorious drunkard having been suddenly destroyed in consequence of the vapour discharged from his stomach by belching, accidentally taking fire by coming in contact with the flame of a candle"), epilepsy, gout, colic, palsy, apoplexy, gangrene, madness. "Ardent spirits," Rush added, "often bring on fatal diseases without producing drunkenness. I have known many persons destroyed by them who were never completely intoxicated during the whole course of their lives."

Among the effects upon intellect and morality he cited impairment of memory and understanding and a general perversion of moral values, leading to falsehood, fraud, theft, uncleanliness and murder.

Rush dismissed nearly all the accepted therapeutic uses of hard liquor:

So great is the danger of contracting a love for distilled liquors by accustoming the stomach to their stimulus, that as few medicines as possible should be given in spirituous vehicles, in chronic diseases. A physician of great eminence . . . who died towards the close of the last century, in London . . . lamented, in pathetic terms, that he had innocently made many sots by prescribing brandy and water in stomach complaints. It is difficult to tell how many persons have been destroyed by those physicians who have adopted Dr. Brown's indiscriminate practice in the use of stimulating remedies . . . but it is well known, several of them died of intemperance in this city, since the year 1790.

Rush conceded only two exceptions to his censure. A few spoonfuls of alcohol, he allowed, could be safely administered to prevent fainting. The second permissible application was both external and internal, a curious treatment of his own invention to guard against chills and fever following exposure to cold, wet weather. ". . . a moderate quantity of spirits is not only safe, but highly proper. . . . They will more certainly have those salutary effects, if the feet are at the same time bathed with them, or half a pint of them poured into the shoes or boots."

For gastric disturbances he considered opium safer and more efficacious than any hard liquor. For mental depression, "the only radical cure . . . is to be found in Religion," but should the sufferer fail to turn to God, wine and, again, opium, would be preferable to spirits. Opium, the doctor believed, created no habit hard to break.

In Rush's view, even the cautious drinker, confining himself to weak toddies, ran the risk of alcoholism. He recounted the case of a Philadelphian, "once of a fair and sober character," who drank nothing but weak toddies for years. Then:

> From this he proceeded to drink grog. After a while, nothing would satisfy him, but slings made of equal parts of rum and water, with a little sugar. From slings, he advanced to raw rum, and from common rum to Jamaica spirits. Here he rested for a few months, but at length finding even Jamaica spirits were not strong enough to warm his stomach, he made it a constant practice to throw a table-spoonful of ground pepper into each glass of his spirits, in order, to use his own words, "to take off their coldness." Soon afterwards he died a martyr to intemperance.

Rush did not feel that alcoholics lay beyond the hope of salvation, and he described several ways of reaching them through religion, psychology and medicine. Belief in Christian doctrine headed the list, for Rush, like every temperance reformer of the age, was deeply religious. The sense of guilt and the fear of punishment in the hereafter, he suggested, could combine to keep the culprit sober, and he recalled the case of another Philadelphia sot who, having attempted to murder his wife while under the influence, was so horrified upon recovering sobriety that he never tippled again. Sudden shame could prove effective, Rush assured his readers, as it did in the case of a dissolute old farmer who never returned from the market town before tossing down a few stiff ones. Omitting the practice one evening because it had started to rain and he wanted to get his cut hay under cover, he overheard his six-year-old son crying out: "O! mother, father is come home, and he is not drunk." Hanging his head, the shamed parent then and there forswore liquor, according to Rush.

The doctor advised restricting the alcoholic's diet to vegetables on the theory that vegetables decrease thirst whereas meat excites it; raising blisters on his ankles and causing massive inflammation, a kind of medical chastisement to wean him away from his vice; inducing him to become an "affidavit man," that is, to swear off liquor before a magistrate at the risk of judical discipline if he backslid; terrifying the drunkard into sobriety with frequent warnings of death. . . . But amid all these absurdities Rush did hit upon a treatment that anticipated by two centuries what modern psychiatry terms "adverse conditioning" and is said to have applied with occasional success not only to alcoholism but to homosexuality and character disorders of various kinds. Rush managed to cure a black alcoholic by secretly doctoring his rum with tartar emetic. The resulting nausea was so violent that ever after the patient could no longer bear the sight or smell of spirits.

Rush appealed to both church and state "to save our fellow-men from being destroyed by the great destroyer of their lives and souls." He called on the government to limit the number of taverns, impose heavier duties on spirits, temporarily deprive convicted drunkards of their civil rights, and impound the property of the habitual drunkard, transferring control of his property to court-appointed trustees to administer for the benefit of his family. At the same time all Christian churches should subject the sale and consumption of ardent spirits to canonical law, as the Methodists and Quakers had already done, and declare them contraband.

To illustrate graphically the drunkard's inevitable downward progress, Rush appended to his *Inquiry* a "moral and physical thermometer of intemperance."

ZERO.	DRINKS.	VICES.	DISEASES.	PUNISHMENTS
	Punch.	Idleness, Gaming.	Sickness.	Debt.
	Toddy and Egg Rum.	Peevishness	Tremors of the hands in morning, puking.	Jail.
	Grog, Brandy and Water.	Quarreling, Fighting.	Bloatedness.	Black eyes and rags.
	Flip and Shrub.	Horse-racing.	Inflamed eyes, red nose and face.	Hospital or poor-house.
	Bitters infused in Spirits and Cordials.	Lying and Swearing.	Sore and swelled legs, jaundice.	Bridewell.
	Drams of Gin, Brandy, and Rum in the morning.	Stealing and Swindling.	Pains in the hands, burning in the hands and feet.	State-prison.
	The same, morning and evening.	Perjury.	Dropsy, epilepsy, melancholy, palsy, apoplexy.	State-prison for life.
	The same, during day and night.	Burglary, Murder.	Madness and Despair.	Gallows.

Reissued year after year, frequently quoted in the press, debated by clergymen, doctors and legislators, *An Inquiry* stirred up the nation. For generations the temperance movement, and prohibitionism after it, would promulgate Rush's basic principles. The year he published his *Inquiry* the Reverend Philip William Otterbein founded the church of the United Brethren of Christ, which withheld communion from any parishioner who took a drink. Two years later the New England Quakers swore its members to abstinence, and the following year, in Litchfield County, Connecticut, more than 200 farmers formed an association to discourage drinking and pledged themselves to use no liquor themselves during the next farming season. In 1791 the College of Physicians of New York sent a memorandum to the U.S. Senate, decrying the use of alcohol and urging high duties on its importation. The first Congress not only raised the import duties, but placed a higher tax on domestic liquor. (Congressman Fisher Ames of Boston sounded a skeptical note: "If any suppose that a mere law can turn the taste of a people from ardent spirits to malt liquors, he has a most romantic notion of legislative power.") In 1796 the General Conference of the Methodist Episcopal Church proclaimed: ". . . the retailing of spirituous liquors, and giving drams to customers when they call at stores . . . are productive of so many evils, that we judge it our indispensable duty to form a regulation against them." The Presbyterian Synod of Pennsylvania pledged its ministers to avoid intoxicating liquors. In Nelson County, Virginia, Micajah Pendleton started the first pledge-signing drive and later organized the first total abstinence group, though it had no formal structure, kept no records and charged no dues. At the installation in 1800 of the Reverend John Cornell as the Presbyterian minister of New Brunswick, New Jersey, the celebrants had consumed four bowls of punch, a pint of brandy, a round of grog, two bottles of wine and three and a half bottles of beer. Five years later, in Allentown, New Jersey, the minister's new parish, his wife founded the Sober Society, whose all-female membership would tolerate no tippling in their homes.

Rush presented a thousand copies of his essay to the General Assembly of the Presbyterian Church in Philadelphia, with a letter urging decisive action. The assembly appointed a committee to weigh the most effective means of fighting the Demon Rum, and ecclesiastical bodies in five other states set up similar committees. Rush predicted, before his death in 1813, that within a century liquor would become as uncommon a drink as arsenic. He had lit a torch. The sparks were kindling fires everywhere. It remained for a phenomenal succession of pulpit orators, circuit riders, dry doctors and lay converts to fan the flames into a major conflagration.

2. "... a sin that excludes from heaven"

God has said to America, as he did of old to ancient Sodom, "I will save you, if ten righteous, sober men can be found." They have been found, and we are redeemed.

—Permanent Temperance Documents of the
American Temperance Society

RAIN, driven by an icy March night wind, lashed the doctor's house and pounded the clay road running past it into a muddy paste. Inside, Billy James Clark, age twenty-three, the only physician within a radius of twenty miles, huddled close to his fireplace, reflecting upon the famous Rush temperance tract he had recently read. The scenes of drunken debauchery it described were painfully familiar to him, "the singing, hallooing, roaring, imitating the noises of brute animals, jumping, tearing off clothes, dancing naked, breaking glasses and china. . . ."

The little upstate town of Moreau, New York, five miles south of Glens Falls, bordering the Hudson where the river takes a wide bend, lay at the heart of rich timberland, and the millowners, raftsmen and loggers who populated it spent a major part of their leisure hours getting rampaging drunk. The half dozen taverns, of which Peter Mawney's, standing opposite the Clark house, was one of the most popular, formed the center of Moreau's social life. The town offered few other diversions. Even the women and children consumed stupendous quantities of hard cider. The men favored a regional version of rum fustian, combining rum, gin, sherry, beer, the yolks of eggs, sugar and nutmeg. It did not take many drafts to topple the toughest lumberjack, and a good deal of Billy Clark's practice consisted of reviving the fallen.

The young doctor's concern for his boozy fellow townsmen was tinged with a sense of personal guilt. At seventeen, just before beginning his medical studies, he had worked as a bartender in Pownal, Vermont, and since then occasionally downed a stiff drink himself. Only a few evenings before, Clark and the Reverend Lebbeus Armstrong, pastor of Moreau's Congregational Church, who was barely a year older than Clark, had taken part in a carousal at Peter Mawney's tavern during which one of their companions, James Mott, drank so much rum so fast that it nearly killed him.

Earlier that winter, remorse and the spirit of reform, aroused by Rush's *Inquiry*, had moved Clark to try to organize a Saratoga County temperance society among the judges and lawyers gathered at nearby Ballston Spa for the sittings of the Court of Common Pleas. To a man they ridiculed the idea as "visionary and impractical." Now, as the doctor warmed himself by the fire, brooding over Moreau's alcoholic intake along with his own lapses, a fresh determination seized him. Slipping into his greatcoat, he hurried out to his stable, saddled his horse and headed at a gallop for the Congregational rectory, a three-mile journey under a black, wet sky, splattering himself from hat to boots with clayey mud. "Mr. Armstrong," he said when the rectory door opened to his knock, "I have come to see you on important business." Then, flinging his hands heavenward (as Armstrong later recalled the visit), he exclaimed: "We shall become a community of drunkards in this town unless something is done to arrest the progress of intemperance."

The equally troubled and penitent minister agreed, and during the following week they managed to round up in Moreau and neighboring Northumberland twenty-three townsmen, among them the resuscitated Mott, for a preliminary meeting. It was held on the very spot where a good many of them had been known to drink themselves into a coma—Mawney's tavern—the proprietor being sufficiently broad-minded to extend his hospitality to them even though they now threatened his livelihood.

1st Resolved [read the minutes], in the opinion of this meeting that it is proper, Practicable & Necessary to form a temperate society in this place, And that the great & leading object of this society is wholly to abstain from ardent spirits.

A committee of five, including Clark and Armstrong, was

appointed to draw up bylaws, and the meeting adjourned until the twentieth.

At this second meeting, augmented by twenty more townsmen, was formally launched the first formal temperance organization in the United States—the Union Temperate Society of Moreau and Northumberland. The deliberations began in Mawney's tavern, but possibly to relieve what must have been a certain strain between the publican and his former clients, the reformers moved across the road to a schoolhouse.

In drafting the bylaws, the committee had gone further than even Rush's strictures. They prohibited not only hard liquor, unless prescribed by a physician for an illness, but also wine, unless served at an official function. The penalties for backsliding were tolerable—25 cents each time. If actually drunk, the offender would have to pay 50 cents and take an oath of reformation. A 25-cent fine was also decreed for anybody who proffered others a drink. Every member was expected to inform against any violator.

In August, at the first quarterly meeting, the Reverend Mr. Armstrong delivered the first recorded temperance oration in America since the country became a nation. Hinting that the Almighty might have taken a special interest in the guzzlers of Moreau and Northumberland, he declared: "We are all liable to the failings and frailties of human nature, and none knows but what God, in His providence, has devised and superintended the erection of this institution to save some of US from unforeseen danger and impending RUIN!"

Within a few months the membership grew to 106. Benjamin Rush was elected an honorary member. During the first annual meeting each member was asked to describe the effects of temperance upon his business and domestic affairs. Captain Isaac B. Payne, a substantial farmer and lumber dealer, testified: ". . . on an average, a hogshead of rum each year [sixty-three gallons] has been consumed by the family, their parties, and visiting friends. After signing the temperance pledge a year ago, instead of a hogshead, I purchased a five-gallon keg of rum. . . . And my reason for doing this was, because my business required a few excellent laborers, not one of whose help I could obtain without some liquor. During the year past, I have exerted the best influence in my power to reduce the quantity of liquor required by them to the lowest mark possible. This morning I examined my keg of liquor and, as nearly as I could judge, without accurate measurement, the keg was half full. We have abandoned all kinds of liquor in the family . . . and my business was never better performed, nor to greater satisfaction."

But the seeds of reform had been planted in stubborn soil. Too many of Moreau's grogshop habitués lay beyond redemption. Of the society's original members ten were expelled during the early years. As Armstrong lamented, "That feeble little band of temperance brethren, holding their quarterly and annual meetings in a country district schoolhouse, without the presence of a single female, were made the song of the drunkard and ridiculed by the scoffs of the intemperate world."

The meetings became irregular. For twenty-two years, from 1821 to 1843, there were hardly any to speak of. In the latter year a reorganized society flickered into faint life again with an affirmation of total abstinence, renouncing even wine at official functions. By 1858, when it held a semicentennial celebration, all but four of the charter members—Clark, Armstrong, Mott and a jurist named Gardiner Stow—had died, resigned or been expelled, but those four could swear that no drop of liquor had passed their lips in half a century.

At the semicentennial gales of incredulous laughter greeted the resolutions adopted by the dwindling membership "that a prohibitory law is required for the protection of property, persons, morality, education, liberty and religion. . . . That a prohibitory law will be ineffectual unless it be founded upon an amendment of that fundamental law—the *Constitution*."

The Reverend Mr. Armstrong died in 1860, and Dr. Billy Clark six years later, and with its guiding lights extinguished the Union Temperate Society fell into inactivity. But it had already served as model and inspiration for countless temperance groups in New York State and New England, such as the Saratoga County Temperance Society over which Judge Esek Cowen, an early Union Temperate, presided; societies in Greenfield and Milton, New York; the Young Men's Temperance Society with members in Moreau and Northumberland. . . . And from a Congregational pulpit in Litchfield, Connecticut, there resounded the thunder of the most powerful temperance orator yet heard, one who not only reiterated Rush's medical objections to strong drink, but raised a new and terrifying spiritual prospect— the peril to the drinker's soul. It was the voice of the Reverend

Lyman Beecher, one of whose thirteen children, Harriet, would later cause a furor of a different kind with her abolitionist novel, *Uncle Tom's Cabin.*

The Reverend Lyman Beecher remembers how he came to deliver his Six Sermons on the Nature, Occasions, Signs, Evils, and Remedy of Intemperance*

There was a neighborhood about four miles out called Bradleysville [Connecticut], where I used to preach on Sabbath afternoon and I have a lecture in the week. The first time I went it was connected with a revival of religion, and —— —— and his wife became pious. He was nearly the first male convert I had after I went to Litchfield, and he was always the most affectionate and kind. His house was my home when I went out there to preach and spend the night. He gave me more presents than any two or three, and was one of the most useful and excellent young men. The meetings about this time had been discontinued for some cause, and on setting them up again I preached at his house again; but it did not go as it used to, and the second time the same. After lecture I went out doors for a few moments, and when I came in found he was abed, and his wife was weeping. I felt a shock of presentiment. I drew up my chair by her side, and said, "What is the matter?" "Oh, matter enough," said she. "Who is it? Is it your father?" I knew he had some liabilities that way. She told me it was her husband too. "Is it possible? is it possible?" "Yes, it is possible."

I thought to myself as I rode home, "It is now or never. I must go about it immediately, or there is no chance of their salvation." These sermons I had projected early. . . . So I began the next Sabbath, and continued as fast as I could write them—one every Sabbath, I think. I wrote under such a power of feeling as never before or since. Never could have written it under other circumstances. Sabbath after Sabbath the interest grew, and became the most absorbing thing ever heard of before—a wonder, of weekly conversation and interest, and when I got through, of eulogy. All the old farmers that brought in their wood to sell, and used to set up their cart-whips at the groggery, talked about it, and said, many of them, they would never drink again.

Nature endowed him with a presence and a voice that could

---

* *Autobiography, Correspondence, Etc.,* 1865.

bring to their knees, sobbing for salvation, the conscience-twitching topers of Litchfield. So horripilating were his depictions of what the damned suffered in hell that one aged sinner cried out for him to stop. No contemporary portrait shows Lyman Beecher smiling. The mouth turns down sharply at the corners as if he smelled some evil effluvium. A long, heavy nose overshadows the short upper lip. Above it rises broad and high a frowning brow, the temples framed by iron-gray locks hanging down to his white collar. Chronic dyspepsia did not soften his normally austere expression.

To the Calvinists earthly existence was but a prelude to everlasting heaven or hell. Under the system developed in the sixteenth century by the Swiss Protestant theologian John Calvin, man, innately wicked since the Fall, was elect—that is, bound for salvation, if God had so predestined him. Otherwise the eternal fires awaited him. There was nothing he could do through his own efforts to alter his fate. In the face of such predestination it would seem that it hardly mattered how he behaved on earth. Yet since no man knew whether he belonged to the elect, it was safer to pursue the path of virtue, to "make your calling and election sure," as the phrase went. By the nineteenth century this rigid creed had been considerably modified. All men, most Calvinist theologians agreed, had the opportunity to accept salvation. By coming to Christ through conversion, they could be redeemed and join the elect. It thus became more urgent than ever for every minister to press the claims of the Gospel and to give believers the assurance of election.

Puritanism, often confused with Calvinism, was largely an Anglo-American doctrine grafted upon the latter. European Calvinists attached no evil to social diversions like dancing and moderate drinking. But the British and American Calvinist-Puritans—the Congregationalists, Methodists, Baptists and other Protestant sects—felt that all sensual indulgence deceived and corrupted the elect, and in the case of liquor injured him physically as well. It is not surprising that the temperance movement drew its greatest strength from the Protestant churches and their converts.

It was in 1810, after attending a boozy gathering of clergymen at an ordination in Plymouth, Massachusetts, where "the maximum amount of hilarity" reigned, that Lyman Beecher first resolved to become a temperance activist. "They were not the old-fashioned Puritans—they had run down; they had a great deal of spirituality on the Sabbath, and not much when they were where there was something good to drink. . . . 'Twas that that woke me up for the war. And, silently, I took an oath before God that I would never attend another ordination of that kind. I was full. . . ."

He began his celebrated series of six sermons on the first Sunday of 1826, choosing as his texts verses from Proverbs and Habbakuk: "Who hath woe? who hath sorrow? who hath contentions? who hath babbling? who hath wounds without cause? who hath redness of eyes? They that tarry long at the wine. . . . Woe unto him that giveth his neighbor drink, that puttest thy bottle to him, and makest him drunken also, that thou mayest look on their nakedness! . . ."

To sell liquor, Beecher declared with a forcefulness of language and gesture that electrified his hearers (even if it did not straightaway cause many tapsters among them to abandon their trade or many drinkers to renounce their revels) was "unlawful in the sight of God," and people who got drunk were "dead, twice dead . . . for drunkards, no more than murderers, shall inherit the earth. . . . Drunkenness is a sin which excludes from Heaven. . . ." Liquor, the preacher concluded in his sixth sermon:

> . . . obliterates the fear of the Lord . . . who are found so uniformly in the ranks of irreligion as the intemperate? Who like these violate the Sabbath and set their mouth against the Heavens? . . . Who can estimate the hatred of God, of his word and worship, and of his people, which it occasions; or number the oaths and blasphemies it causes to be uttered, . . . the impurities. . . . How many thousands does it detain every Sabbath-day from the house of God—cutting them off from the means of grace, and hardening them against their efficacy! How broad is the road which intemperance alone leads to hell, and how thronged with travellers! . . . has not God connected with all lawful vocations the welfare of the life that now is, and of that which is to come? And can we lawfully amass property but a course of trade which fills the land with beggars and widows and crimes, which peoples graveyards with premature mortality, and the world of woe with victims of despair?

Publication in pamphlet form followed the delivery of the sermons. As widely circulated as Rush's *Inquiry*, it coincided with and fortified the vigorous efforts of a group of New England reformers, headed by the Reverend Justin Edwards, pastor of the Congregational Church in Andover, Massachusetts. For almost a year Edwards and a dozen colleagues had been meeting to consider how intemperance could be eliminated from the United States. They met again in Boston on February 13, 1826, after a planning committee had submitted its report, and there founded the American Society for the Promotion of Temperance (soon shortened to the American Temperance Society). The first national organization of its kind, it adopted as its basic principle total abstinence and as its ultimate aim the enactment of state and constitutional laws abolishing hard liquor.

At first, when proselytizing, the society discreetly refrained from demanding complete renunciation of liquor lest it alienate prospective members. But within a few years the name of the society, if taken to imply moderation only, had become decidedly misleading. Emboldened by their successes, the founders now openly denounced as a delusion the long-cherished belief that an occasional nip never hurt anybody. Every drunkard, they reasoned, started out as a moderate drinker; one drink leads to another, a second to a third and so on to intoxication and eventually alcoholism. No doubt exceptions could be found among men of unusually strong character, but the safest course was not to drink at all. So the society now pledged new members to total abstinence, marking after their names on the membership list "T" for "Total," whence the derivation of "teetotaler." (So goes the commonest version of the word's origin, but there is another which attributes it to a stuttering English temperance worker, Richard Turner, who supposedly said at a meeting: "Mr. Chairman, I finds as how the lads get drunk on ale and cider, and we can't keep 'em sober unless we pledge total; yes, Mr. Chairman, tee-tee-total.")

Beecher, Edwards and their co-evangelists ushered in the Augustan age of temperance reform. In March, 1826, a Boston Baptist, the Reverend William Collier, published, with the support of the American Temperance Society, the forerunner of innumerable antiliquor periodicals, the monthly (later weekly) *National Philanthropist*. The masthead carried a double motto—
TEMPERATE DRINKING IS THE DOWNHILL ROAD TO INTEMPERANCE.

. . . DISTILLED SPIRITS OUGHT TO BE BANISHED FROM THE LAND AND
WHAT OUGHT TO BE DONE CAN BE DONE. The medical societies of
Massachusetts, New Hampshire and Connecticut, followed by
dozens of others, passed resolutions acclaiming water as man's
best potable, forswore liquor themselves and undertook to
discourage their patients from drinking it.

The Reverend Mr. Edwards journeyed to the nation's capital,
organizing ten local temperance societies en route, and pleaded
his cause at a joint meeting of the houses. He so impressed a
number of legislators that they formed the American Congressional Temperance Society, electing as its president the Secretary
of War, General Lewis Cass, a lifelong abstainer, and as officers
several influential politicians. General Cass, who blamed the
majority of Army desertions (nearly 6,000 in seven years) on
liquor, had already banned it from all forts, camps and garrisons,
forbidden sutlers to sell it to troops wherever stationed and
substituted coffee for the traditional ration of rum. Secretary of
the Navy Levi Woodbury did not venture quite that far, but he
offered seamen who were willing to forgo their liquor rations a
choice of extra coffee, tea, sugar or cash. Edwards persuaded
hundreds of employers to discontinue the customary daily
allotment of liquor to their workmen and many workmen to
organize temperance groups of their own, a prodigious achievement during a period when the annual consumption of hard
liquor by a population of 12,000,000 ran close to 72,000,000
gallons, or roughly 6 gallons per capita.

By 1833 23 state and more than 5,000 local temperance
societies had arisen with an estimated 1,250,000 members, 10,000
of them reclaimed sots. Four thousand distillers had voluntarily
closed down their plants, and 6,000 liquor retailers had turned to
other occupations. About 1,000 merchant vessels no longer
carried liquor rations for their crews.

In May, 1833, delegates from the 23 state societies held a
convention in Philadelphia. Out of this grew the United States
Temperance Union, embracing and extending the aims of the
Beecher-Edwards crusaders. During a second convention at
Saratoga Springs three years later it changed its name to the
American Temperance Union in order to admit member societies from every part of North America. Upon a motion drafted
by Beecher and Edwards total abstinence was redefined to
include beer, wine and cider.

The new organization chose Philadelphia as its headquarters and there established a national press, whose maiden publication was the monthly *Journal of the American Temperance Union*. For the next fifteen years it remained the affiliate and chief catalyst of the nation's proliferating antiliquor forces.

It was the state of Massachusetts, with its Philadelphia-inspired Temperance Union, which enacted the first American prohibition law.

Brigadier General James Appleton, a jeweler and veteran of the War of 1812, was descended from that John Appleton who became, in 1641, the Massachusetts colony's first brewer. Temperance historians hail the general as "the Father of Prohibition." A native of Ipswich, he took up the dry banner in 1831 after listening to the Massachusetts legislature debate the issue of liquor licensing. In collaboration with several kindred reformers he submitted a petition to the State Senate:

> . . . the laws assume that the sale of Ardent Spirits, to a certain extent at least, is of public benefit and necessity and promotive of individual advantage and happiness. This Assumption, your petitioner humbly apprehends, has been ascertained to be utterly unsupported and unfounded; and if it were possible to separate from our associations long continued habit and universal practice in the commonwealth, it is believed that a license to disseminate the Small Pox, would be thought to be no less proper and reasonable than a License to sell Ardent Spirits. . . .

Ascribing 75 percent of the country's crime and pauperism to liquor, Appleton proposed a law fixing thirty gallons as the minimum amount salable at one time, the idea being that to have to cart home such a quantity whenever a man wanted a few drinks would prove too burdensome. By this the general intended only a preliminary measure. In a letter to the Salem *Gazette* he stated flatly: "A law should be passed prohibiting the sale of ardent spirits."

The majority of legislators were no more prepared than their constituents to curtail the drinking habits of a lifetime. Even the agent of the Massachusetts Society for the Suppression of Intemperance, the Reverend Mr. Hildreth, opposed the petition. Public opinion, he argued, was not ripe for it. In a free society moral suasion, not legal coercion, offered the best hope of reform. The petition was tabled.

The following year Appleton moved to Portland, Maine, where he resumed the battle. Elected to the city's board of aldermen, then to the state legislature, he won a wider following and it was by only a single vote that his proposal for a twenty-eight-gallon minimum purchase law was defeated. A minor victory occurred five years later, though not in his adopted state. His native Massachusetts imposed a fifteen-gallon minimum.

The general could take additional satisfaction in the continually increasing number of societies, publications, orators and legislative factions dedicated to fighting the Demon Rum.

3. Of Washingtonians, Cold Water Soldiers, Rechabites and Others

Whereas, the use of alcoholic liquors as a beverage is productive of pauperism, degradation, and crime and believing it is our duty to discourage that which produces more evil than good, we therefore pledge ourselves to abstain from the use of intoxicating liquors as a beverage.

—The Washingtonian Pledge

. . . The cause itself seems suddenly transformed from a cold abstract theory, to a living, breathing, active, and powerful chieftain, going forth "conquering and to conquer." The citadels of his great adversary are daily being stormed and dismantled; his temples and his altars, where the rites of his idolatrous worship have long been performed, and where human sacrifices have long been wont to be made, are daily desecrated and deserted. The trump of the conqueror's fame is sounding from hill to hill, from sea to sea, and from land to land, and calling millions to his standard at a blast.

—ABRAHAM LINCOLN, Springfield, Illinois, 1842

THEY had been meeting as an informal drinking club almost every evening in Chase's Tavern on Baltimore's Liberty Street, six unquenchable topers—a coachmaker, James McCurley; a carpenter, John F. Hoss; a tailor, William K. Mitchell; a silversmith, Archibald Campbell; and two blacksmiths, David Anderson and George Stears. On the evening of April 2, 1840, a renowned temperance advocate from New York, the Reverend Matthew Hale Smith, was attracting a large crowd to a church nearby. Yielding to a drunken whim, two of the clubmen interrupted their frolic to go and hear him. History does not record what the Reverend Mr. Smith said, but it must have powerfully impressed the two tipplers, for they rejoined their companions, sobered and thoughtful. A noisy discussion ensued, during which Chase, the tavernkeeper, denounced all temperance crusaders as fools and hypocrites. "Of course," retorted one of the habitués, "it is to your interest to cry them down," and he laughingly suggested that they organize their own temperance society with Mitchell, the tailor, as president.

At their next meeting, the following Sunday, while drinking as heavily as ever, the six friends again pondered the merits of the Reverend Mr. Smith's sermon. Mitchell offered to draw up a teetotaler's pledge, as soon as his condition permitted, if they would all sign it, and to this they agreed. Monday evening he called on the blacksmith, Anderson, who still lay abed, nursing a hangover, and showed him what he had written:

> We, whose names are annexed, desirous of forming a society for our mutual benefit, and to guard against pernicious practice, which is injurious to our health, standings, and families do pledge ourselves as gentlemen that we will not drink any spirituous or malt liquors, wine, or cider.

The suffering blacksmith crept from his bed of pain and signed the document. The same evening, hurrying from house to house, Mitchell obtained the signatures of the fellow reprobates. Convening again at Chase's Tavern on April 6, they decided to style themselves the Washington Temperance Society, or Washingtonians, and they conceived a psychological device that anticipated by a century Alcoholics Anonymous—the public confession. Each member undertook to bring to the next meeting some inebriate ripe for reclamation and willing to bare his soul from the podium. The society rejected the dogma of ecclesiastics like Beecher and Edwards who looked upon drunkenness as a sin that could eternally damn the drunkard. They did not consider temperance a religious issue at all. Nor did they hold with the rabid abstentionists who would illegalize drinking. They preferred voluntary teetotaling.

Of the 700 Baltimoreans whom the society pledged at the outset the prize catch was a sodden wretch with a gift for self-dramatization.

John Henry Willis Hawkins remembers the hour of his regeneration*
I was born in Baltimore on the 28th of September, 1797. After some

---

* A public address recorded by the Reverend John Marsh in *Hannah Hawkins, the Reformed Drunkard's Daughter.*

years at the school of the Rev. Mr. Coxe, I was apprenticed for eight years' to learn the trade of a hatter with a master whose place of business was a regular den of drunkards. A few days ago I found the old books of my master; there were the names of sixty men upon them, and we could recollect but one who did not go to a drunkard's grave. . . .

As soon as I was away from paternal care I fell away. All went by the board, and my sufferings commenced. For six months I had no shoes, and only one shirt and one pair of pantaloons. Then I was a vagabond indeed. But I returned, ragged and bloated, to my mother's home. It was customary in those days to let the young people drink with their parents, but neither they nor I thought of my becoming a miserable drunkard.

When I got to the edge of my native town I was so ashamed that I waited till the dusk of the evening, and then I crept along to the house of my mother. She dressed me up decently, did not upbraid me, but only said, "John, I am afraid you are bloated!"

For fifteen years [during which he married and reared two daughters] *I rose and fell, was up and down. I would earn fifteen dollars a week and be well and happy, and with my money in hand would start for home, but in some unaccountable way would fall into a tavern, thinking one glass would do me good. But a single glass would conquer all my resolutions. I appeal to all my fellow-drunkards if it is not exactly so.*

During the first two weeks of June [1840] *I drank dreadfully, bought liquor by the gallon and drank and drank. I cannot tell how I suffered: in body every thing, but in mind more!*

By the fourteenth of the month—drunk all the time—I was a wonder to myself, astonished that I had any mind left; and yet it seemed, in the goodness of God, uncommonly clear. My conscience drove me to madness. I hated the darkness of the night, and when morning came I hated the light, I hated myself, hated existence; was about taking my own life. I asked myself, "Can I restrain? Is it possible?" But there was no one to take me by the hand and say you can. I had a pint of whiskey in my room, where I lay in bed, and thought I would drink it, but this seemed to be a turning point with me. I knew it was life or death as I decided to drink it or not. . . .

Then my daughter Hannah, came up—my only friend, I always loved her the most—and she said,

"Father, don't send me after whiskey today!"

I was tormented before; this was agony. I could not stand it, so I told her to leave, and she went downstairs crying, and saying, "Father

is angry with me." My wife came up again and asked me to take some
coffee. I told her I did not want any thing of her and covered myself up
in bed. Pretty soon I heard some one in the room, and, peeping out, I
saw it was my daughter.

"Hannah," said I, "I am not angry with you—and—I shall not
drink any more." Then we wept together.

I got up, went to the cupboard, and looked on my enemy, the whiskey
bottle, and thought, "Is it possible I can be restored?" Several times
while dressing I looked at the bottle, but I thought, "I shall be lost if I
yield."

Poor drunkard! there is hope for you. You cannot be worse off than I
was, no more degraded or more of a slave to appetite. You can return if
you will. Try it! Try it!

A born actor, Hawkins proved to be the greatest individual
draw that temperance revivalism had thus far produced. His
heart-rending recital of his own redemption packed churches and
auditoriums and brought thousands of drunkards forward,
beating their breasts and crying out for a pen with which to sign
the pledge. In May, 1842, after appearing at the head of a
delegation of Washingtonians before the third National Temperance Convention, Hawkins led them on a cross-country missionary tour. Organizing Washingtonian chapters wherever they
went, they garnered 23,000 pledges in New York, New Jersey
and Pennsylvania, 30,000 in Kentucky, 60,000 in Ohio. . . .
They made a dazzling procession, uniformed and flourishing
gilt-threaded banners with motifs of grapes and grain and the
maxim, FOOD IF EATEN, POISON IF DRUNK, flanked by a women's
auxiliary, the Martha Washington Society, eager to succor the
impoverished families of reclaimed sots.

*Charles Dickens remembers a temperance parade in Cincinnati**

It comprised several thousand men . . . and was marshalled by
officers on horseback, who cantered briskly up and down the line, with
scarves and ribbons of bright colors fluttering out behind them gaily.
There were bands of music too, and banners out of number; and it was
a fresh, holiday-looking concourse altogether.

* *American Notes*, 1842.

I was particularly pleased to see the Irishmen, who formed a distinct society among themselves, and mustered very strong with their green scarves; carrying their national Harp and their portrait of Father Mathew [a Dublin Catholic temperance preacher, credited with having pledged more than 4,000,000 Irishmen] *high above their heads. . . .*

The banners were very well painted, and flaunted down the street famously. There was the smiting of the rock and the gushing forth of the waters; and there was a temperate man with "considerable of a hatchet" (as the standard-bearer would probably have said), aiming a deadly blow at a serpent which was apparently about to spring upon him from the top of a barrel of spirits. But the chief feature of this part of the show was a large allegorical device, borne among the ship-carpenters, on one side whereof the steamboat Alcohol was represented bursting her boiler and exploding with a great crash, while upon the other, the good ship Temperance sailed away with a fair wind, to the heart's content of the captain, crew, and passengers.

By 1842 the Washingtonians had carried their banners as far west as Springfield, Illinois, where they found a sympathizer in Abraham Lincoln, who, though only thirty-three, had already served four terms as a state legislator. On Washington's birthday they staged a monster jamboree, culminating in a ceremony at Springfield's Second Presbyterian Church, with Lincoln appearing as their "orator of the day." Both dry and wet propagandists would forever after invoke Lincoln in their arguments, and both would do so with some justice. He remained all his life a teetotaler. Yet for a while, in 1833, he ran, in partnership with a hard-drinking friend named William Berry, a country store at New Salem, Illinois, that sold liquor. He consistently pleaded for temperance, by which he meant moderation. But in political contention over liquor legislation he never aligned himself with any party. His Whig supporters of 1855, the year he ran unsuccessfully for the U.S. Senate, had adopted a dry plank and referred to the Democrats as "the Whiskey Party." Asked where he stood, Lincoln replied: "I am not a temperance man, but I am temperate to this extent—I don't drink."

Nor did he ever endorse compulsory prohibition. As early as 1840, when a Whig member of the Illinois state legislature, he argued: "Prohibition will work great injury to the cause of temperance. It is a species of intemperance within itself, for it goes beyond the bounds of reason in that it attempts to control a man's appetite by legislation and makes a crime out of things that are not crimes. A prohibition law strikes at the very principle upon which our Government was founded."

In a speech at Columbus, Ohio, on September 16, 1857, he maintained that "each man shall do precisely as he pleases with himself, and with all those things that exclusively concern him; that a general government shall do all those things that pertain to it, and all the local governments shall do precisely as they please in respect to those matters which exclusively concern them."

Even his Washingtonian speech of 1842 contained passages distressing to temperance extremists:

> The warfare heretofore waged against the demon intemperance, has, somehow or other, been erroneous. These champions, for the most part, have been preachers, lawyers, and hired agents; between these and the mass of mankind there is a want of approachability. . . . They are supposed to have no sympathy of feeling or interest with those very persons whom it is their object to convince and persuade. The preacher, it is said, advocates temperance because he is a fanatic, and desires a union of the church and state; the lawyer from his pride, and vanity of hearing himself speak; and the hired agent for his salary. . . .

The former dram seller added:

> Too much denunciation against dram-sellers and dram-drinkers was indulged in. This, I think, was both impolitic and unjust. It was impolitic because it is not much in the nature of man to be driven to anything, still less to be driven about that which is exclusively his own business, and least of all where such driving is to be submitted to at the expense of pecuniary interest or burning appetite. When the dram-seller and drinker were incessantly told, not in the accents of entreaty and persuasion, diffidently addressed by erring man to an erring brother, but in the thundering tones of anathema and denunciation, with which the lordly judge often groups together all the crimes of the felon's life, and thrusts them in his face ere he passes sentence of death upon him, that they were the authors of all the vice and misery and crime in the land; that they were the manufacturers and the material of all the

thieves and robbers and murderers that infest the earth; that their houses were the workshops of the devil, and that their persons should be shunned by all the good and virtuous, as moral pestilence—I say, when they were told all this, and in this way, it is not wonderful that they were slow, very slow, to acknowledge the truth of such denunciations, and to join the ranks of their denouncers, in a hue and cry against themselves.

Possibly Lincoln had in mind his own law partner, William Herndon, a heavy drinker, when he went on to reprove as false Christians those who refused to associate with drunkards even to help them:

"But," say some, "we are no drunkards, and we shall not acknowledge ourselves such, by joining a reformed drunkards' society, whatever our influence might be." Surely, no Christian will adhere to this objection. If they believe, as they profess, that Omnipotence condescended to take on himself the form of sinful man, and, as such, to die an ignominious death for their sakes, surely, they will not refuse submission to the infinitely lesser condescension, from any mental or moral superiority over those who have. Indeed, I believe if we take the habitual drunkards as a class, their heads and hearts will bear an advantageous comparison with those of any other class. There seems ever to have been a proneness in the brilliant and warm-blooded to fall into this vice—the demon of intemperance ever seems to have delighted in sucking the blood of genius and generosity. . . .

The audience was outraged. Herndon, standing at the church door afterwards, heard one man protest: "It's a shame that he should be permitted to abuse us so in the house of the Lord."

It was neither the first nor the last time that Lincoln's humanity or his humor offended respectability. The liquor interests never tired of repeating his reply when a temperance delegation headed by a minister demanded General Grant's removal because he drank too much whiskey: "Doctor, can you tell me where General Grant gets his liquor? . . . for if you could tell me, I would direct the Chief Quartermaster of the army to lay in a large stock of the same kind of liquor, and would also direct him to furnish a supply to some of my other generals who have never yet won a victory."

As President, Lincoln signed the Internal Revenue Act in 1862 which taxed the liquor industry, among others, thereby recognizing its legitimacy and, in effect, making the government its partner.

Before John Hawkins died in 1858, at the age of fifty-nine, he had traveled 200,000 miles up and down the sawdust trail, retelling at least 5,000 times the story of his redemption at the hands of his daughter Hannah.

Hawkins' closest competitor among the Washingtonian evangelists, one, in fact, who eventually surpassed him to become the foremost platform performer of the century, was John Bartholomew Gough, a small, frail, English-born alcoholic with bushy hair and a fan-shaped beard that covered his chest. Gough's chief asset was, like Hawkins', histrionic. During his derelict youth in New York, when not toiling away as an apprentice bookbinder, he had earned extra pocket money doing music hall turns on the Bowery, and he later enlivened his temperance orations with mimicry, songs, jokes and Shakespearean recitations.

The infant Gough, son of a Methodist Army pensioner and a Baptist village schoolmistress, had a precocious command of language. At the age of eight, after a ship foundered off the coast of his native Sandgate, drowning 790 passengers, little John apostrophized the waters thus: "I love you! I love you, even if you are as wicked as the Giant Despair! O sea! O sea! Never be so wicked again or God will dry you up. Mind your rages, sea!"

For ten guineas some neighbors of his impoverished parents agreed to take him to America with them and teach him a trade. They acquired an upstate New York farm, where they set him to tilling the soil, insisting, for his health's sake, that he down his daily tot of rum like all the other farmhands, men and women, children and adults. By the age of twelve he had developed a pronounced liking for booze. But farming never appealed to him; it was the glitter of the big city that beckoned to him, and before his fifteenth birthday he ran off to New York. Injustice soon drove him to his first lapse into total drunkenness. Employed as a binder by the Methodist Book Concern, which published temperance tracts with titles like *The Grave Digger's Pledge*, he was fired when his landlady's sixteen-year-old daughter falsely accused him of trying to seduce her. He made straight for his favorite Bowery saloon, the Brown Jug, and there drank himself comatose. In inebriety Gough tended to indulge a penchant for crude practical jokes that endeared him to nobody. He once staggered into a revival meeting, picked up a cuspidor and, laughing wildly, passed it around as a collection plate. He suffered from another defect incurred in boyhood when a clod from a ditchdigger's spade struck him on the head. Since then, when emotionally overwrought as in the throes of an oration or Shakespearean soliloquy, he would experience a "pricking and darting" inside his skull that caused him to press his hands to his temples.

Barnstorming New England with seedy stock companies, he played a diversity of both comic and dramatic roles, usually drunk, including the lead in a travesty on Lyman Beecher, entitled *Departed Spirits or a Temperance Hoax*. Unhappily married at twenty-two, working at odd jobs on and off the stage, when sober enough to work at all, he lost his wife in childbirth, and the daughter she bore him died a few days later. While trying to drown his grief, he ran into a fervent Washingtonian who led him to a revival meeting in Worcester, Massachusetts. When he was pressed to mount the platform and bear witness to the horrors of the drunkard's life, Gough's theatrical instinct asserted itself, and he delivered an hour-long harangue that nailed his listeners to their seats. He then signed the pledge.

The society was determined never to let such a spellbinder go. They fed him and lodged him, gave him a sizable purse and sent him out on the temperance lecture circuit. It was November, 1842, when Gough started his new career and ever after he could scarcely keep up with the demands for his orations. He liked to conclude them with a cautionary poem chosen for him by his second wife. The author was Mrs. Lydia Huntley Sigourney, a Connecticut poet and frequent contributor to *Godey's Lady's Book*.

> O husband, husband, go not out
> Again this stormy night
> For snowy clouds have hid the earth
> Within a robe of white.—
> Look in the cradle, husband, look.
> There sleeps our baby boy.
> He wakes, he walks to look on thee
> And curl his lip in joy—
> He heeded not her fond appeal
> But thrust his wife aside;
> The gentle being who had been

But one short year his bride.
He braved the snow. He faced the storm
And journeyed o'er the plain
But never to his wife and child
The drunkard came again.

Gough did not soon conquer his own craving for booze, and he
suffered several spectacular relapses. But he was too great an
asset to the cause for banishment. A Washingtonian salvage
squad would sober him up, repledge him and return him to the
lecture platform. His most serious fall occurred in 1845 in New
York City, where, after a week's disappearance, he was found
semiconscious in a lower West Side brothel. Despite the skepti-
cism of the press, the society chose to accept Gough's version of
events, according to which an acquaintance from his old
bookbinding days—probably a secret agent of antitemperance
forces, he surmised—hailed him as he was strolling along
Broadway and invited him into a soft-drink parlor. The raspberry soda that Gough ordered tasted, in retrospect, strangely
like gin, though the villain may have introduced some drug.
Whatever it was, it aroused a fearful alcoholic thirst, and Gough
tore off in search of rum, eventually passing out in the brothel to
which one of its denizens enticed him.

At the outset of his lecture career Gough's living expenses were
defrayed by passing the hat. The collection seldom exceeded $3.
As his popularity grew, he was paid $10 a lecture, the sponsoring
organization retaining the admission fees, which ranged from 25
to 75 cents. But at the peak of his success, when temperance
advocacy generally had become a thriving profession, he received
close to $200 an appearance. Logging 450,000 miles of travel and
delivering 8,000 lectures before audiences totaling 9,000,000, he
acquired a comfortable fortune and a fine house near Worcester,
Massachusetts.

Gough did not confine his lectures to temperance, but
dramatized a variety of moral and religious issues. The master-
piece of his later years was his adaptation of the drama based on
Timothy Shay Arthur's temperance novel, *Ten Nights in a
Barroom*. Gough portrayed all the characters, writhing in the
throes of delirium tremens as the hero, Joe Morgan, one moment,
the next pleading with Joe in the piping tones of the drunkard's
golden-haired little daughter, Mary:

Oh, father, dear father, come home with me now,
The clock in the steeple strikes one.
You said you were coming right home from the shop
As soon as your day's work was done. . . .

Long before apoplexy carried him off in 1866, at the age of sixty-eight, during a superheated performance in Frankfort, Pennsylvania, Gough had broken with the Washingtonians. His reasons were the same as those that removed the society from the mainstream of the temperance movement. They had lost the support of the churches by refusing to involve religion in their pursuit of sobriety and of the temperance politicians by repudiating legal enforcement. John Gough, in the majesty of his snowy-bearded old age, insisted that the religious element constituted the true measure of the movement's success and though originally a "moral suasionist," he ended up championing temperance by law.

Within a decade of its inception the Washington Society had disbanded. But there remained no dearth of troops to pursue the struggle on other levels.

Thomas Poage Hunt, a troll-like, humpbacked little Presbyterian divine from Virginia, who called himself "the Drunkard's Friend," believed that a loathing for liquor could not be instilled in the young too early. Accordingly, he organized, in 1836, large numbers of Sunday school pupils into the Cold Water Army, who would repeat after him poetic pledges of his own composition. The first one he administered ran:

> I do not think
> I'll ever drink
> Whiskey or Gin,
> Brandy or Rum,
> Or any thing
> That will make drunk come.

And a later one:

> Trusting in help from Heaven above,
> We pledge ourselves to works of love,
> With hearts and hands united stand
> To spread a blessing o'er the land.

And now resolve we will not take,
Nor give, nor buy, nor sell, nor make,
Through all the years of mortal life
Those drinks which cause pain, woe, and strife—
Rum, Brandy, Whiskey, Cordials fine,
Gin, Cider, Porter, Ale, and Wine.

At temperance rallies the consecrated tots would parade, as many as a thousand strong, with blue ribbons pinned to the boys' shoulders, white ribbons to the girls', both wearing badges inscribed HERE WE PLEDGE PERPETUAL HATE TO ALL THAT CAN INTOXICATE, and waving white banners bearing such Huntian proclamations as "DRINK A LITTLE" IS THE DRUNKARD'S SONG AND RUIN. . . . THIS FLAG, RUMSELLER, MEANS NO HARM TO THEE, WE LOVE AS BRETHREN, BUT WE WILL BE FREE. . . .

The dwarfish pastor, his metal-rimmed spectacles perched on top of his head, launched his fiercest diatribes against the sellers of liquor. "Children," he would tell his small disciples, "there is a great army of drunkards in the United States. Somewhere near half a million of men and women belong to it. The liquor-sellers, for money, constantly provide them with poison. So about thirty or forty thousand of them die every year . . ." and in his *Life and Thoughts* he wrote: "In a town in Pennsylvania, in which I was lecturing a liquor-seller said he did not know how he could live, if he did not sell liquor. I told him I did not know that it was essential to the world that he should live at all."

The Independent Order of Rechabites of North America took its name and its mission from Jeremiah, 35:5-6, 14:

And I set before the sons of the house of the Rechabites pots full of wine, and cups, and I said unto them, Drink ye wine.
But they said, We will drink no wine: for Jonadab the son of Rechab our father commanded us, saying, Ye shall drink no wine, neither ye, nor your sons for ever.
The words of Jonadab the son of Rechab, that he commanded his sons not to drink wine, are performed; for unto this day they drink none, but obey their father's commandment. . . .

The Biblical Rechabites were pastoral tent dwellers of Israelite extraction, and the new temperance society called its regional divisions tents, the original headquarters tent having been pitched in New York City in 1842. (An international order with the same name and purpose had arisen in England seven years earlier, but there was no other connection.) It was the first American society to combine total abstinence with mutual benefits and secret ritual. Three classes of membership were established under the rule of a High Tent, with Grand Tents controlling the state chapters. The Primary Tents consisted of "white males of good moral character, not under 16 years of age, believing in the existence and omnipotence of God, and willing to sign our pledge"; the Women's Tents of "white women and girls of good moral character and not less than 12 years of age"; and Junior Tents of "white youths of good moral character . . . between the ages of 10 and 18 years." The number of tents grew to 1,000 with a total membership of about 100,000.

On September 29, 1842, sixteen disaffected members of the waning Washington Temperance Society, all of them New York craftsmen, gathered in Teetotaler's Hall, 71 Division Street, at the request of the brothers John and Isaac Oliver, both printers and Washingtonians. Printed invitations under the letterhead "Sons of Temperance" indicated an order like that of the Rechabites, which was then barely a week old. "The object of the meeting," the invitations set forth, "is to organize a beneficial society based on total abstinence, bearing the above title. It is proposed to make the initiation fee at first $1.00 and dues 6 & ¼ cents a week in cases of sickness a member to be entitled to $4.00 a week, and in case of death $30.00 to be appropriated for funeral expenses."

Taking another leaf from the Rechabites, the Sons of Temperance appealed to the boyish love of ritual, regalia and secrecy common among the Americans of that epoch as manifest by nontemperance fraternal orders like the Masons, the Odd Fellows, the Druids. For their emblem the Sons of Temperance chose a triangle enclosing a six-pointed star. The triangle symbolized love, purity and fidelity; the star, the light that temperance had cast upon a world in alcoholic darkness. The Most Worthy Brothers, as the rank and file were called, greeted each other with a secret grip and a password. The top-echelon officers bore titles like Grand Worthy Patriarch, Grand Scribe, Most Worthy Scribe, Most Worthy Patron. The structure of the organization was tripartite with Subordinate (local) Divisions,

Grand (state) Divisions and the National Division. No distinctions of sex, race, wealth or social standing were recognized. The society later created a juvenile branch, the Cadets of Temperance, and merged with a distaff society, the Daughters of Temperance. For the first twenty years of its existence it carried the major burden of temperance advocacy not only in America, but, having developed into an international order, as far away as Australia. At its peak strength, before the Civil War, it numbered in the United States 6,000 divisions with 250,000 brothers.

In Springfield Lincoln donned the initiate's white regalia. But when the Sons of Temperance celebrated their twenty-first anniversary with a march on the White House, he disappointed them. John Nicolay, the President's secretary, described the encounter in his diary dated September 29, 1863:

> Today came to the Executive Mansion an assembly of cold-water men & cold-water women to make a temperance speech at the Tycoon & receive a response. They filed into the East Room looking blue & thin in the keen autumnal air. . . . Three blue-skinned damsels did Love, Purity & Fidelity in Red, White & Blue gowns. A few invalid soldiers stumped along in the dismal procession. They made a long speech at the Tycoon in which they called Intemperance the cause of our defeats. He could not see it, as the rebels drink more and worse whiskey than we do.

The delegation arrived bursting with suggestions for preventing soldiers from drinking. The harassed President said:

> I cannot make particular responses to them at this time. To prevent intemperance in the army is even a part of the articles of war. . . . I am not sure that consistently with public service, more can be done than has been done. . . . I think that the reasonable men of the world have long since agreed that intemperance is one of the greatest, if not the very greatest of all evils among mankind. . . . That the disease exists and that it is a very great one is agreed upon by all.
>
> The mode of cure is one about which there may be differences of opinion. You have suggested that in an army—our army—drunkenness is a great evil, and one which, while it exists to a very great extent, we cannot expect to overcome so entirely as to leave such successes in our arms as we might have without it. This undoubtedly is true, and while it is, perhaps, rather a bad source to derive comfort from, nevertheless in a hard struggle, I do not

know but what it is some consolation to be aware that there is
some intemperance on the other side, too, and that they have no
right to beat us in physical combat on that ground. . . . I thank
you heartily, gentlemen, for this call, and for bringing with you
these very many pretty ladies.

There were the Templars of Honor and Temperance, an
advanced degree of the Sons of Temperance composed of
exemplary members who wished to form a knightly inner circle
to which all might aspire. This elitism led to a division, and the
Templars raised their first independent Grand Temple in New
York in 1845. They wanted still fancier rituals and regalia than
the parent body, adopted lacy white aprons, jeweled robes and
an elaborate seal. At their thirtieth annual convention they could
count twenty Grand Temples scattered through the country,
16,000 adult members, about an equal number of juveniles, and
a Social Temple for their women relatives. . . . And the Knights
of Jericho, another offshoot of the Sons of Temperance, this one
proposing to recruit minors too old for the Cadets and too young
for the Sons. . . . And the Independent Order of Good Templars
organized in 1851 at Castor Hollow, New York, near Utica, by
Knights of Jericho who had attained maturity. It grew into a
national, then an international society with 600,000 members,
each member rising to full-fledged membership through three
degrees—"Heart," which taught him his duty to himself and the
necessity of teetotalism; "Charity," which taught him his duty to
others; and "Royal Virtue," which taught him his duty to God.
The admission of women gave rise to ribald rumors among the
impious and the intemperate that the Good Templars were
actually a free-love society. . . . And the Order of Good Samaritans, starting out in New York in 1857 as an all-white,
all-male order, but within a year opening membership and
privileges to women, the Daughters of Samaria, and to blacks,
the first temperance society to welcome both. Under the
guidance of a Right Worthy National Grand Sire the Samaritans
aimed to rescue those unfortunates who while "passing from
Jerusalem to Jericho have fallen among thieves," and their
initiation rite, reputed to be the most spectacular of all temperance ceremonies, reenacted with mechanical and pyrotechnical
effects the parable of the Good Samaritan. . . . And the
Dashaways, founded in San Francisco in 1859 by four young rips

who met in a saloon for a spree, then unaccountably decided instead to "dash away the flowing bowl." Nearly every California town produced a Dashaway club that year. The following year some kindred Chicago youths formed the Temperance Flying Artillery. . . . And the Royal Templars of Buffalo whose chief object was to enforce the city's Sunday blue laws. . . . And the Sons of Jonadab, who derived their inspiration from the same source as the Rechabites, but considered all other temperance societies too lax. A single misstep, they felt, should suffice to merit permanent banishment without right of appeal. Criticized as illiberal and unchristian, the Jonadabs never won more than 1,200 members. . . . And the Unitarian Temperance Society, which distributed "scientific information" about the effects of alcohol. . . . And the post-Civil War Friends of Temperance, launched in Petersburg, Virginia, to combat the soaring rate of drunkenness after the armistice. It admitted whites only, but created a separate order for blacks, the Sons of Toil. Evolving into the United Friends of Temperance, it forged a popular front consisting of the Sons of Temperance, the Knights of Jericho, the Temple of Honor and Temperance and the Good Templars. Its table of organization listed Most Worthy Primates at the top, followed by Associates, Scribes, Treasurers, Chaplains, Conductors and Sentinels. The Friends fell apart in 1881 after a campaign by their Texas chapter to bring about state constitutional prohibition failed. . . . And the Vanguard of Freedom, devised for the children of freed slaves. . . . And the United Order of True Reformers, organized by and for southern blacks. . . . And the Catholic Total Abstinence Union of Baltimore, a unique society at that time, 1872, the Catholics as a class having shown scant interest in organized temperance, let alone prohibition. . . .

It was easy for America's great wet majority to dismiss the leaders of the dry minority as bigots, crackbrains or hypocrites. Many of them were. But there were also many men among them of intelligence and goodwill whom only the loftiest motives impelled to fight John Barleycorn. They, or their fathers before them, had crossed the Atlantic, hoping to make a better society than the one they had fled, and in the enormous daily consumption of alcohol they saw, with some reason, an obstacle to social progress. Though often simplistic, naïve and humorless, they brought to their struggle for temperance the same moral fervor with which they opposed the evils of special privilege, child labor and slavery. Prohibition aside, no latter-day liberal could quarrel with much of what these early reformers stood for. But only when moral fervor was compromised with political expedience did the temperance movement begin to make real headway.

4. Strange Bedfellows

Mighty reformer! Oft the trump of Fame,
Blown by thyself, has sent abroad thy name!
Sublime Fanatic! who to aid thy cause,
Slights trifles such as Constitutions, Laws!
O Pimp Majestic! whose sharp gimlet eye,
All jugs conceal'd and demijohns can spy!
Astute Smell-fungus! Striving as a goal,
To poke thy nose in every dirty hole!
Pimp, Spy, Fanatic arrogant at heart!
Language would fail to draw thee as thou art!

—ANON.

THE state of Maine, to which General Appleton had removed in 1833, was perhaps the hardest-drinking state in the Union. Its largest city, Portland, with a population of about 10,000, supported 200 licensed liquor dealers, or 1 for every 50 inhabitants, and an incalculable number of unlicensed dram shops, 7 distilleries and 2 breweries. The Portland town hall bell tolled at midmorning and in the afternoon to announce a drinking recess for all employees. Fisheries and lumber mills constituted the chief industries, the various products of which were shipped to the West Indies and exchanged for rum and molasses, the latter being converted into domestic rum. Not many dollars of this trade enriched the state treasury because the Down Easters themselves drank nearly every drop, whether imported or domestic. According to a statistician of the period, they spent on drink, every twenty years, a sum equivalent to the value of all the property in Maine.

Under such circumstances it is not surprising that any efforts to mount a temperance drive met with raillery and sometimes physical violence. A group of teetotaling Portland Quakers who banded together in 1812, when Maine still formed part of Massachusetts, came to be known by the derisory nickname of "Sixty-niners" because only 69 persons responded to their initial appeal for a public meeting. Jeering children chalked the numerals on fences and walks. Some of the older folk, denouncing Quaker moralizing as intemperate in itself, held an anti-Sixty-niner rally in a tavern at which moderate amounts of liquor were consumed to demonstrate "true temperance." Later attempts were made to burn down the Quaker house where the Sixty-niners first met.

For a decade, during which Maine achieved statehood, the Sixty-niners stood alone as champions of total abstinence. Then the wretched end, in 1827, of the governor of Maine, Enoch Lincoln, a Harvard alumnus and a man of impressive intellectual gifts, served to advance the cause. He drank himself to death. Following his state funeral and burial on the grounds of the statehouse, another small temperance organization took shape in the town of Prospect. With a membership of only 101 after a year of recruitment, disaster befell it. In its eagerness to extend its influence it admitted saloonkeepers. They not only continued to guzzle themselves, but seduced other members into resuming their dissolute old ways. The society quickly disintegrated, but reorganizing as the New Prospect Phoenix Temperance Society and taking pains to keep liquor dealers away, it began at length to thrive.

Partly through persistent agitation by crusaders like Appleton, by agents of the American Temperance Society and by various clergymen, partly through civic catastrophes attributable to drunkenness, total abstinence groups gained strength in town after Maine town. In Gardiner, for example, during an orgiastic celebration of July 4, 1833, the town hall was burned to the ground. The soberer residents pushed an ordinance through the town council closing all saloons and appointed a vigilante committee to keep them closed. This was one of the earliest applications of an important legislative principle, first adopted by Maine and later by many states—the principle of local option whereby the state government left it up to the local governments whether to allow saloons and liquor shops to operate within their boundaries.

At about the time that James Appleton changed his residence

there rose to notoriety on the Maine scene an equally implacable foe of liquor, twenty years his junior, and they were soon fighting shoulder to shoulder. If Appleton was "the Father of Prohibition," his young companion-in-arms fully merited the title his admirers bestowed on him—"the Napoleon of Temperance."

Among the prominent Quaker members of the old Sixty-niners had been Joshua Dow, the owner of a flourishing Portland tannery. He had a son, Neal, who so thoroughly assimilated the parental puritanism that he even frowned upon his pious maternal Grandmother Hall when she took to smoking a pipe. Her father had become a legend in the region both because of his baptismal name, Hate-Evil, and his fertility. Before he died at age ninety Hate-Evil Hall could count 497 direct descendants.

After attending public schools in Portland, then the Friends' Academy, Dow wanted to go to college to study law, but his father, believing that licentiousness was rife in college communities, decided against exposing the boy to temptation and instead put him to work in his tannery.

In at least one important respect Dow differed fundamentally with the Society of Friends. Whereas they abjured force under all circumstances, he subscribed to muscular Christianity, considering it the duty of the righteous man, if moral suasion failed, to beat virtue into the sinner's head. He was well equipped to do so. Though short and slight, he carried power in his fists, having learned to box expertly. Quick to take offense, his voice rising to a bellow, his face turning a dark, dangerous red, he could cow opponents bigger than himself. In contemplative repose his wide, thin mouth looked like a crack in a slab of granite. Upon reaching conscript age, Dow refused to claim exemption as a Quaker, defended the use of what the Quakers termed "carnal weapons," when wielded in a just cause, and loudly reproached Federalist politicians for having opposed the War of 1812. Such belligerence obliged the Friends to muster him out of the sect.

At eighteen Dow joined Portland's volunteer fire department partly because it provided him with a ready-made band of brawny youths like himself whom he could lead against the forces of evil, as when, for example, a street mob tried to disrupt an antislavery rally. Abolition ran second only to prohibition among the causes Dow championed. ("His face is white," said a Portland black, intending to express gratitude, "but, God bless him, his heart is black.") Dow also saw in the fire department an opportunity to strike a blow for temperance. What normally attracted new members were the frequent engine company dinners at which liquor flowed copiously. It was a measure of Dow's powers of persuasion that his Deluge Engine Company, of which he was elected captain, actually dispensed with liquor at its next dinner, the first dry festivity in the department's history. Dow failed to move the Portland authorities, however, when he implored them to end the city's immemorial custom of tolling drinking-time bells.

His parentally instilled horror of liquor dealers hardened into an obsession. He uttered his first open declaration of war against them following his marriage in 1830 to Miss Cornelia Durant Maynard, who was to bear him six children. A brother-in-law with a weakness for rum that had cost him job after job managed to find another, and lest he drink himself out of that one too, Dow appealed to the young sot's regular supplier not to sell him any more. "I have a license to sell," said the rum retailer, "and I shall do so."

"So you have a license to sell," cried Dow, quivering with rage, "and you propose to support your family by impoverishing others! With God's help I'll change all that!"

Dow was promoted to chief of the fire department, but his dependability as a fire fighter came into question when he was overheard to remark, as the casks exploded during a blaze that leveled a wholesale liquor store, "Magnificent sight!" Not long after, he allowed fire to reduce another liquor store to cinders without turning on a single hose. When the city's frightened liquor dealers brought an action before the board of aldermen to have him discharged, Dow exonerated himself by claiming that in the first instance he was only giving voice to an esthetic appreciation of the spectacle and, in the second, he had to sacrifice the store to save the buildings facing it.

It was from Appleton that Dow took the idea of state prohibition and made it his lifelong preoccupation. Both crusaders then belonged to the Maine Temperance Society, which focused upon the abuse rather than the use of liquor, an approach too permissive to suit them, and they broke away in 1837 to form the total-abstinence Maine Temperance Union. As chairman of a joint select committee in the legislature, Appleton prepared a report marshaling the arguments for prohibition together with a bill he drafted outlawing the sale of liquor. Both were tabled.

Three years later the Massachusetts drys also suffered a reverse under circumstances that taught Appleton and Dow a lesson in political strategy. At the urging of the state's Democratic Governor Marcus Morton the legislature repealed the fifteen-gallon law. The blow was all the bitterer to the drys in that Morton had been the first president of the American Temperance Union. But though he remained a steadfast temperance champion, he repudiated the law as an infringement upon both individual freedom and property rights. The next week angry delegates from various temperance organizations, 1,500 of them all told, converged upon Boston for a convention and in the course of it adopted a nonpartisan policy which the dry forces would adhere to for eighty years. They resolved to vote thenceforth "only for those men as candidates for legislative and executive offices, who are known and inflexible friends of [prohibition]."

Dow became a rich man, enlarging the family tannery, acquiring extensive timber holdings and assuming directorships in half a dozen Maine corporations. Wealth, the former Quaker believed, was the reward of virtue and sobriety, and as a moral inspiration to others he would flaunt it. He wore velvet vests trimmed with lace and a satin beaver and carried a gold watch that cost $200. Riding with companions in his carriage through Portland's slums, he would point to some dilapidated shanty, observing, "Rum did that."

Dow achieved material success even though he devoted less time and energy to business affairs than to combating the liquor interests. His domestic relations suffered, however. When, at the peak of his temperance activities, his two-year-old son died, he admitted remorsefully to his wife that he had been barely aware of the infant's existence. "My heart, as well as my thoughts, have been, perhaps, too much occupied," he told her. "I have felt willing to sacrifice them to my life and my thoughts have not had time to linger long around the loved ones of my own household."

After the Boston resolution Dow decided to enter the political arena. He began by badgering the Portland aldermen into putting to a referendum the question: Should the liquor dealers' licenses be revoked and all liquor sales illegalized? He then set his temperance troops, many of them recruited from among his employees, to knocking on every Portland door, decrying the evils of drink and distributing admonitory literature. By a margin of two votes the liquor dealers were allowed to retain their licenses. But two years later, as municipal elections approached again, Dow had the referendum resubmitted and this time the dry voters outnumbered the wets 926 to 486.

It was a hollow victory. A few of Portland's dealers went out of business, but most continued to dispense liquor without a license, and since there existed no agency large enough to police them, they suffered no serious inconvenience. The three or four dealers actually arrested and convicted were let off with trifling fines by sympathetic magistrates.

Dow saw that to get a truly prohibitory statute, he must maneuver within the state government, not merely at the local level. He went to Augusta, the capital, to plead with representatives for a bill similar to Appleton's tabled Act for the Suppression of Drinking Houses and Tippling Shops. In 1845 the House voted it down without debate.

Disgusted but dauntless, Colonel Dow, as he now styled himself, having obtained the commission through political favor without ever serving in any military capacity, spent the winter stumping the state and applying the lesson learned at the Boston convention. Ignoring party lines, he rallied various regional temperance societies behind any candidate—Whig, Democrat or member of the abolitionist Liberty Party—who would agree to vote dry. Traveling by sleigh 4,000 miles in two winter months, the colonel collected 40,000 signatures on petitions to the legislature, including one 59 feet long from a Portland woman's society, which Mrs. Dow had circulated. Typical of the impassioned pleas Dow collected was this by two sisters in the tiny, remote settlement of Whitfield: "We beseech you again in behalf of the living—and further, in behalf of your children yet unborn, to stamp an indelible annihilation of the infernal trade."

The legislators, a number of whom owed their ascendance to Dow's backing, finally enacted a prohibitory law in 1846, but so watered down from the Appleton bill by loophole amendments, with only mild penalties prescribed for violations and no provision for enforcement machinery, as to be largely ineffective.

It was nevertheless a victory of sorts, and Dow returned triumphant to Portland, crowing that "there shall not be a

grogshop in this city in ninety days after this date." The "sublime
fanatic," as an anonymous poet called him, tried hard to make
the promise good by spying out and reporting violators. Numerous prosecutions resulted, and one after the other the grogshops
vanished. But the guile of the dealers kept the liquor flowing all
the same. The law said nothing, for example, about giving booze
away. So they would sell, say, a pickle or a wedge of cheese at an
inflated price and with it offer a free drink. Through another
ruse a Portlander could usually get his " 'leven o'clock" in a
certain tavern back room, admission by ticket only. On a kind of
lazy Susan projecting through the wall stood an empty glass. The
thirsty visitor would drop the ticket, for which he had paid the
equivalent of the price of a drink, into the glass, from behind the
wall invisible hands would give the turntable a spin, and the
glass would reappear full of rum. If caught at any of these
dodges, the offenders usually found they could bribe the police.

As Dow intensified his pursuit, his victims retaliated. By dark
of night they strewed his backyard with broken bottles, deposited
dead animals in his carriage, befouled the front steps of his
sumptuous seventeen-room mansion with offal. A person unknown heaved a bottle of asafetida through his parlor window,
and the nauseating stench sickened the whole household. Once,
in broad daylight, a man with a horsewhip grabbed Dow from
behind and pulled him to the ground, but before he could use the
whip, the doughty little crusader fetched him a tremendous kick,
putting him to flight, overtook him and held him down until the
police arrived. His assailant turned out to be a sailor from
another part of the state. Certain that some vengeful liquor
faction had hired him to administer a horsewhipping, Dow was
aghast when the jury failed to convict him. He went about with a
brace of loaded pistols for a time but gave them up after
accidentally discharging one and nearly shooting a small child.

Portland had three seats in the Maine House of Representatives, and in 1847 Dow, resolved to play a more direct role in
state politics, set out to capture one of them. He expected to be
nominated by the Whigs, who controlled the city hall and were
predominantly dry, but the violence and slander of his campaign
offensive, along with his pious implications that Providence had
designated him for the office, repelled all but a handful of
hard-core disciples. He maligned his principal rival, Phineas
Barnes, editor of the Portland *Advertiser*, as a "rum candidate"

and secret tippler and conjured all good temperance men to take heed lest at the polls they prove guilty of "contending against God." Barnes won the nomination and the election.

Dow retired from both political and temperance activity, but only briefly. By 1849 he was back, touting a new state liquor bill and seeking new alliances to smooth its passage through the legislature. The bill empowered justices of the peace to issue warrants for the search and seizure of liquor as evidence against the sellers. Dow found the new alliances among the Whigs and Democrats who had bolted their party because it did not oppose the extension of slavery to the territory conquered in the Mexican War; among the Free-Soilers, a coalition of Whigs and Democrats, and the Liberty Party; among the Antislavery Democrats; and at length among leaders of the Know-Nothing movement. This last element consisted mainly of native-born Protestants hostile to immigrants and Roman Catholics. Originating as the American Republican Party in New York in 1843, when the rate of immigration was rising fast, transplanted to other eastern states as the Native American Party, which declared itself a national party in 1845, Know-Nothingism spawned a number of secret societies—the Order of United Americans, for example, and the Order of the Star-Spangled Banner, whose members gave it its popular name by professing, whenever questioned about their activities, to know nothing. Dow shared their xenophobia, particularly in regard to Irish Catholics, who retained their old-country devotion to cheap whiskey and the shebeen. "Irish cattle," he called them, denounced them as the principal violators of the liquor laws and tried to have them disfranchised on the grounds that they were too ignorant to vote. His association with suspected Know-Nothings grew so close as to suggest that he himself belonged to one of the secret orders.

Fortified by his new alliances, restraining for once his vituperative tongue, Dow ran for mayor of Portland in 1851 and won by a plurality of 396 votes out of a total cast of 2,271. Before a month had elapsed, he was on his way to Augusta with the old Appleton bill, to which he had added still more rigorous clauses. It now prohibited the sale and manufacture of any intoxicating liquor except for medical and industrial use and then only by an officially appointed agent. Unauthorized sellers faced a fine of $10 for the first offense, $20 for the second and for the third $20 plus six months' imprisonment. The penalties for manufacturing liquor without municipal approval ranged from fines of $100 to $200 and four months in jail. Defendants who appealed a conviction were required to post a bond with security equivalent to four times its face value, and if the conviction was upheld, to pay a double fine. Under Dow's toughened search-and-seizure provision any three citizens who suspected illegal sales could obtain a warrant to enter the accused's premises, root out the contraband and turn it over to the police for destruction. But not to antagonize the wealthy, Dow exempted imported liquor consumed in the privacy of the home.

Wearing a blue jacket and frilly figured vest, his hair long and curled after the current fashion, Dow presented his bill to the lower house on May 26. He did so confidently, for he could count 81 allies among the 121 representatives. Three days later the bill was passed. The Senate debate began the following day. Dow's most virulent opponent, Democratic Senator Shepard Cary, a wet proslavery lumber magnate, led off by describing him as Portland's "popinjay mayor . . . a pretty, dapper little man."
The senator went on:

> I train in a different company. I do not expect to have any influence in the party until the reign of niggerism and fanaticism is over. A few years ago the jackdaw Mayor of Portland, this man with the fancy vest . . . was at the head of the nigger movement in that city . . . but even Abolitionism was not strong enough for his diseased palate, and he has added temperance to his former stock of humbugs. Is this Federal-abolition-wringneck to be allowed to dictate to a Democratic legislation what enactments it shall pass?

The answer was a resounding yea. Of the 28 senators voting, a majority of 18, composed of 14 Democrats, 3 Whigs and a Free Soiler, most of them politically beholden to Dow, accepted the bill without a word altered. In his jubilation the victor brushed aside legislative protocol and, clutching the bill, dashed over to the statehouse for the necessary gubernatorial signature.It was Governor John Hubbard's natural inclination to veto the bill, being no teetotaler himself; but he had his eye on another term, and he did not care to forfeit Dow's support. So he signed, consummating the pugnacious little reformer's prodigious feat—

the passage of the first state prohibition law by the wettest state in a predominantly wet nation. (Oregon Territory had adopted a general prohibition law in 1844, but the far northwest was then too remote and sparsely populated for it to have much effect.)

Upon returning to Portland, the mayor announced that he would allow the liquor dealers a period of grace—sixteen days, as it turned out—in which to remove their stocks from the city. A dealer bolder than the rest ventured to test the constitutionality of the law. He not only refused to transport a single bottle, but openly sold some rum. Dow personally supervised a raid. While one officer held the defiant dealer against the wall, three others hauled the stock away in drays, $2,000 worth. At the city hall, as a stunned crowd looked on, the bottles and barrels were smashed and their contents poured down the sewer. The dealer brought suit against Dow. It dragged on for years, costing him a fortune, but he lost. Many of his confreres, meanwhile, shaken by the terrible sight of all that booze drained away, meekly signed an agreement to obey the law, confessing in the same document that they had broken it and thus, should they offend again, providing the court with an open-and-shut case.

Pursuing bootleggers appears to have occupied Dow to the exclusion of his mayoral duties. From his thronelike chair on a dais in the city hall, he began each working day devising new strategies to entrap them. He reinforced the regular police with volunteer agents, hired spies and informers and encouraged vigilante groups. He eventually established a special police court presided over by a judge he could depend on to show no mercy. He exceeded his authority under the law by instructing the police to search incoming trains, steamers and private craft. They uncovered bottles and casks inside big barrels of flour or sugar, in travelers' trunks, in coffins, under mounds of grain, apples, hides, dry goods. Legitimate merchants complained that the police were wrecking consignments by boring holes through the containers with long augers. During his first year in office the relentless mayor saw seventy Portlanders convicted of violating his Maine law.

And yet one could still get a drink in Portland or almost anywhere else in Maine.

*Neal Dow remembers the obduracy of the sinful**

   There were persons, it is true, in Portland, who continued to sell liquors on the sly, but in very small quantities. The authorities were often notified of the places in which the violators of the law had concealed their contraband stocks, and where they were carrying on the outlawed trade. Those hiding places were unknown to the general public and accessible only to the initiated. They were frequently reached through some obscure and filthy alleyway; sometimes they were approached through the front door of a building on one street, thence through that house to the back door, and across areas more or less obstructed with ashes and general rubbish to some shed or out-house connected with a building on another street. Those on whom the appetite for liquor had fastened its relentless grip would pursue these devious and unattractive ways to obtain the means to quench their unnatural thirst. . . .

   The quantity of liquors kept in these places of deposit were very small. The whole stock in some would be contained in a pint bottle or two in the coat pockets of the vendors; some of them would be in a thin tin vessel, fitted to the person, and worn under the vest. One of the places that I remember was in the brickwork of a chimney, a small cask of liquor being enclosed in it, a lead pipe leading out near the floor; another was an opening under the step of chamber chairs, another, under the floor of a pig-pen. Some of these stocks of liquor were hidden in ash-pits under cooking-stoves; some of them in cellar walls; some under chamber floors, the trap covered by the carpet and the bed placed over it; some on shelves in chimneys; some behind mangers in horse-stalls; some under stable floors, and some in unmentionable places.

The liquor interests did not wholly lack political resources. In the municipal elections of 1852 they made common cause with a jumble of anti-Dowites—Democrats who detested the Maine law, Whigs who favored it, but deplored the mayor's roughshod methods of enforcing it, the foreign-born and Catholic victims of his bigotry. . . . Pulling together, they managed to prevent Dow's reelection.

Dow found solace in dazzling triumphs abroad. As author of the Maine Law, for which he and his adherents falsely claimed

* *Reminiscences,* 1898.

total success, he had become a national celebrity. The weekly Maine *Temperance Watchmen*, as well as the press of numerous Protestant temperance organizations, spread his fame through periodicals and tracts distributed by the hundreds of thousands. "The Napoleon of Temperance," reported the *American Temperance Union Journal*, "brought into the battle-field every officer of the State . . . turned its whole artillery against the rum fortifications, and in less than six months . . . swept every distillery and brew-house, hotel-bar, splendid saloon and vile groggery clean from the State."

A throng of New England and Middle Atlantic teetotalers, meeting to express their admiration of the Maine Law, included an overwrought Son of Temperance who leaped to his feet, singing at the top of his lungs:

Come all ye friends of temperance, and listen to my strain,
I'll tell you how Old Alchy fares down in the state of Maine.
There's one Neal Dow, a Portland man, with great and noble soul,
He framed a law, without a flaw, to banish alcohol.

In New York City the National Temperance Society of the United States held a banquet in Dow's honor at which the renowned educator Horace Mann acclaimed him as "the moral Columbus" and gave the Maine Law an importance equal to "the discovery of the magnetic needle, the invention of printing, or any other great strides in the progress of civilization." The president of the society, General Sam Houston of Texas, once a tosspot of Cyclopean capacity, pinned a gold medal to Dow's pride-swollen chest.

After the passage of the Maine Law Dow had forwarded copies of it to temperance groups in other states and challenged them to duplicate his victory. "You can do it if you try," he assured them. He now followed up his exhortation with a wide-ranging lecture tour, drawing immense crowds, who were enthralled by his fiery recital of how Maine had been purged (though according to the enemy back home, there was more drinking in Portland and other Maine cities than at any time during the previous twenty years). To the local dry leaders, he expounded the strategy of supporting those political candidates, no matter what their party or ideological bent, who would swear fealty to the temperance banner.

No one man, of course, could be credited for the wave of prohibitionism that swept the country during the next four years, but none did more to stimulate it than Dow. Eleven states and two territories enacted laws as tough or tougher than Maine's. They were, in the order of their enactment, Minnesota Territory, Rhode Island, Massachusetts, Vermont, Michigan, Connecticut, Indiana, Delaware, Iowa, Nebraska Territory, New York, New Hampshire and Pennsylvania.

Riding the crest of his national fame, vowing death to the liquor traffic "if it takes all the hemp in Kentucky," Dow bid again in 1855 for the Portland mayoralty. The local arm of the newly emergent Republican Party, largely composed of Know-Nothings and sundry antislavery partisans, nominated him. Arrayed against him were what one of his campaign publicists termed "Rum, Hunkerism,* Catholicism and Corruption." Dow squeaked through by forty-seven votes.

Once invested, he made no secret of higher political aims—the Vice Presidency of the United States no less. If successful, his drumbeaters pointed out, "the scenes of drunkenness which disgraced the last Congress would scarcely be repeated." But Dow had served barely two months of his second mayoral term when he blundered into a trap of his own making. At his behest the state legislature had revised the Maine Law to stress the search-and-seizure provisions and increase the penalties. Inadvertently, Dow himself violated the law. Choosing the city hall as the place to store liquor authorized for medicinal and industrial uses, he ordered $1,600 worth. No agent had been appointed, and under the law only the agent could buy or sell liquor. Thus, to his enemies' glee, the mayor was technically guilty of an offense punishable by a fine of $20 and thirty days in jail, and they lost no time exploiting his blunder. The city's shrillest anti-Dow newspaper, the *Eastern Argus*, demanded that "the lash which Dow has prepared for others' backs be applied to his own." A distiller charged him with stockpiling liquor for personal profit and called upon the court to issue a search-and-seizure warrant. The deputy sheriff who obtained the warrant and seized the liquor, being a Dow appointee, could bring himself neither to remove it nor to arrest the mayor. A mob formed outside the city

---

* "Hunkers" was slang for the Conservative Democrats supposedly "hunkering"—that is, hankering—for office.

hall, shouting for the destruction of the liquor. To Dow's order to disperse, they responded with obscenities and rocks. He called out the militia. "I want every man of you to mark your man," he shrieked. "We'll see whether mob law shall rule here or whether the Chief Magistrate shall!" As the mob tried to force the doors of the city hall, he cried: "Fire!" The volley wounded seven men and killed one before the mob scattered.

When a doctor reported the fatality to him, the mayor glanced up from the cheese and crackers with which he was reinvigorating himself after the strain of the hostilities and coolly asked: "Is the body Irish?" The dead man happened to be a native-born sailor's mate, age twenty-two. Unmoved, Dow pronounced the killing entirely justified.

A substantial segment of public opinion and of the nation's press failed to share this view. A Connecticut newspaper described Dow as "a remorseless, unscrupulous tyrant, who wants only power to commit atrocities that would affright a Nero." Other periodicals conferred martyrdom upon the slain seaman, whose grave, according to one editorial, would be covered with floral tributes long after Dow's was "lost among the wild grasses and weeds that spring from carrion carcasses in places hideous to human tread." Broadsides were circulated, depicting the Portland militia shooting down unarmed citizens. A general clamor arose for the mayor's impeachment and prosecution as a murderer.

Retaining a Republican senator as his attorney, Dow was acquitted of illegally possessing liquor and, at a coroner's inquest, of homicide. But his political standing underwent a decline so steep that he did not trouble to run for reelection in 1856. Worse, the state legislature replaced his hard-won Maine Law with a licensing system which allowed innkeepers to sell liquor by the glass. Dow departed for a temperance missionary tour of England.

Home six months later, he recovered a measure of political power through bargains and compromises. He gained the support of Maine's dominant Republican Party for a new prohibitory law. This became the central issue in the 1858 state elections, with the Democrats backing the license system. The Republicans scored a smashing victory. The legislature then passed a law somewhat less stringent than the initial Maine Law, imposing lighter penalties and permitting the sale of wine and, as

a concession to the farm constituencies, whose fondest tipple it
was, hard cider. At the insistence of the new Republican
governor, Anson P. Morrill, the final choice between prohibition
and licensing was submitted to a referendum. In a light turnout
prohibition won by 28,865 ballots to 5,912. The plurality hardly
reflected the true picture of temperance in Maine, with its
population of about 600,000, for it retained its reputation as one
of the nation's drunkest states.

In recognition of Dow's services to the party, the Portland
Republicans returned him to the legislature in the fall of 1858.
By then a pall had fallen over the entire temperance movement.
Of the thirteen states which had enacted prohibitory laws since
1851 seven had repealed or radically modified them, and before
many more years elapsed Maine would stand alone as a dry
state.

The causes of this reform recession were manifold, the most
obvious being the insuperable problem of policing such thirsty
multitudes. From 1850 to 1860, the very decade during which the
temperance reformers achieved their greatest legislative victories,
the per capita consumption of beer, wine and whiskey increased
from 4.08 gallons to 6.43.* Beer-drinking took the sharpest rise.
From less than 37,000,000 gallons in 1850 the manufacture of
malt liquor had increased almost threefold by the end of the
decade, a change in national taste ascribable to the hordes of
German and other middle European immigrants with their love
of lager and skill at brewing it. The beer garden, resounding with
brass bands, belly laughter and sudsy sentimentality, was for
generations a favorite social environment of the masses, and
under German brewmasters beer and ale came to rank among
the country's leading industries.

But the major deterrents to further temperance progress were
such overriding concerns as the sectional differences—social,
economic, political and psychological—between North and
South, abolitionism and the secession of the Southern states,
culminating in the firing on Fort Sumter. Moral reforms
appeared inconsequential by comparison as the nation plunged
into civil war. Membership in temperance societies dwindled.
Soldiers and civilians alike sought relief from the agonies of the

* Computed from statistics of the U.S. Department of Commerce and the Bureau of
Internal Revenue.

conflict in drink. When the Union administration in order to replenish its war chest, levied a $20 license fee on liquor retailers and taxed the manufacturers at the rate of $1 per barrel of malt liquor and 20 cents per barrel of distilled liquor, it not only sanctioned the industry, but furnished the wets forever after with one of their most cogent arguments against prohibition—the immense loss of government revenue.

New Hampshire in 1855 had been the last state to adopt prohibition. Not for a quarter of a century would another state enact such a law.

II. The Party, the Union, the League 1869–1919

5. James Black for President

We will be as harsh as truth, and as uncompromising as justice. Urge us not to use moderation in a cause like the present. We are in earnest—we will not equivocate—we will not excuse—we will not retract a single inch, and we will be heard.

—THE REVEREND JOHN RUSSELL at the first convention of the National Prohibition Party

IN its darkest hours, following the Civil War, the nearly moribund temperance movement began to stir with fresh life. The stimulus arose mainly from the challenge posed by the arrogant, heavy-handed United States Brewers' Association, the first organized opposition to prohibitionism. Launched in New York City in the fall of 1862, four months after Congress passed the Internal Revenue Law, it numbered so many Germans that most of the speakers at its opening convention spoke in German.

> Cooperation is necessary [read the preamble to the association's charter]. Owners of breweries, separately, are unable to exercise a proper influence in the legislation and public administration. It appears especially necessary for the brewing trade that its interests be vigorously and energetically prosecuted before the legislative and executive departments. . . .

For its operating expenses the association levied upon all major establishments selling beer an assessment of $1,000 and upon small retailers $25 to $50, according to the volume of their trade. In addition, each member solicited contributions from the wholesalers eager for his patronage, such as the hop growers and the barrelmakers.

The association pursued two paramount objectives: first, to get the beer tax lowered and second, as expressed in a resolution at

its 1867 convention in Chicago, copying the political strategy of
the prewar drys, to "sustain no candidate of whatever party, in
any election, who is in any way disposed towards the total-abstinence cause." With a combined annual production now exceed-
ing 200,000,000 gallons, the brewers further resolved to place
their advertisements only in periodicals advocating the same
views.

Drawing upon its ample propaganda funds, the association
proceeded to distribute 30,000 circulars extolling legislative
candidates favorable to their interests, to patronize sixty different
newspapers which published sympathetic editorials and to enlist
the support of the German-American population.

The first of its sworn objectives was soon achieved. Within a
year the government had been prevailed upon to reduce the beer
tax from $1 a barrel to 60 cents. During a later convention,
attended by the Commissioner of Internal Revenue himself,
David Ames Wells, a well-known economist who championed
free trade and opposed a federal income tax, the brewers were
assured that "no imposition or increase of tax will be placed on
malt liquors by the government without first communicating
with this association and getting their views upon it." Although
the distillers did not effectively organize themselves for another
decade, they, too, benefited from the friendly commissioner's
pledge to "bring about a cordial understanding between the
government and the trade." Congress accepted Wells' recom-
mendation to lower the tax on spirits from $2 a gallon to 50
cents.

Such enemy conquests galvanized the depleted temperance
troops into renewed militancy. Their chief rallying grounds were
the lodges of the Good Templars, the only temperance society
which had not only retained a sizable membership during the
Civil War, but increased it afterward. Most of the lesser groups
either merged with the Templars, bringing the total membership
to almost 400,000, or closely associated themselves. When the
brewers threw down the gauntlet during their Chicago convention, the fast-growing temperance order was quick to pick it up.
Pennsylvania's Grand Lodge of Good Templars, meeting in
Pittsburgh at the same time, resolved: ". . . we do accept the
issue thus made, and declare that we will not vote for men who
countenance the liquor traffic, or degrade their official positions
by the use of intoxicating liquors."

This recall to political action, echoed and reechoed at Grand Lodge sessions the country over as well as at state and national temperance conventions, led to a radical departure in prohibitionist politics. With neither Republicans nor Democrats any longer willing to include a dry plank in their platforms, the drys moved to create a party of their own. First Michigan in 1867, then Illinois a year later, the latter proclaiming, "We acknowledge our dependence on God, and in His name we set up our banners in the cause of temperance," organized a third party at the state level. In an editorial, following the Illinois convention at Bloomington, the Chicago *Tribune* summarized the new prospect:

> For once the Temperance party have acted wisely. In too many cases they have attached themselves to other parties, and have then demanded that these other parties should adopt compulsory temperance as a part of their platform. If temperance be a question of such magnitude, morally and politically, that it must be presented at the polls, and candidates elected or defeated, as they may favor or oppose a prohibitory or liquor law, then it is of sufficient importance to command a party of its own. The country is divided politically between the Republican and Democratic parties. Both of these have, in every State including Massachusetts, refused to make prohibitory or liquor laws part of their policy. The reasoning in both cases is not an objection to temperance, or any disposition to favor drunkenness, but because such laws, wherever they have been enacted, have proved to be utter failures; and because such laws are wrong in principle.
>
> The advocates of prohibitory liquor laws are to be found among the most exemplary and estimable citizens, but there are others equally respectable, equally religious and exemplary, who oppose all such laws. The result is that the policy of prohibition is not, and can never be, made part of the policy of any existing party. It is, and must be, a policy of itself, distinct of all other questions. As well endeavor to make the Republican party adopt the peculiar faith of any one religious sect, and make that a political issue.
>
> The temperance advocates of Illinois have, therefore, done well in relieving both political parties of prohibition, and in relieving prohibition of other and incongruous questions. A temperance party composed of Democrats and Republicans, advocating prohibition, is better for that party, and all other parties, than a Republican party with a temperance plank, temporarily inserted in the platform until after the election.

Neither the Illinois nor the Michigan third party actually drafted a ticket for any election. The distinction of first doing so fell to the Prohibition Party of Ohio, which entered the Cleveland municipal elections in the spring of 1869. Its principal candidate received barely 1,000 votes.

The most persuasive of the moving spirits behind the third-party trend was James Black of Lancaster, Pennsylvania, a Methodist of Scottish descent, former Washingtonian, co-founder of Lancaster's Conestoga Division of the Sons of Temperance, of its Good Templar Lodge and of the Ocean Grove Camp Meeting Association in New Jersey with its seaside temperance resort. Black served the Templars successively as Grand Worthy Chief Templar and, a lawyer by profession, as Right Worthy Grand Counsellor. His abhorrence of liquor developed early in life when, as a muleskinner of sixteen on the Pennsylvania and Union Canal, he joined the older workers in a prolonged carousal. Awakening next day with pounding head and aching limbs, "he prayed to God to preserve him from another such humiliation."

Among Black's prolific literary contributions to the cause was a tract warning against the unsuspected dangers of cider—not hard cider, but ordinary fresh sweet cider. What his argument, embedded in eight pages of medical and Biblical citations, boiled down to was that cider, once exposed to air, quickly starts to ferment, and only a chemist can tell exactly how much alcohol it contains. "Though its use when quite fresh from the press . . . may be comparatively harmless to one who has never felt the drunkard's raging appetite, for the sake of our brother who is *in danger,* we abstain, and make a rule that the drinking of cider is a violation of the Good Templar's obligation." Thereafter any Templar who touched the stuff risked immediate expulsion.

Black was the principal organizer, in 1865, of the National Temperance Society and Publication House, whose New York City presses ground out during the next sixty years more than a billion pages of temperance literature. It published three monthly periodicals—*The National Temperance Advocate* for adults, *The Youth's Temperance Banner* for adolescents and *The Water Lily* for children—which reached a combined circulation of about 600,000. Its 2,000-odd books and pamphlets included the novels of Mary Anna Paull, notably *Tom's Trouble, Sought and Saved, Blossom and Blight* and *Packington Parish and What Happened in It;*

BENJAMIN RUSH, M.D.
His inquiry inspired a generation of temperance reformers.

America's first temperance society and the house in which it was organized in 1808. The organizers *(left to right)*: The Reverend Lebbeus Armstrong, Dr. Billy James Clark, Gardiner Stow, James Mott.

SOME EARLY TEMPERANCE LEADERS

THE REVEREND THOMAS P. HUNT
"The Drunkard's Friend and the
Liquor Seller's Vexation."

THE REVEREND JUSTIN EDWARDS
". . . shall we declare a war of
extermination and root it out?"

JOHN BARTHOLOMEW GOUGH
"Apostle of Cold Water"

JAMES APPLETON
". . . a license to disseminate the
Small Pox would be thought to be
no less proper and reasonable than
a license to sell Ardent Spirits."

THE REVEREND LYMAN BEECHER
"Woe to him that giveth his neighbor drink. . . ."

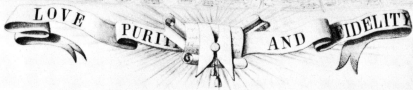

LOVE PURITY AND FIDELITY

Division No. State of

This is to Certify

That Brother _____ *was regular*
initiated and invested with the badge of the Order of t.

Sons of Temperance

on the _____ *day of* _____ *in the year of our L.*
One Thousand Eight Hundred and _____ *I*
witness whereof we hereunto annex our names.

_____ 18 ___

W.

R.

Published by Brother Edw. R Blattner 925 Coates St Philadᵃ

Entered according to Act of Congress in the Year 1851 by Edwᵈ R Blattner in the Clerks Office of the District Court of the Eastern District of Pennsylvania

L. N. Rosenthals Lith Philadᵃ

PROHIBITION PARTY:
Candidates for President of the United States, 1880–1904

THE TEMPERANCE CRUSADE.
FOUR HOURS IN A BAR ROOM.

1ST HOUR
CYNICAL INDIFFERENCE.

2ND HOUR
MOCKERY AND DEFIANCE.

3RD HOUR
RAGE AND DESPAIR.

4TH HOUR
UNCONDITIONAL SURRENDER.

J. FISHER 98, NASSAU St NEW YORK.

Women's Crusaders at work in Ohio (*circa* 1879)

Abraham Lincoln's tavern license, authorizing him to sell whiskey, gin and wine.

Frances E. Willard

"The uncrowned Queen of American Womanhood"

(Bettmann Archive)

In an Indiana saloon (*circa* 1880) Women's Crusaders keep tabs on the customers, while a deep-dyed villain prepares to rout them with the aid of a skunk.

"Organized mother love"—The General Staff
of the World's WCTU.

Seated (*left to right*): Anna A. Gordon, assistant secretary; Frances E. Willard,
president; Mary E. Sanderson, treasurer. Standing (*left*): Agnes E. Slack, secretary, and Lady Henry Somerset, vice-president-at-large.

Mrs. Bent of the Maine WCTU blows her golden cornet.

BOYHOOD.
The First Step.

YOUTH.
The Second Step.

MANHOOD.
A Confirmed Drunkard.

OLD AGE.
A Total Wreck.

A cautionary illustration from *Grappling with the Monster or The Curse and Cure of Strong Drink* by Timothy Shay Arthur, who also wrote *Ten Nights in a Bar-Room*.

Carry Nation at prayer in jail.

". . . a bulldog running along at the feet of Jesus, barking at what He doesn't like."

Daddy's in There---

And Our Shoes and Stockings and Clothes and Food Are in There, Too, and They'll Never Come Out.
—Chicago American.

WANTED--A FATHER; A LITTLE BOY'S PLEA
JULIA H. JOHNSON

A shy little boy stood peering
　Through the door of a bright saloon;
He looked as if food and clothing
　Would be thought a most welcome boon.

And one of the men, in passing,
　As if tossing a dog a bone,
Asked, "What do you want this evening?"
　In a rude and unkindly tone.

"I am wanting"—the boy's lips trembled—
　"I am wanting my father, sir."
And he gazed at the little tables
　Where the careless onlookers were.

It was there that he saw his father,
　But the man only shook his head,
And the boy, with his thin check burning,
　Ran away with a look of dread.

Oh, the fathers—the fathers wanted!
　How the heart-break, and bitter need,
With the longings, deep and piteous,
　For the wandering children plead.

May the children's call arouse them,
　May the fathers arise and go
With the young souls waiting for them,
　For the little ones need them so!

SERIES G. NO. 23.

The American Issue Publishing Co
Westerville Ohio

An object lesson from the Anti-Saloon League

DR. MARY EDWARDS WALKER (1832–1919)
Surgeon, suffragette and temperance fighter; she was several
times arrested for wearing male attire but persisted to the end
of her life.

THE REVEREND HOWARD HYDE RUSSELL, founder of the Anti-Saloon League.
"I prayed to God to stay the tide of the sun and shame. . . ."

WAYNE BIDWELL WHEELER, general counsel of the Anti-Saloon League.

"We'll make them believe in punishment after death!"

Mrs. D. O. Clark's *Slaying the Dragon*; Lydia Rouse's *Catherine Grafton's Mistake, or, Light at Eventide*; Margaret Winslow's *Saved by Sympathetic Kindness and the Grace of God*; Mrs. Julia McNair Wright's *Nothing to Drink: A Temperance Story* and *Jug-or-not* (Wherein Squire Arnot's entire household, "father, mother, children and servants were all under the demon." The frontispiece shows a neighbor's child, Solomon Tot, already on the road to ruin, as he sips a glass of bourbon the squire has carelessly left about and exclaims: "I love it!") For Publication House Mrs. Lizzie Penney edited a series of "Little People" booklets crammed with inspirational anecdotes, adages and verse, typically:

> If dogs could vote,
>   Then very, very soon,
> There'd be more meat and baker-shops
>   And not one rum saloon.

One Conant S. Foster contributed a lengthy verse sequence, *The Temperance Telescope*, beginning with a rake's progress:

> "Drop Inn!" Ay, in and after *down;*
> Who drops in here doth lose the crown
> Of Independence, and is curst
> With serfdom to the tyrant Thirst.
> Gaze on the self-reliant air
> With which the youth descends the stair;
> He only thought to take a glass
> With some attractive waiter lass,
> A moment listen to her talk
> And then continue on his walk.
> Deluded fool! his *glass* was ten;
> He sought the place again, again;
> Became the most debauched of men.
> The only walk he took that night
> Was downward from the path of right.

But none of the Publication House versifiers surpassed the fervor of Ella Wheeler Wilcox, sometimes called "the People's Poet," who composed this appeal in her best-selling *Drops of Water*:

> Don't drink, boys, don't!
>   There is nothing of happiness, pleasure, or cheer

D

In brandy, in whiskey, in rum, ale, or beer.
If they cheer you when drunk, you are certain to pay
In headaches and crossness the following day.
    Don't drink, boys, don't!

    Boys, let it alone!
Turn your back on your deadliest enemy—Drink!
An assassin disguised; nor for one moment think,
As some rashly say, that true women admire
The man who can boast that he's playing with fire.
    Boys, let it alone!

    No, boys, don't drink!
If the habit's begun, stop now, stop today!
Ere the spirit of thirst leads you on and away
Into vice, shame and drunkenness. This is the goal
Where the spirit of thirst leads the slave of the bowl.
    No, boys, *don't* drink!

    Boys, touch not, nor taste!
Don't think you can stop at the social "First Glass."
Too many have boasted that power, alas!
And found they were slaves to the seeming good friend,
And have grown into drunkards and knaves in the end.
    Boys, touch not, nor taste!

    Don't drink, boys, *Don't!*
If the loafers and idlers scoff, never heed:
True men and true women will wish you "God-speed."
There is nothing of purity, pleasure, or cheer
To be gotten from whiskey, wine, brandy, or beer.
    Don't drink, boys, *Don't!*

In addition to armchair reading, Publication House released a
steady flood of textbooks, broadsides, flyers and vade mecums to
aid the temperance campaigners, such as *One Thousand Temperance
Anecdotes, Jokes, Riddles, Puns and Smart Sayings, suitable for speakers,
readings and recitations.* The flyers rang innumerable changes on
the theme of the blessings that attended the teetotaler compared
to the miseries that overwhelmed the drinker. The Reverend
Edward Carswell, a Canadian Methodist and an artist, proved
particularly adept at producing illustrated temperance homilies,
of which a widely circulated example appears below:

No. 130.

THE ABSTAINER AND THE DRINKER

BY EDWARD CARSWELL.

I am worn by a man who works and thinks.

And I by one who don't, and drinks.

We guard his feet from damp and dust.

Like him we are always on the "bust."

I am the coat my master wears.

I resemble mine in terrible tears.

When master thirsts he comes to me, I cost him nothing; to all I'm free.

My master's throat I only burn. And cost him all he can borrow or earn

"Wherefore do ye spend money for that which is not bread? and your labor for that which satisfieth not?"—ISAIAH lv. 2.

Published by the National Temperance Society and Publication House,
273 Fourth Avenue, New York   Price $1.00 per 1000.   Postage 30 Cents.

Among James Black's chief collaborators in the mammoth publishing enterprise were Neal Dow and Edward Cornelius Delavan, an Albany newspaper proprietor. The resilient Dow had bounced back into public life after a financial scandal that ruined him as an officeholder. In 1857, following his reelection to the Maine legislature, he had borrowed state funds from a defalcating state treasurer, a lapse which, when exposed, led one temperance leader to lament: "Every grogshop in Maine resounds with fiendish scoffings." The Civil War offered Colonel Dow an opportunity to refurbish his tarnished reputation. He marched off at the head of the Thirteenth Regiment of Maine Volunteers, which was dubbed "the Hymn Singers" and extolled by Maine's dry reformers as "the most temperate and moral of all the regiments of the state." Promoted to brigadier general, Dow saw little of the action he craved, mainly because his commanding officer, General Benjamin Franklin Butler, so disliked him. Finally, during an attack against the Confederate redoubt at Port Hudson, Louisiana, in the spring of 1863, he was wounded twice and captured. After eight months in Libby Prison at Richmond, Virginia, he was exchanged for the Confederate cavalry general Fitzhugh Lee. Dow returned to Maine, a patriarchal figure at the age of sixty, with whitening muttonchop whiskers and an expression of marmoreal gravity. Traveling extensively in England and the United States, he perfected his skills as a temperance publicist, and in that capacity he contributed yeoman service to Black's National Temperance Society and Publication House.

Edward Delavan, a rotund old man, clean-shaven save for a massive white beard that sprang from beneath his jaw and flowed across his chest, had attained heroic stature in the eyes of his fellow prohibitionists when, in 1835, his Albany *Evening Journal* ran an exposé of local brewers, charging that they used water from a pond polluted by the refuse of a slaughterhouse and a glue factory. The brewers filed eight separate suits for damages aggregating $300,000 and lost them all after defense witnesses not only confirmed Delavan's allegations, but testified to having seen dead dogs, cats and cesspool drainings befouling the same pond.

Delavan retired permanently from commerce at the age of forty, having made millions as a real estate operator, hardware dealer and wine merchant. Once converted to the temperance cause, he emptied his wine cellars. For spiritual counsel Delavan leaned upon Dr. Eliphalet Nott, a Presbyterian clergyman who had delivered Alexander Hamilton's funeral oration, become president of Schenectady's Union College and, as a scientific experimenter, devised, among many other patented inventions, the first stove for burning anthracite coal. Nott was also responsible for starting an interminable "Bible wine controversy" when he advanced the theory that the Bible recognized both fermented and unfermented wine, but sanctioned the latter only. With Nott, Delavan organized the New York State Temperance Society in 1829. Five years later he called upon Justin Edwards to draw up a manifesto:

> Being satisfied from observation and experience, as well as from medical testimony, that ardent spirit, as a drink, is not only needless, but hurtful, and that the entire disuse of it would tend to promote the health, the virtue and the happiness of the community, we hereby express our conviction that should the citizens of the United States, and especially the young men, discontinue entirely the use of it, they would not only promote their personal benefit but the good of our country and the world.

To this document, Delavan managed eventually to obtain the signatures of twelve Presidents of the United States, from James Madison to Andrew Johnson.

Delavan spent a good deal of his fortune footing the bills for the state society's voluminous publications. He sent out from Albany more than 13,000,000 copies of temperance papers. He was particularly impressed by a Dr. Thomas Sewall's *Diagrams of the Human Stomach in Various Conditions*, illustrating the doctor's contention that "no one who indulges habitually in the use of alcoholic drinks, whether in the form of wine or more ardent spirits, possesses a healthy stomach." At a cost of $7,000 Delavan circulated 150,000 copies of the diagrams. They showed what purported to be a series of six dissected stomachs, the first captioned "Healthful," a smooth pale orange; the second ("Moderate Drinking"), heavily veined; the third ("Drunkards"), veined with patches of gray; the fourth ("Ulcerous"), exhibiting myriad dots; the fifth ("After a long debauch"), a phantasmagoria of brown, tumorlike excrescences; and the last ("Death by Delerium Tremens"), a mottled dark brown and black.

As chairman of the American Temperance Union's executive committee Delavan sailed for Europe in 1838 with 800 volumes of its *Permanent Temperance Documents* to distribute among notable personages whose aid he planned to solicit in a world war against booze. King Louis Philippe agreed to sign a declaration that liquor was harmful, if the American crusader thought this would benefit France.

Black, Dow and Delavan were conspicuous presences at the numerous meetings held during the late sixties to create a national prohibition party. Others included the Reverend John Russell, Colonel John Sobieski and Gerrit Smith. Russell, a Michigan Methodist and one of the Good Templars' Right Worthy Grand Lodge Lecturers, published, in 1867, the first prohibition newspaper, Detroit's *Peninsular Herald*, which advocated a separate political party.

Sobieski, a Polish-born Minnesotan, could trace his ancestry in a direct line back to King John III of Poland, who routed the Turkish invaders of Europe in 1683. The prohibitionist's father, Count John Sobieski, was executed in 1847 after leading an insurrection against his country's Russian occupiers. Mother and son roamed Europe as refugees, finally reaching England, where the countess died in 1854.

The boy entered the United States that year at the age of thirteen, a stowaway aboard the famous frigate USS *Constellation*, unable to speak English and never having spent a day in any school. He joined the Army as a bugler and took part in expeditions against the Indians. At the outbreak of the Civil War he enlisted in the Army of the Potomac and fought with it right up to the hour of final victory. He refused a colonel's commission because the troops to be assigned to him were all blacks, a prejudice he overcame in later life when he championed suffrage for both blacks and women. He did accept a colonelcy conferred by the Mexican Army of the Republic which he joined after the Civil War, when Mexico was struggling to throw off the French imperial yoke. Sobieski guarded the captured Emperor Maximilian during the last hours of his life and commanded the reserve firing squad.

Throughout these military adventures, the Pole always claimed, he never drank, gambled or blasphemed, a conduct which, together with his espousal of prohibitionism, he ascribed to a pledge his mother exacted from him on her deathbed. "The love which I cherished of a noble memory made me strong against every temptation," he said, "and all that I am, and all I expect to be, and all the good I have accomplished in fighting the liquor traffic—all belong to her."

Returning to the United States, his mastery of English now complete, Sobieski settled in Dayton, Minnesota, a suburb of Minneapolis, and studied law. A Republican, he was elected within a year to the state House of Representatives, where he immediately introduced a bill outlawing liquor. It was laughed out of the House without debate. The same year he joined the Right Worthy Lodge of Good Templars and embarked upon a career of temperance writing and lecturing that took him to every state in the Union and Europe. Before he was buried fifty years later, an American flag flying above his coffin and a military band playing "The Star-Spangled Banner," as he had requested with his dying breath, Sobieski founded 2,086 Good Templar lodges and initiated 90,000 members.

The most arresting figure among the prohibition separatists was seventy-year-old Gerrit Smith of Peterboro, New York. Towering and bush-bearded, with a lordly manner and a lordly paunch, he owned more land than any individual in his state and one of the country's great fortunes. A substantial part of that fortune he bestowed upon a bewildering diversity of cults and causes. Reared in a Presbyterian family, he espoused the teachings of William Miller, the founder of Adventism, who predicted that Judgment Day would fall between March 21, 1843, and March 21, 1844, and exhorted the godly to prepare themselves for heaven. Following the "First Disappointment," as the Millerites called it, when the world remained intact beyond the predicted dates, doomsday was put forward to October, occasioning the "Great Disappointment," then to various other dates and finally to an indefinite future not given to man to know. Smith's wife, whom he regarded so highly that he would greet her appearance at the breakfast table with a rapturous cry of "Heaven has broke loose!", fully shared his faith in Adventism. She happened to be absent from Peterboro when the Millerite organ, the *Midnight Cry*, specified October 22, 1844, as the day to expect the Second Coming, and Smith, a prey all his life to fears of damnation verging on the psychotic, wrote to her:

> My Dearly Beloved,—We have just had family worship—perhaps for the last time . . . the extra Midnight Cry . . . declares that the world will end at three tomorrow morning . . . that time may possibly continue until the 23rd or even the 24th. . . .
>
> I know not my dear Nancy, that we shall meet in the air. You will be there—for you have long loved and served your Saviour. I cast myself on his mercy, like the thief on the Cross. I seek salvation though it is in the last hour. . . . Ah, the treasures of religion. How mad I have been to make so little account of them. . . .

After the Great Disappointment Smith swung to the opposite pole of rationalism, or the religion of nature, which repudiated divine revelation and recognized reason alone as the path to spiritual verities. By the time he entered prohibition politics he had involved himself with Christian missions, domestic and foreign; with vegetarianism; women's rights, including the right to vote; women's dress reform, calling for greater simplicity of dress and freer physical movement, led by Amelia Jenks Bloomer, who gave her name to the bifurcated garment (though Smith's daughter Elizabeth actually invented it); land reform; prison reform and the abolition of capital punishment; opposition to government-financed institutions such as public schools and post offices; crusades against tobacco and Freemasonry; relief for Greek, Italian and Irish refugees; the American Peace Society, African colonization for freed slaves, the Extreme Abolitionists, who nominated him for President of the United States as did the Liberty Party, of which he was an organizer. . . . To such causes, to needy or oppressed individuals, to his alma mater, Hamilton College, to hospitals, orphanages, old age homes, insane asylums, churches, libraries and schools, he gave more than $8,000,000, which was roughly eight times the value of his estate at his death.

Smith inherited the nucleus of his fortune and possibly some of his mental peculiarities from his father. Peter Smith, a man obsessed by gloomy forebodings of the afterlife, earned his first wages in New York City at sixteen as a clerk for an import house and a part-time actor. Within a year he had started his own small store, selling books, stationery and theatrical supplies. A meeting with John Jacob Astor, a German immigrant then dealing in musical instruments and furs, led to a brief partnership and Smith's removal in 1789 to the newly established settlement of Utica, New York, where he set up a trading post close to a forest crossroad traveled by Indian fur trappers. He ended the partnership the following year, though from time to time he and Astor collaborated in land speculations.

Smith contrived a slick method of acquiring real estate with little financial outlay. He would buy a tax-defaulted property offered by the government for a nominal sum, withhold the taxes due until the government repossessed it, then buy it back. In this fashion he amassed hundreds of thousands of acres scattered through nearly every New York county. At one period he owned more land than the state itself. From the Oneida Indians, with whom he traded regularly, he leased a tract of 80,000 acres straddling Oneida and Onondaga counties and, when the state took title to it by treaty, bought it outright. Toward the middle of this tract he established a village and a township, naming the first Peterboro and the second Smithfield. He always signed himself thereafter "Peter Smith of Peterboro."

In 1792 he married Elizabeth, daughter of James Livingston, a Revolutionary hero and state assemblyman. She bore him six children in less than eight years, then died. Only three sons and a daughter survived infancy. The firstborn was named Peter Skenendoa after an Oneida chieftain who was a reformed drunkard and convert to Christianity. But Peter Skenendoa failed to profit from his namesake's example and became an alcoholic, dying in an insane asylum. Augustus Lent, the second son, was a hopeless psychotic from childhood, while Gerrit, the youngest son, suffered from not only religious mania like his father, but hypochondria. Only the daughter, Cornelia Wyntje, appears to have enjoyed normal mental health. The father took a second wife, Sarah Pogson of Charleston, South Carolina; but his eerie behavior soon drove her away, and he sank deeper into religious fantasy and melancholy.

A brilliant student, Gerrit Smith graduated from Hamilton College at twenty-one with the highest honors. For a birthday present his father gave him the entire town of Florence in Oneida County. The same year Gerrit married the curiously named Wealthy Backus, daughter of Hamilton's president, the Reverend Azel Backus. She died seven months later.

The young widower had been out of college barely a year, helping manage the parental holdings, when his father, whose morbidity was rendering him unfit to conduct business affairs, turned over all his interests to him. Smith, Sr., then retired to a house he had bought in Schenectady, where he lived another eighteen years, "a trouble to himself [as a biographer put it] and a vexation to those around him."

When a financial panic in 1837 threatened to force Gerrit Smith to sacrifice his properties, his reputation for integrity enabled him to borrow $250,000 from old John Jacob Astor on a mere verbal promise to execute land mortgages as security. Thus weathering the crisis, Smith repaid the debt and went on to ever more spectacular real estate coups.

Three years after his first wife's death Smith had married a girl from Maryland, Ann "Nancy" Carroll Fitzhugh, by whom he had four children. Her father was a slaveholder, and the close view of slavery the relationship afforded Smith led him to embrace abolitionism, for which he became one of the country's most impassioned and widely known pleaders. Having also decided that the kind of land monopoly he and his father had exercised was immoral, he gave away 200,000 acres in lots of 50 acres to both freed or fugitive slaves and poor whites. In his opulent Peterboro mansion, where he entertained regally, seating as many as twenty guests at his dinner table, he received blacks and whites on an equal social footing.

Second only to slavery in the intensity of Smith's aversion was liquor. "I would that no person were able to drink intoxicating liquors without becoming a drunkard," he said, "for who, then, would . . . drink the poison that always kills, or jump into the fire that always burns?" Like his friend and fellow prohibitionist Edward Delavan, he built at enormous cost a temperance hotel, with the motto painted over the entrance, "Temperance and the Bible," and the Scriptures prominently displayed in every room. The flyers advertising the place read:

PETERBORO HOTEL
Cleanliness; Quiet; Comfort

1. No intoxicating liquors.
2. Persons, so unfortunate, as to use tobacco, are requested to observe the spit-boxes.
3. The traveller is assured that he shall not be disturbed by dancing parties; that this house shall not, like many a village tavern,

be the resort of ungoverned and idle boys.
4. The office is closed on Sunday.

It was all the information needed to turn away most travelers, and after two years Smith abandoned the hotel as an economic disaster.

In 1852, running on a platform of abolition and temperance, he was elected to Congress by a coalition of Whig and Democrat voters from Madison and Oswego counties, a victory which moved the teetotaling publisher Horace Greeley to editorialize in his New York *Tribune*:

> We are heartily glad that Gerrit Smith is going to Washington. He is an honest, brave, kind-hearted Christian philanthropist, whose religion is not put aside with his Sunday cloak, but lasts him clear through the week. . . . We heartily wish more such great, pure, loving souls could find their way into Congress. . . .

As a politician Smith proclaimed it a guiding principle that "in all matters of fundamental morality, the ruler is bound to consult, not the will of the people, but the will of God." None of the causes he pleaded in the House won any adherents, and embittered, he resigned after a single term.

Smith's hatred of slavery led him into a perilous involvement with John Brown. For years Smith, along with other prominent Northern reformers, had idealized the violent and fanatical Kansas abolitionist, applauding him even after Brown, two of his sons and some followers murdered five proslavers "to cause a restraining fear." (The Brown heredity, as tainted as Smith's, would lend weight to the theory that father and sons were deranged. The insurgent's mother, several maternal relatives and his dead first wife had all been psychotic.) With tears in his eyes, Smith later publicly acclaimed Brown as "the man in all the world I think most truly Christian." Though vice-president of the American Peace Society, Smith condoned force when used in the name of abolition. "Much as I abhor war," he wrote, "I nevertheless believe that there are instances in which the shedding of blood is unavoidable. . . . I and ten thousand other peace men are not only ready to have it [slavery] repulsed with violence, but pursued even unto death, with violence." Smith himself helped several fugitive slaves slip across the Canadian border.

Among the gifts of land he made to free blacks were 140,000 acres in the Adirondacks. Brown journeyed to Peterboro in 1848 with a proposal that his family (which eventually numbered twenty children—seven by his first wife, thirteen by his second) settle on an adjacent tract and teach the ex-slaves agriculture. What he really intended was to train them as guerrillas for a general antislavery insurrection. Smith not only gave him a farm at North Elba, near Lake Placid, but after Brown returned to the Midwest in 1851, the black colony having proved unamenable to either farming or armed combat, periodically sent him money. The gaunt old zealot revisited upstate New York in February, 1858, and again in April, 1859, to obtain additional funds from Smith and other Northern sympathizers. He did not conceal from them his madbrain scheme to secure a Southern mountain stronghold as a refuge for escaped slaves and a staging area for slave uprisings throughout the South. He thereby made his hosts accessories to murder and treason.

The following October U.S. marines raided the government arsenal at Harpers Ferry, West Virginia, which Brown had seized with a handful of whites and blacks, and captured him in a skirmish that cost the lives of ten marines and seven guerrillas, among them two of Brown's sons. Swiftly tried and convicted, Brown died bravely on the hangman's scaffold, a martyr to some, a maniac to others. Lincoln, in his address at Cooper Union College in New York City the following February, described the abortive rebellion as "so absurd that the slaves, with all their ignorance, saw plainly enough it could not succeed."

Smith went to pieces. His mind unhinged by accusations in the proslavery press of criminal complicity, by fear of prosecution and a deep sense of guilt, he was committed, five days after Brown's conviction, to the Utica Asylum for the Insane. Upon his recovery and discharge seven months later he denied ever having aided Brown or known anything about his plans, a position he maintained in the face of overwhelming evidence to the contrary for the rest of his life.

John Brown was buried by his sons on the New Elba farm Smith had given him ten years before.

After the Civil War and Reconstruction, during which Smith campaigned for the Republican Party and Lincoln's reelection and urged, in speeches and writings, moderation toward the

Southern whites and black suffrage, he resumed his temperance work. The initiative toward a national prohibition party was taken on May 27, 1869, at a meeting of the Right Worthy Grand Lodge of Good Templars in Oswego, New York. A five-man committee, including the Reverend John Russell and James Black, undertook to transmit a call for an organizing convention to every temperance group throughout the country. Attended by 500 delegates from nineteen states, the convention followed on September 1 in Chicago's Farwell Hall. Gerrit Smith delivered the keynote speech:

> We must inspire the government with a sense of the sacredness of its mission—of the responsibility to High Heaven. . . . Let the government decide in the light of the divine will, and in that light only . . . let the government listen to the voice of God, and permit no crime to be practised anywhere within its jurisdiction. Do you doubt, my dear brother and my dear sister, for a moment that dram-selling is not to be excluded with crime. In the light of its effects, compared with the effects of stealing, of getting goods under false pretences, of forgery, of perjury, these crimes sink into mere peccadilloes. . . . A great mistake has been made in some of the States by naming in the prohibitory laws the proscribed liquors. They never should be named. The law-making power in this matter should know only one distinction, and that is between maddening and non-maddening drinks, between crazing and non-crazing drinks. Let the prohibitory law forbid the drinking of crazing and maddening drinks, and leave it to the jury in every case prosecuted to decide whether the drink in question is or is not maddening, is or is not crazing. . . .

Smith also composed the party's first official document, *An Address to the People of the United States*:

> Slavery is gone, but drunkenness. . . . The lot of the literal slave, of him whom others have enslaved, is indeed a hard one; nevertheless it is a paradise compared with the lot of him, who has enslaved himself—especially of him who has enslaved himself to alcohol. . . .
>
> What can we do towards saving our millions of drunkards? Just what we have been doing. We are to continue the power of persuasion with them, and the power of prayer of God for them. And what can we do to prevent the recruiting of the ever rapidly thickening ranks of drunkenness? None of the recruits come from

those who abstain from intoxicating drinks. The "temperate drinkers" furnish all. Our work, therefore, at this point, is to warn and beseech the rising youth to take not the first step in the pathway, the second in which sinks the unwary and ill-fated traveller into drunkenness. It is, in other words, to warn and beseech them to "Touch not, taste not, handle not" the drinks which transmute more than one-tenth of the "temperate drinkers" into drunkards. It is, we might add, to persuade them—yes, and the old as well as the young—that there is no security from drunkenness but total abstinence from all intoxicating drinks. . . .

We proceed to ask whether Government may be called upon to advance the cause of temperance. . . . We have no occasion to question the conclusion of those who hold that Government has not the right to espouse the temperance reform or any other reform. . . . For two sufficient reasons, nevertheless, we call upon the Government to suppress the dramshop.

First. The province of Government being to protect person and property, it is clearly its duty to forbid the existence of the dramshop. That abomination is the great peril to person and property; for it is the great manufactory, not of paupers only, but also of incendiaries, madmen, and murderers. Not a few of its frequenters go forth from it to burn and kill. Government is surely very false to its trust, and very delinquent in its duty, in licensing or permitting the dramshop. . . .

Second. The other reason for our calling on Government to rid the land of the dramshop is that the cause of temperance would, though incidentally, be nevertheless benefited by this measure for protecting person and property. . . .

We shall, of course, have to encounter, continually and everywhere, the utter but effective falsehood that in asking Government to put away the dramshop we are asking it to enact that most odious of all laws—a sumptuary law. How insidious as well as disingenuous to confound with a sumptuary law a law enacted for the protection of society from the dramshop, the manufactory of madmen and murderers—from peril to person and property far greater than the sum total of all the other perils which they incur! In the legislation we call for we do not propose, as does the sumptuary law, to interfere with the household. We do not propose the searching of families, nor the hindering of them from drinking their domestic drinks or eating their spoiled meats. But we do propose that they shall be effectually debarred from bringing their dram-bottles into the public markets, as they are from bringing into it such meats. As temperance men we are opposed to all intoxicating drinks any and everywhere. As such we would do all in our power to persuade every home to relieve itself of the presence of this preeminent destroyer of the peace of the home. As temperance men we aim to make millions of rum-ruined and unutterably wretched homes the paradise they would have been but for this evil presence—the paradise they would have been had not the devil entered them. But nothing of all this domestic beauty and blessedness will be the object of our new political organization. This organization will war upon rum-selling only. Its war, however, will be upon all rum-selling—upon that in the fashionable as well as the unfashionable hotel; upon that in the gilded parlor as well as that in the dirtiest den. . . .

Our words are ended. We may not succeed in shutting up the dramshop, but we will work very faithfully and very hopefully to this end. And then, even though we shall have utterly failed of our object, and the dramshop shall remain wide and deep and fixed a curse upon poor humanity as ever, a great success will nevertheless be ours—the great success of having done our duty.

The press generally took a skeptical view of the party aborning. According to a Chicago *Tribune* editorial, "When our senators and representatives come reeling to their desks in a state of intoxication and when all the avenues of political life are crowded with debauchees, it is idle to hope that prohibitory laws could be enforced."

Smith wanted to call it "the Anti-Dramshop Party" with the idea that the public would then pin the pejorative label of "Dramshop Party" on the opposition, but the majority opted for the National Prohibition Party. Its first Presidential candidate, James Black, ran in the elections of 1872, which the whiskey-loving Republican incumbent, Ulysses S. Grant, won, partly with the help of the United States Brewers' Association. (The nominee of both the Democrats and the Liberal Republicans, Horace Greeley, crushed by the double blow of a smashing defeat and his wife's death, collapsed mentally and died insane.) The third-party platform achieved a high distinction in electoral annals, for in addition to prohibition, it included two other planks which eventually formed parts of the Constitution—the direct election of U.S. Senators and suffrage for all citizens of voting age regardless of sex or race.

At the time of the party's first massive popular repudiation there began to emerge from an unexpected quarter a new element destined to become a mighty ally.

6. "... they shall be devoured as stubble fully dry"

"Why did the women choose such a strange method of carrying on this reform?"

"They did not choose it; it was the work of God marked out for us, and we simply did it according to orders."

—THE REVEREND W. H. DANIELS, The Temperance Reform and Its Great Reformers

IT was a sight to strike terror into the stoutest-hearted publican—hundreds of women, jaws outthrust, eyes ablaze with moral indignation, marching toward him two abreast through the cold February drizzle and chanting Psalms to the tune of "John Brown's Body." Of the forty-one saloons enlivening the social life of Xenia, Ohio, in 1874, nine stood within a stretch of 600 yards along Whitman Street, the town's main thoroughfare, most of them so rowdy that respectable townsfolk referred to them by such names as Shades of Death, Certain Death, Mules' Ear, Hell's Half-Acre, The Devil's Den. The embattled women, advancing between curbside lines of gaping onlookers, divided into small bands, each band coming to a halt before a different saloon. Miss Laura Hicks, a girls' school teacher, brought along her entire flock, who lustily sang in front of the Devil's Den: "Say, Mr. Barkeeper, has father been here?" The women read from Scripture at the top of their lungs, then knelt on the damp, chilly pavement while one of them loudly prayed:

> Oh, Lord, our hope in time of need, we prostrate ourselves in the dust before Thee to beg for the lives of our fathers, our brothers, and our sons. Oh, God, help us to save dying men; help us to rescue the idols of our love;—dying men are all around us,

they crowd us in the streets; we look upon them in our homes, we shed tears of bitter anguish because we cannot save them from this traffic of death. . . . Come, dear Lord, and touch the hearts of the dealers in ardent spirits; send down Thy spirit on this poor man who still turns a deaf ear to our pleading—he will not listen to us. . . . Give us access to the heart of this man. . . . Oh, Lord, our God, wilt Thou not listen to the prayer of those made desolate by rum? Here, bowed before Thee, are widows and orphans, made such by this traffic . . . bring us all, both the dealer and those who fall by the traffic, to see more clearly the light of Thy truth. . . .

The invasion of Whitman Street had started at nine o'clock in the morning. At three in the afternoon a cry went up from the spectators: "The Shades of Death has surrendered!" The shaken owner, Steve Phillips, stood in his doorway, inviting the praying, singing women to step inside. He would, he announced, hand over his entire stock to them; never again would he sell any intoxicants. "Praise God from whom all blessings flow," the women sang, the crowd joining in. As Phillips began hauling barrels of beer and cases of whiskey out into the street, a group leader announced that whatever business he might switch to they should all patronize him. They then set about what they euphemistically termed "ax application to barrel heads" and "fire application to whiskey" until the gutter was awash with the condemned beverages and the whole street reeked of alcohol. An elderly ax wielder, near hysteria, shrieked: "Bless the Lord! Bless the Lord!" Members of the National Grange of Husbandry, who happened to be holding a convention close by, hearing of Phillips' capitulation, burst into cheers and ran out to ring all the town bells. The same day four more Xenia saloonkeepers voluntarily closed their doors, bringing the total that week to twenty-nine.

This technique of coercion by prayer, of religious blackmail, was originally promoted by a temperance lecturer and physical culture pioneer, Dr. Diocletian (Dio for short) Lewis. His title was self-conferred. The son of an alcoholic Welsh farmer, whose wife, Delecta, used to flee to the garret, whence her despairing cry could be heard ringing through the house: "How long, Oh, Lord, how long!", left school at twelve and at fifteen started a private school of his own. After attending Harvard Medical School for only a year, he began practicing homeopathic medicine without a license in Port Byron, New York, near his native Aurora, adopting the system of the German physician Samuel Hahnemann, whose therapeutic formula was *Similia similibus curantur* ("Like cures like"). Treatment consisted of dosing patients with minute amounts of drugs that produced the same symptoms as the disease—for example, Spanish fly for inflammation of the bladder, croton oil for dysentery, opium for lethargy. Lewis eventually obtained an honorary medical degree from the Homeopathic Hospital College of Cleveland, Ohio.

He presently abandoned homeopathy in favor of physical culture and hygiene for women, an area in which he ventured far ahead of his time. In his popular book *Our Girls*, he prescribed dresses with low necks, short sleeves and short skirts and loose garments in general to enhance "the body beautiful," suspenders instead of belts in order to free the pelvis "for more worthy purposes," nude sun bathing. For elegance of carriage he recommended walking with a heavy weight on the head, such as a sack of corn. He coined the slogan "A clean tooth never decays." An exponent of what he touted as "the New Gymnastic," he introduced from Germany the light wooden dumbbell with which women could exercise without undue strain, and he invented the beanbag. He sharply criticized the fashionable wasp waist. "What a mortification," he wrote, "when a lady is in company, to hear from her bowels, that gurgling, glug-glug noise." He ascribed it to tight stays, an affectation which he insisted, in a chapter on how to get a husband, put men off. "I never could join my fortunes with those of a woman with a *small waist*. It means the organs of the abdomen jammed down into the pelvis . . . it means a delicate, nervous individual . . . and not a vigorous helpmate."

In a day when women were not supposed to have pelvises or abdomens, such talk was considered indecent, and it exposed Lewis to scathing attack, especially from the clergy. Public outrage flared up when he established first in Boston, then in Lexington, Massachusetts, a girls' school for girls who had failed to adjust elsewhere. Nathaniel Hawthorne's daughter Una was enrolled. Under a shockingly progressive policy, Lewis kept no record of attendance, deportment or even scholastic achievement. The girls remained free to receive visitors without supervision, an unheard-of permissiveness that gave rise to rumors of sexual misbehavior. A devout feminist, Lewis considered women as well qualified as men for almost any occupation or profession —carpentry, dentistry, law, banking.

Lewis scored his greatest success as a temperance lecturer. With his silky red hair and beard, his athlete's physique and resonant voice, he thrilled female audiences from New England to the far West. One lecture which he delivered more than 300 times was entitled "The Duty of Christian Women in the Cause of Temperance." In it he would recount how his long-suffering mother finally fought back. Leading other wives with drunken husbands in a praying campaign against the saloonkeeper who furnished the booze, she prevailed upon him to seek a different means of livelihood. "Ladies," the lecturer concluded, "you might do the same here if you had the same faith." The first to take up the suggestion were the women of Dixon, Illinois, a town with thirty-nine saloons. In 1859, they managed to pray them all closed within a week. A few months later, following Lewis' standard lecture, the fifty-odd groggeries of Battle Creek, Michigan, were, as he put it, "swept away like chaff before the wind." In Greenfield, Ohio, shortly after the Civil War, the accidental shooting of a young man as he passed a saloon aroused a band of women to violence. Storming the saloon with hatchets and hammers, they smashed every receptacle containing liquor. The sheriff arrested them, but the grand jury refused to indict them. These were isolated local incidents, without major significance. Not until Christmas Eve, 1873, in the quiet southern Ohio town of Hillsboro (population: 5,000; saloons: thirteen; hotels and drugstores selling liquor: eight) did the Women's Crusade get under way as a national phenomenon.

In a tiny, frail woman nearing sixty, Mrs. Eliza Jane Trimble Thompson, daughter of Ohio's ex-Governor Allen Trimble and wife of a prominent lawyer, the Crusaders found their Joan of Arc. Domestic duties prevented Mrs. Thompson from attending the Lewis lecture in the Presbyterian church; but her son was there, and his account deeply moved her. About seventy-five women, he reported, proclaimed their willingness to emulate Lewis' heroic mother, while as many men swore to shield them from the hostility of the liquor sellers. They then called upon Mrs. Thompson *in absentia* to join them at a church meeting next morning.

"What tomfoolery is all that?" Lawyer Thompson asked when he got home from a day in court.

"Men have been in the tomfoolery business a long time,"
retorted his wife. "It may be God's will that the women should
now take a part."

After praying for guidance and interpreting the 146th Psalm,
at which her daughter had randomly opened the family Bible, as
a divine message intended for her ("the Lord loveth the righteous
. . . but the way of the wicked he turneth upside down"), she
tied on her white winter bonnet and trotted around to the
church, where she was unanimously elected president of what
was later called the Committee of Visitation.

"Let us form in line, two and two," Mrs. Thompson instructed
her sisters, "and let us at once proceed to our sacred mission,
trusting alone in the God of Jacob."

Convoyed by male members of the congregation, they descended first upon the pharmacy of Dr. William Smith with a
"druggists' pledge" for him to sign. After lengthy contention he
acceded and agreed to confine his liquor sales to those amounts
for which he, as a physician, wrote prescriptions. His chief
competitor, William Dunn, whose Palace Drug Store the women
visited the day after Christmas, did not care to face them,
transmitting instead a promise to furnish no liquor "to any
person whose father, mother, wife, or daughter send me a written
request not to make such a sale." Considering this inadequate,
the women erected a tabernacle opposite the store and spent the
rest of the day there in prayer for Dunn's soul, disbanding only
after he obtained a court injunction. Dunn also filed a $10,000
"action of trespass." The jury awarded him $5. He had,
meanwhile, delivered himself into the enemy's hands by committing such illegalities as allowing drinking on his premises and
selling liquor to minors. The Crusaders saw to it that he was
prosecuted. Heavily fined, he eventually declared bankruptcy.
Recalling this victory years later, Mrs. Thompson alluded to
Nahum, 1:10: "For while they be folden together as thorns, and
while they are drunken as drunkards, they shall be devoured as
stubble fully dry."

After the druggists, the Crusaders tackled the Hillsboro hotel
proprietors, then the saloonkeepers. Initially they got only
evasive responses, but persistence was rewarded. The Boston
Watchman and Reflector, an organ of the Baptist Church, described
the conflict thus:

If any think this is a work to be sneered at, let them read the
following report. . . . We confess we did not read it with dry eyes.

I came unexpectedly upon some fifty women kneeling on the pavement and stone steps before a store. . . . There were gathered here representatives from nearly every household of the town. The day was bitterly cold; a cutting north wind swept the streets, piercing us all to the bone. The plaintive, tender, earnest tones of that wife and mother who was pleading in prayer, arose on the blast, and were carried to every heart within reach. Passers-by uncovered their heads, for the place whereon they trod was "holy ground." The eyes of hardened men filled with tears, and many turned away, saying that they could not bear to look upon such a sight. Then the voice of prayer was hushed; the women began to sing, softly, a sweet hymn with some old, familiar words and tune, such as our mothers sang to us in childhood days. We thought, Can mortal man resist such efforts?

Evidently not. When Henry Uhrig, a young German tapster, locked his doors at the approach of the women, they knelt en masse and launched into a marathon prayer service. To ease their discomfort, the pavement being sleek with ice, some of the neighborhood housewives brought them doormats to kneel on. A venerable Mrs. Foraker carried her mat to the top step of the saloon and with her mouth close to the keyhole raised her voice in apostolic orisons. "Why did you do that?" a sister Crusader asked her afterward. "When a man locks his door on good women's prayers," replied Mrs. Foraker, "he is apt to be listening inside to hear what they have to say about it." In the end Uhrig accepted their offer to buy him out and remorsefully helped them destroy his entire stock.

Robert Ward, an Englishman, whose High Street saloon was "made famous by deeds the memory of which nerved the heart and paled the cheek of some of us," withstood a siege of weeks only to fall to his knees in the sawdust among the praying women. For years Joe Lance had defiantly run Hillsboro's most squalid pothouse, the Lava Bed, but he too ultimately yielded and turned to selling fish from a street stand, which the Crusaders, to show their appreciation, all patronized.

From Hillsboro the crusading fever spread with epidemic fury through Ohio and the Midwest, thence to the Deep South and westward all the way to California. The most spectacular mass manifestation of the day, it made daily front-page headlines. Essentially a religious movement, it typified the revivalist, camp-meeting fanaticism common in rural America. Like Justin

Edwards and the early temperance firebrands, the Crusaders denounced liquor not merely as a danger to body and mind, but as an offense against God, a theme that runs through the entire history of prohibition.

Dio Lewis' next stop after Hillsboro was Washington Court House, Ohio. A "very drunken town," he found it, with 3,000 inhabitants, eleven saloons and three drugstores dispensing liquor. The women started street prayer services on December 27, kneeling in the snow that had fallen heavily the night before, and by January 2 the last of the fourteen drinking places had struck its colors.

On the outskirts of Washington Court House a beer garden flourished under the ownership of a German immigrant, Charley Beck, whom the women were especially eager to reform, for they learned that a cabal of wholesale liquor dealers had promised him all the beer he could sell without charge if he managed to stem the advance of the Crusade. "Go vay, vimmins, go home," said Beck (as Lewis later reproduced his speech). "Shtay at home, and tend to your papies; vhat for you wants to come to my peer garten? Dis is de blace to trink peer; ve don't want no brayer-meetings in dis garten."

The women not only ignored his plea, but pitched a tent nearby and set up a locomotive headlight which threw its glare full upon the entrance. In four-hour shifts around the clock they sang, prayed, read the Scriptures and harassed people entering or leaving the beer garden by ostentatiously jotting down their names. With his clientele rapidly dwindling, the hapless German finally walked into the tent, crying: "O, vimmins! I quits, I quits."

Recognizing the publicity value of martyrdom, the Crusaders deliberately sought abuse, and they often received it. In the little Ohio village of New Vienna there was a dive known as the Dead Fall. Its proprietor, a knobby-headed, foul-mouthed ruffian named John Van Pelt, gloried in the title of "the wickedest man in Ohio." Forewarned of an impending visitation, he armed himself with an ax and stalked up and down behind his windows, viciously brandishing it. This failed to deter a platoon of about forty women from crowding into the saloon twice a day every day. "May the Lord baptize him with the Holy Spirit," they prayed, which so infuriated Van Pelt that he picked up a bucket of dirty water and, bellowing, "I'll baptize you!", emptied it over the supplicants. When they stood their ground, he filled the bucket with beer and let them have a shower of that. They finally retreated to the snow-blanketed street, where, teeth chattering, drenched and reeking of beer, they concluded the service, while Van Pelt hurled obscenities at them.

Public indignation brought about his arrest and a week behind bars, from which he emerged impenitent and in vile mood. The women, meanwhile, having found that the land adjoining the Dead Fall belonged to the railroad, obtained permission to camp on it, and there, beyond range of Van Pelt's counteroffensive, they resumed their prayers. The conflict raged on for three weeks. Then, on February 2, a correspondent for the New York *Tribune* telegraphed his editor:

> Today the people of New Vienna witnessed the complete surrender of the notorious Van Pelt. . . . A procession of about a hundred ladies marched to his saloon at two o'clock P.M. Some rumor had spread which led the people to close the stores and workshops and join the gathering throng. When the crowd was assembled at the "Dead Fall" saloon, Van Pelt appeared and announced that he was ready to give up his entire stock for the good of the temperance cause. He said with emotion and apparent sincerity, "I make a complete surrender, not because of law or force, but to the women who have labored in love. It has reached my heart." Narrating the circumstances later, he said, ". . . I then asked the ministers to please carry out the whiskey. They were terribly willing and out it went. I gathered up the same axe that I had threatened the women with, and drove it as near through those barrels as I could, and out ran the whiskey. Such a shout went up I never heard before, and never will again till I stand before God. The tears ran down their cheeks like a fountain stream."
>
> Devotional exercises closed the scene. All the bells of the town were rung in honor of the occasion. Tonight an earnest temperance meeting was held, and Van Pelt made a brief address, confessing his wickedness and admitting that he could not reconcile himself to the business. He referred to his saloon as a low groggery, saying, "Yes, I'll call it a low groggery, for no man can keep a high one." At the close of the meeting a purse of $150 was presented to Van Pelt as an expression of the feeling of the community towards him. . . .

As the Crusade spread, the praying women were beaten,

kicked, hit with brickbats, drenched with water ("O Lord," ecstatically cried the leader of a Clyde, Ohio, contingent, "we are now baptized for the work!"), splattered with mud, eggs and rotten vegetables, stoned, dragged through the streets, menaced with knives, hatchets, clubs, firearms and vicious dogs. . . . In Bucyrus, Ohio, hoodlums deputized as special police by the mayor to enforce his decree against street praying broke up a procession of Crusaders, shoved their small, frail seventy-year-old leader, Mrs. O'Fling, down a flight of cellar steps and mutilated her arms with bludgeons. In Shelbyville, Indiana, a saloonkeeper placed a charge of gunpowder under the floor and threatened, if the women set foot in the place, to blow them all to smithereens. The Pittsburgh police arrested scores of Crusaders as common nuisances who were violating an ordinance against hindering legitimate business, but they raised such a din with their prayers and hymns and they so overcrowded the jail that they had to be released next day. A mob then turned fire hoses on them. In Carthage, Missouri, hirelings of the liquor dealers disrupted the Crusaders' prayers by tooting tin horns. An Adrian, Michigan, barkeep locked them inside a backroom from dawn to dusk, when their husbands and sons finally broke down the door. In Cincinnati, a third of whose population was then of German origin, a German saloonkeeper drew up an ancient cannon before his entrance, loaded it to the muzzle and, holding a lighted torch, swore to blast the first Crusader to approach. More than 100 Crusaders lined up within cannon range, while their commander hoisted herself onto the barrel and led them in song. The saloonkeeper dropped his torch. "I vas not afraid of dem voomans," he explained afterward, "but I could not shtand dot singin'."

Elsewhere in the Midwest saloonkeepers blocked up their chimneys to send the women gasping and coughing into the street, sprinkled pepper over burning coals to make them sneeze, opened their doors and windows to freeze them and sloshed filthy water across the floor to discourage kneeling. In Wheeling, West Virginia, a saloonkeeper named Savegant agreed to let the women pray unmolested to their heart's content, then, once he had them inside his establishment, barred the exits and assailed them in language to bring blushes to a drill sergeant's cheeks. "It was as if a putrid carrion had burst and poured out a mass of corruption," one horrified member of the captive audience

recalled. During the resultant brawl between Savegant's chival-
rous customers and his ungallant ones the police rescued the
women before serious injury befell them. In Alameda, California,
on July 2, 1872, a referendum was held on a proposal to enact
prohibitory laws under local option. To sway the voters, a
Crusade leader, Miss Sally Hart, put up a tent tabernacle near
the polling place. From San Francisco a force of 150 mercenaries,
hired by German beer sellers, marched against Miss Hart behind
a U.S. Fourth Artillery band, shouting: "Down with her! . . .
Drive her from the streets! . . . Take her home or we'll kill her!"
She managed to escape, badly bruised from the stones they
hurled at her.

In their spiritual transports the Crusaders felt sure that God
would sustain them and chastise their foes, a conviction fortified
by the misfortunes that overtook several assailants. When, in
Ripon, Wisconsin, the driver of a buggy drove straight at a band
of marching Crusaders, the horse reared back so violently that he
smashed the buggy. "It was said," recalled Mrs. Annie Wittenmyer, the leading Philadelphia Crusader and a historian of the
movement, "that an 'angel' restrained the horse." A Xenia
barkeep kicked a Crusader down his steps. A few minutes later,
as he was tapping a beer barrel, the bung shot out, struck him in
the eye and permanently blinded him. In Bellefontaine, Ohio, a
kneeling Crusader, who was being berated in vile language by a
saloonkeeper's wife, prayed: "Lord, silence this woman!" The
woman was instantly struck dumb and remained so to her death
two years later. Appalled by the Crusaders' smug satisfaction at
these seemingly supernatural disasters, a German-language
newspaper of Covington, Kentucky, commented: "They pray
that their God may strike the saloonists and their families dead.
(Very Christian, is it not?)"

The Crusaders met their greatest challenge in Cincinnati.
Here was a city with the country's biggest production and
consumption of alcoholic beverages—3,000 saloons, breweries
and distilleries together capitalized at $40,000,000 and grossing
$33,000,000 a year. So important a part did liquor play in the
city's economy that its merchants, whatever their line, tended to
discourage their wives from temperance activities lest they
undermine the general prosperity. The panicky liquor wholesalers pooled $5,000 as a purse for anybody who could repulse
the advancing Crusaders.

*Mrs. Abby Fisher Leavitt remembers the battle for her hometown of Cincinnati**

> Good Friday of 1874 was one of our great days. We had a band of
> about a hundred and twenty of the best ladies in Cincinnati that day.
> . . . Our route was to go down to the esplanade and hold a
> prayer-meeting on the flagstones near the fountain.
>
> When we came in sight of the place we saw a crowd of roughs,
> evidently waiting for us, the leader of which had sworn a terrible oath
> that no woman should set her foot on the esplanade that day. I did not
> know of it at the time, so we marched right along, two by two, up to
> where the crowd were trying to block up our path and, going up to this
> leader, a big burly fellow, half full of whisky, I said:—
>
> "My brother, you must help us to keep order. We are going to hold a
> prayer-meeting."
>
> A great change seemed to come over him all at once, for he said—
> "Break ranks, boys! These women are coming through!"
>
> The crowd obeyed him, and allowed us to pass to our station, formed
> in hollow square around us, and the leader detailed some of them to act
> as a special police to keep order while we held our meeting, saying,
> "We are going to see these ladies through."
>
> We began to sing "Rock of Ages;" next "Jesus the Water of Life
> will give," and then a dear Quaker lady began to exhort those roughs to
> give their hearts to God. We forgot all about temperance, and held a
> real gospel meeting, which made a profound impression on the crowd.
> . . . then we asked who would come forward for prayers, and the
> very first man who came was the ring-leader of the gang; and the poor
> fellow was saved then and there. . . .
>
> You see the Crusades were breaking in so on the liquor business that
> the dealers and manufacturers were alarmed. Liquors sent out to
> dealers in the country began to be sent back again because there was no
> sale for them, so the liquor men besought the mayor to try and stop the
> work of the women! They made a mistake there: it was not the work of
> the women but the work of God that troubled them so.
>
> You know we were arrested and had to go to jail. Just think of it!
>
> There was a Sidewalk Ordinance which forbade the obstruction of
> the streets, and under that we were arrested, though we were careful to
> use only the two feet in width that the law allowed us when we stood in
> front of a saloon and sang at it, and quoted texts of Scripture at it, and
> knelt down and prayed against it and for the souls of those who kept it.

---

* Recorded in *Broken Fetters* by Charles Morris, 1888.

The seven policemen who were detailed to arrest us were crying like whipped children; but they had to do it, and we, like good, law-abiding citizens, submitted, and went in procession to prison—forty-three of us—singing all the way. . . .

We were released after about four hours. Bail was offered us, but we refused it, on the ground that we had done nothing against the law, and those who arrested us should take the full responsibility of their outrageous act. . . .

Nothing could dampen the Crusaders' militancy, no indignity, no amount of physical hardship, and in their determination to vanquish the Demon Rum they stopped at nothing. With fine disregard for the rights of individuals and, frequently, for the law, they began picketing saloons in groups of five or six, eventually forcing them out of business for lack of customers. Pad and pencil in hand, they would halt the thirsty male at the entrance, asking, "Do you love Jesus?" and urge him for his soul's sake to sign the pledge. If he dared brush past them, they would take down his name. It was a rare tippler with the pluck to brave the displeasure of those implacable guardians of morality. Let him try to sneak through a back door or come first thing in the morning when he thought the women would not be about yet, there they were, waiting. The pretendedly reformed liquor dealer, however ingenious, found it equally difficult to elude their vigilance. Evidently they had developed an intelligence system that kept them informed of prospective liquor shipments, for when one arrived, they would be patrolling the railroad depot to point the finger of scorn at the spurious penitent. Suspicious of a Cincinnati dealer, despite his public profession of remorse, they set a twenty-four-hour watch on his house. Late one night a wagon rolled up to his door, and the dealer began helping the driver unload some barrels of beer. Interrupted by a sudden flood of light from the watchful women's lanterns, they quickly reloaded the wagon, and away it went. ". . . no place so hardened the Crusade cannot reach it," boasted Eliza Daniel Stewart, a Methodist schoolteacher from Springfield, Ohio, popularly called "Mother Stewart" because of her ministrations to the Union soldiers during the Civil War, "and no place so given over to drunkenness and its accompanying vices but was greatly blessed. . . . It looked as if we were going to take over the world."

In carrying the Crusade beyond the borders of Ohio no torchbearer played a greater role than Mother Stewart. She had made her first contributions to the cause after the Civil War as a special pleader in lawsuits against violators of Ohio's Adair Law, which enabled the wife or mother of a drunkard to sue the saloonkeeper for civil damages. With Mother Stewart's aid one plaintiff won a judgment of $100 and another of $300. In April, 1874, a bill sponsored by the harried liquor dealers to amend the state laws so as to remove from municipal administrations the power to prohibit the sale of ale or beer and the licensing of saloons was presented to the legislature. Mother Stewart sat in the gallery, a figure of granitic strength, surrounded by 300 Crusaders, singing, praying and shrilly deploring the proposal until at midnight the exhausted legislators adjourned without voting.

Mother Stewart remembers the Children's Crusade*

I was driven out to visit the Washington County Orphan's Home, the model institution of the kind in the State. . . . Nine-tenths of these little ones, so carefully sheltered there, were subjects of the public charity because their fathers, and some, because their mothers too, were drunkards.

The children here had, with everybody else, become greatly excited over the Crusade, that they hoped was going to shut up all the saloons and stop all the drinking.

Mrs. Hart, the matron and a real mother too to the little ones, as they loved to call her, told me that the children one day asked her if they too might have a prayer-meeting. She said they might; they gathered in the play-room, and as they knelt, she said, now we will first have a season of silent prayer. In a few moments, she said, a little girl eleven or twelve years old, broke out in supplication, stifled with sobs and tears, for her father, that the Lord would save and make a sober man of him. Then there was silence again, and next a little colored boy eight years old broke forth for his father; he would choke and break down, then go on again. And so the Orphan's Crusade prayer-meeting went on. It was not long till a man came to the Home to take away two of

* Memories of the Crusade, 1890.

the little ones. He had been a very intemperate man, so much so that his wife had been obliged to bring her children to the Home and seek employment for herself as a servant, to obtain food and shelter. But the dear Crusaders had got hold of the man and induced him to sign the pledge. And when he came to himself, he sought out his wife and besought her to live with him again. . . . About the same time a poor inebriate, whose wife was dead and his five children in the Home, came to see them. His children gathered about him and began to plead, "Father, sign the pledge," "Father, sign the pledge," "O, father, please sign the pledge." The youngest was not able to talk, but it joined the rest, clapping its little hands, and with pleading, inarticulate sounds besought father to sign the pledge. It was more than the poor, broken father could stand, but he made excuse that he could not write his name. "Oh," they cried, "Mother Hart will write your name. Mother Hart will write your name." And she did.

Who would like to persuade those little ones that they were mistaken, that God does not hear even the cry of a little child? Those children learned a lesson of faith in prayer that will never be forgotten. . . .

I reached home on Friday evening, March 21st [1874] and hastened up on Saturday morning to learn what news of the battle. On Market Street a gentleman came hurrying along and asked me if I wasn't going to the "liquor pouring." "Is there a surrender?" "Yes, around on Main Street." I fell into line on "double quick." When I arrived upon the scene, the sisters and everybody else were there. Mrs. Kinney, Mrs. Mast, and others were making lively work in that saloon. And amid great rejoicing the bottles, flasks, jugs and casks were brought out and hurled into the ditch.

My pulpit, an empty beer-cask, being just in place, I was helped up onto it and proceeded to address the crowd. . . .

I have frequently spoken of the interest the children everywhere took in the Crusade. In our city this was especially the case. The boys were always on hand, often acting as volunteer scouts to go forward and explore, and bring back information of the situation. I called them my body-guard, and I believe if the saloon-keepers had attempted to molest me—of which I was in fear—the boys would have fought my battle for me.

Some of the young ladies had organized a band of little girls and taught them to sing appropriate pieces, and would lead them out to visit the saloons on Saturday afternoons. On this Saturday I led them; we visited several places, and it was a touching sight to the throng of

people gathered to see and hear them. The people from all over the
country were in the habit of coming in on Saturdays to witness the
Crusade. What wonder that many a stalwart farmer, as he looked
upon the women kneeling on the curbstone, praying to God to soften and
change the saloon-keeper's heart and make him give up his business,
were often wrought up to a high degree of excitement. And seeing those
little things standing there, more than one knowing from bitter
experience what it meant, sing
                    "Father, dear father, come home,"
or
             "Pray, mister saloon-keeper, has father been in here?"
was it surprising that as he furtively brushed away the tears he would
exclaim: "Seems to me it would relieve a fellow's feelings a good deal to
go in and clean 'em out!"

A little later on, a Children's Association was formed under the
leadership of Mrs. Guy, our Secretary, the more to interest the children
and teach them to hate and shun the drink as their deadliest enemy.
They met on Saturday mornings. To one of these meetings came a wee
bit of a boy, in dress and long curls—Forest Lehman—with a penny to
give to Mother Stewart, and with a little speech, expressing his idea of
the cruelty of the saloon-keepers, that made it necessary for such aged
women as Mother Stewart to go out against them. A gentleman held
him up in his arms as he made his little speech.

That penny is among my richest treasures, and that baby boy is
growing up to a sober young manhood.

Some children were indoctrinated with a thoroughness that
must occasionally have irritated their parents. During a Boston
Sunday school rally one bright-eyed little girl asked Mother
Stewart in a whisper if she could sign the pledge and still eat
mince pies. "Why, yes, my dear," the Crusader replied, "if your
mamma will not put brandy in her pies. She could then sign the
pledge and eat mince pies too." Promising to carry the message
home, the moppet signed. "The mother of that little girl was a
Christian lady," Mother Stewart wrote later, "but had not
dreamed of the stumbling-block she was putting in the way of her
child. The child, though so young, saw the inconsistency."

An Ohio mother, testifying to the achievements of the
Crusaders, told how one morning, walking to market with her
six-year-old son, she felt him grasp her hand and quicken his

pace. "What is the matter, my son?" she asked. "Why do you hurry mamma along?" "Why, mamma," said the child reproachfully, "don't you want to hurry? Don't you know we are passing a saloon?"

The motive force that impelled some Crusaders transcended the cause of temperance. The constant marching, the trapping of sinful men in the very commission of their sins, storming halls of legislature theretofore barred to women, the tumult, the martyrdom, the public attention—all this was adventure that liberated them from the tyranny of wifehood, motherhood and domestic duty.

> The infectious enthusiasm of these meetings [an anonymous "Chastened Crusader" admitted in a letter to a newspaper], the fervor of the prayers, the frankness of the relations of experience, and the magnetism that pervaded all, wrought me up to such a state of physical and mental exaltation that all other places and things were dull and unsatisfactory to me. I began going twice a week, but I soon got so interested that I went every day, and then twice a day in the evenings. I tried to stay home to retrieve my neglected household, but when the hour for the morning prayer meeting came round I found the attraction irresistible. The Crusade was a daily dissipation from which it seemed impossible to tear myself. In the intervals at home I felt, as I can fancy the drinker does at the breaking down of a long spree.

The hostility aroused by these pious valkyries was not confined to liquor dealers and their clientele. Many staunch temperance men were horrified by what they considered unwomanly conduct. (A notable exception was the teetotaling Baptist multimillionaire John Davison Rockefeller of Cleveland, who hired detectives to obtain evidence against violators of the local liquor laws and contributed handsomely to the Crusade.) The feeling against the Crusaders ran highest in the South, where women's role was still more restricted. When a fiery proselytizer visited Andrew Johnson's town of Greeneville, Tennessee, the ex-President stood watching, hands in pocket, muttering imprecations against "the damn Yankee women who come down here to make the Southern ladies unsex themselves." Nearly everywhere the press opposed the Crusade.

Though the women accomplished a good deal less than they claimed, they were instrumental in obtaining indictments of about 1,000 Adair Law offenders. (Here again Rockefeller's private detectives helped.) Under their influence the Ohio Republican Party adopted a resolution condemning "intemperance and its causes" (reversed the following year, thanks to the brewers' lobby). At the height of the Crusade 17,000 small-town Ohio saloons, drugstores and other dispensers of drink by the glass went temporarily out of business, 1,000 followed in New York State, and all together, throughout the country, almost 30,000 closed. Eight of Ohio's biggest distilleries suspended operations, as did 750 breweries elsewhere, with a consequent decline in beer consumption close to 6,000,000 gallons. The loss to the government in liquor taxes exceeded $1,000,000.

But these temperance victories were transient. In a concluding note to the case of the miscreant John Van Pelt, Mother Stewart sorrowfully reported: "He was heard of afterwards in Wilmington, keeping a very low, disreputable place, and was suspected of setting fire to the house of the Friends' minister who had attempted to prosecute him. The last I heard of him he was in a Western penitentiary. Alas, the seed had not the depth of earth."

The same could be said of most saloonkeepers. The Crusade having failed to substantially change any liquor law, nearly all of them reopened within six months to a year after the Hillsboro uprising. The Crusade itself, meanwhile, had run out of steam. It could scarcely have continued without major disruption to the women's homes. But by then they had forged a weapon more effective than prayer on a barroom floor.

7. Organized Mother Love

ON the dining room wall of Josiah Flint Willard's modest house in Oberlin, Ohio, there hung his certificate of membership in the Washingtonian Society, dated 1835. Elaborately decorated and colored, it deeply impressed his six-year-old daughter, Frances Elizabeth, the fourth of five children, two of whom had died in infancy. A few years later Frances cut from her favorite periodical, *Youth's Cabinet*, a rhyming temperance pledge, which she pasted in the family Bible and insisted that every member of the family sign:

> A pledge we make, no wine to take,
> Nor brandy red that turns the head,
> Nor fiery rum that ruins home,
> Nor whiskey hot that makes the sot,
> Nor brewers' beer, for that we fear,
> And cider, too, will never do;
> To quench our thirst we'll always bring
> Cold water from the well or spring.
> So here we pledge perpetual hate
> To all that can intoxicate.

Willard had moved to Oberlin from Churchville, New York, where Frances was born, in order to study for the Congregational

E

ministry at the new Oberlin Collegiate Institute. Founded in
1833, it was the country's first coeducational college, and Mrs.
Willard, a schoolteacher, decided to study theology there too.
After four years tuberculosis forced Willard to seek a drier
climate, and having packed their meager belongings into a
wagon, parents and three children drove westward, settling
finally on farmland near Janesville, Wisconsin, a hotbed of
Methodist fundamentalism. The wife resumed her schoolteach-
ing, the husband farmed, and both joined the Methodist Church.

On the Sabbath the activities of the otherwise industrious
family slowed down almost to the point of immobility. Willard,
Sr., would not shave, black his boots, write or read a letter, even
look up a word in the dictionary, receive or make a visit. About
the only occupations he sanctioned were prayer and Bible study.
The farm being too far from church for regular attendance, he
usually conducted Sunday services at home. When Frances, a
fledgling artist, wanted to wile away the heavy hours sketching,
she got permission to do so by promising to sketch only churches.

Willard held equally rigid views concerning the physical
well-being of his family. He considered a cold-water compress the
sovereign remedy for practically every ailment from infections to
broken bones. With a few exceptions his "Golden Rules of
Health," which he imposed upon the household, were sensible
enough.

> Simple food, mostly of vegetables, fish or fowls.
>
> Plenty of sleep with very early hours of retiring.
>
> Flannel clothing next to the skin all the year round; feet kept
> warm, head cool, and nothing worn tight.
>
> Just as much exercise as possible, only let fresh air and sunshine
> go together.
>
> No tea or coffee for the children, no alcoholic drink or tobacco
> for anybody.
>
> Tell the truth and mind your parents.

Neither Frances nor her younger sister, Mary, was permitted
to go anywhere unaccompanied by a parent until they reached
the threshold of womanhood. To friends who found such
chaperonage excessive, their father would reply: "These are 'two
forest nymphs that dwell in the depth of the woodland shade,'
and I propose to keep them *innocent*." Frances, who received her

elementary education partly at home from her parents, partly in a one-room schoolhouse her father helped to build, recalled in after years: "We were literally never left alone with children or work people; there was always quiet but careful supervision. . . . Only two persons, one of them a child and one a girl in her early teens, ever said to me things that were calculated to mar the purity of my thoughts in the formative years of my life, and these were neither of them persons who had influence with me. . . ."

She had carroty hair, which she cut as short as a boy's, and a body as thin and flat as a plank. She wore trousers up to the age of sixteen. At play she could keep pace with her brother Oliver, climbing trees, walking on stilts, shooting marbles, pitching horseshoes and firing a double-barreled shotgun. Having mastered all of her father's carpentry tools, she could fashion a cart, sled, crossbow or whip handle. In the winter snows, borrowing an old overcoat of her father's and a pair of Oliver's boots, she would construct and set figure-four traps for quails.

She was subject to intense crushes on girls. She wrote in her mature years:

I was hardly sixteen years old when the flame of the ideal burned in my breast for a sweet girl of sixteen, Maria Hill by name. . . . That was my first "heart affair," and I have had fifty since as surely as I had that one. . . . Then came the vision of my cousin Mary G. . . . little dreaming of the commotion that her presence stirred in the wayward heart of her Western cousin. . . . My boy cousins I liked, my other girl cousins I loved, but for my cousin Mary I felt nothing less than worship. . . . That soft, white hand on mine seemed to complete the circuit that brought me into harmony with the electric tides of God's universe. . . . Next came the sweet-faced blind girl, Carrie, with her gift of music, sending my blithe spirit up to heaven's gate; then Anna C., the superintendent's daughter, but she liked my sister Mary best and my budding hopes were swiftly nipped . . . the next enshrined ideal of my life was Marion, "whose soul was like a star and dwelt apart," the high-bred girl with whom in 1857 I contested the palm for scholarship in Milwaukee Female College [Frances won]; then Susie B., the rich merchant's daughter in that same city, who was a very Saint Cecilia to my ardent fancy; and then Maggie H., of early Evanston fame, the "wild girl" of the school. . . .

A temporary estrangement occurred when the wild Maggie

tried to lure her into a moonlight ride with three college Lotharios. "I refrained from speaking to my *inamorata* for three weeks, but finally made up our difficulty when she admitted I was right in saying no 'self-respecting girl would ever make a clandestine appointment of any kind with a young man.' "

She wrote to Maggie during a summer vacation: "I love you more than life, better than God, more than I dread damnation!"

When she repeated to her mother what she had written, Mrs. Willard exclaimed: "Oh, Frank! pray Heaven you may never love a man!"

She never married. The few young men whom she grew to know well she tended to speak of as brothers. With her short hair and tomboyish ways she became, in the sexually segregated schools and colleges she attended, a masculine symbol, a swain figure, courting and courted.

She began her advanced education in 1857, when she was eighteen, at the Milwaukee Female College, boarding in a minister's home. The following year the Willards moved again, this time to Evanston, Illinois, a "Methodist heaven," Frances called it, the seat of Northwestern Female College and bone-dry by charter. Entering Northwestern as a sophomore, she was graduated two years later with distinction, her major studies having consisted of belles-lettres, natural science and Scripture. For the next sixteen years she taught in ten different schools and colleges. During one of her first teaching appointments, in the Chicago suburb of Harlem, she boarded with a family named Thatcher. She was then twenty-one. According to Clara Thatcher, the daughter of the family, "She was a most affectionate girl and her girl friends seemed to arouse in her the devotion and love that are usually lavished on the other sex. I recall a number of these girls who loved and were loved in turn by her as I have never seen elsewhere."

After teaching at her alma mater, she joined the faculty at the age of twenty-three. Her emotional involvements with some of her pupils were intense. A girl named Emma, anguished by her attentions to another, slipped a letter under her door:

MY OWN DEAR FRANK,
   No, not mine any longer either. How very natural it came for me to say those words, and yet I must tutor myself to change them, for your love has gone from me, like "a beautiful dream," gone to

Ada! . . . Oh Frank pity me! Oh God pity me! Yes, I ask pity of you! It isn't hard for you; you can't have loved me as I have loved you! It is impossible, you couldn't give it up so soon. . . . Never till now have I felt this truth in all its force, that "of all griefs a strong love unreturned, or unfulfilled is the sorrow which most blights a human life." Blights? Sears and corrodes! My life will not be very long I believe tonight, I pray that it will not. . . .

The favorite of Frances Willard's late twenties was an Evanston neighbor, Kate Jackson. They traveled together to Europe for two years of study and tourism, Kate paying all expenses. In Berlin a married American woman, whom they met in a pension, pressed gifts upon Frances until, to assuage Kate's jealousy, the two travelers moved on to Paris. There Frances received a letter from her bereft devotee:

MY OWN DARLING,
   . . . "Do I think of you?" "Have I thought and longed for you?" "Could I whisper in your ear the old sweet words, were you beside me?" Oh! Frank, dearest, little do you know, will you ever know of all that I have thought and longed and suffered, since I last saw you. . . .
   I thought . . . to return to the house from which the dear form had gone forever, to go up the stairs, where I used to kiss you, where I afterwards longed to and did not dare, the sofa where we sat that last night. . . .
   What I would whisper were you here this moment by me, but words fail me. I think if you were here, I should ask first, "can you kiss me" and then I should lay my head on your dear shoulder, and listen for the loving words. . . .
   If I never look upon your sweet face again, I will never let you forget my love is for you. . . .

In 1871 Frances Willard became president of Northwestern Female College, the first woman in the country to hold such a position. When the college merged with the men's Northwestern University, she was named dean of women and professor of esthetics. But the appointment of a new president made her situation untenable. He was Charles Henry Fowler, later a bishop of the Methodist Episcopal Church. A decade earlier she had broken her engagement to him. It was probably Fowler she meant when she wrote in her autobiography: "In 1861-62, for three-quarters of a year I wore a ring and acknowledged an

allegiance based on the supposition that an intellectual comrade-
ship was sure to deepen into unity of heart. How grieved I was
over the discovery of my mistakes the journals of that epoch
would reveal."

Her resignation coincided with the tapering off of the Woman's Crusade, a movement she had followed with profound
concern. The blooded warriors had no intention of abandoning
the field. In what Frances Willard termed "a sober second
thought" they formed temperance leagues or unions in state after
state, starting with Ohio under Mother Stewart's leadership.
After going East to confer with Dio Lewis, John Gough, Neal
Dow and other temperance strategists and stopping in Pittsburgh
on the way back to help pray a saloon closed, Miss Willard
declared her total dedication to the cause. On November 7, 1874,
delegates from seventeen state unions met in Cleveland's Second
Presbyterian Church and voted into existence the National
Woman's Christian Temperance Union, later described by Mrs.
Hannah Whitall Smith of Philadelphia, its National Superintendent of Evangelical Work, as "organized mother love." As
their emblem they adopted a white ribbon, symbolizing purity
and distinguishing them from the Blue Ribbon Clubs and the
Red Ribbon Clubs, both consisting of reformed male drunkards;
as their motto, "For God, Home, and Native Land." In addition
to pledging themselves to the destruction of the liquor traffic,
they affirmed their belief in a living wage for all workers, an
eight-hour day, equal civil rights for both sexes and a single
moral standard. Miss Willard refused a nomination for the
presidency, preferring to work at first under the tutelage of more
experienced antiliquor combatants. She was elected recording
secretary, the presidency going to Mrs. Annie Wittenmyer,
celebrated as a heroic Civil War nurse and founder of Homes for
Soldiers' Orphans. Miss Willard succeeded her five years later,
holding the office to the end of her life. But by whatever title,
Frances Willard *was* the WCTU, its policymaker, master tacti-
cian and guiding light.

A woman of inexhaustible energy, she averaged a speech a day
for ten years, frequently in addition to writing a sheaf of letters to
influential persons and an article or two for the temperance
press. At deliberative sessions she used a bung starter from a
closed-down saloon as a gavel. The agenda of the early
conventions included a lyceum bureau to furnish speakers and

organizers for the formation of local unions within states; a training school for young temperance missionaries; a medical committee to investigate the effects of alcohol on the nation's health; a committee to evaluate Biblical doctrine concerning wine. This last undertaking produced an unending debate since both drys and wets could, like the devil, cite Scripture for their purpose. Thus: "Wine is a mocker, strong drink is raging" (Proverbs 20:1) *versus* "And wine that maketh glad the heart of man" (Psalms 104:15); "Woe unto them that are mighty to drink wine, and men of strength to mingle strong drink" (Isaiah 5:22) *versus* "Drink no longer water, but use a little wine for thy stomach's sake and thine often infirmities" (Timothy 5:23); "Look not thou upon the wine when it is red" (Proverbs 23:31) *versus* "For in the hand of the Lord, there is a cup, and the wine is red" (Psalms 75:8); and so on *ad infinitum*.

The supreme objective of Frances Willard and the WCTU was constitutional prohibition, and one of their acts, in 1875, was to petition Congress. They thereby lost an old ally. Dio Lewis had always preached moral suasion as against legal coercion. "While we are waiting for the constable to do the work," he argued, "we cannot employ with the needed fervor those social, moral, and religious forces which alone can triumph over human vice. . . . It is not the clumsy fingers of the law which restrain us from a vicious life, but reason and public sentiment." Miss Willard visited Lewis in Boston because "I wished to see and counsel with the man whose words had been the match that fired the powder mine." She found "a considerate and kind old gentleman who could only tell me o'er and o'er that 'if the women would go to the saloons they could close them up forever.' But we had already passed beyond that stage, so I went on to broader counsels."

Among the purposes declared at the first WCTU convention had been the temperance education of the young. "For they [the saloonkeepers]," as Miss Willard put it, "must constantly recruit their patronage from the ranks of our youth, or it will ultimately fail." In 1880, the year following her election to the presidency, the WCTU created a Department of Scientific Temperance Instruction in Schools and Colleges, appointing Mrs. Mary Hannah Hunt of Massachusetts to superintend it. She and the shock troops under her command harried state and territorial legislatures so relentlessly that within twenty years every one of them except Arizona had enacted laws making such education compulsory in its public schools. Congress imposed the same law upon all schools under federal control.

The WCTU's Temperance Publishing Association, originally set up in Chicago, then moved, along with its national headquarters, to Miss Willard's hometown of Evanston, proceeded to grind out tons of textbooks, graphics, parables and miscellaneous propaganda designed to capture the minds of the young. Sunday school beginners began to receive a series of *Envelope Leaflets,* like the one entitled *Counting Fingers.* It showed an outspread hand, each finger numbered, followed by the homily:

One, two, three, four, five fingers on every little hand;
Listen, while they speak to us; be sure we understand.

1.—THERE IS A DRINK THAT NEVER HARMS
   It will make us strong.
2.—THERE IS A DRINK THAT NE'ER ALARMS
   Some drinks make people wicked.
3.—A DRINK THAT KEEPS OUR SENSES RIGHT
   There are drinks that will take away our senses.
4.—A DRINK THAT MAKES OUR FACES BRIGHT
   We should never touch the drinks that will put evil into our hearts and spoil our faces.
5.—GOD GIVES US THE ONLY DRINK—'TIS PURE, COLD WATER

According to another leaflet:

APPLES ARE GOD'S BOTTLES

The sweet juice of the apple God has placed in His own bottle. What a beautiful rosy-red bottle it is! These red bottles hang on the limbs of a tree until they are all ready for us to use. Do you want to open God's bottle? Bite the apple with your teeth and you will taste the sweet juice God has put in His bottle for you.

GRAPES ARE GOD'S BOTTLES

These purple and green bottles you will find hanging on a pretty vine. See! So many little bottles are on a single stem! Put a grape in your mouth and open God's bottle. How nice the juice tastes! Some men take the juice of apples and grapes and make drinks that will harm our bodies. They put the drinks in glass bottles, but we will not drink from such bottles. We will DRINK FROM GOD'S BOTTLES.

Kindergarten pupils learned to shout in unison: "Tremble, King Alcohol, we shall grow up!" and to sing songs by Florence Marshall, "a gifted woman," according to a footnote in the songbook, "who has put scientific information from the syllabus into rhymes easy to remember." Before leading her charges in Miss Marshall's *Keep It Outside*, for example, teacher would demonstrate to the class that "alcohol and water are exactly opposite; that alcohol is useful outside the body but injurious taken in beer, wine, whiskey." Then, all together:

> Who ever heard of blacking
>   The INSIDE of a shoe.
> It's all right on the OUTSIDE—
>   And so I'm telling you
> Some folks are just silly,—
>   Yes, brains they surely lack,
> They're using alcohol to drink,
>   And not to rub the back!
> Yes, blacking's good; so's alcohol;
>   But everyone should know
> They get OUTSIDE, not INSIDE,—
>   Or trouble's bound to grow.

For first-grade students there was a *Think a Minute Series*, of which a representative example was entitled *Fool Decimals*:

> Daddy was disgusted with Neighbor Jones. "Swigs beer like a sponge! Drank ten glasses, one after another,—made a fool of himself,—and had to be carried home dead drunk!"
> Billy asked, "Daddy, how much did you drink?"
> "Only one glass," said Daddy virtuously.
> Billy has been studying fractions. "One glass is ten per cent of ten glasses," he calculated. "Mr. Jones was a fool to drink ten glasses. Were you ten per cent of a fool, Daddy?"

The textbooks which the WCTU foisted upon high school

students reflected the views of extremists like Sir Benjamin Ward
Richardson, a British physician whom one disciple acclaimed as
"the Father of Scientific Total Abstinence," and Dr. Alonzo
Benjamin Palmer, dean of the Medical Department at the
University of Michigan. According to Richardson, any quantity
of alcohol in any form was toxic and when consumed regularly
produced inheritable disorders unto the third generation. Palmer
agreed that "idiocy, deafness, and other defects of the nervous
system are painfully common in children of the intemperate."
Piously, he added: "Theologians generally consider drunkenness
in all its forms as a vice and there seems ground for this opinion
in the Scriptural declaration, 'No drunkard shall inherit the
Kingdom of Heaven.'"

In a standard classroom demonstration the teacher would
place part of a calf's brain in an empty glass jar. After
discoursing on the nature of the brain and the nature of alcohol,
she would then pour a bottle of alcohol into the jar. The color of
the calf's brain would turn from its normal pink to a nasty gray.
And that, the teacher would conclude in sepulchral tones, is what
would happen to her pupils' little brains if ever they drank
Satan's brew.

Nowhere in all this gallimaufry of misguidance and religiosity
aimed at children, or in any of the prohibition literature and talk
addressed to adults, did there linger the ghost of a suggestion that
perhaps one might drink moderately without damage to oneself
or to others. The very word "moderation" inflamed the WCTU
and the Prohibition Party. It was "the shoddy life-belt, which
promises safety, but only tempts into danger, and fails in the
hour of need . . . the fruitful fountain from which the flood of
intemperance is fed. . . . Most men become drunkards by trying
to drink moderately and failing." Even conceding that a rare few
could conceivably imbibe in moderation at no risk to themselves,
they should nevertheless refrain lest they set a bad example for
the weaker majority of the human race. In 1880 the Reverend
Howard Crosby, chancellor of the University of the City of New
York, organized the Businessmen's Society for the Encouragement of Moderation, which offered its members a choice of
pledges, varying from total abstinence for a specified period of
weeks or months to daily abstinence until 5 P.M. Following a
lecture Crosby delivered in Boston, expressing "a calm view" and
defending moderate drinking, he drew fire from the prohibi-

tionists' heaviest artillery. ". . . the malignancy of the Evil One," stormed the New York *Witness*, "could not devise a greater injury to society in general than to put the advocacy of moderate drinking in the mouth of an influential and generally esteemed minister of the Gospel."

Frances Willard's hopes rose high when James Abram Garfield, the Republican candidate and WCTU favorite in the Presidential elections of 1880, defeated General Winfield Scott. By religion a Campbellite, or Disciple of Christ, Garfield had frequently mounted the pulpit as a lay preacher to advance the rigorous temperance principles of his sect. On March 8, 1881, four days after his inauguration, Miss Willard led a WCTU delegation to the White House, bearing a gift—a portrait of Lucy Hayes, the wife of Garfield's predecessor, Rutherford B. Hayes, who had refused to serve any liquor at official dinners. It was a disillusioning encounter. Miss Willard reported:

> His manner to us seemed constrained. He was not the brotherly Disciple preacher of old, but the adroit politician "in the hands of friends" and perfectly aware that the liquor camp held the balance of power.
>
> Surprised and pained by his language, we at once adjourned to the Temple Hotel, and such a prayer-meeting I have seldom attended. The women poured out their souls to God in prayer that total abstinence might be enthroned at the White House, that a chief magistrate might come unto the kingdom who would respond to the plea of the nation's home-people seeking protection for their tempted loved ones.

"Home Protection" became a key phrase of her political vocabulary. In 1880 she had organized a party so named and two years later merged it with its natural ally, a supporter of women's suffrage, the Prohibition Party, which took the name, Prohibition Home Protection Party.

As president of the WCTU Frances Willard did not limit her objectives to the abolition of alcohol. Had she done so, she might never have acquired the title which a worshipful Canadian follower bestowed upon her—"the Uncrowned Queen of American Womanhood." But like her sister reformers whose programs embraced the general betterment of their sex, like New York's Elizabeth Cady Stanton, Massachusetts' Lucretia Coffin Mott,

Texas' Helen Maria Stoddard, Miss Willard associated liquor, traditionally a male indulgence, with the inequities of woman's social condition. An errant husband could besot himself night after night, squandering his wages on drink, could frequent brothels (and defile the purity of his home), could brutalize his wife and children—the law offered them scant protection or relief. Divorce, if obtainable, meant social obloquy for the ex-wife. Property rights were weighted in the husband's favor. In nearly every area that did not involve her immemorial functions as child rearer, cook and churchgoer, she encountered gross injustices. Her opportunities for advanced education were narrowly circumscribed. Most colleges and universities had been founded by men for men. Single women obliged to earn their living received far less pay than men in equivalent jobs.

Under Frances Willard's leadership the WCTU, until then concerned solely with promoting temperance, became a rallying ground for a vast diversity of causes, adopting, in the phrase of its president, a "do-everything" policy. Forty-five departments were eventually established, each focusing upon a different aspect of social reform. Its Department of White Cross and Shield, in which Miss Willard took a particular interest, assuming the office of superintendent, attacked the double standard of morality, though the remedy it proposed was not, heaven forfend!, to encourage "free love," as advocated by a few shameless Bohemians, but rather to elevate the concupiscent male to the same degree of chastity as women, uniting the sexes in what the department termed "a white life for two." White Shielders pledged themselves "to uphold the law of purity as equally binding on men and women; to be modest in language, behavior and dress; to avoid all conversation, reading, pictures, and amusements which may put impure thoughts into my mind; to strive after the special blessing promised to *The Pure in Heart*."

The departments of Health and Hygiene, of Heredity, and of Physical Culture condemned patent medicines containing alcohol, vivisection, intercollegiate athletics on the grounds that they distracted students from their textbooks, and narcotics, which, according to the Department of Health and Hygiene, included tobacco. Concerning tobacco, one departmental "expert" contended that as liquor impaired the moral sense, so nicotine impaired the capacity to love and thus contributed to broken marriages. Nicotine could also inflict instantaneous physical injury, a Health and Hygiene pamphlet reported and, to prove it, cited the case of a boy whose face was totally disfigured after he had smoked a few cigarettes, and of another, a fourteen-year-old, who dropped dead immediately after his first cigar. Juvenile WCTU recruits were urged to pulverize every cigarette and cigar butt they might spy in the street to prevent others from picking them up and relighting them. The Department of Scientific Temperance Instruction taught as scientifically proved fact that:

The majority of beer drinkers die from dropsy.

When it [alcohol] passes down the throat it burns off the skin leaving it bare and burning.

It causes the heart to beat many unnecessary times and after the first dose the heart is in danger of giving out so that it needs something to keep it up and, therefore, the person to whom the heart belongs has to take drink after drink to keep his heart going.

It turns the blood to water.

[Referring to invalids], A man who never drinks liquor will get well, where a drinking man would surely die.

The Department of Social Purity, created and headed by Miss Willard, demanded harsher penalties for white slavers, the establishment of rehabilitation centers for penitent prostitutes, an increase in the age of consent, or as she more delicately put it, "the age of protection," at least to eighteen, having been horror-struck to learn that in twenty states it was ten years and in the state of Delaware seven. The department also viewed prevailing feminine fashion as a menace to social purity. "Women who parade what ought to be the mysteries of the dressing room before the public gaze of men," Miss Willard scolded, "who, bewilderingly attired, emulate in the waltz the fascinations that in haunts of infamy beguile these same men to dishonor and whose effrontery in defending their outrageous conduct with the time-worn phrase: 'Evil to him who evil thinks,' proves them to be as bare-faced mentally and bare-footed morally as they are bare-necked and shouldered in the dance-delerium." Contemporary portraits of Miss Willard customarily show her wearing a black bombazine dress of severe cut, high-necked and long-sleeved. Her hair worn short, pulled tight behind her ears and parted straight down the middle, pince-nez perched on her thin nose, further defeminized her.

Miss Willard developed close relations with the founder and chief agent of the New York Society for the Suppression of Vice, the luxuriantly mutton-chop-whiskered Anthony "Uncle Tony" Comstock, whose slogan was "morals, not art or literature." The WCTU's Department of Purity in Art and Literature upheld Comstock in his crusade against nude paintings and sculpture like the Metropolitan Museum's "Bacchante," a gift which the White Ribboners bade the museum reject, and the advertising brochures of the Art Students' League with their anatomical drawings; against entertainment like the side shows at the Chicago World's Columbian Exposition of 1893 ("I have been to the mouth of hell today," reported a Comstock investigator); and against literature deemed morally pernicious like the *Thousand and One Nights* ("too vile to translate and of no literary merit"), Walt Whitman's *Leaves of Grass*, Tolstoy's *Kreutzer Sonata*, which the Postmaster General banned from the mails and whose author Teddy Roosevelt called "a sexual and moral pervert," dime novels and the *Police Gazette*.

Polygamy, what Miss Willard denounced as "Utah's monstrous lust," brought into existence the Department for Work among Mormon Women. The Department of Christian Citizenship took up cudgels against gambling, with particular attention to racetrack habitués, while the Department for the Suppression of Sabbath Desecration flooded the country with petitions decrying the use of the mails, travel by train, steamboat or bicycle, the publication of newspapers, getting a haircut, unessential labor and entertainment of any kind on Sunday.

In the field of temperance proper the WCTU overlooked no possible point of purchase. The Department for the Suppression of Social Evil specialized in demonstrating connections between crime and alcohol. The Department of Unfermented Wine at the Lord's Table called upon the clergy to confine their sacramental beverages to grape juice. The Department for Inducing Corporations to Require Total Abstinence in Their Employees won considerable support among employers with its plea that drinking increased the danger of occupational accidents, wasted man-hours and generally reduced efficiency. Still other departments were set up for temperance missions to special groups such as blacks, Indians, immigrants, soldiers and sailors, railroad workers, lumbermen and miners.

Side by side with these encroachments upon private morality and religious practice there arose departments devoted to a variety of humanitarian causes. The White Ribboners fought hard, and with occasional success, for improved employment codes, prison reform, world peace and international arbitration, child welfare and laws against child labor, adult education classes for both native and foreign-born illiterates, the easing of racial tensions. . . .

But their hardest-fought cause next to prohibition, without which neither prohibition nor any of the other causes stood much chance of lasting success, was woman suffrage. "To deny her the use of that most efficient weapon, a vote," wrote one suffragist to the New York *Herald Tribune* in 1874, "and then urge her into a physical contest with [the liquor trade] is very like saying that women cannot use artillery, or Spencer rifles, but ought to form the advance in an attack on an army well drilled in their use, and sending them forward with broadswords, javelins, and other implements of medieval warfare." At first a large faction within the WCTU, headed by its first president, Mrs. Annie Wittenmyer, opposed suffrage lest it alienate the churches and Southern society, but with the election of Frances Willard the majority sentiment shifted, and a Franchise Department was organized to advise and aid suffrage groups wherever they might arise. The liquor interests were quick to recognize the deadly threat: Woman suffrage could only hasten the advent of prohibition, and they marshaled every counterforce at their disposal. When a state suffrage amendment was proposed, as in Nebraska during the early eighties and later in Oregon, they would line up the saloonkeepers and their customers against it. The foreign-born voter, to whom the notion of renouncing his daily nips of rum or seidels of beer was unthinkable, proved especially receptive to antisuffrage propaganda. Where persuasion failed, the saloon politicians bought votes. In both Nebraska and Oregon the wets won by substantial majorities. Up to 1911, in fact, only four states—Utah, Colorado, Idaho and Wyoming—had enfranchised its women, and nine more years would elapse

before women could vote in a national election. Yet long before
that the WCTU had become the world's biggest, best organized
and most powerful temperance society.

When Frances Willard took office as president, the WCTU
had established auxiliaries in twenty-five states and scores of
intrastate branches. Determined to organize the entire country,
she set out on an odyssey that covered every town with a
population of 10,000 or more. Her first target was the South,
where the prospect of an emancipated womanhood was regarded
with scarcely less dismay than the enfranchisement of the black.
She spent three months there, returned north to add a Department of Southern Work to the other White Ribbon enterprises
and within seven years welcomed into the fold delegates from
every state below the Mason-Dixon line. "The first time I heard
her," one Southern recruit remembered, "I lay awake all night
for sheer gladness. It was a wonderful revelation to me that a
woman like Miss Willard could exist. I thanked God and took
courage for her humanity." Miss Belle Kearney of Mississippi,
who organized her state under Miss Willard's guidance, described the WCTU as "the golden key that unlocked the prison
of pent-up possibilities, the discoverer, the developer of southern
women," to whom it gave "a new vision of woman's life."

Concerning the most wildly visionary and unpent of all the
women it had inspired, Carry Amelia Moore Gloyd Nation,
organizer of its chapter at Medicine Lodge, Kansas, the WCTU
was of two minds. "Mrs. Nation is a White Ribboner," noted its
official organ, the *Union Signal*, "but she has a method all her
own, and one which is not found in the plan of work of the
W.C.T.U. . . . whose weapons . . . are not carnal but spiritual.
While we cannot advise the use of force . . . we are wide awake
to the fact that Mrs. Nation's hatchet has done more to frighten
the liquor sellers and awaken the sleeping consciences of Kansas
voters than the entire official force of the state has heretofore
done." But after a series of particularly destructive sorties the
Signal concluded: ". . . more harm than good must always result
from lawless methods."

Though "hatchetation," a term she coined, became Carry
Nation's weapon of choice in her one-woman war against the
law-defiant saloonkeepers of dry Kansas, she did not confine
herself to it. At various times she also used her fists, rocks,

brickbats, a sledgehammer, an iron bar, prayer and invective.

"Carry" was the way her semiliterate father, George Moore, a slaveowning Kentucky planter and devout member of the Disciples of Christ sect, inscribed her name at birth (November 25, 1846) in the family Bible. She herself preferred the conventional "Carrie" until she embarked upon her lifework. It then occurred to her that God had guided her father's hand. "My right name is Carry A. Nation—carry a nation for temperance," she explained. ". . . my father had christened me 'Carry' for a purpose."

Signs of dementia flickered fitfully through Carry's family history. Her mother believed herself to be Queen Victoria, affected regal robes, received her relatives by appointment only and rode around in a magnificent coach drawn by silver-caparisoned horses which her husband had bought to humor her. She died in an insane asylum. Her mother, brother, sister and a nephew were also mentally unbalanced.

Carry, who described herself as "a bulldog, running along at the feet of Jesus, barking at what He doesn't like," exhibited odd behavior early in life. Such was her devotion to her father ("an angel on earth . . . one of the noblest works of God," she called him in her stupefying autobiography, *The Use and Need of the Life of Carry A. Nation*) that she longed to resemble him physically. Moore, Sr., had somehow managed to wear down all his teeth on the right side, possibly by unconsciously grinding them. So Carry tried to wear down hers. She failed, fortunately, for she could ill afford the sacrifice, being an excessively plain girl, who grew into a woman of forbidding aspect, square-jawed and blunt-nosed, with a large, grim mouth, scraggly hair gathered in a bun on top of her head and a heavy frame. At various stations of her pilgrim's progress she suffered from intense nervous depressions, "consumption of the bowels," convulsions and amnesia. She had celestial visions and reported several intimate conversations with Jesus Christ.

Carry's aggressions vented themselves upon four principal objects: saloons, freemasonry, tobacco and sex. All four shared a common source in the wretchedness of her marital experiences. The Civil War brought ruin to the Moores, forcing them to seek a home farther west. After a painful hegira they came to rest in Belton, Missouri. There, when Carry was nineteen, she married a handsome young physician named Charles Gloyd despite her family's warnings against his drinking. "I was so hungry for his caresses and love," she recalled years later. But Gloyd drank so heavily that he could seldom respond to her hunger. She grew to hate the Masons, to which Gloyd belonged, as fiercely as the saloonkeepers. "A great curse to Dr. Gloyd. These men would drink with him . . . secret societies are unscriptural and the Masonic Lodge has been the ruin of many a home and character."

Excessive smoking did not improve Gloyd's health either. His distraught wife wrote:

> I believe that, on the whole, tobacco has done more harm than intoxicating drinks. The tobacco habit is followed by thirst for drink. The face of the smoker has lost the scintillations of intellect and soul. The odor of his person is vile, his blood is poisoned. . . . Prussic acid is the only poison that is worse. . . . Tobacco users transmit nervous diseases, epilepsy, weakened constitutions, depraved appetites and deformities of all kinds to their offspring. . . . Deterioration of the race is upon us. . . . The tobacco user can never be the father of a healthy child. Therefore he is dangerous for a woman to have as a husband. If I were a young woman, I would say to the men who use tobacco and who would wish to converse with me: "Use the telephone; come no closer!" I would as soon kiss a spittoon as to kiss such a mouth. . . .

Carry's sexual frustrations led her to follow courting couples to their tryst, surprise them as they embraced and, brandishing her umbrella, cry hell and damnation upon them. The sight of nude paintings such as adorned saloon walls plunged her into foaming fury. "Cover that wicked and shameful object!" she would scream. "You're insulting your mother by having her form stripped and hung in a place where it is not even decent for women to be when she has her clothes on!"

One child, a sickly girl, Charlien, was born of Carry's union with Gloyd. Husband and wife were living apart by then, he drinking himself rapidly to death, she back in her parents' home. A bout of delirium tremens finished off Gloyd six months after Charlien made her appearance. Desperate for money to support her sick daughter and demented mother, Carry prayed to God for another husband. "Ten days later," as she told the story, "I was walking down the street and passed a place where Mr. Nation was standing. . . . He was standing in the door with his back to me, but turned and spoke. There was a peculiar thrill which passed through my heart and made me start. The next day I got a letter from him asking me to correspond with him. . . . I knew this was the answer to my prayer, and David Nation was to be the husband God had selected for me."

Nation turned out to be a minister of the Christian Church, a lawyer and editor of a religious newspaper. Until they were divorced twenty-five years later, they shared a life of utter misery, Nation having managed to muster no sympathy for his wife's reform mania.

In the afflictions that now befell little Charlien, Carry saw the curse of a tainted heredity, the sins of drink and tobacco visited upon the innocent second generation. "Her right cheek was very much swollen, and so on examination we found there was an eating sore inside her cheek . . . at last the whole right cheek fell out, leaving the teeth bare. . . . I said: 'Oh, God, let me keep a piece of my child.' " A minister advised her against praying for Charlien's survival because he felt she would be better off dead. But Carry persisted, and a recovery of sorts took place. The wound shrank to a hole about the size of a twenty-five-cent coin. Then, despite constant prayer and repeated surgery, the child's jaws clamped shut, not to open again for eight years. Charlien's physical ailments were at long last brought under control. She even married a Texan named MacNabb. But her mind grew progressively weaker, and Carry's only child spent most of her last years in an insane asylum, a prey to "chronic mania."

To support themselves and Carry's feebleminded kin, not to mention a daughter, Lola, by a previous marriage of Nation's, the ill-matched couple tried their hands at many different occupations. Drifting through Missouri, Texas and Kansas, they farmed cotton and ran a hotel. Carry taught Sunday school for a time, while Nation worked as a Campbellite pastor, newspaper correspondent and lawyer searching in vain for litigants. Between them they earned only the barest subsistence.

In 1890 the Nations were living in Medicine Lodge, Kansas, the husband enjoying for the first time some small success as a lawyer, his wife serving the WCTU local as a jail evangelist. The state had adopted prohibition ten years before. Yet in Medicine Lodge alone seven saloons, or "joints," to use the regional term, were operating more or less openly with political protection. Holding liquor chiefly responsible for the downfall of the prisoners she visited, Carry began harassing the "jointists," confining herself at first to the well-tried methods of the Women Crusaders—identifying the offenders by name in church and public meetings, praying in the street before their establishments, and shrilly denouncing them wherever encountered as a "Maker of drunkards and widows! Rum-soaked rummy! Ally of Satan!"

With her sister White Ribboners Carry kept up such a clamor that the town officials finally closed all seven joints. That left a druggist named O. L. Day, who, Carry learned, had received a secret shipment of a ten-gallon keg of whiskey, though he lacked a license to sell it for medicinal purposes. Seconded by Mrs. Wesley Cain, the Baptist minister's wife with whom she had organized the WCTU local, Carry determined upon decisive measures. Sledgehammer in hand, she stormed the drugstore and staved in the keg. When the WCTU later successfully blocked Day's efforts to obtain a medicinal permit from the town authorities, he left. Medicine Lodge was clean.

Carry had not yet received the word from the Almighty which she hoped would sanctify her work. That did not come until the evening of June 6, 1900, when she opened her Bible at random and fell upon Isaiah 60:1: "Arise, shine; for thy light is come, and the glory of the Lord is risen upon thee."

There was no restraining her after that. Dashing into the street, she cried to the first White Ribboner she met: "There is to be a change in my life!" A further heavenly communication reached her at dawn. A voice commanded: "Go to Kiowa." This was a town about ten miles distant, swarming with bootleggers and saloons. Driving a buggy filled with what she called smashers—that is, brickbats, rocks and bottles wrapped in paper to conceal them from the foe—she set out for Sodom, telling her husband she planned to spend the night with a friend.

Carry's swift passage through Kiowa was cyclonic. As her first target, she chose a joint run by one Dobson. "Mr. Dobson," she announced, "I told you last spring . . . to close this place, and you didn't do it. Now I have come with another remonstrance. Get out of the way. I don't want to strike you, but I am going to break up this den of vice." A few well-aimed brickbats shattered the mirror and demolished every bottle below it.

Proceeding to the neighboring joint, ". . . there was quite a young man behind the bar. I said to him: 'Young man, come from behind that bar, your mother did not raise you for such a place.' I threw a brick at the mirror, which was a very heavy one, and it did not break. . . . I was standing by a billiard table on which there was one ball. I said: 'Thank God,' and picked it up, threw it, and it made a hole in the mirror. . . .''

Altogether, Carry reduced three Kiowa joints to shards. Such destruction of private property exposed her to prosecution. On the other hand, the local authorities were guilty of malfeasance for failing to padlock the joints. It was a standoff, and they had to let Carry go. As she rolled out of town, standing bolt upright in her buggy, both arms raised to heaven, she cried: "Peace on earth, goodwill to men!"

Carry Nation entered legend.

Soon after her Kiowa foray, she bought from a Medicine Lodge hardware store the implement that became both her weapon and her symbol—a hatchet—and at the age of fifty-four sallied forth on a smashing campaign that carried her across the country, shouting: "Smash! Smash! For Jesus' sake, Smash!"

The counties of Kansas were the first to bear the full brunt of Carry's ire. In Wichita she stormed the famed Carey Bar armed with rocks and a cane and iron rod lashed together. She heaved the rocks through "Cleopatra at Her Bath," demolishing the $1,500 glass and mutilating the canvas. With the rod and cane she swept the counters free of glassware and bottles. She was pounding the cherrywood bar with a spittoon when the police bundled her off to headquarters. Had the Wichita jointists sensibly lain low that night while Carry languished in jail, the onslaught might not have so perturbed the state legislature about to convene in Topeka. But instead they encouraged their clientele in an all-night celebratory orgy, thereby prompting the enactment of stiffer enforcement laws. Carry, serene in her martyrdom, happily knelt on the stone flagging of her cell, Bible in hand, while a news photographer clicked away. So posed, she became one of the most familiar front-page figures of the era.

Provided with defense counsel by the WCTU, Carry was shortly released. Her mind, the county attorney feared, might collapse under prolonged incarceration. But she had not yet done with Wichita. Deaf to her husband's pleas to come home, she laid waste with her hatchet to two more Wichita joints and was about to complete the destruction of the Carey Bar when two detectives barred her path.

Then it was on to Enterprise, Topeka, Des Moines, Chicago,

St. Louis, Cincinnati, Atlantic City, Philadelphia, New York, trailed by thousands of slack-jawed citizens, slowed down here and there by a night or two in jail, but unstoppable, a sainted heroine to the church and the drys, a lunatic vandal to the wets. A whole literature sprang up around the Kansas maenad, exemplified by such verse as "SHE'S COMING ON THE FREIGHT, or, The Joint Keeper's Dilemma":

> Say, Billy, git ten two-by-four
>   'Nd twenty six-by-eight,
> 'Nd order from the hardware store
>   Ten sheets of boiler plate,
> 'Nd phone the carpenter to come
>   Most mighty quick—don't wait,
> For there's a story on the streets
>   She's coming on the freight.
>
> There, Billy, now we've got her—
>   Six-eights across the door,
> 'Nd solid half-inch boiler iron
>   Where plate glass showed before;
> But, Bill, before that freight arrives
>   Y'd better take a pick
> 'Nd pry that cellar window loose,
>   So we can git out quick.

and "That Little Hatchet":

> A century was fading fast
> When o'er its closing decade passed
> A matron's figure, chaste, yet bold,
> Who held within her girdle's fold
>   A bran' new hatchet.
>
> The jointists smiled within their bars,
> 'Mid bottles, mirrors and cigars—
> The woman passed behind each screen,
> And soon occurred a "literal" scene—
>   Rum, ruin, racket!

By 1901 Carry was no longer waging a lone combat. Fired by her example, women all over the country were seizing hatchets and wreaking havoc upon their local joints.

Many New York jointists, forewarned of Carry's approach, quietly bolted their doors and waited for the tempest to blow over. John L. Sullivan, the retired heavyweight, who ran a Manhattan saloon, had boasted: "If she comes to my place, I'll throw her down the sewer." Carry headed straight for the Sullivan saloon, demanding to see him. When told of her presence, he said: "Not on your life. Tell her I'm sick in bed," and he refused to budge until she left town.

A little prosperity lightened Carry's closing years. She earned sizable fees as a lecturer. In Topeka she published a semiweekly newspaper, *The Smasher's Mail*, which enjoyed as much popularity among the wets as the drys because of its unintentional hilarity and spectacular vilification. Under the rubric "Letters from Hell" Carry lashed out at all her old bugbears. She especially detested President McKinley, calling him "a whey-faced tool of Republican thieves, rummies and devils." When he was assassinated, she applauded the deed. In addition to selling subscriptions to *The Smasher's Mail*, she peddled autographed pictures of herself praying and souvenir hatchets. "The paper accomplished this much," Carry commented after she suspended publication to devote more time to lecturing, "that the public could see that I was not insane."

Eventually, Carry Nation joined that galaxy of yellow press eccentrics and sideshow freaks serving chiefly to amuse and titillate. Under the aegis of a toping, cigar-smoking impresario, who sweetened his breath with cloves when near her, she toured the Chautauqua circuit, county fairs, carnivals and amusement resorts. As the climax of a burlesque show in Springfield, Massachusetts, she delivered one of her rousing antijointist harangues. She acted in a version of *Ten Nights in a Barroom*, retitled *Hatchetation* and revised to include a saloon-smashing scene.

In her sixty-fourth year Carry's strength began to fade, and on January 11, 1911, after lecturing at Eureka Springs, Arkansas, she broke down. She entered a hospital in Leavenworth, Kansas, where she died five months later, her mind quite dimmed.

How great Carry Nation's "use and need" may have been in the prohibition movement remains moot. Some will disagree with her two most skilled biographers, Robert Lewis Taylor and Herbert Asbury. The first concluded that "she inspired women to revolt on other levels . . . she was the first real catalyst," and the second, "that she, more than any other one person, transformed it [prohibition] from an apologetic weakling into a militant giant of overwhelming power." Those achievements would seem more properly credited to cooler, better balanced intellects like Frances Willard.

What Carry's headline-catching antics did accomplish was to fix attention upon the pestholes of the liquor industry—the low-grade saloons. Her harshest critics could scarcely quarrel with her self-assessment, murmured as she collapsed on her last lecture platform: "I have done what I could."

The WCTU set the example for a good many women's temperance societies overseas, and in 1883 Miss Willard founded the World's WCTU with the dual purpose of integrating these scattered foreign societies and creating new ones. The international missionary work, first undertaken by Mrs. Mary Clement Leavitt, a New England veteran of the Women's Crusade, eventually established unions in fifty-one countries, girdling the globe from Canada to Argentina, from England to Japan. Through this endeavor Miss Willard formed the warmest and longest-lasting attachment of her mature years.

When the British Women's Temperance Association elected Lady Henry Somerset president in 1889, Miss Willard, who had yet to meet her, wrote a congratulatory letter. "In that letter," Lady Somerset recalled later, "she sent me a little knot of white ribbon, and all these years that little bow has been pinned into my Bible. It came as a promise of the most beautiful friendship that ever blessed my life."

Isabella Caroline Somerset had inherited from her father, Earl Somers, vast country properties, including Eastnor Castle in Herefordshire, and when her marriage to Lord Henry proved an unhappy one, she retired there. It was the drunkenness among her tenantry that turned her toward temperance work. She began by assembling forty of her tenants in a schoolhouse near the castle gates and persuading them to sign the pledge.

As guest of honor at the first convention of the World's WCTU in Boston in 1891 Lady Somerset finally met Miss Willard. Enchanted by her, she eagerly accepted her invitation to return with her for a prolonged visit to "Rest Cottage," as Miss Willard called her Evanston retreat. The first night there Lady Somerset noted in her Bible: "October 28, 1891—A Day to be remembered in thanksgiving." To the eleven-story Temple on Chicago's La Salle and Monroe streets, the WCTU headquarters during the nineties, Lady Somerset donated a marble bust of the president for which John Greenleaf Whittier composed an inscription:

> She knew the power of banded ill
> But felt that love was stronger still,
> And organized for doing good,
> The world's united womanhood.

Miss Willard had interrupted her travels in 1882 to present to the Presidential nominating conventions a memorial, asking them to advocate constitutional prohibition. She appealed first to the Greenback Labor Party, which declared itself "in favor of submitting to a vote of the people an amendment to the Constitution in favor of suffrage regardless of sex, and also on the subject of the liquor traffic," a response too insipid to suit Miss Willard.

At the Republican convention in Chicago's Exposition Hall the platform committee grudgingly allowed her fifteen minutes for a hearing. They listened with glacial indifference. Their final report did not even mention prohibition, and afterward the crumpled memorial was found on the convention floor, splattered with tobacco juice. The discourtesy backfired. A temperance periodical, the *Lever*, published a photograph of the befouled document, and the WCTU broadcast copies as evidence of "the perfidy of the Republican party to the interests of the American home."

Miss Willard did not delude herself that the Democrats, "the whiskey party . . . whose drink bill [she estimated] was no larger than that of the Republicans—in both cases immense," would prove any more hospitable, but she considered it her duty to offer them the opportunity. The Democratic platform committee reported against "sumptuary laws that vex the citizen."

This left the Prohibition Home Protection Party, which Miss Willard had striven so diligently to fortify. At its convention in Pittsburgh the following July her heart was gladdened by the contrast with the other bibulous, antifeminist conventions, by "the crowd not only of 'real folks' but of 'our folks'—non-drinking, non-tobacco-using home-people, almost without exception

members of the church." They accepted the WCTU memorial
with enthusiasm. Miss Willard's only disappointment was the
decision to drop the words "Home Protection" and substitute
"National Prohibition Party."

Meanwhile, the former Republican governor of Kansas, John
Pierce St. John, a rock-ribbed dry and champion of women's
rights, had been so outraged by his party's treatment of Miss
Willard that he bolted, declaring: "I will condemn such
cowardice, such disregard of the best interests of the people with
my voice and vote." A majestically hirsute figure, veteran of the
Indian wars and the California gold rush, youthful drunkard,
self-educated ex-miner, lumberman, sailor and lawyer, St. John
had served two terms as Kansas governor, losing a third
campaign to a coalition of wet Republican and Democratic
politicians. "The Lion-hearted [so one White Ribbon Kansan
apotheosized him], leading the crusade of the nineteenth century, not to the rescue of the empty sepulchre of our risen and
ascended Lord from Moslem hands, but to rescue and reclaim
the temple of the soul where should ever dwell the spirit of the
Crucified," was the Prohibition Party's choice for President.

He polled only 150,626 votes (still almost fifteen times more
than the previous Prohibition candidate) as against the victorious
Democrat Grover Cleveland's 4,911,017 votes. But St. John's
campaign demonstrated the growing power of prohibitionism. It
was a major cause of the defeat of the Republicans' James G.
Blaine, the price they paid for ignoring the WCTU memorial.
They feared as much, for they tried to persuade St. John to quit
the race. Since Blaine lost by only 62,683 votes, St. John's total,
small though it was, proved to be one of the decisive factors.
Another was the blunder committed by the Reverend Samuel D.
Burchard. At a reception which the Republican ministers of New
York City held for Blaine, Burchard characterized the opposition
as the party of "Rum, Romanism and Rebellion," thereby
antagonizing Catholic voters throughout the country. The Republicans, who had dominated national politics for a quarter of a
century, never forgave St. John. They reviled him and the
WCTU, which they accused of playing politics behind the
hypocritical mask of moral reform. In more than a hundred
towns party zealots burned St. John in effigy. But armored in his
conviction of righteousness, he spent the rest of his life happily

serving the dry cause as both propagandist and political adviser
to the National Prohibition Party.

The Republican rout was the high-water mark of the second
prohibition wave to sweep the nation since the fifties, when
thirteen states enacted anti-liquor laws. Those laws were all
statutory and so relatively easy to dilute or repeal according to
the shifting winds of politics and public opinion. What chiefly
characterized the prohibition wave of the eighties and early
nineties was the determination of its proponents to dry up the
states by constitutional amendment, a measure requiring a
popular vote. In three-fourths of the states and territories the
pressure exerted by the dry politicians obliged the legislature to
submit such an amendment to the people. Four states, in
addition to Kansas—Maine, Rhode Island, South Dakota and
North Dakota—actually adopted constitutional prohibition,
while Vermont and New Hampshire maintained their statutory
laws, the former strengthening them. President Cleveland imposed prohibition upon the territory of Alaska.

At the federal level Republican Representative Henry William Blair of New Hampshire had introduced in 1876 the first
resolution for a national prohibition amendment, a relatively
feeble one that would outlaw distilled liquor only and not take
effect until 1900. It never left the committee room. Ten years
later, as a Senator, Blair presented a new amendment, the joint
production of Frances Willard and two of her male colleagues,
banning all alcoholic beverages. Prodded along by the increasingly effective dry lobbyists, this one got as far as the Senate floor,
where it was defeated by a vote of 33 to 13. During the same
period fifteen states passed local option laws, while every dry
state stiffened its existing laws with wider powers of search and
seizure and heavier penalties for violators.

In 1886 the Reverend George Channing Haddock, pastor of
the Sioux City, Iowa, Methodist Episcopal Church, suffered
martyrdom for prohibition. Sioux City then had about 20,000
inhabitants and 100 saloons operating in violation of statutory
laws. It also had fifteen churches, which the saloonkeepers
threatened to burn down should their pastors prove obstructive.
This failed to intimidate Haddock, who continued to denounce
the lawbreakers from his pulpit, gathered evidence against them

in pending court cases and canvassed the townsfolk for moral and financial support. On the evening of August 3 a band of saloonkeepers and saloon regulars, among them a prosperous, influential brewer named John Arensdorf, surrounded him in the street. Arensdorf drew a pistol and fired it in the minister's face, killing him instantly.

So tightly did the liquor dealers control the municipal authorities and the local press that almost a year elapsed before any action was taken against Arensdorf. It then came out that Haddock had fallen victim to a conspiracy. The day before the murder, at a meeting of the Sioux City Saloonkeepers' Association, Arensdorf had drawn attention to the $700 in the association's treasury, with which, said he, it could reward anybody willing to "do up" the minister. The belated trial of the brewer, who had finally decided to pull the trigger himself, ended in a hung jury, 10 to 1 for acquittal, with the dissenter accusing defense counsel of having suborned the other jurors. After a second trial Arensdorf went free, even though one of his proven co-conspirators, a desperado named Munchrath, had meanwhile been convicted and imprisoned. Defendant and jurors together commemorated the verdict by going to a photographer's studio and posing for a group portrait. The next annual convention of the United States Brewers' Association opened on a self-congratulatory note. "With pride and gratification," read a collective statement, "we record the fact that the fanaticism of the Iowa Prohibitionists was frustrated in at least one instance, namely, the attempt to fasten the crime of murder upon a member of our trade."

The following year the Mississippi prohibitionists were similarly frustrated. In Jackson the foe set fire to the office of their state organ, *Sword and Shield.* Its twenty-one-year-old editor, Roderick Dhu Gambrell, the son of a Baptist preacher, armed himself with a pistol and resumed publication in new quarters. At that time the top-ranking local antiprohibitionist, a Colonel J. S. Hamilton, had been renominated for a state senatorship. Gambrell's editorial attacks, exposing him as an embezzler of state funds, forced him to withdraw his candidacy. A few nights later the sound of pistol shots, of heavy blows and shouts of "Murder!" brought a crowd on the run to a street near Gambrell's office. They found the young editor dying from a beating that had mutilated his face. He had evidently discharged his pistol before he fell, for towering above him was Hamilton, his coat sleeve smoldering from close pistol fire and blood trickling from two superficial bullet wounds. With him stood a saloonkeeper, one Albrecht, holding a pistol whose butt dripped blood; a hireling of Hamilton's named Eubanks; a professional gambler, Figures; and City Marshal Carraway, an old Hamilton crony.

Two trials followed. The first resulted in prison sentences for Hamilton and Eubanks, the release under bond of Albrecht, and the unconditional release of Figures. On appeal Hamilton won a new trial and change of venue to the adjoining county, where a deputy sheriff, another Hamilton ally also under indictment for a felony, summoned the jurors, bribing four of them, as he later boasted. Hamilton was acquitted.

Such murders and perversions of justice, together with the gloating of the brewers, incensed people on both sides of the liquor controversy. Many who might otherwise have remained neutral or even opposed to prohibitory measures now felt in conscience bound to support them.

The churches of every major Christian denomination spurred their members on to political action against the liquor traffic. With a warning that "it can never be legalized without sin," the Methodist Episcopal Church declared:

> We recommend all members . . . who enjoy the elective franchise, to so use that solemn trust as to permit the rescue of our country from the guilt and dishonor which have been brought upon it by a criminal complicity with the liquor traffic.
>
> We do not presume to dictate the political conduct of our people, but we do record our deliberate judgment that no political party has a right to expect, nor ought it to receive, the support of Christian men so long as it stands committed to the license policy, or refuses to put itself on record in an attitude of open hostility to the saloon.

The United Presbyterian Church:

> We regard the traffic as an evil which can never be removed without political action and we regard its entire prohibition as the most pressing political question of the times; and it, therefore, becomes our duty as Christian citizens, in the careful and prayerful use of the ballot, to meet the question directly. . . .

No party is worthy of the support of Christian men that fails to antagonize the saloon.

In a letter to the priest of his Columbus, Ohio, diocese, the Roman Catholic Bishop·John Ambrose Watterson ruled:

> . . . No one who engaged . . . in the manufacture or sale of intoxicating liquors can be admitted to membership [in any Catholic society in the diocese]. . . . If there are saloonkeepers in your parish who . . . carry on their business in a forbidden or disedifying way . . . you will refuse them absolution . . . unless they promise to cease offending.

Nor did the advancing dry forces neglect the college campuses. In 1887 student delegates from forty-four of them formed the Intercollegiate Prohibition Association, and by 1893 it had organized chapters in 146 colleges.

Like the first prohibition wave, the second was not accompanied by a decrease in the consumption of alcohol. On the contrary, it rose from an annual average of about 62,000,000 gallons of distilled liquor during the decade 1870–80 to more than 76,000,000 during the succeeding decade, from almost 21,000,000 gallons of wine to 27,500,000, and from 647,000,000 gallons of malt liquor to about 1 billion, all together representing an increase in the per capita consumption from 8.79 gallons to 13.21. These figures, computed by the U.S. Statistical Abstracts, could not, of course, include the incomputable amounts of illegal liquor consumed. Again, as in the fifties, bootleggers and speakeasies* thrived wherever prohibitory laws existed.

The crest of the prohibition wave carried Frances Willard to new heights of fame and power. She became the most celebrated American woman of her day. As she pursued her missionary work across the country, traveling, on the average, 15,000 to 20,000 miles a year, flourishing the twin banners of temperance and women's rights, she aroused the kind of veneration normally

---

* The word had been used as early as 1889, and an Irish variant appeared in an anonymous rhyme alluding to Saint Patrick almost two decades before that:

No wonder the Saint himself
To take a drop was willin'
For his mother kept a spake-aisy
In the town of Enniskillen.

accorded to the sanctified. Said her Philadelphia disciple, Mrs. Hannah Whitall Smith: "If Frances Willard should push a plank out into the ocean, and should she beckon the white ribbon women to follow her out to the end of it, they would all go without question. . . . She seemed like a person who, as someone expresses it, 'changed eyes with Christ.' She looked at everybody and everything through his eyes. . . ." The Pundita Ramabai, a Brahmin widow, converted to Christianity, who had taken the temperance pledge at Miss Willard's hands when they met in England and, after returning to her native Poona, became vice-president of the India WCTU, recalled: "Saint Frances was truly one of those who in life, in death, in resurrection followed the Lord; she was the spotless sainted queen of womanhood . . . a miracle of Christ." A later president of the American WCTU compared her to St. Francis of Assisi, saying: "We follow not the woman Frances Willard, but the leader sent by God, we believe, for a special purpose." So potent was the leader's charismatic effect upon a Boston girl, Anna Gordon, that she gave up a promising musical career to serve as her organist, secretary and Boswell.

Miss Willard's "gospel politics" (a term she craftily employed to lull those ultrapurist White Ribboners who shrank from sectarian or partisan entanglements) ended in bitter frustration. It was her vision to merge into a single huge party a number of mutually supportive reform organizations—the Prohibition Party, the WCTU, suffragists; the socialistic Knights of Labor, 700,000 strong, who welcomed women and blacks, demanded higher wage scales and an eight-hour workday and had successfully struck the Union Pacific Railroad; the Federation of Organized Trades and Labor Unions, precursor of the AFL; the agrarian Grangers, struggling to crack the big-business monopolies with their own cooperative enterprises; the Populists, who wanted silver instead of paper currency, government ownership of unused lands, railroads, and telegraph and telephone utilities and a graduated income tax. . . .

Miss Willard managed to bring together representatives from such groups at a mammoth St. Louis "People's Convention" in 1892. Had a merger resulted, prohibition might well have captured a majority of state legislatures. But her hopes were dashed chiefly by the preconvention committee intrigue of two Prohibition Party bigwigs, John St. John of Kansas, who wished

to keep the Prohibition Party a force distinct and apart, and Mrs.
Helen Mar Gougar of Indiana, a lawyer and White Ribboner,
who bore Miss Willard a personal grudge. "I'll teach her she
doesn't own the Prohibition Party as she did the W.C.T.U.,"
Mrs. Gougar told a reporter. She succeeded. Frances Willard left
St. Louis in abject defeat.

The prohibition wave again began to recede. There were
many causes. The liquor industry organized a National Protective Association, which, with its immense resources, subsidized
newspapers, subverted politicians and engineered fraudulent
elections wherever a prohibitory amendment confronted the
voters. A Pennsylvania brewer, Harry Crowell, who directed a
campaign against an antiliquor amendment submitted in 1889,
made no bones about how he handled the press. "I visited the
editors in person or had some good man do so," he disclosed
later, "and arranged to pay each paper for its support a certain
amount of money. Throughout the state we paid weekly
newspapers from $50 to $500 to publish such matter as we might
furnish either news or editorial, but the city dailies we had to pay
$1000 to $4000. . . ." In Providence, Rhode Island, an association member paid the chairman of both Democratic and
Republican state committees thousands of dollars to manipulate
city and county campaigners on the liquor question. In Nashville, Tennessee, the Democratic collector of Internal Revenue
compelled his entire personnel on pain of dismissal to contribute
to an antidry chest. Since their inception the United Brewers had
been circularizing every candidate for public office to determine
where he stood on antiliquor legislation. They spared no expense
to defeat at the polls those who approved or returned evasive
answers.

The prohibitionists were no match financially for such moneyed foe. Internal dissension, moreover, weakened them politically. A sizable faction within the WCTU was so antagonistic to
President Willard's policies, especially her alliance with the
Prohibition Party, that it seceded to form an independent
nonpartisan union. A new quasi-prohibitory concept, the high
license, widened the breach. All this amounted to was the
imposition of higher fees to operate a saloon, which, so its
proponents argued, would reduce the number of saloons and
consequently the amount of liquor sold and oblige the surviving
owners to run a law-abiding, respectable place lest they forfeit

their costly fee. Thirty-two states and territories welcomed high license as a compromise satisfactory to both camps and the elimination of a disruptive factor in politics. It only proved a boon to the liquor industry. A few shabby little saloons were forced out of business, but the majority, financed by the brewers and distillers in order to secure outlets for their products, expanded and flourished as never before. High license not only gave the liquor industry control of the retail market, but staved off state prohibition.

Finally, President Cleveland's condemnation of high tariffs on imports overshadowed prohibition, as well as every other issue. He was defeated for reelection in 1888 by the Republican Benjamin Harrison, a bête noire of the temperance groups, who drank wine at public functions, while Vice President Levi Morton, as owner of Washington's Shoreham Hotel, permitted liquor to be sold over the bar, and Secretary of State James Blaine instructed the consular service in Latin America to drum up business for the home beer trade. The dry recession gained momentum until by the early 1900's only three states—Maine, Kansas and North Dakota—retained constitutional prohibition.

Physically drained by her struggle to stem the ebbing tide and grief-stricken by the death, in 1892, of her mother, Miss Willard sought tranquillity abroad. Lady Somerset was overjoyed to shelter her at Eastnor Castle. During her long sojourn the guest could not refrain from advising her hostess on the management of the British WCTU, stressing the interrelationship of temperance with other reform movements. This was not unanimously appreciated by her ladyship's fellow White Ribboners, one of whom protested: "There is in many countries, perhaps even America herself may not be quite free from it, a little sensitiveness in regard to plans and methods and interference from abroad . . . ," and a British temperance paper suggested that Miss Willard stay home and administer her "Yankee" union without meddling in British affairs.

Every year after to the end of her life Miss Willard spent several months with Lady Somerset either in England or America. She wrote in her memoirs:

> The loves of women for each other grow more numerous each day, and I have wondered why these things are. That so little

should be said about them surprises me, for they are everywhere. Perhaps the "Maids of Llangollen" [in Wales] afford the most conspicuous example; two women, young and fair, with money and position, who ran away together, refusing all offers to return, and spent their happy days in each other's calm companionship within the home they there proceeded to establish [a reference to Lady Eleanor Butler and Sarah Ponsonby, a pair of eccentric eighteenth-century Dubliners, given to wearing semimasculine garb; they shared the same Welsh cottage for fifty years, never leaving it a single night]. . . . In these days, when any capable and careful woman can honorably earn her own support, there is no village that has not its examples of "two heads in counsel," both of which are feminine. Oftentimes these joint-proprietors have been unfortunately married, and so have failed to "better their condition" until, thus clasping hands, they have taken each other "for better or for worse. . . ."

And what was it, in Miss Willard's view, that kept so many men and women apart, what were "the great separatists" between them? Drink and tobacco.

Once they used these things together, but woman's evolution has carried her beyond them; man will climb to the same level one day. . . .
The friendships of women are beautiful and blessed; the loves of women ought not to be, and will not be, when the sacred purposes of the temperance, the labor, and the woman movements are wrought into the customs of society and the law of the land.

After the debacle of the People's Convention Miss Willard played only a minor role in prohibition politics. Mainly she wrote and lectured on a wide range of reform topics and edited the *Union Signal*. During her travels abroad she had also developed an intense interest in such arcana as phrenology, theosophy, spiritualism and reincarnation.

In February, 1898, while visiting New York City, she contracted a fatal case of influenza. As she lay near death in a suite at the Hotel Empire, the faithful Anna Gordon by her bedside, her thoughts turned to Isabella Somerset, from whom she longed for a cabled message of love. When it came shortly before the end on February 17, she asked her companion to read it to her. "Oh, how sweet," were the dying words Anna Gordon recorded in her *Beautiful Life of Frances Willard*, "oh, how lovely, good—good!"

Thirty-four years earlier the old House of Representatives in Washington had been converted into the National Statuary Hall, each state being privileged to raise there statues of two of its eminent natives. Upon Anna Gordon's plea the Illinois legislature appropriated $9,000 for a white marble statue of Frances Willard standing at her lectern, which Congress accepted in 1905, so honoring a woman for the first time.*

* Only three other women have been admitted to Statuary Hall since: the Colorado scientist Dr. Florence Rena Sabin, the Wyoming suffragette Esther Hobart Morris, and the Minnesota educator Maria Sanford.

8. *"Ethics be hanged"*

The League was born of God. It has been led by Him and will fight on while He leads. The one thing that stands out is that those things in the way of progress of the Kingdom of God must get out of the way.

—THE REVEREND FRANCIS SCOTT McBRIDE, General Superintendent of the Anti-Saloon League of America

The Reverend Mark Revell Sadler Shaw remembers the Prohibition Party's finest hour

I wasn't quite four years old, but I can still see that big homemade flagpole going up in our front yard as clearly as if it happened yesterday.

We'd just moved from Grand Rapids, where I was born, the fourth of ten children, to Baldwin, a little railroad junction in the northern part of Michigan. My father, Solomon Shaw, was a Free Methodist minister. My mother, Etta Sadler, had also been ordained, but to the ministry of the Primitive Mission Church, because at that time the Free Methodists did not ordain women. Both churches were somewhat more evangelistic and fundamentalist than the Methodists generally, but in later years when my parents joined the Methodist Episcopal Church, it recognized Mother's ordination.

Up to the middle of the century there'd been two kinds of temperance groups—those who favored total abstinence, who thought the right way, the only safe way, was to sign the pledge, get on the wagon, and never drink at all. Others felt it was enough to be temperate in the generic use of the word—that is, moderate, not drinking to excess. Gradually, temperance came to be in common usage synonymous with total abstinence. Throughout the churches, particularly the Methodist, Congregational and Baptist churches, it was taken for granted that they stood for total abstinence, not moderation, total abstinence. But then they found that a man might sign the pledge and his friends would urge him to take a drink and he would weaken and yield to temptation and start in again. So the idea grew up that it wasn't enough to get individuals to take the total abstinence pledge. You had to remove the source of temptation. You had to get rid of liquor itself. Out of that attitude grew the Prohibition Party.

My parents, who had always been total abstainers, became active members of the party. Their work as ministers was evangelical rather than pastoral. While we children were still young, Mother taught school, but later she spent twenty years traveling as a WCTU lecturer.

Mother compiled from magazines and newspapers many examples of remarkable answers to prayer, and Father published them in a book, which I believe sold a quarter of a million copies. Then he got out a children's edition, and there was one story he read to me that has stayed with me all my life. It was a story about a little boy named Tim who needed a new pair of shoes to go to a Sunday school picnic, but his mother told him the shoes had gone into a jug, which was her way of saying that his father had spent the money on whiskey. So Tim smashed the jug with a brickbat to get the shoes. His heart sank when he found nothing but an evil-smelling liquid. He was still sobbing when his father came home that night and between his tears he explained why he smashed the jug. "I'm really sorry, Father," he said, "I'll never do it again." "No, I guess you won't," said his father, deeply moved, and laid a loving hand upon the little head. The day before the picnic he handed Tim a parcel. Inside was a pair of new shoes. "Oh, Father," exclaimed the happy lad, "did you get a new jug and were they in it?" "No, my boy," replied his father, "there ain't going to be any new jug. Your mother was right. Everything went into the jug, but you see getting things out ain't an easy matter, so I'm going to keep them out from now on."

Not long after that I spoke in public for the first time. I got up in Sunday school and took the pledge of the cold water boy.

It was about the same time, in 1892, that my three older brothers went out into the woods with an old baby carriage. They cut down a big pine tree, chopped all the branches off, stuck the trunk into the axle of the baby carriage and hauled it back to our front yard. Then they dug a deep hole and planted the tree there, and they hoisted a flag Mother had sewn to the top of it. It said BIDWELL AND CRANFILL. Those were the Prohibition Party candidates for President and Vice President.

[General John Bidwell, a seventy-three-year-old Civil War veteran and California rancher, had been one of the

first white men to cross the Rocky Mountains into California. A friend of the Indians, he let 200 of them live free on
his property, which covered 25,000 acres of some of the
richest soil on the Coast. It once produced wine grapes, but
when the general saw how drunk Californians got on wine,
he destroyed all his vineyards. He had held office in both
Democratic and Republican state machines until his temperance convictions led him to join the Prohibition Party.
His running mate, James Britton Cranfill, a physician and
Baptist minister from Texas, half his age, had resigned from
the state Democratic Party when it tabled his resolution
against the liquor traffic, and gone on to organize the
Prohibition Party in Texas.]

*I trotted along to the voting place with my whole family. It's my
earliest recollection of politics. Our candidate got over 270,000 votes,
the most the party ever polled. In fact, we never came close to it again.*

*The trouble was we couldn't get enough people who'd been lifelong
Republicans or Democrats, like their fathers and grandfathers before
them, to leave their party and vote for the Prohibition Party, even
though they were against liquor. A completely new approach was
needed.*

The Midwest was the heartland of prohibitionism. The Right
Worthy Grand Lodge of the Independent Order of Good
Templars, the Women's Crusade, the WCTU, the Prohibition
Party, the Intercollegiate Prohibition Association and scores of
lesser antiliquor movements originated there. Since 1828 Ohio
alone, the most abundant in temperance societies of the Midwestern states, had produced at least a dozen major ones, plus a
great many of the country's most persuasive dry leaders. The
latter came chiefly from rural areas, bringing with them a
curious traditional amalgam of liberalism and bigotry. Abolitionists, most of them, before the Civil War, they demanded equal
rights for blacks after it, as well as reforms in working conditions,
education, penology and women's rights. At the same time they
tended to equate rectitude, sobriety and piety with country life
and vice, drunkenness and irreligion with the cities. The entire
temperance movement came to reflect a conflict of cultures—
agrarian against industrial, the native-born Yankee against the
immigrant micks, dagos, bohunks and krauts, Protestants against

Catholics and Jews—and by exploiting the prejudices of the rural masses the dry fanatics won their biggest following.

In the fall of 1832 two young Presbyterian ministers set out together to find land upon which to build a college—wilderness land remote from the corrupting influences of cities. The Reverend John Jay Shipherd was the pastor of the Plan-of-Union Presbyterian Church at Elyria, Ohio; the Reverend Philo Penfield Stewart, his friend since school days, had been a missionary to the Choctaw Indians of southern Mississippi until poor health forced him to seek less taxing duties. What they envisaged was a college within a Christian community where ministers and teachers would be trained "in the diffusion of useful science, sound morality and pure religion among the growing multitudes of the Mississippi Valley" and thence among the populations of the West. Toward the end of November they came upon a 500-acre tract of virgin forest, 34 miles southwest of Cleveland, that struck them as ideally situated. When Shipherd found the owners, two devout Connecticut merchants, they pledged it to him, and the following December he and Stewart inaugurated, with thirty-four students, the Oberlin Collegiate Institute, so named after an Alsatian pastor and educator, Jean Frédéric Oberlin, whose inspirational biography the two friends had recently read. In 1836 the tract was incorporated as the village of Oberlin.

From its first day Oberlin seethed with reformist ardor. It was not only the country's first coeducational college, but the first to admit blacks as the equals of whites. Gerrit Smith donated to Oberlin 21,000 undeveloped acres in Virginia to cultivate as a haven for free blacks. Owen Brown, the father of John Brown, was an Oberlin trustee, and John Brown surveyed the acreage for the college. When, in 1835, almost the entire student body and several professors walked out of Cincinnati's Lane Theological Seminary in protest against the reactionary trustees who had tried to disband their antislavery society, Oberlin warmly welcomed them.

The new college became a station on the Underground Railroad that smuggled fugitive slaves across the Canadian border to safety. On September 11, 1858, four Kentucky slave catchers, armed with legal documents and accompanied by a U.S. marshal, came hunting for an escaped black named John Price. They recaptured him in Oberlin, where he had been living for two years, and whisked him to a hotel in the nearby village of Wellington, pending his return to his Kentucky master. Before they could leave, more than 600 Oberlin students, teachers and townsmen besieged the hotel, rescued Price and hid him in the home of Oberlin's president, James H. Fairchild, whence he was shortly sneaked into Canada. Thirty-seven rescuers were indicted under the Fugitive Slave Law and kept prisoners in a Cleveland jail for three months awaiting trial. The slave catchers were also liable to prosecution under Ohio's recently enacted Personal Liberty Law. Extralegal negotiations ended in the release of all parties, the Oberlin rescuers emerging to cheers and a hundred-gun salute.

Given Oberlin's cultural and sectarian orientation, prohibitionism was bound to find fertile soil there. To keep the community liquor-free, it formed in 1874 the Oberlin Temperance Alliance under President Fairchild's leadership, which soon extended its operations beyond the community, securing a local option law first for all of Ohio's college towns, then for all of its townships. In May, 1893, a ministerial graduate, the Reverend Howard Hyde Russell, revisited his alma mater with a new plan to foil the Demon. His credentials were positively celestial. The preceding winter, in a Conneaut, Ohio, church, the pastor introducing Russell as an antiliquor fighter, proclaimed: "There was a man sent from God whose name was John; it is equally true there was a man sent from God whose name was Russell." Commenting on this endorsement, Russell said: "I was compelled to believe the statement was true." A later follower attested: "To him, under God, is traceable the conception and execution of that plan. Every step in his career has been evidenced by divine guidance in preparation for this apostolic task."

A Minnesotan by birth, Russell had successfully practiced law in Iowa until his conversion. He prepared for the Congregational ministry at Oberlin and for ten years held pastorates at Amherst and Berea, Ohio; Kansas City, Missouri; and Chicago. An alcoholic brother had early turned him against liquor. At Berea his temperance sermons resulted in the closing of six saloons and cost him a severe beating by a dispossessed barkeep. In Kansas City his way to church led past the Rochester Brewery. "Always when I passed this devil's-broth factory," he recalled, "I prayed God to stay the tide of sin and shame flowing therefrom . . .

whenever I passed a saloon I sent up a prayer, 'O, God, stop this!' At length God plainly said to me, 'You know how to do it; go and help answer your own prayers.' " The decisive moment came in Chicago during the funeral service for an alcoholic woman. As Russell used to tell the story,

> . . . there was the father intoxicated, sitting upon the floor. The undertaker's driver was tipsy, and there were three or four neighbor women with liquor upon their breath. The mother was asleep in the cheap box of a coffin. . . . Then I asked the boy, "Do you know what caused your mother's death?"
> "It was the drink."
> "Are you going to drink, my boy?"
> "I'll never touch it," and the boy clinched his little hand as he said it.
> I then made a solemn promise also:
> "I promise to go out to my brothers and sisters of the churches, regardless of their name and creed, and I will appeal to them to join their hearts and hands in a movement to destroy this murderous curse."

Ever since attending Oberlin, Russell had collaborated with the Temperance Alliance. It was he, in fact, who had led the successful fight for a statewide local option law. Now, at his request, the Alliance's executive committee assembled in the college library to hear his new plan. The date was May 24, 1893. What Russell proposed was neither an exclusively Protestant organization nor an independent political party like the Prohibition Party, but an interdenominational, omnipartisan state league, working with any church and supporting any candidate opposed to the liquor traffic. Nor would it attempt the kind of do-everything policy that diffused the energies of Frances Willard and the WCTU, but concentrate all its fire upon the single enemy—alcohol. The committee immediately accepted the proposal, passed a resolution to organize what it later named the Ohio Anti-Saloon League and elected Russell superintendent at an annual salary of $2,000.

Russell's concept aroused great excitement in temperance circles and stimulated similar activities throughout the country. In fact, before the Ohio league was formally instituted, a group of Washington drys had formed the Anti-Saloon League of the District of Columbia. Not long after, two noted clergymen found themselves traveling on the same train from Chicago to Philadelphia. They were the Reverend Alpha Jefferson Kynett, founder of the Methodist Church's Board of Temperance, and Archbishop John Ireland of the St. Paul, Minnesota, Catholic diocese, another forceful proponent of total abstinence. They fell to discussing the burgeoning movement, and before they reached their destination, they had agreed upon the need for a merger of all national, state and local prohibition agencies along the lines formulated by the Oberliners. Accordingly, at Kynett's urging, the District of Columbia Anti-Saloon League summoned the country's prohibitionists to a convention in Washington's Calvary Baptist Church. Lasting two days (December 17 and 18, 1895), it resulted in the formation of the Anti-Saloon League of America, from which future state leagues would take their direction. For national superintendent the logical choice was Russell, who forthwith set about organizing chapters. By the early 1900's they had been established in nearly every state and most American territories and dependencies.

The Anti-Saloon League had been shrewdly named. Its ultimate purpose was to illegalize all alcoholic beverages, not simply those dispensed over a bar, but the average saloon presented the most vulnerable point of attack, being a noisome dive infested by the neighborhood riffraff. The majority scarcely merited the status ascribed to them by their defenders, that of a "workingman's club," offering a respite from daily cares, where a weary man could find good fellowship and relaxing, innocent conviviality, sympathetic bartenders ever ready to listen to his joys and sorrows, beer at a nickel a stein and a free lunch, where in close harmony with kindred souls, eyes dimmed by sentimental memories, he could release his emotions through such sob songs as:

> They say we are aged and gray, Maggie,
> As spray by the white breakers flung;
> But to me you're as fair as you were, Maggie,
> When you and I were young. . . .

or

> Then cherish her with care and smooth her silv'ry
> hair;

> When gone, you will never get another;
> And wherever we may turn, this lesson we
>   learn—
> A boy's best friend is his mother!

or

> Sweet Ad-e-line, my Ad-e-line,
> In all my dreams,
> Your fair face beams. . . .

Fan-cooled in summer, heated by a coal stove in winter, the best of the neighborhood saloons generated a congenial atmosphere in which to read the newspapers provided by the bartender at no charge. Some of them had billiard and pool tables, some bowling alleys, and nearly all would make their back rooms available for union or fraternal meetings, wedding or christening celebrations and Saturday-night dances. The lordly bartenders served a number of community needs, feeding the starving, keeping clean rest rooms, rushing first aid to people injured in fights or accidents. Among the best-informed members of the community, they also functioned as a kind of free employment agency, steering laid-off workers to new job openings.

Such benevolent establishments, however, bore no more resemblance to the average neighborhood saloon than did the glossy drinking places of the big cities, all cut glass, gilt and mahogany, frequented by the rich and famous, like New York's Hoffman House bar with its enormous paintings of mythological nudes by the French artist Bouguereau; Peoria's Alcazar, its floor inlaid with marble and onyx, its fifty-foot bar of rubbed cherry wood curving gracefully across a room dotted with gleaming outsize brass spittoons; the barroom of San Francisco's mammoth Palace Hotel, the first luxury hotel on the Coast; New Orleans' Ramos and Sazerac, respective fonts of Ramos gin fizzes and absinthe cocktails. . . . As early as 7 A.M. some of these deluxe groggeries were open to administer to patrons who may have overindulged the night before with such classic panaceas as the prairie oyster (a raw egg in Worcestershire sauce), a "brain duster," whose ingredients varied from region to region, but generally included brandy, or simply a hair of the dog. As the tippler tippled, he could help himself at no additional expense, or for a quarter tip have a waiter help him, from a buffet table laden with imported cheeses, sausages, cold chicken and turkey, smoked salmon, salads, rich stews, pies and pastries. . . .

But not even the natural enemies of prohibition could find much to say in favor of the ordinary beer-and-whiskey saloon. ". . . a nuisance and a loafing place for the idle and vicious," complained the New York *Wine and Spirit Gazette*. "It is a stench in the nostrils of society and a disgrace to the wine and spirit trade." At election time politicians would seek votes for sale among the hoodlums and derelicts gathered there. When riots threatened, the first police action would be to close the saloons.

The choicest location for a saloon was a busy street corner where its gaudy signboards would catch the eye of passersby coming from all directions. A corner building offered the further advantage of doors on two streets so that a thirsty customer, eager to elude family vigilance, could slip through one, toss down a slug and duck out through the other. The next best location was by a factory gate in the path of workers with their paychecks, which the saloonkeepers were only too happy to cash. An Illinois manufacturer found that of 3,600 checks issued on a single payday every one had been cashed in a saloon.

The activity inside the average saloon frequently grew rowdy, and to conceal it from the gaze of respectable passersby, the doors would be shuttered and the windows blocked by advertising posters, potted plants or a pyramid of bottles. The interior decor invariably included a deep carpet of sawdust to absorb the beer suds dripping from the bar and the tobacco juice that fell short of the spittoons. Behind the bar hung chromos of opulently proportioned, reclining nudes intermingled with colored photographs of bareknuckle prizefighters, their dukes up, their handlebar mustaches bristling. For many years a favorite subject of saloon art was John L. Sullivan, "the Boston Boy," "the Great John L.," who won the last professional bareknuckle fight in 1889 by knocking out Jake Kilrain after seventy-five rounds and more than two hours. Sullivan himself lost the title three years later to James J. "Gentleman Jim" Corbett. What especially endeared the Boston Boy to the saloon crowd was his way of swaggering up to the bar, slapping down a huge bill and inviting everybody to join him. He was known to have slugged bartenders who tried to give him change. It was an occasion for lamentation throughout the drinking fraternity when Sullivan, having entered middle age and run through a million dollars of prize money, climbed aboard the water wagon and began touring the country as a temperance speaker.

Placards carrying maxims festooned the walls. A recurrent one ran: IF DRINKING INTERFERES WITH YOUR BUSINESS, CUT OUT BUSINESS. There was more truth than jest in this. The barkeepers' geniality might mask hearts of stone. Semicriminal types many of them, they would serve a customer liquor, no matter how drunk he was already, as long as he remained conscious and solvent, then, when his legs or his credit collapsed, have the bouncers throw him into the street. These important functionaries, with their bulging biceps, generally came from the ranks of retired prizefighters. Few bartenders hesitated to serve minors, and it was no uncommon sight to see a throng of teen-agers lined up at the bar after school hours. For poker players and crapshooters tables in the rear were usually available, provided the house got a cut of each pot. Some bartenders excelled as short-change artists. Others watered the whiskey and added red pepper to give it bite. To maintain a pose of bonhomie and join boozy celebrants in a toast whenever asked without himself getting drunk, a common bartender's dodge was to keep within reach a tiny glass called a snit, filling it as required with a few innocuous drops of beer or colored water. Another was the drink on the house, intended to create an obligation of honor requiring the groups of customers so favored to keep drinking until each of them had stood a round for all the others. Thus twenty companions meant twenty drinks apiece. To increase the size of the rounds, the bartender would herd several boozy groups together.

The highly touted free lunch was largely a fraud. If a man's hunger exceeded his thirst, a bouncer would likely usher him out of the place. The fare provided was designed primarily to stimulate thirst and consisted of heavily salted pretzels, salted peanuts, pickles, sauerkraut, overseasoned sausages, dried herring, sardel, a cheap cousin of the sardine, and similar briny preparations.

If the saloonkeeper did not operate some nearby brothel himself, the chances were he maintained close liaison with those who did. Usually he kept a list of brothels to which he could refer his clients. He might also allow an allied whoremaster to post a pimp in the saloon to serve as a tout and guide. Many saloonkeepers harbored free-lance whores, letting them, in return for a share of their earnings, use the back room to arrange assignations. During the early 1900's Big Jim Colosimo, the prototypal Chicago vice czar, ran a score of saloons, many of them connected to a neighboring bordello by a secret passage.

The typical saloon hardly needed to advertise itself. The reek of spilled beer, mingling with the general filth littering the pavement in front, carried half a block or more. Derelicts and drunks no longer able to stand slumped before the swinging doors, and where several saloons occupied the same block, women would zigzag from one side of the street to the other rather than pass them.

Lowest of the low were the tenement district saloons. Albert J. Kennedy, a settlement worker who made a national survey of slum areas between 1908 and 1920, ascribed the alcoholism he found there to the prevalence of saloons:

> There were in many neighborhoods [he reported] a heavy proportion of men and a great many women who, from one year's end to the other, were never for a single hour completely sober. They were always slightly muddled. Every dance and party, every political rally, most trade-union and lodge meetings got underway in a slightly maudlin manner. Going in and out of a public gathering always involved passing through a barrage of men in various stages of drunkenness. One of the most desired qualities in a chairman or leader of a meeting was ability to squelch drunks. The tone of all gatherings had to be scaled down to a level just above the individual who was not quite all there. Dances of young people suffered severely from the prevailing alcoholism. There was always a proportion of seventeen-, eighteen-, and nineteen-year-old boys who were beginning to go the way of their fathers in the matter of inebriety. Getting the drunks edged out of a dance without a fight, or the threat of gun or knife play, was the first and most important duty of the director of boys' work in a settlement.
>
> Drunken men were a source of demoralization to neighborhood children. A mob of small boys and girls trailing and pestering an unsteady man or woman was one of the most unedifying sights. . . . It was a regular practice for boys and young men to entice drunks into alleys and rob them of whatever money and other valuables they had on their person. Crime, as an important by-product of the liquor traffic, was also widespread. . . .

Approximately three-fourths of the country's saloons were

owned or controlled by the big liquor wholesalers, who could have imposed decent behavior upon the consignee by threatening to cut off his supplies. They might thus have disarmed the antisaloonists, but greed blinded them to their danger. They might have forestalled prohibition indefinitely. Instead, they hastened its advance. During a convention of Columbus, Ohio, liquor dealers, in 1874, the question of serving minors was raised, whereupon a delegate argued: "Men who drink liquor, like others, will die, and if there is no new appetite created, our counters will be empty as well as our coffers. . . . The open field for the creation of appetite is among the boys . . . and I make the suggestion, gentlemen, that nickels expended in treats to the boys now will return in dollars to your tills after the appetite has been formed."

An anonymous New York saloonkeeper remembers his occupational hazards*

> . . . the relations between the brewer and the saloon-keeper are close and complicated. . . . I had found that every [saloon] was really owned by a brewery. . . . The saloon is leased, the fixtures are supplied, and the license is paid by the brewer.

> When I "bought" my place, I discovered that the brewery held a mortgage of $4000 on its fixtures. These fixtures, when they were new, had cost perhaps $2000. The fact that the mortgage was so much larger than the value of the property it covered made it practically certain that it would never be paid off, and that the saloon would remain the property of the brewery. . . .

> My saloon, like all others in that vicinity, was opened at five in the morning by the bartender and porter. . . . There was a great deal of transient trade all through the daytime, especially from the teamsters who passed by our place, and came in to get a drink or a cigar, while their horses got their fill of water at the trough outside.

> The bartender's working day averaged, therefore, fourteen hours, from five in the morning until one in the afternoon, and from six in the afternoon until after midnight; my own hours were even longer, usually sixteen. It was seldom earlier than one in the morning when I got home, and to be at my place again at eight gave me less than five hours of actual sleep . . . [such hours] began to tell on my general health. . . .

---

* From *McClure's Magazine*, January, 1909.

Tom Ryan, the bartender whom I took over with the saloon, seized the opportunity afforded him by several unavoidable absences of mine, to drink in excess, so that . . . I found him in a state of intoxication. While in this condition, he knocked down a regular patron of the place. The latter retaliated, and Tom issued from the fight with a badly split nose. . . .

It became known at once in the neighborhood that I meant to discharge him, and . . . about thirty men applied for his place. . . . I picked out an experienced German bartender, Henry Kurz by name. . . . He showed me "recommends" of a high character. But none of them stated he was honest. So I asked him: "Henry, are you honest?"

He smiled a sad and derisive smile. "As honest as any bartender. The really honest bartender does not exist. You can take that from me."

Well, there seemed to be a certain rugged honesty in his dishonesty, so I hired him. . . .

But from the first my receipts were smaller than they had been before his advent. . . . I noticed, too, the disappearance of sundry bottles of French cognac. Two days later Henry got speechlessly drunk, so drunk he fell down behind the bar, and the last time he was unable to rise. So I left him go, and only then, on taking stock, discovered that Henry had been robbing me right and left. . . .

The average weekly wages of a barkeep vary between ten and fifteen dollars. . . . Too many of them succumb to the perpetual temptation and become drunkards. . . .

My customers, as a rule, took very large drinks of whiskey—of a size about nine to a quart bottle. This grade of whiskey cost me $1.90 per gallon, making the bottle stand me about forty cents. Nevertheless, this meant a profit of one hundred per cent, and over, to me. On the finer grades of whiskey, brandy, gin, etc. my profits were larger. I gave my patrons what they called and paid for. That is, if they wanted Old Crow or Hunter whiskey, they got it—at fifteen cents a drink. But many saloon-keepers fill the original bottles up with whiskey costing them but $2.00 or so a gallon, and sell this for any brand of liquor that is called for. One of my competitors, for instance, told me in a burst of confidence that he had only one grade of whiskey behind his bar and that only cost him $1.40 per gallon. . . .

A saloon week begins on Saturday, when the laboring men are paid, and from morning to midnight Saturday my bar was continually wet. But Sunday receipts average much more than those of any other day except Saturday. . . . Wednesdays and Thursdays I found to be the worst days, from a business point of view. On those days men and women hand over nothing but pennies, nickels, and dimes, the larger coins and the bills being all gone. Vest pockets and stocking feet were being emptied of their "chicken feed"; the week's earnings were exhausted. Then came Saturday and Sunday again, with fresh money.

So I found very soon that it was necessary to keep open on Sunday in order to make both ends meet. . . . Drugan, the former owner had . . . said: "You will have to pay fifteen dollars a month for police protection. Then you won't be interfered with on Sundays . . ." *

A day after . . . the go-between looked me up. He proved to be the secretary of a Democratic club.

"But why should I keep open Sundays at all?" I ventured to ask him. . . . "I don't feel much like risking arrests."

"Just as you please," answered the man curtly. "Only in that case, you might as well shut up your place at once. It wouldn't pay."

I didn't pay any bribe, however, neither did I join the Liquor Dealers' Association (who attended for you to excise arrests), and on the second Sunday my bartender was arrested while serving a drink to a "plain-clothes man."

I made up my mind to keep my place closed hereafter on Sundays, even if to do so should spell heavy loss.

My experience, however, was not to be confined to a political "hold-up." I soon had an experience with the genuine article. During my first week as a saloon-keeper, I left my place a little after midnight . . . two fellows rushed out upon me, and while one pinned my arms behind me with incredible swiftness and skill, his pal went through my pockets. . . .

The police afforded me and my place absolutely no protection. The men patrolling my beat rarely showed themselves until late at night, and then only to partake of a friendly glass at my expense. . . .

The population in the neighborhood of my saloon was what is technically called . . . "a good drinking one." It was made up of Irish and Germans in about equal parts, and with a good-sized Italian section, and a few Americans thrown in. There were scarcely any Jews. . . . Drugan . . . had dwelt on this last fact, saying that Jews were no drinkers and therefore "N.G. for our trade."

. . . An overwhelming majority of the people living near me were working men—day laborers, teamsters, furniture movers, and mechanics. . . .

Being German-born myself, and all my life accustomed to the

* Under New York's Raines Law saloons could not sell liquor on Sunday.

moderate use of beer and wines, I had never had much sympathy with the movements against saloons and drinking. But here in my place . . . the drinking habits of most of my patrons appeared frightful . . . intoxication to the point of senselessness—and this not once in a while, but frequently or daily was common . . . my unmarried patrons spent about seventy-five per cent of their earnings in drink. . . .

Some of my regular patrons habitually consumed their four quart bottles of whiskey a day, not reckoning the beer, etc., that they drank besides. One-, two-, or three-bottle men I counted by the score.

There were curious types among them. One bricklayer, a man earning good wages, on coming home Saturdays, always provided liberally for his family. Then, his mind freed of that responsibility, he would issue forth, dressed in his best clothes, on a "glorious drunk." He would return home late Sunday night or early Monday morning, with not a cent left. . . .

A great deal of "rushing the growler" was done at my place, and all over the district, in fact. I had occasion to observe the evil effects of this drinking by women and children all through the day and evening. True, it is an inexpensive mode of becoming intoxicated. On thirty cents a whole family of topers can become drunk. . . .

I found in my short experience that it was almost impossible for me to make money decently in the business. I lost patronage because I refused to allow my saloon to become a hang-out for criminals, and a place of assignation; I lost a big source of revenue because I refused to encourage hard drinking among my patrons; and finally I lost all possibility of a margin of profit by refusing to pay politicians a monthly bribe to break the law. . . .

The gallery of Oberlin's Old First Church projected so far over the main floor that anybody sitting up there in the front row could see the color of the speaker's eyes. On June 4, 1893, the Reverend Mr. Russell returned to the pulpit to expound the aims of the recently formed Anti-Saloon League of Ohio. Resorting to a standard device of public speakers, he fixed his gaze upon a single listener in the gallery close above him. This was a third-year student named Wayne Bidwell Wheeler, whom Russell so profoundly impressed that when he appealed for financial aid, Wheeler, though a poor boy, working his way through the college, signed a pledge card, committing him to a monthly contribution of 25 cents.

The following spring Russell asked various members of the Oberlin faculty to name the graduating student they considered best qualified to help him advance the Anti-Saloon League. Without exception they named Wheeler. A good deal of time during his senior year, in fact, Wheeler had spent lecturing in the area on the evils of alcohol. "I poured out my soul in youthful ardor," he recalled years later, "anathematizing the saloon, and predicting its final overthrow." He was a physically unimposing figure, standing barely five and a half feet tall, but with a steely will and an irresistible drive. A classmate dubbed him "the locomotive in trousers."

Born in Brookfield, Ohio, to a cattle dealer, the third of four children and the only son, he observed at an early age the perils of intoxication. An uncle who lived a mile from the Wheeler farm used periodically to topple senseless off his wagon after a night in the village saloons, and the whole family, assisted by their neighbors, would have to search the countryside for him. "I never could understand why the saloons were allowed to make him drunk," the nephew said. Two other episodes in his boyhood left him a permanent enemy of anybody who sold liquor. One night when Wheeler, Sr., was absent, a village drunkard staggered into the farmhouse and proceeded to reenact *Ten Nights in a Barroom* with such violent sound and gestures as to terrify mother and children. Not long after, a farmhand, pitching hay while under the influence, thrust a tine of his hayfork through the boy's leg. "I hope," the bleeding victim told him, "that some day there won't be any more liquor to make men drunk."

When he graduated from the Brookfield high school and wanted to go on to college, his father pleaded penury. It was the only parental objection. So the son taught school locally for two years until he had saved enough money to pay the entrance fees to Oberlin, which he chose because of its proximity, low tuition and lofty moral tone. During his four years there he not only supported himself, but put aside part of his earnings as a janitor, waiter, business manager of the *Oberlin Review*, publisher of score cards and sports programs, and salesman of books, rugs, school blackboards and desks.

At the time Russell approached him Wheeler had decided to pursue a business career. The minister begged him to reconsider. The pay would be small, he told him, and the work heavy, but the results would justify the sacrifice. They knelt together and

prayed for guidance. A few days before graduation Wheeler
agreed to devote a year to the League, but would not commit
himself beyond that. "The New David . . . who will hurl his
missile at the giant wrong," as he was introduced to his
co-workers, devoted the rest of his life to it. He undertook his first
assignments on bicycle, pedaling from one legislative district to
the next in quest of political sponsors. Sundays he paused to
deliver a temperance sermon in church. With the nationalization
of the League, Russell foresaw the need for a coadjutant versed in
law. Wheeler accordingly studied for an LLB degree first
privately under a Cleveland attorney, then at Cleveland's
Western Reserve University, continuing, meanwhile, to serve the
League whenever his curriculum permitted. Graduating in 1898,
he was appointed attorney for the Ohio League, then state
superintendent, and, in 1916, general counsel of the national
League.

Wheeler proved himself a peerless machinator, unfettered by
scruples, who brought low one wet Goliath after another. Many
years later his somewhat disillusioned former personal publicity
representative, the Reverend T. Justin Steuart, in an unauthorized biography entitled *Wayne Wheeler Dry Boss* wrote without
much exaggeration:

> [He] controlled six Congresses, dictated to two Presidents of the
> United States, directed legislation for the most important elective
> state and federal offices, held the balance of power in both
> Republican and Democratic parties, distributed more patronage
> than any dozen other men, supervised a federal bureau from the
> outside without official authority, and was recognized by friend
> and foe alike as the most masterful and powerful single individual
> in the United States.

John D. Rockefeller was a particular admirer of Wayne
Wheeler. After hearing him speak at a Baptist church service in
Cleveland one freezing winter morning, the old oil billionaire
presented him with $5,000 for the League, a paper vest
supposedly proof against the fiercest cold and an admonition to
guard his health. Wheeler never wore the vest but preserved it in
pristine condition among his memorabilia.

So pervasive was the giant killer's influence that the press and
public tended to consider the League and "Wheelerism" synony-

mous and to ascribe to him every important dry victory. This overstated the case. Though the most effective and conspicuous member of founder Russell's cabinet, Wheeler was abetted by formidable collaborators, nearly all of them Ohio clergymen.

In 1898 the League opened a Washington office and appointed the Reverend Edwin Courtland Dinwiddie, an Evangelical Lutheran and defector from the Prohibition Party, as the country's first national legislative agent concerned solely with temperance enactments. Within two years he had prevailed upon Congress to pass the Anti-Canteen Act, banning liquor from Army canteens, post exchanges and military transports. When Oklahoma entered the Union in 1907, it was largely as a result of a Dinwiddie-led campaign that it did so as a dry state.

The Reverend Purley Albert Baker, a Methodist preacher, whose fiery evangelism reportedly snatched thousands of Ohio sots from the clutches of the Demon, first superintended the Ohio League, then, in 1903, succeeded Russell as national superintendent. Baker, who resembled Buffalo Bill, believed in the boycott as a means of compelling the support of businessmen and industrialists.

As general manager of the League's publications, Ernest Hurst Cherrington developed, in Westerville, Ohio, an immense propaganda mill that produced a newspaper, *The National Daily*; two weeklies, *The American Issue* and *The New Republic*; two monthlies, *The American Patriot* and *The Worker*; a quarterly, *The Scientific Temperance Journal*, which disseminated horrifying statistics (for example, "Nearly 3000 infants are smothered yearly in bed by drunken parents"); and *The Anti-Saloon League Year Book*. Their combined circulation eventually exceeded 15,000,000. In addition, Cherrington's American Issue Publishing Company spewed out millions of books, pamphlets, leaflets, charts, window cards, color posters and marching songs, notably " 'Tis Time to Swing Our Axes," "The Yellow Dog Voter Is Dead," "Nobody Knows but Mother." In support of a proposed dry law or League-approved candidate for office carloads of such materials would be sped to the appropriate area from the never-idle Westerville presses.

The League financed its enterprises mainly by "prying open the churches," as the Reverend Homer W. Tope, its Pennsylvania superintendent, bluntly put it—that is, persuading individual pastors, often paying them a fee, to allow the use of their pulpits as a launching platform for antisaloon missiles and to solicit contributions from their congregations. What more logical recourse than to the churches for an organization that claimed to be divinely inspired and guided? But not every pastor proved amenable. With the predominantly urban Jewish and Catholic churches, which opposed prohibition while encouraging abstinence as a personal choice, the antisaloonists made little headway. Because the League was essentially secular and political, despite its spiritual stance and ministerial leadership, many of the Protestant churches as well balked, fearing to violate the traditional separation of church and state. Others placed their need for contributions ahead of the League's. Nevertheless, the League managed ultimately to win over about 60,000 churches, a small fraction of the nation's total, yet enough to yield it more than $2,000,000 a year, plus a substantial number of dry votes. Its principal adherents consisted of rural Methodists, followed, in order of importance, by Bible Belt Baptists, Presbyterians, Congregationalists and several smaller fundamentalist sects. "The movement was dependent upon the church, first of all, for financial support," Cherrington wrote in his *History of the Anti-Saloon League*. "It was also dependent upon the church for the necessary influence and power to turn the tide along nonpartisan lines in the election of members of the legislatures favorable to temperance legislation and in the election, as well, of public officials who would enforce the law." With some justice the League could describe itself, in the words of its New York superintendent, William H. Anderson, as "the church in action."

The League's foremost pry-opener was undoubtedly the founder himself. Russell extracted large sums not only from the churches, but by combining moral and religious appeal with the promise that prohibition would increase industrial efficiency, from several billionaires, among them John Wanamaker, Samuel Kresge, Andrew Carnegie, Pierre Du Pont, Henry Ford and the Rockefellers, Sr. and Jr., the last two donating between them, during the years 1900 to 1926, $350,000. The bulk of the League's millions, however, came in small-change contributions from teetotaling, churchgoing pledgers.

To propitiate the large numbers of clergymen who still preferred moral suasion to prohibition, Russell also founded the pledge-signing Lincoln Legion, a misnomer, as noted earlier, since Lincoln did not favor legally enforced abstinence. When the Southern proselytizers failed to obtain many signatures, the League remembered that Robert E. Lee had been a total abstainer and so renamed it the Lincoln-Lee Legion.

Of the hierarchs whom the League enlisted, few served it more assiduously than Virginia's Reverend (later Bishop) James Cannon, Jr., of the Methodist Episcopal Church, South, whom it named to its executive committee in 1902. The supreme dry politician in his home state, on the national scene Cannon ranked second only to Wayne Wheeler, from whom he jealously schemed to wrest control of the League. After liquor he hated most Roman Catholicism. "The mother of ignorance, superstition, intolerance and sin," he called it. On issues of public decency he out-Comstocked Comstock, inveighing against dancing, the theater, various games and sports and art that afforded any glimpse of "the female person." He expressed horror at the prospect of Sarah Bernhardt playing *Camille* in a Southern auditorium—"a French actress of brilliant powers but unsavory moral ideals, presenting to the public at high rate the life of a fallen, debauched character." He accepted as truth the slander circulated by enemies of Madame Curie, the co-discoverer of radium, that she had been the "affinity" of a married French professor. "Affinity in Bible language is an adultress," said Cannon. "She has lost forever her claim to a place among the great men and women of the world."

Like most dry energumens, he could cite a traumatic boyhood encounter with a drunkard. The house where he grew up in Salisbury, Maryland, adjoined a hotel that had a barroom. One night a patron with a large, savage mastiff drunkenly let the dog off the leash. It attacked a hunting dog belonging to Cannon's Uncle Josiah, who flew to the rescue and was bitten on the arm. Blood poisoning set in, and he died a few days later. "Knowing that the hotel barroom was the underlying cause of my dear uncle's death," Cannon recalled, "I have always charged that up as a debt on the balance sheet." Cannon's mother, a Woman Crusader, who founded a local WCTU, often took him along when she went to pray against the saloons, of which Salisbury had twelve. She was buried with a white ribbon pinned to her dress, the only personal adornment she ever allowed herself.

Astute in business affairs as well as politics, Cannon turned at least two failing enterprises into successes. The first was a Methodist girls' school at Blackstone, Virginia, chartered to

provide "Thorough Instruction under Positive Christian Influence at Lowest Possible Cost." When the trustees asked him,
in 1894, to become its principal, it consisted of a single unfinished
building, six acres of undeveloped land, an $11,000 indebtedness
and no funds for teachers' salaries or equipment. Within twenty
years he developed the Blackstone Female Institute into a
flourishing junior college, meanwhile paying himself a compensation whose exact amount he never revealed. A good many of
his fellow Methodists suspected it was excessive.

Cannon also made the Baltimore and Richmond *Christian
Advocate*, an impoverished Methodist journal of which he acquired control in 1903, pay him a profit, partly by accepting ads
for patent medicines of dubious value, an accommodation that
typified the practical side of his career. The Richmond *Virginian*,
a daily newspaper which he established in 1910, started out with
the announcement that it would "in no way promote any form of
species of gambling, prize fighting or sport that is forbidden by
law or detrimental to good morals." But as Cannon quickly
discovered, such omissions did not appeal to many readers, and
by the third week the *Virginian* was covering not only prizefights,
horse races (prohibited under state law) and card games, but
news of the stock market, which Cannon had always professed to
consider an insidious form of gambling. He had also denounced
as ungodly newspapers with Sunday editions. Realizing, however, that they could not meet competition otherwise, the board
of directors voted to bring out a Sunday *Virginian*. Cannon, the
majority stockholder, went through the motions of resigning in
protest, but actually continued to direct policy from behind the
scenes.

He was a distant and humorless figure. One League associate
found him "cold as a snake." Another, with whom he worked
side by side for forty years, could not remember ever having seen
him laugh or often seen him smile. His omnifarious activities
demanded such long, hard hours as to leave him little time for
shaving, and so he grew a stubbly mustache and beard that
intensified his dour aspect. In later life he kept only the
mustache. He wore high shoes with buckles, long woolen
underwear the year round, and carried a walnut cane, for which
he had to substitute a crutch when arthritis crippled him.

In that Good Templar from Nebraska, William Eugene
"Pussyfoot" Johnson, the League acquired its most zealous spy

and *agent provocateur.* "I have told enough lies 'for the cause' to make Ananias ashamed of himself," Johnson unblushingly admitted toward the end of his career. "I have told to sinners a thousand lies for the purpose of decoying them into telling the truth. . . . I bribed many bad men to give me information about their associates. . . . Did I ever drink to promote prohibition? . . . In seeking hidden information, in perfecting criminal cases, I have drunk plenty of the stuff."

What initially aroused the admiration of prohibitionists was Johnson's technique of entrapment. When, in 1890, the Nebraska legislature submitted a prohibition amendment to a referendum, he wrote to the state's leading liquor dealers under a fictitious letterhead, "JOHNSON'S PALE ALE," asking their advice on how to thwart the drys. They replied with self-incriminating directions for buying politicians, which Johnson promptly published. The voters nevertheless rejected the amendment.

Moving around the country as a correspondent for various temperance periodicals, Johnson exposed vote frauds by Omaha's antiprohibition forces, drinking in colleges and camps, bootlegging in the South, the serving of liquor without license in Washington's Senate and House restaurants and violations of New York's Raines Law. He was occasionally mobbed and beaten, but, a burly and pugnacious man, he managed to administer severe punishment in return.

In 1906 Congress appropriated $25,000 for the suppression of liquor sales in the Indian Territory of Oklahoma, a traffic conducted by some of the roughest Western desperadoes who ever escaped hanging. At the suggestion of the Anti-Saloon League Teddy Roosevelt commissioned Johnson a special officer to enforce the ban. With a pistol belt strapped around his massive torso and a ten-gallon hat on his head, he turned up in Muskogee, the heart of the territory, where he deputized a squad of gunslingers as doughty as himself. "I spilled liquor wherever found, without bothering about any legal process."

Singly or en masse, their pistols and rifles cocked, Johnson and his hearties would break into poolrooms, gambling dens and brothels that sold liquor, smash every bottle and with fine disregard for legal niceties put the torch to the furnishings. It was Johnson's practice of approaching his prey stealthily, by dark of night, that earned him the sobriquet "Pussyfoot." For years brewers from outside the territory had been shipping in beer of supposedly low alcoholic content as allowed by law, but actually potent, under labels like "Non Tox," "Uno," "Ino," "Long Horn," and "Tin Top," while whiskey distillers flooded the territory with gut-searing "red-eye." To prevent distribution, Johnson posted a deputy at every railroad depot. At the Ardmore Express Office he himself once intercepted and destroyed 2,000 bottles of "temperance beer." Shortly before Christmas of his first year as chief "Booze Buster" a McAlester newspaper addressed a poem to him:

> Say, Mr. Johnson, turn me loose
> And let me have my Christmas juice.
> Don't break these bottles; let them be;
> There's plenty there for you and me.
> Just shut your eyes, don't make a row;
> Be good this once, right here and now.
>
> Say, Mr. Johnson, please go 'way,
> And come around some other day.
> Be good this Christmas, what's the use
> Of spilling all our good red juice?
> Say, Mr. Johnson, you're too fly;
> Come, old man, just wink your eye.
> Just let expressmen turn it loose;
> It's Xmas now, a good excuse.
>
> Say, Mr. Johnson, what's the use
> Of spilling all the good bug juice?
> You won't make good, there'll come a time
> When you must find another clime.
> Say, Mr. Johnson, just you skiddoo,
> Let 23 be good for you.
> You're on the slate when we're out loose;
> We'll then get plenty of red juice.

But never within the memory of territory dwellers had they endured so dry a Christmas.

"On the slate" was an allusion to a $3,000 reward offered by a gang of bootleggers for anybody who would liquidate Pussyfoot. A professional killer named Jack Patman nearly collected it. He mistook a deputy marshal for Johnson and shot him dead. He drew a five-year sentence, which was considered a stiff penalty for murder in those parts.

The owner of a pool hall-*cum*-saloon in the town of Haskell, Oklahoma, publicly notified Johnson that if ever he set foot there, he would shoot him on sight. Disguising himself and feigning drunkenness, Johnson staggered into the pool hall a few nights later, slapped a dollar bill on the bar and shouted for some "real hell-fire." When the owner turned to pick up a bottle of red-eye, Johnson whipped out two pistols, pressed a muzzle against each of the owner's ears and marched him off to justice.

Johnson's contempt for due process attained its boldest expression on the border between Kansas and Indian Territory where a gambler named Ernest Lewis claimed to have discovered a strip of land belonging to neither state nor territory and so outside the jurisdiction of either. He erected a building sixty feet long and ten feet wide, with a bar at one end and gambling tables at the other. The Muskogee *Phoenix* reported:

> The Sheriff and Marshal from Montgomery County, Kansas, can sit upon the outside of the building and see the thirsting patrons pass in and out; they can hear the monotonous rattle of the ball around the roulette-wheel—but they are powerless. On the other side of the structure the United States Marshals of Indian territory sit astride their ponies and roll cigarettes as the dice bounce on the table and they can hear the pop of the bung from a fresh beer-barrel of Budweiser—but they are helpless. Lewis insists that he will go on forever, unmolested by the law. It will remain for Congress to take some action before Lewis can be ousted from his gambler's paradise.

Lewis reckoned without Pussyfoot. Shrugging aside such niggling considerations as what land belonged to whom, the special agent put him out of business overnight by simply invading the place with two heavily armed deputies, wrecking all the gambling paraphernalia and dumping all the beverages.

Back in Washington representatives of the liquor industry protested to Teddy Roosevelt against Johnson's highhandedness. "Let him alone," retorted the President, "more power to his elbow," and promoting him to Chief Special Officer, he extended his sphere of operations throughout all Indian reservations. In Minnesota, Idaho, Montana, New Mexico and the Dakotas liquor dealers and gamblers felt the weight of Johnson's elbow. Whenever threatened, he made it a principle immediately to confront the threatener eye to eye. A California badman, who bragged that he used to kill Indians to get their teeth for rifle sights, publicly promised, should Johnson ever venture into his part of the world, "to meet him in the road with a rifle." Johnson trailed him to a desert hideaway, roped him and dragged him to the nearest jail. At sight of his captor in court the badman burst into tears. All together, during Johnson's five years in the Indian service, he and his cohorts shot to death twenty-five outlaws, destroyed hundreds of thousands of dollars' worth of liquor, barroom equipment and gambling apparatus and brought to trial 5,473 captives, of whom 4,400 were convicted. The Pussy-footers did not escape casualties. Eight deputies were killed, and many wounded by knife or bullet.

Johnson's star began to wane in 1909 under the administration of Roosevelt's successor, William Howard Taft. A new Commissioner of Indian Affairs proved less sympathetic to his rough-and-ready methods. Several bootleggers convicted of supplying whiskey to Indians received Presidential pardons. One of Johnson's most valued lieutenants was charged with murder, though eventually exonerated. Johnson resigned in disgust.

During his post-Indian period, as a publicity agent for the Anti-Saloon League, he reverted to his old trap-baiting tactics. In West Virginia a prohibition amendment awaited the will of the people. The League had reason to suspect that a large percentage of the state's press would sell their news and editorial columns to the highest bidder. Signing himself "C. L. Trevitt, Literary Agent," Johnson wrote from Washington to seventy West Virginia papers, proffering generous payment in advance "for the privilege of laying arguments against prohibition before your readers." How much per line would they charge, he inquired, "for pure reading matter without advertising marks?" Sixty editors bit. "I am in the market for business," ran one typical reply, "and I accept your proposition. I am hard up too, and the sooner you send your matter and a small cheque, the better it will be for me." Johnson circulated photocopies of such replies, probably swaying a fair number of voters in favor of the amendment. The majority voted dry.

By now a legend, Johnson went on to become managing editor of the League's American Issue publications, then, as a propagandist for its worldwide crusade, to lecture abroad. It was in the latter capacity, when British college students chanting

> Pussyfoot, Pussyfoot, why are we here?
> We've come to prevent you from stopping our beer.
> Pussyfoot, Pussyfoot, there'll be a big riot.
> We drink in pubs, you on the quiet,

mobbed him and somebody threw a stone, that he lost an eye.

Johnson exemplified the League's pragmatism. "Ethics be hanged," said he. "I more than accomplished what I was driving at." In the opinion of James A. White, attorney for the Ohio League, "No money is tainted if the Anti-Saloon League can get its hands on it," and Wayne Wheeler's Cotton Mather-like battle cry was "We'll make them believe in punishment after death!" Unlike those drys who scrupled at working through the existing political machines and so formed the independent Prohibition Party or unlike the WCTU, which divided and weakened itself bickering over moralistic issues, the Leaguers were prepared to strike a bargain with the devil if it advanced their grand design of drying up America. Nor did they dissipate their energies in promoting extrinsic liberal causes, as the Prohibitionists and the White Ribboners had done. They hewed to the single purpose of making drinking a crime.

When it came to elections, no candidate was required to forgo liquor himself to win the League's approval. As long as he agreed to endorse temperance legislation, the hardest-drinking politician could count on its support. Better a sinner who voted dry than a saint who voted wet. The *Anti-Saloon League Catechism* made this clear:

> May the League properly favor the election of candidates who are not wholly in faith and practice acceptable to friends of temperance reform?
> While it is desirable that candidates for office should be in all respects acceptable, it may be necessary at times, in order to secure some desired end, to vote for candidates committed to the object, though not wholly committed to the plan and purpose of the League.
> How shall the League choose between candidates partially acceptable?
> It should choose the one committed to the most desirable measures and of whose election there is a reasonable probability.

When the Cincinnati press exposed a League-backed candidate for mayor as the owner of two saloons, Wheeler coolly remarked: "Owning saloons doesn't have anything to do with official actions."

Such trimming produced anomalous situations. In a 1908 Illinois election the League and the liquor interests endorsed the same thirty-four legislative candidates.

No more than the brewers or distillers did the League hesitate to buy venal politicians. But if neither bribery nor threats could break down an opponent's resistance, it would seek his destruction through its Westerville propaganda arm with a fusillade of slander. Tennessee, for example, went dry in 1909, whereupon snooping agents of the League proceeded to swear out warrants against lawbreaking saloonkeepers. Judge A. B. Neil of the Davidson County Criminal Court was a man of unassailable integrity, who later became chief justice of the State Supreme Court. Though no intransigent dry himself, he stressed the necessity, in his charges to the grand jury, of enforcing the new law. During the 1913 Nashville mayoralty campaign more than 200 violators were indicted. Yet the League contended that these indictments did not represent a sincere effort to close the saloons, but only a political maneuver in the conflict of two Democratic factions, both wet. The *New Republic*, founded and edited by Pussyfoot Johnson, reviled the judge as one of the "chief officers of the crime trust in Nashville," responsible for "open saloons, gambling houses, houses of prostitution, houses of assignation, Sunday baseball and every form of vice."

Itinerant evangelists like Sam Small and Sam Young of Georgia, who later joined the League, were masters of the big lie. Small, a reformed drunkard, felt that "all this about personal liberty is trash" and claimed to find liquor the root cause of various national catastrophes. On May 3, 1886, in a clash between workers striking against Chicago's McCormick Harvest Machine Company and professional scabs, six men were killed. The next night anarchists held a protest meeting on Haymarket Square. When the police tried to disperse it, a bomb exploded, killing seven of them and wounding many others. Though the bomb thrower was never identified, four anarchist leaders went to the gallows, one to prison for life, another for fifteen years, and a seventh committed suicide. The crimes of the anarchists, Sam

Small assured his audiences, originated in beer. Anarchy, he said, fed upon whiskey; the saloons bred nihilism, treason and rebellion.

The Leaguers played upon every traditional fear and prejudice of race and religion, color and class. Throughout the South they exploited the myth of the black as rapist of white women. Alcohol, their evangelists warned, inflamed his lust; prohibition would reduce both sex crimes and lynchings. A cheap brand of gin popular among blacks, distilled by the Lee Levy Company of Minnesota, bore a label depicting a seminude woman in a seductive attitude. During the summer of 1908 the Tennessee Democrats were rent by a primary contest for the gubernatorial nomination between the incumbent, Malcolm Patterson, a temperance moderate, and Edward Ward Carmack, a dry extremist. At the height of hostilities a Shreveport, Louisiana, black raped and murdered a fourteen-year-old girl and was lynched. The Nashville *Tennessean*, a newspaper favorable to both Carmack and the Anti-Saloon League, printed an interview with a Methodist clergyman, who said: "This gin, with its label, has made more black rape fiends, and has procured the outrage of more white women in the South than all other agencies combined. It is sold with the promise that it will bring white virtue into the black brute's power."

The Carmack camp took the cue and exhibited specimens of the supposedly aphrodisiac beverage with the implication that Patterson was to blame for its wide distribution. To lure away an influential Patterson supporter named Crotzer, the president of the Tennessee League, the Reverend Edgar Estes Folk, told him: "Brother Crotzer, I have a thing in my pocket which if you will let me show you, you will go home a Carmack man and for state-wide prohibition." He showed him the gin bottle, manipulating it in such a way as to emphasize the salient anatomical features of the nude on the label. But these tactics failed to delude enough voters, and Patterson carried both the nomination and the election.

The same year a confraternity of German-born Michiganders, the Arbeiter Bund, announced its opposition to prohibition, thereby moving Ernest Cherrington to a characteristic outburst of xenophobia in his *American Issue*. "Really, is not the country growing rather tired of having a lot of swill-fattened, blowsy half-foreigners getting together and between hiccoughs laying down definitions to Americans regarding the motive of our constitution and laws?"

In persistent appeals to organized labor the *American Issue* set forth: "There is no Union-Made Whiskey . . . every barrel or case of beer delivered in Chicago is delivered by non-union men . . . in Milwaukee breweries . . . girls are paid only 75 or 85 cents for three or four days' work a week." Furthermore, ". . . seventy per cent of the drink bill of the United States is contributed by the American laboring man . . . liquor money is usually bread money, meat money, shoe money and money that ought to go for clothing."

Crime, truancy, divorce, insanity, the "social diseases" in the euphemism of the period—meaning tuberculosis, gonorrhea and syphilis—these and countless other evils the League ascribed in principal part to liquor. One of its greatest propaganda weapons was handed to it by the Kentucky Distillers & Distributing Company, which upon going out of business in 1913 had the folly to write to the Keeley Institute, the famous sanatorium for alcoholics: "Our customers are your prospective patients. We can put on your desk a mailing list of over 50,000 individual consumers of liquor. The list of names is new, live and active. . . . We furnish this list in quantities at the prices listed below. . . ." Photocopies of the self-convicting letter were disseminated at League meetings and sent to newspapers.

The Leaguers fought with the patience of driver ants. They fought a war of attrition. No community was too small, no proposed prohibitory measure too trivial to merit their attention. The conquest of Ohio, the native state of no less than thirty-four top-ranking officers, demonstrated the procedural model later applied to other states and ultimately to the nation.

Young Wayne Wheeler led the way on his bicycle. He achieved his first victory early. In 1888 Ohio had adopted township local option largely through the efforts of the Reverend Mr. Russell. Five years later, shortly after Russell founded the Anti-Saloon League of Ohio, it sponsored the Haskell bill, calling for state local option. All but thirty-six legislators voted nay. The most influential opponent was the boss of Madison County, John Locke, who warned them: "If you would protect your state from fanaticism and lawlessness, vote against this revolutionary measure. If you want to dig your own political

grave, vote for this Haskell bill." The Leaguers thereupon
resolved to back any of the thirty-six dissenters who might seek
reelection, and to fight the majority, Locke first of all. The
following year Locke became a candidate for state senatorship.
Wheeler persuaded a prosperous Madison County grain dealer,
W. N. Jones, to run against him on a dry platform, then,
pedaling furiously the length and breadth of the state, recruited
delegates for Jones to the senatorial convention and got church
dignitaries and civic leaders to support them. Locke's partisans
felt so confident that they did not trouble to campaign vigorously. They were flabbergasted when Jones won. WHO DEFEATED
LOCKE? crowed the League in pamphlets and broadsides,
WHEELER AND HIS WHEEL.

During the next eight years the same strategy, directed chiefly
by Wheeler, brought about the ouster of seventy Ohio legislators
inimical to the League program. "If these church people get
busy," said the wet Republican U.S. Senator Marcus Hanna in
grudging tribute, "they'll knock the devil out of politics." Before
an election the League would ask both Republican and Democratic candidates how they stood on temperance legislation. If
both replied to its satisfaction, it would abstain from further
interference in the race; if only one, it would back him; and if
none, it would put forward an independent candidate of its own.

The climactic demonstration of the Ohio League's omnipar-
tisan policy revolved around the Republican Governor Myron T.
Herrick. Having secured control of a legislative majority, the
League pushed through a bill in 1904 enabling residential
districts to vote out saloons only to have Herrick emasculate it.
When he ran for renomination that year, the League deluged
Republican leaders with petitions of protest. But the wets within
the party prevailed and Herrick again won the primary,
cocksure of reelection in the predominantly Republican state.
The Democratic Party, meanwhile, nominated a staunch dry,
John M. Pattison, president of a life insurance company. One
hundred thousand letters then went to voters from the League,
lauding Pattison and representing Herrick as a tool of liquor
lobbyists. The charge was hard to deny after Wheeler laid his
hands on a circular letter mailed by the Brewers' Association to
its Ohio members, requesting them to lend some of their
employees to the Herrick campaign forces, but to do so with
utmost secrecy. Wheeler sent thousands of photocopies to the

churches, staged 3,000 anti-Herrick rallies and ordered from the Westerville plant 75,000,000 pages of denunciatory literature. Though nearly every other Republican candidate was elected, Herrick, who had won his first term by a plurality of 113,000, lost by 43,000. "Never again," Wheeler predicted, "will any political party ignore the protests of the church and the moral forces of the state."

Between 1896 and 1908 the League engineered the extension of dry laws through local option from townships to residential districts to counties. As a result, seventy-five of Ohio's eighty-eight counties voted themselves dry, and almost 3,500 saloons closed their doors (with the usual concomitant increase of blind pigs and bootleggers). All together creeping prohibition encompassed 85 percent of the state's territory and 60 percent of its people, most of whom inhabited the rural areas, with the cities remaining, as everywhere, the principal centers of resistance.

Statewide statutory or constitutional prohibition was still a distant prospect in Ohio and most other states. None of them, the League policymakers reasoned, would be ripe for it until the great preponderance of its communities had adopted temperance reforms. So they settled temporarily for fragmentary victories, drying up towns and counties wherever local option presented the opportunity. There existed many variants of local option, and with serpentine flexibility the League adapted its maneuvers accordingly. Tennessee, for example, had a law prohibiting the sale of intoxicants within four miles of schools in any town of 2,000 inhabitants or less, provided that town incorporated. The Tennessee Anti-Saloon League successfully agitated for the extension of the law first to towns of 5,000 inhabitants, then to towns of 150,000. The Four Mile Law became the League's principal instrument for drying up all Tennessee.

Only when the League had consolidated large intrastate dry areas did it raise its sights to the state as a whole. Georgia was the first to succumb, its legislature adopting statutory prohibition in 1907. Oklahoma followed the same year with a constitutional enactment. The League usually preferred legislative action to a popular vote, the latter being less easily controllable. Before the decade ended, thirteen states, plus Alaska, Puerto Rico and the District of Columbia, had gone bone-dry (in law if not in fact) and twenty states had passed statutes severely restricting the manufacture and sale of liquor. Together with local option districts in wet states, this indicated that all but 5 percent of the land, and more than two-thirds of the population were wholly or partly deprived of legal liquor.

Enforcement remained the overriding problem. Few dry districts had either the legal apparatus or enough incorruptible police and politicians to abolish booze. It was bound to flow in torrents when no law prevented liquor dealers in wet states from exporting their wares into dry states. Only the federal government could regulate interstate traffic. The League began bombarding Congress with angry petitions. The upshot was the Webb-Kenyon bill (after Democratic Congressman Edwin Yates Webb of North Carolina and Republican Senator William Squire Kenyon of Iowa)—the product of "a few rabid, misguided professional prohibitionists," its opponents called it—which Congress passed in 1913 over President Taft's veto. It outlawed the interstate transportation of liquor when intended for sale in violation of the laws of the state to which consigned. But no penalties were provided until an amendment in 1917 imposed heavy fines and/or imprisonment.

The League had meanwhile achieved a signal diplomatic coup. Recognizing it as the most effective temperance organization in American history, both the Prohibition Party and the WCTU submerged their misgivings about its ethics and decided to cooperate with it. Thus reinforced, the League plunged full steam ahead toward the real objective it had had in view from the first.

9. The Barrage

Congress is made up eternally of petty scoundrels, pusillanimous poltroons, highly vulnerable and cowardly men: they will never risk provoking the full fire of the Anti-Saloon League.

—H. L. MENCKEN

COLUMBUS, OHIO. November 13, 1913. The Jubilee Convention celebrating the twentieth anniversary of the Anti-Saloon League. James Franklin Hanley, ex-governor of Indiana, concludes his attack on the liquor industry with a resolution:

"We therefore declare for its national annihilation by an amendment to the Federal Constitution which shall forever prohibit throughout the territory of the United States the manufacture and sale and the importation, exportation and transportation of intoxicating liquor to be used as a beverage."

For an instant the vast assembly of clergymen, politicians, Prohibition Party members, White Ribboners and League delegates sit in tense silence. Then, leaping to their feet, they let out a roar of approval as wild as the blizzard raging outside. The resolution passes without a single dissenting voice.

The mask is off. The League will no longer pretend concern for states' rights and home rule, will fight no more for temperance legislation through local option or for any moderate prohibitory measures that reserve freedom of choice to communities. In the perfervid language of John Granville Woolley, a Prohibition Party demagogue, "the crime of crimes . . . must go . . . We will crowd it to the ropes. We will not break away in the clinches. And when it lies dying among its bags of bloody gold and looks up into our faces with its last gasp and whispers 'Another million of revenue for just one breath of life,' we will put the heel of open-eyed national honor on its throat and say 'NO! Down to Hell and say we sent thee thither!'."

On the morning of December 10 a small boy, carrying the American flag, marched down Washington's Pennsylvania Avenue. Behind him stepped fifty little girls wearing white Sunday-go-to-church frocks, and behind them 2,000 Leaguers and 2,000 White Ribboners in separate phalanxes with banners inscribed NATIONAL CONSTITUTIONAL PROHIBITION. Amid the gibes of foe and hurrahs of friends, they converged upon the Capitol, singing "Onward, Christian Soldiers" and the WCTU favorite, "A Saloonless Nation in 1920," composed by Professor J. G. Dailey of Philadelphia and pronounced by Mrs. Ella Alexander Boole, a New York White Ribboner, as "dignified but catchy music." Waiting for them on the east steps of the Capitol were Congressman Richmond Pearson Hobson (Democrat, Alabama) and Senator Morris Sheppard (Democrat, Texas).

Hobson was the beau ideal of the drys, especially the women, upon whom he customarily bestowed kisses during his public appearances. A tall, slender Annapolis alumnus, with a Barrymoresque profile, Hobson had emerged from the Spanish-American War a hero for having scuttled the USS *Merrimac* in Santiago Harbor to prevent the escape of the blockaded enemy squadron. The attempt failed. He was captured and briefly imprisoned, but his feat brought him military honors. Retiring from the service as a captain in 1903, he became a temperance orator, delivering over and over in churches and camp revival meetings a polemic entitled "The Great Destroyer" in which he contended that alcohol killed five times as many people a year as all the wars ever fought. Half the country's economy and half its population, according to Hobson, were already vitiated by alcohol. It was the main cause of feeblemindedness and sexual perversion in women. A thorough racist, he warned that the yellow peril would overrun the earth unless the Great Destroyer were destroyed. Addressing himself to his fellow Southern Congressmen: "Liquor will actually make a brute out of a Negro, causing him to commit unnatural crimes. The effect is the same on the white man, though the white man being further evolved, it takes longer to reduce him to the same level."

Temperance advocacy was a profitable pursuit for Hobson. As a League fund raiser, he received varying percentages of every dollar he could charm out of his lecture audiences. The annual total averaged $22,000, and in nine years he pocketed more than $170,000. The hero of Santiago remained on the League's payroll throughout his eight years as a Congressman.

The Texan, Morris Sheppard, was a Yale Law School graduate and a millionaire, owning extensive properties around Austin. His small stature and mild manner belied his aggressiveness as a prohibitionist. The Democrats sent him to Washington for the first time in 1902 to complete the unexpired term of his late father, Congressman John Levi Sheppard. In 1913 he was elected to the Senate, where he served three terms, during which he sponsored the most radical prohibitory legislation yet proposed. "Long live prohibition!" he wrote later in the *Anti-Saloon League Year Book*. "Its benefits will become more evident as the years separate us from the era of the nation's shame when misery, poverty, and ruin were the sad harvest of a traffic in one of the deadliest poisons known to man."

On the Capitol steps the Reverend Purley Baker handed the two dry legislators copies of a proposed Eighteenth Amendment to the Constitution which he, Wheeler, Cannon and other Leaguers had helped draft. The same day Sheppard introduced it in the Senate:

> *Whereas*, exact scientific research has demonstrated that alcohol is a narcotic poison, destructive and degenerating to the human organism, and that its distribution as a beverage or contained in foods, lays a staggering economic burden upon the shoulders of the people, lowers to an appalling degree the average standard of character of our citizenship, thereby undermining the public morals and the foundation of free institutions, produces widespread crime, pauperism and insanity, inflicts disease and untimely death upon hundreds of thousands of citizens, and blights with degeneracy their children unborn, threatening the future integrity and the very life of the nation; *Therefore be it resolved:* By the Senate and House of Representatives of the United States of America in Congress assembled (two-thirds of each House concurring therein), that the following amendment of the Constitution be, and hereby is proposed to the States, to become valid as part of the Constitution when ratified by the legislatures of the several States as provided by the Constitution.
>
> Article
> Sec. 1. The sale, manufacture for sale, transportation for sale, importation for sale, and exportation for sale, of intoxicating

liquors for beverage purposes in the United States and all territory subject to the jurisdiction thereof are forever prohibited.

Sec. 2. Congress shall have power to provide for the manufacture, sale, importation, and transportation of intoxicating liquors for sacramental, medicinal, mechanical, pharmaceutical or scientific purposes, or for use in the arts, and shall have power to enforce this article by all needful legislation.

Known thereafter as the Hobson-Sheppard resolution, it was referred to the Senate Judiciary Committee, which never reported it. The next day Hobson introduced it in the House. The hour of reckoning was nigh, he warned his fellow Democrats. "If the Democratic Party can only live by joining the liquor interests to debauch the American people, then in God's name let it die!" At this the wet Republican Congressman Richard Bartholdt of Missouri sarcastically proposed that the House adjourn to some place remote from Washington, inaccessible to the pressures of the dry lobbyists. "Never mind!" he apostrophized the enemy. "You may intimidate village councils and members of the state legislature, but you cannot cow or intimidate me," and to his fellow Congressmen: "I predict that not one of you who vote for it will ever come back to tell the tale."

The resolution remained for five months in the House Judiciary Committee, which finally reported it in May, 1914. This was an election year, and the League mobilized its every resource behind dry candidates. Wheeler left a vivid account of its tactics.

Back of the drive were virtually all the Protestant denominations which compose and control the League, and through the churches of the country the Washington headquarters was in close touch with every section of the United States. Through the state leagues, which directed the campaign locally, we were at all times intimately in touch with the battle on all fronts.

The first step, it seemed to us, was to appeal to Congress. So we started out to let Congress hear from the people back home. Word went out from Washington and state headquarters to send letters, telegrams, and petitions to Congressmen and Senators in Washington. They rolled in by tens of thousands, burying Congress like an avalanche. . . . From that December day in 1913 when we wired back to our people in every State in the Union, "Open fire on the enemy," until the final vote of submission, the country kept up a drumfire upon Washington.

We started off, early in 1914, with about 20,000 speakers, mostly volunteers all over the United States. They spoke at every opportunity to every sort of gathering. As the campaign increased in intensity, the number of speakers also increased. During the final stages of the battle there were approximately 50,000 trained speakers, volunteers and regulars, directing their fire upon the wets in every village, town, city, county and State, a vocal army storming the enemy trenches.

There was literature, too, to be distributed to these speakers and through them to the rank and file of voters. We already had a pretty big printing plant in Westerville, Ohio, but soon it became a bigger one. When the fight got hot it became the biggest prohibition printing plant in the world. . . . As the climax approached we doubled our forces. Even that wasn't enough, so for a time the world's largest prohibition printing establishment ran three shifts a day, every hour of the twenty-four, grinding out dry literature. It was and is a union shop. Most of the distillers and many brewers ran non-union shops.

This literature found its way to every spot in the United States. It was no uncommon thing for carloads of printed material to roll out of Westerville in one day for the front.

We went into every Congressional district where there was a chance to elect a dry and waged as strong a fight as candidates have ever seen. Congress sat long those days, and while we were fighting back in the districts, we were also bombarding the House and Senate at Washington. Scores of the members of Congress took their political lives in their hands during the struggle, as up to the time of submission of the amendment there was strong feeling both ways and members did not know, in a great many cases, what the folks back home really did want.

Our Washington headquarters opened correspondence with every possible friend in Congress. We also went to see them personally. We got word at frequent intervals from the States as to the way the fight was going there, and when we received such information we would place it at once before members of Congress who were wavering or whom we wanted to convert.

The information obtained in our correspondence and interviews with members of Congress at Washington was sent back to the States. We kept the field workers advised of the attitude of every individual member of Congress and suggested ways to the local workers of winning converts.

While all this was going on, we kept informed daily as to what the wets were doing. We knew what their arguments would be every time they changed them. . . . We also knew, often in advance, just what their plans were for influencing this, that or the other member of Congress. Whenever they opened up on a member of Congress we would wire back to that member's State or district and tell the local drys to start a counter-attack.

They would do the rest. Within twenty-four hours a storm of telegrams would break over that member's head and he would realize that a revolution had broken loose back home. We confirmed it at Washington.

Under the terrific pace our finances expanded. Our expenses gradually increased until they reached the greatest figure in our history, about $2,000,000 a year.

As Wheeler intimated, the enemy was not laggard. Like the League, the United States Brewers' Association, with a membership, in 1908, of 1,747 breweries, and the National Wholesale Liquor Dealers' Association, representing 1,200 distilleries, threatened boycotts, coerced and bribed politicians and disseminated tons of literature. The Brewers' Association maintained a blacklist of unfriendly companies that were not to be traded with, among them the Delaware, Lackawanna & Western Railroad because it forbade its employees to drink, Cleveland's Grasselli Chemical Company because some of its executives donated money to a Billy Sunday revival meeting, the Heinz Pickle Company because its president belonged to a Sunday school organization that promulgated temperance, the Liggett drugstores because they would sell no liquor.

Again, like the League, the brewers and distillers bought pledges from political candidates with campaign contributions. In 1914 the candidate for the Republican nomination for Senator from Illinois, wrote to a Brewers' Association agent: "I am enclosing you those parts of my platform pertaining to the subject of personal liberty and to the malt liquor industry. I want to circulate one million of those pamphlets as well as to wage an educational campaign through the state, if I can get the required assistance. . . . I would appreciate your aid." Preceding a 1911 Texas referendum on statewide prohibition, the Milwaukee beer magnate Adolphus Busch informed the association: "I will not mind to give $100,000 extra if necessary. Missouri recently went through a most strenuous campaign winning out by an enormous majority. Well, you can hardly imagine the cost of that campaign. If we sacrifice one-half our earnings in 1911 in order to make up this campaign fund it is not so serious." But the Texas wets lost.

Neither brewers nor distillers lacked for funds. During the first decade of the twentieth century the national drink bill averaged around $2 billion a year. It was therefore no great strain upon its members when the Brewers' Association imposed a 3-cent barrelage tax for its war chest. The levy yielded an annual $750,000. Nor did the association have much trouble raising additional sums to subsidize friendly voices. The Hearst editor Arthur Brisbane while professing temperance convictions, defended beer drinking, a position which prompted the president of the association, Christian Feigenspan, to write to him, "I and a number of friends have for years felt very strongly that the public welfare and *our own industry*—because of your well-known convictions—would be benefitted by your personal ownership of a newspaper," and to enable Brisbane to buy the Washington *Times*, Feigenspan collected $375,000 from fifteen prominent brewers.

The liquor men fought as ruthlessly as the League, but they were less adroit. Whereas the League at least paid lip service to women's suffrage, the brewers antagonized the opposite sex by resolving during one of their early conventions: "We oppose always and everywhere the ballot in the hands of woman, for woman's vote is the last hope of Prohibitionism." For the most part the League operated openly. The brewers and distillers set up dummy organizations with high-sounding names—the Taxpayers' Union, the National Association of Commerce and Labor, the Civic Liberty League—through which to control secretly periodicals and political groups only to have these false fronts quickly stripped away by the League. They repeatedly fell afoul of laws governing political campaigns and electioneering. No corrupt practice was ever proved against the League. In 1916 seven Texas breweries paid $281,000 in fines plus court costs after pleading guilty to assorted illegalities in elections all over the state. Two years later a federal grand jury indicted the national association, its Pennsylvania chapter and almost a hundred corporations connected with brewing for conspiracy. Most of the defendants pleaded guilty and paid fines aggregating $100,000.

But more than any specific dereliction, what damaged the pre-World War I liquor industry was its gross greed. The League could wrap itself in the robes of morality and piety. The liquor industry could delude hardly anybody that its profits did not come first. The League used the churches as a staging ground for political action. The brewers and distillers used the saloons. In the end they defeated themselves. Charles Merz, one of the sharpest analysts of prohibition politics, wrote in *The Dry Decade*: "There was never a moment in the history of those years when the brewers could not have reformed the institution which was the chief point of attack . . . the saloon. . . . Reformation by the brewers and distillers of their own trade might have averted national prohibition. . . . [They] refused all reformation and compromise."

There were many Americans outside the liquor industry who wanted no part of prohibition—how many it is impossible to calculate—but they were unorganized. They had no powerful lobby to oppose the League and the WCTU—a failure of imagination. Few of them could conceive of a dry America. They lost by default.

In the 1914 Congressional elections the drys gained seats in both houses. A month after the House of Representatives convened the Hobson-Sheppard bill came up for debate. The galleries were jammed. From the balconies floated long bands of paper inscribed by more than 6,000,000 dry petitioners. The dashing Hobson, standing before quasi-medical charts depicting the destructive effects of liquor, delivered his Great Destroyer oration. The session lasted almost twelve hours. (Among the 105 speechmakers was the dry Republican Congressman from Minnesota, Charles August Lindbergh, Sr.) The bill won by 197 votes to 190—61 short of the needed two-thirds majority.

To have prompted the first House debate on national prohibition would by itself have constituted an important League victory. That a majority of the Congressmen voted for the Hobson-Sheppard resolution boded a still greater victory. But on Wheeler's advice the Leaguers did not press for a resubmission during the next two years. They wished first to assure themselves of the two-thirds majority. Wheeler recalled:

Back in the field we got busy again. All the energy we put into the 1914 election campaign boiled and bubbled with hotter fire in the campaign of 1916. We laid down such a barrage as candidates for Congress had never seen before, and such as they will, in all likelihood, not see again for years to come. . . . We knew late election night that we had won. . . . We knew that the Prohibition Amendment would be submitted to the states by the Congress just elected.

As a further result of the League's barrage, nine more states adopted prohibitory statutes, bringing the total to twenty-three, while dry areas were expanded through local option in twelve states. Then occurred the momentous event without which the League's crowning victory might have eluded it for many more years.

On April 16, 1917, President Woodrow Wilson called a special session of the newly elected Sixty-fifth Congress to declare the existence of a state of war with Germany. By now the League felt confident that Congress would pass a resolution to submit to the states for ratification a revised Hobson-Sheppard bill, or Eighteenth Amendment. At the President's request, however, it held off to allow him first to present his war program. A vital part of that program was a food control bill. The Leaguers saw in it a superb opportunity to force through some dry legislation under the guise of food conservation. Because the production of liquor used up huge quantities of grain, sugar and other foodstuffs needed for the armed forces, they could now argue that drinking was unpatriotic, as well as sinful and impious. Besides, they insisted, alcohol impaired military efficiency. Major General Leonard Wood pointed to Kansas, a dry state since 1881, as proof. According to the general, it bred "the finest, the cleanest, the healthiest and the most vigorous soldiers . . . that we have ever known. . . . Kansas boys were brought up in a clean atmosphere. They started right."

The League excoriated the beer industry as pro-German and treasonable. In the climate of war hysteria, when sauerkraut was renamed "liberty cabbage," it was not hard to whip up popular hatred of the big brewers with their German names and background. The U.S. Brewers' Association, purblind as ever, facilitated the assault by contributing large subsidies to the antiprohibitionist National German-American Alliance. A sociopolitical organization founded in 1901 by Dr. Charles John Hexamer, composed of German-born or German-descended citizens, and dedicated to the furtherance of German *Kultur*, it spawned numerous beer-loving *Turnvereine*, *Sängerfeste* and *Män-*

nerchöre. Kaiser Wilhelm did not enhance its popularity among non-German-Americans when he proclaimed: "If ever a man was worthy of high decoration at my hand, it is Herr Doktor Hexamer, the president of the Alliance, who may justly be termed, by my grace, the acting ruler of all the Germans in the United States."

Following the outbreak of World War I, the Alliance became an instrument of propaganda to glorify the German cause and keep America neutral. With sublime tactlessness, President Hexamer publicly told the membership:

> We have long suffered the preachment that "you Germans must allow yourselves to be assimilated, you must merge in the American people; but no one will ever find us prepared to descend to an inferior level. . . ."
>
> Many are giving our German culture to this land of their children, but that is possible only if we stand together and conquer that dark spirit of muckerdom and Prohibition just as Siegfried slew the dragon . . . we are giving to this people the best the earth affords, the benefits of German *kultur*.

An investigation instigated by Wayne Wheeler resulted in the revocation of the Alliance's charter and its disbandment. "Kaiserism abroad and booze at home must go," Wheeler declared, carefully confusing the issue. "Liquor is a menace to patriotism because it puts beer before country."

His pursuit of the culprits led him into a ludicrous misadventure. On a train carrying him to a church meeting in Elizabeth, New Jersey, with some documents incriminating the Alliance, he accidentally dropped a paper calling on all German-Americans to aid the Kaiser. The conductor who picked it up believed he had detected an enemy agent and wired ahead to the Elizabeth police. Upon the train's arrival a brace of policemen hustled Wheeler to the stationhouse, where he spent a painful half-hour before he could establish his identity. With characteristic foxiness, he then turned the incident to advantage. You see, he said, in effect, how alert good Americans are to the enemy's schemes and how they detest Germans, particularly those connected with the beer business.

The League Congressmen amended the food control bill to exclude all foodstuffs from the manufacture of alcohol, and thus worded, it passed the House. The liquor forces realized they could never stop the prohibition of distilled liquor, but figured perhaps they could save beer and wine. In the Senate the hulking Republican Boies Penrose, Pennsylvania political boss and leader of the wet faction, threatened a summer-long filibuster unless the bill was so modified. President Wilson then asked the League to accept the compromise lest Senatorial conflict delay more urgent phases of the war program. Donning the mantle of patriotism, the League agreed but at the same time served notice that its docility was strictly temporary. "We are glad that your request applies only to the pending food legislation," the League's legislative committee wrote to Wilson. "It will be our purpose to urge the passage of the legislation prohibiting the waste of foodstuffs in the manufacture of beer and wines at the earliest date, either in the form of a separate bill or in connection with other war legislation."

The Cincinnati *Enquirer* echoed the fury of the wets in an editorial: "For brazen effrontery, unmitigated gall, superegoism, transcendent audacity, supreme impudence, commend us to the legislative committee of the prohibition lobby. . . . Here we have the President of the United States under orders to an officious and offensive lobby."

Congress passed the food control bill without the beer and wine proviso and with the addition of a clause authorizing the President to restrict beer and wine as he deemed fit. The bill took effect on September 8, 1917.

The League, meanwhile, had determined to forge ahead with the Eighteenth Amendment, advocating it primarily as a war-time measure. The wets, fearful it would pass, devised a snare and to bait it, they chose Boss Penrose and the Republican Senator from Ohio, Warren Gamaliel Harding, who, though an habitual drinker, was politically beholden to Wheeler and other dry potentates from his home state. While aware that he not only tippled but gambled, they backed him because he voted their way.

As Senator Sheppard reconstructed the crucial episode years later, Penrose lumbered across the Senate floor and, towering above him, rasped: "I'll let that joint resolution of yours come on to the floor from the committee, if you'll agree to one change in it."

"What's the change?" the little Texan quietly asked.

"You'll have to fix that amendment of yours so that it won't go into effect unless two-thirds [*sic*] of the states have ratified it within six years."

Sheppard agreed. Later he recalled:

What else could I do? Washington was full of drys who were depending on me to put the law through. I had to think fast, while Penrose waited. . . . I knew Penrose was playing a trick on me. He thought that six years were too short for thirty-two different state senates and thirty-two state legislatures [*Sic*. Three-quarters of the states—thirty-six, not thirty-two—were required to ratify a constitutional amendment] with their five or six thousand different members to meet and act. Why, there are proposed amendments still dangling in space after a century waiting for a sufficient number of states to ratify them. Half a dozen years seemed an awfully short time to me. . . . But I had to take a chance. It was the first time in American history we had ever had a chance to get a dry amendment onto the floor for a vote. . . . So I decided in a hurry, made the compromise, and agreed.

That night, at a certain hotel in Washington, there was a great jubilation among the wets . . . they were sure the prohibitionists were whipped. To speak the truth I was heartsick myself that night, and so were my friends. "You'll never get enough states to ratify within a mere half-dozen years," they said. "Why, the war may last that long and the state legislatures will be all tied up with war measures and war excitement."

During the same Senatorial session, Harding summoned Wheeler from his customary perch in the gallery. "You fellows ought to agree to have some limitation put on the time for ratification," he told him. Otherwise the liquor issue might be kicked around as a political football for ages. Besides, the future President reminded him, there were several irresolute Senators likely to flop over to the wet side if ratification was protracted. Wheeler took a more sanguine view than Sheppard. No man alive understood better than the Leaguer the extent and nature of the country's dry sentiment or how to handle state legislatures, and he considered six years time enough. Congress later spotted the liquor industry an additional one-year period of grace to settle its affairs.

The seven-year clause, introduced by Harding, was one of three major elements in which the final form of the Eighteenth

Amendment differed from the original Hobson-Sheppard resolution. They betrayed the crafty lawyer's hand of Wayne Wheeler. Section 1 now read:

> After one year from the ratification of this article the manufacture, sale or transportation of intoxicating liquors within, the importation thereof into, or the exportation thereof from the United States and all territory subject to the jurisdiction thereof for beverage purposes is hereby prohibited.

Sheppard, whose target was not the drinker of alcohol, but the saloonkeeper, the brewer and the distiller, as it was the chief target of many Anti-Saloon Leaguers, later told a reporter: "I didn't intend to stop the making of liquor in homes. I didn't even have in mind the idea of preventing gifts of liquor, or the carrying of liquor from point to point, unless these things were done for commercial purposes. Private making of booze and private drinking thereof were not aimed at." But by omitting the original qualifying "for sale" after the words "manufacture," "transportation," "importation" and "exportation," Wheeler hoped to end all making and drinking of liquor, private or otherwise.

Again, a number of legislators and Leaguers felt it would be dishonest not to make the buyer of liquor as guilty of crime as the seller. But Wheeler, foreseeing that no buyer would likely testify against the seller, if by so doing he would expose himself to prosecution, dissented, and his will prevailed. The word "purchase" was not included.

An entirely new section inserted by Wheeler seemed to preserve states' rights while actually making a mockery of them.

> The Congress and the several states shall have concurrent power to enforce this article by appropriate legislation.

Section 1 abolished local option throughout the nation. It stripped state legislators of their authority as far as liquor went. To soften this reality, Section 2 granted the states a meaningless power—namely, to assist the federal government in the exercise of *its* power to enforce the law. In short, the states could no longer enact their own liquor laws; they could only prohibit liquor.

Among Wheeler's most useful allies was Secretary of the Navy

Josephus Daniels and former Secretary of State William Jennings Bryan, total abstainers both. At his request they besought the President to stifle his natural impulse and not oppose the amendment. If enacted and proved salutary, they reasoned, his administration would reap the glory. If otherwise, no blame could attach to him. The President complied.

On August 1, 1917, the Senate adopted the amendment 65 to 20. Jubilant over the trap they imagined the League had fallen into, the wet Senators adjourned to a Washington hotel for a celebratory libation.

The following December 18 the amendment was put to a vote in the House of Representatives. "Every Congressman knows," commented Brisbane's Washington *Times*, "that if the ballot on the constitutional amendment were a secret ballot, making it impossible for the Anti-Saloon League bosses to punish disobedience, the amendment would not pass." It passed by a majority well in excess of the requisite two-thirds—282 to 128. Once again the self-deluded wets rejoiced, certain that thirty-six states would not ratify within the stipulated seven years.

The League did not wait to hear from the states before demanding interim measures in the name of the war effort. It drew added encouragement from the British Prime Minister, David Lloyd George, who cried: "We have three foes—Germany, Austria and drink—and the greatest of these is drink." Though President Wilson did exercise his discretionary power to reduce sharply the amount of foodstuffs the breweries could use, it still left too much to suit the League, and its legislative committee rebuked him in a letter dated April 1, 1918:

> . . . we cannot believe that you are fully aware of the deep and widespread unrest in the minds of the great majority of patriotic citizens of the nation caused by the continuance of this waste . . . when fathers and mothers are giving their sons, and sons are giving their lives, there is an ever-increasing tide of indignation and resentment that the liquor traffic should continue to prey upon the strength—even the very life—of the nation. . . .
>
> The intimation that any large number of workmen in factories, mines and munition plants would rebel against the surrender of intoxicants in order to save bread, sugar and fuel, and thus help win the war, is a reflection upon the loyalty, patriotism and character of the workingman of the country which has been started by the liquor traffic to save itself from its well-deserved destruction. . . .

We are convinced that it is the duty of our committee . . . to
ask you . . . to ask Congress to pass speedily such legislation as
will prohibit the sale of all kinds of intoxicants for beverage
purpose during the period of the war and demobilization thereafter.

Receiving no reply or any satisfaction from a conference with
Wilson, the committee proceeded to draft and to recommend to
various legislators war emergency dry measures of its own. The
most stringent of these was cunningly introduced as an amendment to the Agricultural Appropriation bill and threatened to
withhold desperately needed pending appropriations unless the
President banned the manufacture of beer and wine until the
war ended and demobilization ended. He had no choice.
Disagreements between House and Senate over the bill delayed
its passage until November 21, 1918, by which date the League's
pretext for attaching the dry rider no longer existed. The
armistice had been signed ten days earlier.

To the stupefaction of the wet Senators, who had fancied
themselves so crafty by establishing a seven-year limit for the
ratification of the Eighteenth Amendment, thirty-six states
ratified it within thirteen months of its submission. During the
fourteenth month nine more states ratified it. Of these forty-five,
twenty-eight had already adopted statewide prohibition so their
assent should have been no great surprise to the wets. New Jersey
did not ratify until 1922. Only Connecticut and Rhode Island
never ratified. The Eighteenth Amendment, for which the
League's strongest argument had been wartime urgency, became
law on January 16, 1919—two months after hostilities ceased.

The liquor industry was cheated of its promised year of grace
by the Agricultural Appropriation bill, whose dry clause remained in effect during demobilization. Only the absence of
enforcement provisions enabled it to operate without penalties
for a few more months. Many law-abiding members of the
industry hastened to dispose of their stocks and shut down their
plants or convert them to a different line of production. Others
prepared to carry on *sub rosa*. They did not lack precedents. Amid
the plethora of long-standing town, county and state dry laws,
the techniques of smuggling, bootlegging and running speakeasies had been solidly established the country over. Under the
liquor tax laws moonshining had become a fine art. Since 1876
Bureau of Internal Revenue agents had seized 66,794 stills.

Wayne Wheeler drafted the National Prohibition Act, providing for enforcement of both wartime prohibition and the Eighteenth Amendment. But it took its popular name from the Republican Congressman who introduced it in the House, Andrew Joseph Volstead of Minnesota. The wets pictured Volstead as the archetype of bluenose, killjoy fanatic, a misconception to which his appearance and manner lent credence. A bony, cadaverous figure, his mouth hidden by a thick, downdrooping mustache in the style of a Mack Sennett Keystone Kop paste-on, he spoke sparingly and seldom with any flicker of humor. Chewing tobacco seems to have been his only vice. The son of immigrant Norwegian Lutherans, who settled near the southern Minnesota-Wisconsin border, he was born in a log house built by his father. Educated at St. Olaf's College, Minnesota, he resisted parental efforts to interest him first in the Lutheran ministry, then in agriculture. He chose the law, practiced at Lac qui Parle and other obscure Minnesota communities, married Nellie Gilruth, and moved to Yellow Medicine County, which embraced both wet and dry townships.

In 1886 Volstead was elected county prosecutor, an office he served for fourteen years. Contrary to his later national reputation, he held no extreme views regarding liquor. He never delivered a temperance speech, never joined a temperance society and never signed a temperance pledge. "I just kept in the middle of the road," he said. He even admitted to having taken a nip. "I don't know that there's any harm in one drink." He devoutly believed that "law regulates morality, law has regulated morality since the Ten Commandments," and because the law in many townships under his jurisdiction prohibited liquor, he considered it a moral imperative, as well as an official duty, to prosecute violators diligently. In the process he learned a good deal about the loopholes of prohibitory legislation, the wiles of bootleggers and the corruption of enforcement agents. "I have seen sheriffs and prosecuting attorneys drinking at clubs in dry territory," he recalled, "and I have seen solid and prosperous business men who were made sots and bankrupts while members of such clubs."

Yet in none of the six elections to Congress which Volstead won did he run on a prohibition platform. Twice, in fact, he opposed prohibitionist candidates. It was as chairman of the House Judiciary Committee that the final preparation of the Wheeler-drafted act fell to him, and he shouldered the task in the spirit of his Yellow Medicine County prosecutions as a moral obligation to arm the law rather than a personal commitment to prohibition. The general public never understood this and unfairly identified him with the country's most bigoted Grundyist element.

Volstead added little to the Wheeler draft, nor did he greatly alter it. His principal contribution was to verify its constitutionality. (The Supreme Court later voted 5 to 4 in its favor.) Introduced in the House on May 27, 1919, H.R. 6810 was debated for three months, passing on July 22 by a vote of 255 to 136. The Senate then debated it until September 5, passed it, slightly amended, without a roll call, and returned it to the House, which finally adopted it on October 10 by a vote of 321 to 70.

President Wilson, now a sick man after the strain of the Versailles peace treaty negotiations and the blighting of his hopes that the United States would join the League of Nations, vetoed the Volstead Act. Congress, he objected, had combined wartime prohibition with constitutional prohibition, whereas the war emergency had long been over. Though he expressed himself somewhat ambiguously about the act as a whole, he appeared to disapprove on constitutional grounds. "In all matters having to do with personal habits and customs of large numbers of our people," he wrote, "we must be certain that the established processes of legal change are followed. In no other way can the salutary objects sought to be accomplished by great reforms of this character be made satisfactory and permanent."

On October 28, two hours after receiving the President's message, Congress overrode his veto, and the Volstead Act became law.

In its original form, before unforeseen pitfalls necessitated numerous changes and additions, it consisted of three titles and sixty-six sections. Title I—"To provide for the enforcement of War Prohibition"—was finally rendered irrelevant by the end of demobilization. Title III—"Industrial Alcohol"—defined the conditions governing the manufacture of nonbeverage alcohol, the denaturation of distilled spirits, the transformation of distilleries and the penalties for converting the product back into potable liquor—not over $1,000 fine or 30 days' prison, or both, for the first offense; from $1,000 to $10,000 fine and from 30 days to a year's imprisonment for subsequent offenses. Title II—"Prohibition of Intoxicating Beverages"—was what chiefly affected the individual.

"No person," it decreed, "shall . . . manufacture, sell, barter, transport, import, export, deliver, furnish or possess any intoxicating liquor except as authorized in this act, and all the provisions of this act shall be liberally construed to the end that the use of intoxicating liquor as a beverage may be prevented." The exceptions, requiring a government permit, included sacramental wine, medicaments containing alcohol, hard liquor if prescribed by a physician—but no more than a pint per patient within any ten-day period—alcoholized patent medicines unfit for beverage, undrinkable toilet preparations, flavoring extracts and syrups. Beer was allowed as long as the alcoholic content had been reduced from the normal 3 or 4 percent to less than half of 1 percent. Another exception reflected the tender regard of Congress for the farm vote. Section 3 exempted "vinegar and preserved sweet cider" without mentioning fermentation.

Advertising liquor was unlawful. Also, advertising, making or selling any contrivance for the production of liquor. "Any room, house, building, boat, vehicle, structure, or place where intoxicating liquor is manufactured, sold, kept, or bartered in violation of this title, and all intoxicating liquor and property kept and used in maintaining the same, is hereby declared a common nuisance, and any person who maintains such a common nuisance shall be guilty of a misdemeanor and upon conviction thereof shall be fined no more than $1000, or be imprisoned for no more than one year, or both. . . ." Under Section 25 no property rights existed in liquor stored for sale or premises maintained for the manufacture of such liquor and were liable to search, seizure and destruction. So were vehicles used to transport the liquor. In the privacy of the home possession of liquor was permissible, if the liquor was intended to be drunk by the owner, his family or guests.

The range of penalties, covering the thirty-eight sections of Title II, went from a first-offense $500 fine to a fine of $2,000 and five years' imprisonment for repeated offenses.

The Volstead Act assigned the task of investigation to the Bureau of Internal Revenue, which was to refer cases for prosecution to the appropriate district U.S. attorney. For the first fiscal year under national prohibition, ending June 30, 1920, the act authorized an appropriation of $2,000,000 for the extra expenses to be incurred by the tax bureau and $100,000 for those of the Department of Justice—a supreme instance of financial optimism.

When a Washington correspondent for the St. Paul *Pioneer Press* observed, during an interview with Andrew Volstead, that the new law seemed drastic, the Congressman readily agreed, adding: "It will be made even more severe after the country has learned what prohibition means."

Did the majority of the American people really want prohibition? The drys have always replied with a resounding "Yes!" The wets have maintained that a small but powerful political pressure group foisted prohibition upon the country without warning while its attention was distracted by World War I.

The accessible evidence confirms neither claim. It precludes any flat answer and leaves the question forever unsettled. For half a century the principal arguments have run as follows:

The wets. We had our hands full with the war. The antiliquor crowd pushed through the amendment while the youth of the land was at the front.

The drys. In 1914, three years before America entered the war, before a single soldier had been drafted, the House voted for prohibition by a 197–190 majority, thereby giving ample warning which way the wind blew. Two years later, with America still neutral, the Congressional elections sent a majority of dry representatives to Washington, and by 1917 twenty-six states had adopted prohibition.

The wets. Most of them by legislative action, not direct popular vote.

The drys. Just the reverse. In only nine states was prohibition adopted by the legislature. The other seventeen adopted it by referendum. And the majorities were overwhelming.

The wets. Not if you combine the totals of all twenty-six states. Then you get 1,967,337 for and 1,437,402 against, or 14 out of every 19 voters opposed. The total represented barely 4 percent of the national population.

The drys. All the same, by 1917 most of the U.S. territory was under some kind of prohibitory laws and so prepared to accept the Eighteenth Amendment.

The wets. Some kind. That's the point. You can't compare the bone-dry federal law with laws of varying severity as adopted by the states. Only thirteen states went bone-dry before the Eighteenth Amendment—thirteen states with a combined area of about a third of the country, inhabited by a seventh of the total population. In the other states the prewar dry laws allowed a great many exceptions to absolute prohibition. Indiana, for example, forbade neither the fermentation of grapes nor serving any kind of drink to guests in one's home. Virginia allowed adult males not attending school or college to buy a quart of hard liquor or a gallon of wine or 3 gallons of beer once a month. Alabama, while banning the manufacture of liquor, permitted its citizens to import every two weeks 2 quarts of liquor or 2 gallons of wine or 5 gallons of beer. . . . So many exceptions that during the years 1906–1917, the per capita consumption of legal hard liquor increased from 1.47 gallons to 1.60. Malt liquors declined slightly per capita, but the total consumption increased from about 17 billion gallons to more than 18 billion gallons.

The wets advanced at least two propositions hard to refute. Contrary to the Anti-Saloon League's sweeping claim, prohibition before 1917 was primarily a regional grass-roots movement, not one that truly expressed the national will. Of the twenty-six dry states twenty-four lay either west of the Mississippi or south of Ohio and two in the rural northern part of New England, whereas the thirteen predominantly industrial states from Massachusetts to Missouri included only two that the drys had captured, Michigan and Indiana. Significantly, in Michigan, which held a referendum, its only big city, Detroit, voted wet. In sum, it appeared that rural, agricultural America with its large Protestant, native-born population thrust prohibition upon urban, industrial America, with its heterogeneity of races, religions and foreign backgrounds.

It was also true that during the Congressional debate over the Eighteenth Amendment and the state legislative actions following it, neither press nor public paid much attention. There was relatively little organized opposition because a deeper concern overshadowed the issue. America had entered the war; its sons were fighting alongside the Allies. And so, though the Anti-Saloon League never took its eye off the state legislatures, people generally were looking in another direction until the thirty-sixth state had ratified the amendment and prohibition was upon them.

Had no seven-year limit on ratification existed and had time allowed for a state-by-state popular referendum, the result can only be conjectured. But whatever the majority of Americans really wanted it was not what they got.

III. The Noble Experiment
1920–1934

. . . a great social and economic experiment, noble in motive and far-reaching.

—PRESIDENT HERBERT HOOVER

10. "This law will be obeyed . . . "

in cities, large and small, and in villages, and where it is not obeyed it will be
enforced. . . . We shall see to it that it [liquor] is not manufactured. Nor sold,
nor given away, nor hauled in anything on the surface of the earth or under the
earth or in the air."

—JOHN F. KRAMER, the first Prohibition Commissioner

in cities, large and small

JEAN BOYER, a French film director, stopping over
with his wife at New York's St. Moritz Hotel en route to
Hollywood, was perplexed to see, upon awaking from a postpran-
dial siesta, a handbill sliding under his door. Picking it up, he
read:

> Why come to us—we come to you
> CALL
> "Sonny"
> JOhn 4-1443

The reverse side carried a price list, ranging from "Bacardi
(Carta de Oro)" at $1.75 a quart to "Mumm Champagne" at
$7.50. For customers who preferred to concoct their own potions
Sonny offered "190 Proof Government Tested Grain Alcohol" at
$2 a quart.

Though both thirsty and curious, the Boyers did not call
Sonny because they had barely an hour to catch their westbound
train. At their Hollywood hotel, the Garden of Allah, another
opportunity presented itself. From a similar list that appeared
mysteriously beneath their door they telephoned for an assort-
ment of wines and cognacs. It was delivered within fifteen
minutes by a man driving a black Cadillac limousine.

That evening Boyer's producer gave a dinner party in his honor at the Coconut Grove. Midway through the festivities, one of the guests, a strapping portrayer of Western badmen, returned unsteadily to the table from the dance floor, teetered a moment by his chair, then pitched forward like a felled tree. As a contingent of waiters nonchalantly bore the body away, Mme. Boyer turned in consternation to her neighbor, a scriptwriter. "What happened to the poor man?" she asked.

"Just can't hold his liquor," he explained, his speech a trifle blurry. "Always passes out early in the evening."

"But he was only drinking water," said Mme. Boyer, naïvely indicating the innocent tumblers at each place.

"Look under the table," suggested the writer.

Lifting a corner of the tablecloth and glancing down, she beheld before every chair a partly consumed bottle of booze.

"You can't very well carry the rest of it home," her informant went on. "Wouldn't look right. But it's pretty fancy stuff—right off the boat. You never know when you're going to get real quality again. So you drink it all up here."

With perverse pride drinkers in dozens of cities claimed theirs to be the nation's wettest. The distinction was probably New York's, but in the public mind the depredations of Chicago gangsterism under Al Capone together with the permissiveness of its corrupt, clownish Mayor William "Big Bill" Thompson came to symbolize the bootleg era. Chicago was the scene of the first recorded prohibition thefts of liquor—three of them, in fact, committed almost simultaneously. Within one hour of the moment the Volstead Act took effect, 12:01 A.M. of January 17, 1920, six armed, masked bandits invaded a Chicago railroad switching yard, bound and gagged the watchman and emptied two freight cars full of whiskey reserved for medicinal use and valued at $100,000. At about the same time another gang lifted four barrels of grain alcohol from a government bonded warehouse, while a third gang hijacked a competitor's truck transporting whiskey, the first known instance of what would become routine intergang practice.

During the hours remaining before dawn of the seventeenth agents of the Prohibition Unit (later renamed the Prohibition Bureau), which the Secretary of the Treasury had created as a branch of the Internal Revenue Service, raided two stills in

Detroit and Hammond, Indiana, intercepted liquor-laden trucks rolling through Peoria and New York City and arrested twelve upstate New Yorkers for sundry infractions of the new law. Chicago distinguished itself again eleven days later as the scene of the first federal speakeasy raid, when Prohibition Unit agents invaded a North Side blind pig, the Red Lantern, and collared forty merrymakers. By June more than 500 indictments for Volstead Act violations clogged the Chicago trial calendars, with thousands of offenders carrying on unhampered for lack of enough police able or willing to arrest them. At the same time Captain Hubert Howard, the federal prohibition administrator for Illinois, estimated that since the Volstead Act took effect, Chicago physicians had issued about 300,000 spurious prescriptions for liquor. A staggering increase in liquor prescribed as medicine occurred during those five months throughout the country: more than 15,000 doctors and 57,000 retail druggists applied for licenses to dispense intoxicants. Where approximately 400 wholesale drug houses formerly sufficed to meet all medicinal liquor requirements, more than 3,000 new ones sprang up.

In the next three years the number of Chicago saloons, "soft-drinking parlors," and "wet cabarets" increased to a total of more than 7,000. Twenty-six breweries were wholesaling thousands of barrels of beer a day at $55 to $65 a barrel. The cash needed to buy off both state and federal enforcement officers (according to Chief of Police Morgan Collins, about $1,000,000 a year) represented but a minute fraction of the gross profits. Though the chief investigator for the state's attorney, Pat Roche, would later maintain that "a one-legged prohibition agent on a bicycle could stop the beer in the Loop in one day if he was honest," no state authority ever closed a single Chicago brewery. Under the supervision of a new district U.S. attorney, appointed in 1923, the breweries were temporarily closed and their equipment was destroyed. But the beer barons simply imported beer from other states.

Of "Satan's Seat," as Bishop Cannon referred to New York City, Congressman Fiorello La Guardia, an embattled wet, predicted at the outset of the Noble Experiment: "In order to enforce prohibition it will require a police force of 250,000 men and a force of 250,000 men to police the police." By 1922 about 5,000 speakeasies dotted the metropolis, and a few years later its bandboxical Police Commissioner Grover A. Whalen, with his glistening top hat and gardenia boutonniere, was estimating the number at 32,000 or more than twice as many as the legal drinking spots existing before prohibition. "All you need is two bottles and a room and you have a speakeasy," he observed. But Congressman William P. Sirovich considered the commissioner's estimate far too conservative. He put the total closer to 100,000.

Variety, the Bible of the entertainment world, frequently published the fluctuating prices of liquor as charged at selected speakeasies or other retail sources. Before prohibition the average New York saloon price of a highball or cocktail, containing one ounce of liquor, ran two for a quarter, straight whiskey 10 to 15 cents a shot, and beer a nickel a schooner. With prohibition prices doubled, tripled and quadrupled, but supplies were so plentiful and competition among bootleggers grew so fierce that they eventually dropped back.

A pioneer among New York speakeasy operators, penologically speaking, was Barney Gallant, a Latvian-born charmer, the friend of Eugene O'Neill, Theodore Dreiser, Edna St. Vincent Millay and numerous distinguished Villagers, whose Greenwich Village Inn had already won him personal and professional esteem throughout Bohemia before Congress passed the Volstead Act. It never occurred to Gallant, after the enactment, to stop selling drinks openly at his usual charge of 50 cents a drink, and so on October 30, 1919, he became one of the first New Yorkers to be jailed for violating the new law. A petition signed by thousands of his clients, including a priest and a police captain, moved the sentencing judge to halve the thirty-day term. Two years later Gallant opened the Club Gallant at 85 West Third Street, the forerunner of a succession of his modish Village speakeasies, serving scotch at $16 a quart and champagne at $25.

The principal uptown initiators consisted of a fellowship of discriminating high livers, who reasoned that they could elude prosecution by forming a private chartered cooperative. With Harris Fisher, an artist, as president and a restaurateur named John Steinberg as provisioner, they rented a room over a garage at 129 West Fiftieth Street, naming it the 50-50 Club in double allusion to the street and to the original membership limitation of fifty. Each member contributed $100 toward furnishing the premises. Steinberg's starting stock included 100 cases each of rye and scotch, for which he paid $4,000, the first important purchase of bootleg liquor in Manhattan. There was no bar, only lockers to store the members' purchases. Steinberg made the first sale within twenty-four hours of the Volstead deadline, on January 18, 1920, and the 50-50's fictive status survived unchallenged for two years, chiefly because the authorities had their hands full investigating cruder violations. Most of the early speakeasies attempted the same dodge, many with success. But eventually it failed them, and they had to resort to more reliable methods such as bribery.

Another notable innovator was one James Perkins, who in 1922 introduced the speakeasy bar. Before he opened his establishment in a brownstone house on Fortieth Street, just off Fifth Avenue, the practice was to pour the customers' drinks at their tables straight from bottle to glass. Then, if raided, the pourers would slip the bottles into the customers' overcoat pockets and claim that they had been serving nothing but setups. With the advent of the speakeasy bar it was an inevitable step to the full-panoplied restaurant, and there dawned the golden age of forbidden guzzling.

The city's reputedly wettest street was Fifty-second between Fifth and Sixth avenues, and while it is apocryphal that liquor could be bought in any building there, certainly nobody had to take many steps along the brownstone-lined thoroughfare to slake a thirst. The humorist and connoisseur of speakeasies Robert Benchley once counted thirty-eight of them on Fifty-second Street. Such was the street's reputation that a lady who occupied a guiltless brownstone between two speakeasies was obliged to post a sign: THIS IS A PRIVATE RESIDENCE. DO NOT RING. Among the more renowned neighborhood oases were Tony's, favored by magazine editors, writers and illustrators, whose owner, Tony Soma, practiced yoga and sang operatic arias while standing on his head; razzle-dazzle Leon & Eddie's with its entrance sign, THROUGH THESE PORTALS THE MOST BEAUTIFUL GIRLS IN THE WORLD PASS OUT, the owners' names parqueted into the dance floor, and Eddie Davis, a former carnival wheelman turned singer, convulsing the clientele with such ribaldry as "She Came Rolling Down the Mountain" and "Virgin Sturgeon"; the Town Casino Club, glorying in a neon-lit, electrically operated fountain that sprayed a nude naiad with jets of multicolored water; Janet of France, a theatrical rendezvous and the only speakeasy (according to its proud patronne, Janet Martire) ever

visited by the abstemious George Bernard Shaw; Jack &
Charlie's or Club 21 (after its address, 21 West Fifty-second
Street), perhaps New York's farthest-famed speakeasy, a status it
achieved largely through the early patronage of *New Yorker*
magazine wits like Benchley, Dorothy Parker and Alexander
Woollcott. To shield its habitués from the prying eyes of
newspaper columnists, the co-founders, John Karl Kriendler and
Charles Berns, allowed none to cross the threshold. In an effort to
generate snob appeal, they were also known to turn away, or
relegate to back tables, persons they deemed insufficiently
ornamental.

Charlie Berns* remembers the Redhead and the Fronton

*In 1919, when I was eighteen, I went to the New York University
School of Commerce to study accounting. Jack Kriendler was a distant
cousin—our families had immigrated from Austria and we lived near
each other on the Lower East Side—and he attended Fordham. In the
evenings we both worked as salesmen for Jack's uncle, Sam Brenner,
who owned a shoe store on the corner of Essex and Rivington streets.
He also owned a saloon across the way, and we made ourselves
generally useful there as well. For instance, there came a time when the
government slapped an additional tax on whiskey of 25 cents a barrel.
So whenever the tax collector was due to drop around, Jack and I
would cart away a few barrels and hide them at home until the danger
passed.*

*The year I graduated, 1922, Jack and a classmate named Eddie
Irving bought a controlling interest in a type of place near the campus
known as a "Village [Greenwich Village] tea room." They called it
the Redhead. In addition to food they sold liquor in one-ounce flasks,
miniatures, which the customers could drink right there if they wished
or take home. They asked me to keep the books. They couldn't afford to
pay me a salary. So they made me a partner. Our only idea behind the
enterprise at the start was to earn enough money to continue our
education, I having decided to practice law instead of accountancy and
Jack to become a pharmacist. The way things developed, neither of us
realized his ambition.*

*The Redhead served good, solid, simple food—Jack had a natural
culinary gift—and the best liquor we could find. We dealt with two*

---

* Who died in 1971 a few weeks after taping these reminiscences.

neighborhood bootleggers who would deliver the merchandise to Jack's home on East Fourth Street. When we needed fresh supplies, Jack's kid brothers, Mac and Pete, would wheel it over, a few bottles at a time. Who was going to suspect a couple of kids that age? We never did discover the original source of our liquor, but it was always authentic imported stuff.

We attracted a small but choice crowd, young people mostly from the schools and colleges, and an occasional tourist. We were a success. But even before we started, we had been approached by a group of Village gangsters who declared themselves in. Being innocent college boys, we refused to discuss the matter. A couple of weeks later they came around again. They told us unless we paid for certain protective services, they would wreck the joint. We remained unimpressed. A few nights later, as Jack and I were walking home, a couple of them jumped us. We gave a pretty good account of ourselves, and they took quite a licking. The next time I wasn't so lucky. Jack survived in one piece; but my attacker had a razor, and I wound up in St. Vincent's Hospital with a dozen stitches in my throat. A third fight took place a month later, but again we managed to drive them off.

Meanwhile, we had become acquainted with the district police captain through friends in the James Heron Association. This was a very powerful Lower East Side Democratic organization. These friends let the captain know that Jack and Charlie were decent people who ran an orderly place, no bookmaking, no gambling, no hookers. He came to see us. "Why didn't you let me know about these things that have been happening to you?" he asked. Jack said: "We didn't understand how serious it was." "I'll see what we can do," he said. And nobody ever bothered us again the whole time we operated in the Village.

Every speakeasy had to make some arrangements with the cops to survive. In our case it wasn't exactly a shakedown, nothing on a regular basis, more like an act of friendship. We would slip the captain a $50 bill from time to time and a box of cigars to the cops on the beat. They could always count on us for free meals and drinks, and at Christmastime, of course, we had a gift for everybody.

In 1925 we sold the Redhead (we had bought out Eddie Irving meanwhile) and opened a place we called the Fronton at 88 Washington Place, a basement nightclub this time with dancing and entertainment. Our star attraction was Al Segal, a great jazz pianist, who later coached performers like Ethel Merman. At the Redhead the door was always open. People just wandered in, paid a 50-cent cover charge on weekend nights and drank their miniature flasks. But the

Fronton was a bigger, riskier operation. We felt we had to know our customers. So we kept the front door locked and looked people over carefully through a peephole before we admitted them.

The Fronton prospered, too, and it wasn't long before we heard from our gangster friends again. But we got an unusual break, thanks to a boyhood chum of mine. His name was Jimmy Kerrigan. His father once ran a saloon on Fiftieth Street and Broadway before the Capitol Theater was built there. I peddled newspapers in the area at the age of thirteen, and that's how my path crossed Jimmy's. Well, Jimmy grew up to be a revenue agent, which may explain why we never had any trouble with the feds back at the Redhead.

The minute I got the word from those hoodlums that they were planning to visit us on a certain night I got in touch with Jimmy. He arrived in a car with five of his fellow agents, parked across the street and waited. When the gangsters showed, the agents swarmed all over them. They held a long conversation out there on the sidewalk, and that's the last we ever heard from that particular group.

First a flood, then a flash fire hit the Fronton, and it taught us the importance of having friends in the fire department, as well as the police. Chief Purdy headed the fire brigade nearest us. Off duty he liked to drop in for a few snorts with the missus, and we never charged him anything. One spring day it rained so hard the sewers backed up. Our main room being below street level, the water started rushing up through the toilet bowls and flooding the place. Chief Purdy answered our distress call with powerful pumps and pumped us dry.

Not long after, the flash fire broke out. We never found out how it started. This time Chief Purdy and his men arrived with axes and started to wreck the premises. "Think of all the money you're going to get from the insurance," he said. "My God!" I told him. "We're not insured!" He felt terrible. "Never mind," he said, "we'll fix it all up." And they did, too.

The construction of the Sixth Avenue subway forced us to abandon the Fronton in 1926, and we moved uptown into a brownstone house with an iron gate at 42 West Forty-ninth Street. The main reason we chose it was that the Italian bootlegger who owned it and wasn't doing too well because he couldn't speak much English agreed to guarantee our mortgage payments if we would buy all our stock from him. We found both him and his liquor reliable. In fact, if we overbought, he would always take back a few cases. We quickly established a reputation for our French and Italian cooking and our cellar.

Soon after we opened, a police captain from the Forty-seventh Street

station came to pay his respects and explain that to protect himself, he
had to make a friendly arrest—that is, to put it on the record that we
sold liquor. "Now you just leave a couple of pints out in the open," he
told us. "We'll have a man come by and pick them up. But don't
worry. You'll go free on bail, and that'll be the end of the matter."
Which is exactly how it worked out.

A certain group of federal agents presented a more serious problem.
They were young men of good families, socialites, who saw a means of
making some extra easy money by joining the Prohibition Unit. To put
it crudely, they were shakedown artists. The way we handled them, a
number of us speakeasy operators in the neighborhood created a sort of
informal association. John Perona of the Bath Club, who later founded
El Morocco, was the main negotiator who spoke for us all. When one
of those agents tried to make a case against us, we'd tell him: "You
know John Perona. Call him. He'll tell you we're all right and he'll
take care of everything." Then we'd square it with John. It cost us
about a thousand a year, not including free meals and drinks.

Our Forty-ninth Street place changed its name every year in order to
avoid continuity in the IRS records—the Iron Gate, the Grotto, 42,
Jack & Charlie's, the Puncheon Club. One evening a Yale student
named Ben Quinn came in, took a quick look around and cried: "My
God, this is my old home! I grew up here!" He was right. The house
had passed through several hands since his father sold it. Ben became a
regular visitor, and the place was sometimes called "Ben Quinn's
kitchen."

In spite of all the payoffs we did have one serious raid. It was
ordered personally by Mabel Walker Willebrandt.* Two things put
her on our trail. First, the rumor that we were the only New York
speakeasy in continuous operation that had never been bothered by the
city police or the feds. Secondly, a valued customer, a Southern
gentleman, who didn't trust his local brew, telephoned to ask us to send
him some of our whiskey. The employee who took the call stupidly sent
it through the mail with the return address on the package. The post
office spotted it, reported it to the prohibition authorities and made Mrs.
Willebrandt doubly determined to get us, selling liquor through the
mail being an additional offense.

It was a long-drawn-out case, but thanks to our able counselor-at-
law we reached a compromise. We pleaded guilty to possession of

---

* The Harding-appointed Assistant Attorney General in charge of prohibition
nforcement.

*liquor and paid a fine. Ironically, the raid turned out to be the best
advertising we ever got. It made us. Because the confiscated liquor was
analyzed by federal chemists, who declared it to be of the finest quality.
The press cheered. H. L. Mencken wrote, as nearly as I can remember:
"Why raid a place that is serving good liquor and not poisoning
anybody?"*

*Although we owned the building on Forty-ninth Street, we only
leased the ground, and in 1929 the lease ran out. By then the
Rockefellers, who had bought up or leased a lot of land in the Forties
and Fifties, including our location, were planning to construct
Rockefeller Center. So we had to move again. We didn't want to leave
the neighborhood, not after the good relations we had established there
with various prohibition agents. We considered several houses in West
Fifty-third and West Fifty-fourth, but there were Rockefellers living on
both those streets, and they didn't like speakeasies. Nobody exactly liked
to have a speakeasy as a neighbor, but some people were more
broad-minded than others. We finally settled for the brownstone we've
occupied ever since at 21 West Fifty-second.*

*The last night on Forty-ninth Street, which was not long before a
wrecking crew started to tear down the building, we threw a private
farewell party for some of our favorite customers. Bea Lillie, for
example. And Bob Benchley. We gave every guest a crowbar or spade
and let them go to work breaking down the walls and digging up the
floor. Then we all loaded the bottles, crockery, furnishings and so forth
onto carts and wheeled them three blocks north to our new address.*

*We weren't there very long before three hoodlums paid us a visit.
They represented Jack "Legs" Diamond.* [Of all the gang
overlords, possibly the most barbarous. The nickname
derived from his fleet-footedness as an adolescent thief. It
amused him, a kidnapper, as well as bootlegger, hijacker,
extortioner and dope dealer, to burn the bare soles of his
captives' feet with matches. He killed, or ordered to be
killed, dozens of competitors. He himself was shot up so
often that the underworld dubbed him "the Clay Pigeon."]
*It was like the old days in the Village again. Diamond wanted a piece
of our business. The doorman threw the hoodlums out. We were lucky.
Before Diamond had a chance to strike back at us, he was shot to
death.*

*We continued on friendly terms with the prohibition agents. We also
became quite friendly with some of the assistant U.S. attorneys, who
would drop in for an occasional drink or when they needed a good bottle*

as a gift would ask us to help them out. But you could never be sure. You could never relax completely. Some new officials might be appointed to the New York district or the agents you took care of might be reassigned elsewhere, and the first thing you knew you got raided.

We had this engineer we trusted, and he installed a series of contraptions for us that worked on different mechanical or electrical impulses. For example, the shelves behind the bar rested on tongue blocks. In case of a raid the bartender could press a button that released the blocks, letting the shelves fall backward and dropping the bottles down a chute. As they fell, they hit against angle irons projecting from the sides of the chute and smashed. At the bottom were rocks and a pile of sand through which the liquor seeped, leaving not a drop of evidence. In addition, when the button was pressed, an alarm bell went off, warning everybody to drink up fast. We once put too many bottles on the shelves and they collapsed under the weight. Another time a bartender pressed the button by mistake. But we had only one serious raid. The agents searched the building for twenty-four hours. They never found a single contraption.

The most important was the secret door to our wine cellar. [Here Berns led the author down to the subterranean depths of the building. We paused before an alcove, its white walls bare, and he produced a long, thin steel rod.] Unless you know exactly where to look, all you can see are solid walls, no visible cracks of any kind. But there's this tiny aperture here. You'd have to have an eagle eye. [He shoved the rod through.] When I push this a little further in, you'll hear a noise. That's the tongue lock being released on the other side. It takes very little pressure on my part, even though with the steel frame support the thing weighs over a ton. It works like a trigger on a gun. Listen. [I heard a sharp, metallic click, and the wall swung back on silent hinges, revealing bin upon bin of bottles cradled on their sides.] This is the only entrance or exit. No other way in or out. If the mechanism broke, we'd have to dig through the concrete and pull out the whole lock. But that never happened. And no agent ever discovered the cache either. We still keep the contraption because people like to come down here and see the way things were in the old days.

However distressing to the Rockefellers, the blocks they lived on soon became almost as wet as Fifty-second Street. In fact, the majority of the city's smartest, highest-priced speakeasies, many of them owned or controlled by gangsters, clustered within a radius of half a mile from Rockefeller Center. On Fifty-eighth Street the suave ex-bootlegger Sherman Billingsley introduced at his first Stork Club the predinner bowl of celery, olives, radishes and scallions buried in crushed ice, gave his patrons silk neckties emblazoned with a stork and their ladies, perfume. In her Fifty-fourth Street nightclub Helen Morgan drew rivers of tears from her clientele as, perched upon a piano, she sobbed, "He's just my Bill." The Five O'Clock Club, on the same block, owned by the gang bosses Owen Victor "Owney the Killer" Madden and George "Big Frenchy" De Mange, originated a custom, soon adopted by a number of speakeasies, of identifying the celebrities present by having the orchestra strike up some tune associated with them. Two blocks north, at the Merry-Go-Round, Paris-gowned women and their dinner-jacketed escorts bestrode wooden horses as they sipped cocktails, while a circular bar revolved to the music of an electric organ. Zito, the Daumier of the speakeasies, had adorned the walls with caricatures of the better-known customers, like Lily Pons, Vincent Astor, Dudley Field Malone and Maurice Chevalier.

Merely to set foot inside Belle Livingstone's five-story Country Club on East Fifty-eighth Street cost $5. Well advanced in years when she inaugurated what she described as "a salon of culture, wit and bonhomie," ex-wife of a Chicago paint salesman, an Italian count, a Cleveland millionaire and an English engineer, friend of European royalty and American tycoons, Belle custom-arily wore Chinese red lounging pajamas and, being fairly tall and husky, personally ejected customers who failed to meet her standards of decorum. Abandoned as an infant, she claimed to have been found under a sunflower by an Emporia, Kansas, newspaperman, who adopted her and had her educated in a convent. Stage-struck, she left her first husband to join a barnstorming comic opera company. For a stage name she borrowed that of the explorer David Livingstone, "because it connoted to me a daring spirit." Reaching Broadway, she was variously publicized as "the Kansas Sunshine Baby," "the Belle of Bohemia" and "the Girl with the Poetic Legs." Upon inheriting a sizable sum from her first husband, who died young, she sailed for Europe, stayed abroad thirty years and married three more times. It was in 1927 that Belle returned to the States broke, and announced: "I wish to have a civilized, delightful, joyous, witty group of people about me. Something of Rabelais, something of Madame de Staël, everything of happiness."

The main salon of her Country Club, which had a capacity of 400, was decorated in Louis Quinze style. The upper floors offered such divertissements as ping-pong and miniature golf, available only to players who ordered drinks at frequent intervals. Prices started at $2 for an ordinary whiskey and soda and peaked at $40 for a bottle of champagne.

Belle's only rival for the crown of Queen of the Speakeasies was Mary Louise "Texas" Guinan from Waco, a thrice-married former circus bronco rider, vaudevillian and star of early two-reel Westerns, billed as "The Female Two-Gun Bill Hart." Less elegant, but as expensive as the Livingstone resort, Texas' El Fey Club at 107 West Forty-fifth Street, backed by the racketeer Larry Fay, netted $700,000 during its first year. Though El Fey featured a variety of bizarre entertainers, among them a girl calling herself Nerida, who danced with an eight-foot python twined about her nude torso, the stellar attraction was Texas herself, a calliope-voiced dyed blonde, sheathed in ermine and flashing a bracelet encrusted with almost 600 diamonds. Her *shtick* consisted of chaffing the customers. "Hello, sucker!" she would bellow at them as they entered, a greeting that became a catchphrase of the dry decade. "He's a good fellow!" she would exclaim, pointing to some blushing male, sitting with his wife. "But for another woman. . . . See that girl over there? I knew her when she was a bathing beauty—and she's still all wet. . . ." A "big butter-and-egg man," meaning a big spender from a small town, was another Guinan coinage. If the cash register failed to ring often enough, Texas would blow a whistle and raise her gravelly voice above the jazz band and the wooden clappers: "Come on, suckers, open up and spend some jack!" Texas Guinan's fortunes were already on the decline when, in 1933, a disgruntled doorman employed by Larry Fay at another speakeasy, Club Napoleon, put four bullets in him.

At the opposite pole from these opulent playgrounds was a vast outcropping of dives by comparison to which the vilest of the old-time saloons seemed benign. The raw liquor they dispensed at best seared the throat, at worst blinded or killed the consumer. The "shock houses" of the Bowery and the Lower East Side did not hesitate to serve wood alcohol when their stocks of less noxious beverages ran low. During the single year of 1928 the poison killed more than 700 people in the Bowery alone.

A man venturing alone into such dumps was a likely mark for an ancient swindle. A pretty girl would join him at the bar, eyes full of promise, and, pretending to let him ply her with drink, down glass after glass of colored water, all duly added to his bill at the price of the genuine article. When, thoroughly drunk, he had paid it and suggested they leave together, the temptress would ask him to wait and head for the ladies' room, not to reappear until he had collapsed or staggered away. Other common practices of the "creep joints" included padding the bill, with a beating by the bouncer if the victim protested too vigorously; raising the numbers on bank checks offered in payment; doctoring the rotgut with knockout drops and lifting the unconscious drinker's wallet; blackmailing men accompanied by women other than their wives. . . . In a speakeasy off lower Fifth Avenue, run by a veteran pickpocket named Charles Fern, a policeman who tried to rescue a prospective victim was shot dead. An ornate and seemingly respectable uptown resort, the Chantee Club was operated by a killer, Richard Whittemore, and staffed almost exclusively by felons, among them the brothers Jake and Leon Kraemer, whom the police ranked among the deftest safecrackers on record, also "Shuffles" Goldberg and Tony Paladino, equally distinguished as thieves. A fire eventually razed the Club Chantee, and Whittemore ended up on a Maryland gallows after murdering a man in Baltimore.

Between these upper and nether extremes there evolved an agglomeration of modest, relatively decent saloons and cafés selling drink by the glass or bottle at no great risk to the customer's health or wallet. In addition, a variety of establishments, most of them originally unconnected with the liquor traffic, began carrying liquor as a sideline. Without too taxing a search, it became possible to find a drink on almost any block in the city. The New York *Telegram* once assigned a team of reporters to investigate the availability of liquor in the borough of Manhattan alone. They managed to buy it in "dancing academies, drugstores, delicatessens, cigar stores, confectionaries, soda fountains, behind partitions of shoeshine parlors, back rooms of barbershops, from hotel bellhops, from hotel headwaiters, from hotel day clerks, night clerks, in express offices, in motorcycle delivery agencies, paint stores, malt shops, cider stubes, fruit stands, vegetable markets, groceries, smoke shops, athletic clubs, grillrooms, taverns, chophouses, importing firms, tearooms, moving-van companies, spaghetti houses, boarding-houses, Republican clubs, Democratic clubs, laundries, social clubs, newspapermen's associations."

The Lower East Side harbored two of the city's oddest speakeasies. One was a converted bowling alley running between Water and Cherry streets, with an address on both streets, a bar one hundred feet long and sixteen bartenders. The prohibition agents who raided it several times, to the inevitable cries of "Set 'em up in the other alley!," evidently failed to connect the two addresses, or so pretended, because they would padlock only one entrance. Then, after a discreet interval, the management would resume business as if at a different address, readmitting its customers through the unpadlocked door. The other speakeasy curiosity in the area was Duke's, on the second floor of a Division Street building. A professional pedicurist, Duke would administer foot care at no extra charge to any customer who desired it.

The diversity of receptacles used for carrying liquor home, to a sporting event, picnic or restaurant showed the resourcefulness of the drinker under pressure. Besides the conventional hip flask, without which no sophisticated collegian would be caught dead at a football game or debutante's coming-out party, there were dummy books, coconuts drained of their natural contents and replenished with liquor, boots expansible at the ankles, hollow canes, ladies' muffs, baby carriages with storage space beneath the baby, pants with extra large pockets.

When Chicago dry agents caught a banker named Charles Thomas with a flask in his hip pocket, the U.S. district court was asked whether his trousers should not be considered a vehicle and therefore subject to confiscation and sale at auction. After ponderous debate, the court ruled otherwise, merely fining the offender.

In certain New York social circles the line between hospitality and profit grew thin. The New York *Times* of June 6, 1922, reported:

> Many individuals, some prominent socially, have fitted up regular bars in their living apartments and have engaged drink mixers. The patronage is restricted to the set in which the owner of

the place moves. Several persons have greatly added to their
finances through the operation of the apartment bar. At some
places drinks of the best grade are sold for 40 to 50 cents.

Bootleggers were omnipresent. One of them went so far as to
scatter his handbills through the Federal Building, where, despite
the assurance of New York's chief revenue agent, Colonel Daniel
Porter, that nobody would be so foolhardy as to risk the drastic
penalties imposed by the Volstead Act, an average of 50,000
alleged violators were arraigned every year. In 1925 the Department of Justice appointed Emory S. Buckner U.S. Attorney for
the Southern District of New York. The following year Buckner
testified before a Senate subcommittee: "I found the fifth floor of
the Federal Building a seething mob of bartenders, peddlers,
waiters, bond runners, fixers. . . . Federal judges have told me
. . . that the whole atmosphere of the Federal Building was one
of pollution, that the air of corruption had even descended into
the civil parts of the court, and reports were made . . . of
attempts to bribe jurymen even in the toilets of the building."
In line with Section 2 of the Eighteenth Amendment ("The
Congress and the several states shall have concurrent power to
enforce this article by appropriate legislation") most states
enacted supplementary liquor laws. New York modeled its
Mullan-Gage Law, adopted in April, 1921, on the Volstead Act.
During the next three years the grand jury heard 6,904 cases. It
dismissed 6,074. Of those that went to trial only 20 ended in
convictions. Judge Alfred J. Talley of the Court of General
Sessions, who believed that as a result of prohibition, the United
States had become "the most lawless country on the face of the
earth," summoned the grand jurors to his chambers to ask them
why they so rarely returned an indictment. The foreman
explained: "The men tell me that they will not indict men for
offenses which they are committing themselves."

*Major Maurice E. Campbell remembers his woes as prohibition
administrator for the Eastern District of New York**
      *Tuesday, Oct. 25, 1927. Conference with Hotel Association of New
York City. Mr. Campbell mentioned about placing notices at the
elevators, and in the rooms, of the hotels calling attention of the hotel to*

* From Campbell's unpublished diary.

uphold the Prohibition law insofar as possible . . . *any infringement on the part of the clerks in knowingly and willfully serving ginger ale or cracked ice to a room where liquor is in prominence would be cause for immediate dismissal. . . .*

Friday, Dec. 9, 1927 . . . discussed with Tuttle [U.S. Attorney Charles Tuttle] *the advisability and plan of raiding a nightclub and hauling out all the furniture, etc. He thought it bad as a general principle but when I stated I wanted to do it as a horrible example, he thought that was good. . . .*

[On December 29 Campbell chose the Helen Morgan Club as his first horrible example, personally leading a raid in which his agents demolished the place and removed all the furniture. He acted without a warrant, citing as justification a federal statute under which the property of a person who had not paid the tax on liquor could be confiscated.]

Friday, Dec. 30, 1927. Most of the day I have been worried by reporters asking questions which I refused to answer.

Wed., Jan. 4, 1928. Had dinner at the Commodore Hotel with son looking for violations. . . . Not a sign of whiskey drinking at any table. Check $4.85; tip 50¢.

Friday, Jan. 6, 1928 . . . proceeded to the Parisian Restaurant, 304 West 56th Street, to make observations. The check was $3.65, tip 40¢; hat check 25¢. Observed three waiters serving liquor. . . .

Tuesday, Feb. 9, 1928 . . . I was being inundated with letters of complaint regarding Agent Kupferman shaking restaurants, etc. down. . . .

Tuesday, March 27, 1928. It seems there is considerable litigation between the [Washington Avenue Baptist Church] *congregation and this minister* [Reverend Robert McCaul] *in an effort to oust him from the church. Mr. Field* [an attorney] *told me that this preacher was now conducting a speakeasy in connection with a tailor in Brooklyn. . . .*

Oct. 2, 1928. 9:15 A.M. *Campbell to Brewery Squad: I don't want to have to watch you. It's most irksome to send a man out to do a job and then have to send somebody else to see that he does it; that's a hell of a situation. I told you you would have temptations, and I told you then that they would try to reach you—but it's up to you to stick fast. I have several men on the squad who I may have to relieve. . . . Stay on the job at the breweries as I told you—right at the door. . . . Let your presence be seen at all times. . . . Your instructions are to*

remain at the entrance of the brewery or exit; take samples of any
trucks. . . . Don't let any trucks get away without taking a sample.
   Saturday, Jan. 25, 1930. I went to the dinner at the St. Regis Hotel
of the Owl Alumni [an association of newspaper editors,
Campbell having formerly been city editor of the New York
Herald]. . . . *It was a very "wet" celebration; whiskey was displayed*
everywhere; a great many were drunk, and I withdrew at 10:30. . . .

The city, like most American cities, abounded in shops selling
malt, hops, wort, yeast, bottles, crown caps, capping machines,
rubber hosing, alcohol gauges and other paraphernalia for home
brewing. As an anonymous New York rhymster wrote:

> Mother's in the kitchen
> Washing out the jugs;
> Sister's in the pantry
> Bottling the suds;
> Father's in the cellar
> Mixing up the hops;
> Johnny's on the front porch
> Watching for the cops.

Around these homely activities there grew up a major
industry. Some economists believed that the sums expended for
brewing materials, especially malt syrup, absorbed a large part of
the average American household budget. In New York City
alone more than 500 malt and hops shops flourished, with almost
100,000 dispersed through the country, plus 25,000 outlets for
assorted home brewing apparatus. The national production of
malt syrup in 1926 and 1927 came close to 888,000,000 pounds.
Allowing a normal 10 percent for nonbrewing uses, enough
remained for 6.5 billion pints of beer. The available hops crop,
after export and the manufacture of near beer, was, according to
the estimate of Hugh F. Fox, an officer of the United Brewers'
Association, about 13,000,000 pounds. For malt, hops, sugar,
yeast and machinery, Fox further estimated, the consumer spent
$136,000,000.

In addition to the independent shops, the big food chains like
Kroger Grocery, Piggly-Wiggly and the A&P displayed great
pyramids of malt syrup cans. Such was the extent of the trade

that it gave rise to two associations of wholesalers and retailers, the National Association of Malt Syrup Manufacturers and the Interstate Products Association. The former published a monthly journal called *Sips.*

The courts had ruled that there was nothing inherently illegal in any of these products—not unless sold to make alcohol. Intent determined guilt or innocence. Accordingly, the associations obtained a ruling from the Patent Office defending malt syrup as a food, and they enjoined their members from running any ads that suggested guilty applications. One member manufacturer drew a severe rebuke for his ad illustrating the "food virtues" of malt syrup with a drunken camel leading a quartet of drunken camels in a rendition of "Sweet Adeline."

The end product of amateur brewing usually fell short of preprohibition standards. If the corks did not pop out or the bottles explode before their contents matured sufficiently to drink, you got a mud-brown liquid, smelling sourly of mash and tasting like laundry soap. As for the effect, one imbiber reported: "After I've had a couple of glasses I'm terribly sleepy. Sometimes my eyes don't seem to focus and my head aches. I'm not intoxicated, understand, merely feel as if I've been drawn through a knothole."

Basing its calculations on the sale of hops, malt, etc., the Prohibition Bureau estimated the quantity of beer brewed at home in 1929 to be almost 700,000,000 gallons.

In a store on lower Fifth Avenue, facing the Marble Collegiate Church, one of the Reformed Churches in America, whose general synod had declared itself "solidly and squarely back of . . . the Volstead Act," a salesgirl was demonstrating to a fascinated audience a new product. On the counter before her stood a brick of grape concentrate, a gallon glass jug and various accessories. "You dissolve the brick in a gallon of water," she explained, suiting the action to the words, "and it is ready to be used immediately." She then hastened to add some cautionary instructions:

"Do not place the liquid in this jug and put it away in the cupboard for twenty-one days, because then it would turn into wine.

"Do not stop the bottle with this cork containing this patented red rubber siphon hose, because that is necessary only when fermentation is going on.

"Do not put the end of the tube into a glass of water, because that helps to make the fermenting liquor tasty and potable.

"Do not shake the bottle once a day, because that makes the liquor work."

By the end of the day she had sold several hundred "blocks of port," "blocks of sherry," "blocks of Burgundy," and "blocks of Rhine wine," or, to use the popular generic term, "bricks of Bacchus," which, if her warnings were ignored, would produce a beverage with an alcoholic content of 13 percent.

Section 29 of the Volstead Act, permitting the manufacture and possession of fruit juices for home consumption (under a later stipulation, up to 200 gallons per household), had been framed mainly to appease the farmer. But it proved a boon to viticulture. The California grape grower who killed himself, believing he faced ruin, could scarcely have imagined that during the next five years in his state alone grape acreage would expand sevenfold from 97,000 to 681,000. Similar increases benefited the four other leading grape states—Michigan, Ohio, Pennsylvania and New York. The produce reached the customers as fresh grapes, bricks of Bacchus or grape juice, the last labeled CAUTION: WILL FERMENT AND TURN INTO WINE. From 1925 to 1929 Americans drank more than 678,000,000 gallons of home-fermented wine, three times as much as all the domestic and imported wine they drank during the five years before prohibition. This figure did not include the wine made from backyard vineyards, from dandelion, currants, cherries and other fruits. Like home brew, winemaking stimulated the manufacture of numerous related products—grape crushers, winepresses, fermenting tubes, gelatine to settle the sediment, crocks, kegs and bungs, bottles and corks—on which the home winemakers spent about $220,000,000 a year.

Far simpler than brewing beer or fermenting wine at home was distilling alcohol. One primitive method called for nothing more than a little corn sugar mash, a tea kettle and a bath towel. The home distiller would heat the mash inside the kettle over a slow fire. Alcohol volatilizes at between 180° and 200° Fahrenheit and as the mash gave off its fumes, he would drape the towel over the kettle spout to absorb them. When he cooled the towel and wrung it out, it would yield a few drops of a vile-tasting but potent liquid. With patience he could collect enough to jollify the whole household. Steam cookers, coffee percolators and wash boilers were also commonly used as receptacles for mash. But at a cost of only $5 or $6 the home distiller could buy the more sophisticated portable one-gallon copper still. For technical guidance he needed only visit the public library, where he would find books and trade periodicals devoted to the subject. A series of *Farmer's Bulletins* published by the government between 1906 and 1910 and still available for the asking would show him how to distill alcohol from fruits of all sorts, from grain, sugar beets, potato peelings. Once he had a batch of alcohol, he could quickly and simply simulate almost any desired type of liquor with additives. To produce a large quantity of gin, he would combine alcohol, water, glycerine and juniper oil in a bathtub. Because it was cheap and its taste readily disguised in cocktails, "bathtub gin" enjoyed considerable popularity during the early years of prohibition, as indicated by the sudden increase of juniper oil imports. Most of it came from Italy and Austria and served little purpose outside of flavoring gin. An ounce sufficed to flavor several gallons. In 1920 almost 9,000 pints were imported; in 1925, almost 11,000.

By 1921 the one-gallon still had become a commonplace domestic utensil, and over some sections of the big cities the reek of sour mash hung like a miasma. "The worst crime a child can commit," said Will Rogers, "is to eat up the raisins that Dad brought home for fermenting purposes." The bloodthirsty, bootlegging Genna brothers of Chicago's "Little Italy" hired hundreds of its immigrant slum dwellers as "alky cookers" at $15 a day, installing stills in their kitchens and supplying them with the ingredients and operating directions. In New York City, as early as the second week of prohibition, home distillation was so widespread that a squad of federal agents were assigned to what the first prohibition administrator for the district, Charles O'Connor, called "the greatest campaign ever conducted against violation of the prohibition law." O'Connor advised every New Yorker with a still to surrender it to him or risk jail. Nobody responded. At the same time commercial stills, priced around $500, were producing 50 to 100 gallons a day at a cost of 50 cents a gallon and selling at $3 or $4. With only 178 agents to police more than 1,000,000 New York homes, seizures were few.

Wet though his constituency was, New York's Democratic Congressman Emanuel Celler rose in wrath when Assistant U.S. Attorney Mabel Walker Willebrandt singled it out as an example of extreme lawlessness. "During my six years in Washington [1923-29]," he said, "I have witnessed more drinking in the national capital than in New York."

Bootleggers roamed the Senate and House office buildings, doing business almost openly with the occupants. For three years the police tried to identify a bootlegger named George Cassidy known to them only as "the man in the green hat," who fled the House corridors after dropping a briefcase and breaking the liquor bottles it contained. They finally caught Cassidy on the steps of the building as he was about to deliver some more whiskey.

Under the Capitol dome itself, a few steps from the chamber where Congress passed the Volstead Act, there nestled a small, inconspicuous room, furnished with half a dozen chairs, an empty desk and book-lined shelves. It was designated "the Board of Education" room, but initiates knew it better as "the Library." What took place there bore scant relation to either education or literature. Set up jointly by Congressmen Nicholas Longworth, Republican of Ohio, and John Nance Garner, Democrat of Texas, whose common fondness for whiskey enabled them to surmount their political antagonism, it provided a snug retreat to which they and a selected group of their associates could conveniently withdraw from the hurly-burly of legislative debate and refresh themselves with a draft. The books concealed an abundance of liquor.

"Senators and representatives," attested Mrs. Willebrandt, "have appeared on the floor of the Senate and the House in a drunken condition. During the closing days of a recent session, one senator objected to and prevented the passage of important legislation while in such a condition that he had to hold to his desk to keep himself upright."

Following the 1926 Senatorial elections a New York stockbroker named William Fahey invited the victorious candidates to a dinner in a private room at Washington's New Willard Hotel "just to get acquainted." Senator Smith Wildman Brookhart of Iowa, a vehement dry, was scandalized by the gift Fahey pressed upon his guests. He bade them lift the cloth that covered a large table at one end of the room and help themselves to what they found there. Underneath the cloth was an array of silver hip flasks filled with whiskey. Brookhart, who walked out, later expressed his indignation on the Senate floor, though he refrained from naming any of his colleagues who accepted a flask.

The dry block numbered a good many legislators with no personal aversion to booze. Illinois' Republican Congressman M. Alfred Michaelson, who voted for harsher penalties than those imposed by the Volstead Act, was a notable example. In January, 1928, he landed at Key West from a West Indies cruise ship, accompanied by his wife, brother-in-law and two Chicago friends. Granted free entry privileges upon his assurance that nobody's baggage contained any liquor, he got fourteen pieces through without examination. En route north by railroad, a trunk sprang a leak, causing it to be held for inspection by prohibition agents. Inside they found thirteen bottles of whiskey. Another trunk, specially constructed to accommodate it, yielded a ten-gallon keg of rum. Michaelson stood trial in a federal court, but thanks to his brother-in-law, who swore the liquor-laden trunks belonged to him, he was acquitted. Indicted in his turn, the brother-in-law pleaded guilty and got off with a $1,000 fine. The following year leaking luggage brought another dry legislator, Republican Congressman Edward Everett Denison of Ohio, to grief, after he returned from a winter jaunt to Panama. Tipped off by the railway express employee who handled the Congressman's baggage, two agents visited his office and from the trunk which had been delivered there removed thirty quarts of assorted liquor. Denison, too, went to trial, but the jury accepted his defense that he was "the innocent victim of a mistaken shipment." Among the hardest drinking, dry-voting legislators were some of the Deep Southerners whose chief concern was to keep liquor away from the black lest it impair his capacity for cheaply paid work.

In the fall of 1922 the whiskey-loving President Harding called a conference of state governors for the following spring to formulate more efficient methods of enforcing the law. A gesture calculated to retain his dry support, it drew a scornful speech in the House from Congressman William David Upshaw of Georgia, a co-founder of his state's Anti-Saloon League:

> If these governors . . . really wish to get anywhere, let them remember what the beloved and immortal Sam Jones [the Georgia evangelist] said: "If you want to reform the world, begin on yourself, and then you will have one rascal out of the way."

. . . Let the President issue a ringing proclamation calling every
citizen, and especially every official, to total abstinence. Too many
of these officials are striking a grandiose posture and calling upon
the people with tears in their eyes to respect and honor the laws of
our nation, and then going the back way and buying blind-tiger
bootleg whiskey for their personal consumption. . . .

Equally incensed by the ubiquity of the Capitol bootleggers,
Kansas' dry Republican Senator Charles Curtis announced: "No
influence, however strong, will protect a bootlegger hereafter
from arrest and prosecution if he invades the Senate end of the
Capitol or the Senate office building." Even as he spoke, the
Senate restaurant resounded with the crash of a whiskey bottle
that had slipped from the grasp of a clumsy waiter.

Hard upon Senator Curtis' battle cry, the police arrested one
of Washington society's favorite bootleggers, dashing young
Raymond "Razor" Gray, a stockbroker by legitimate trade. In
his apartment they uncovered 500 quarts, together with correspondence and account books listing numerous Congressmen and
Senators among his steady customers. All of them, the books
indicated, were awaiting deliveries for the approaching Christmas holidays.

To the treasurer of the Republican National Committee, Fred
Upham, fell the task of procuring whiskey for the White House,
where twice a week the President played poker and drank with
his cronies of the Ohio gang, comprising some of the most
rapacious grafters ever to hold high government office. Upham
did not have to look far. According to the Consolidated Press
Association's Washington correspondent, David Lawrence, at
least 500 bootleggers operated within rifle shot of the White
House.

But not even the White House was better provisioned than the
"little green house" at 1625 K Street, the rented home of
Harding's old campaign manager, Howard Mannington, and
the meeting place of the Ohio gang, headed by Attorney General
Harry M. Daugherty. Privileges of many kinds were for sale at
No. 1625, and through the green-trimmed door passed a
procession of eager buyers—aspirants to judicial office, tax-delin-
quent businessmen, lawyers seeking pardons or parole for jailed
clients. . . . When the police took Razor Gray into custody, his
lawyer threatened to complain to Attorney General Daugherty
should any delay occur in granting his release on bail. None did.

By 1922 the government held roughly 138,000,000 gallons of pre-1920 liquor in 296 bonded warehouses. It still belonged to the original owners who had been compelled by the Eighteenth Amendment to deposit it there, but they could not remove a drop without government authorization and then only for nonbeverage use or export. Occasionally thieves of exceptional skill and daring would loot a government warehouse.

Morris "Red" Rudensky, ex-convict, ex-thief, remembers his biggest haul

I was on the lam at the time from the Illinois State Penitentiary at Menard, where I'd been doing ten years to life for bank robbery. I'd been apprenticed to a master locksmith before I became a gonif, and although I was only twenty-one, I was considered the best box man in the country.

I headed for Chicago to meet up with the team I'd worked with on heists all over the Midwest. There was Smitty Krueger, a box man like me; Dago Mike Vanelli, an electrician and a genius at defusing alarm systems; and a Spaniard named Sauro, another ace electrician. Shortly after I got to Chicago, I met the Big Fellow himself—Al Capone—in Colosimo's café. We pulled off a few small capers for him, among others—we were strictly free lance—but we wanted something really big to swing on our own. Then we learned about this government whiskey warehouse in St. Louis that covered about ten acres. It stood a couple of blocks from police headquarters, but that didn't bother us. We moved to St. Louis.

For financial backing we went to an Irish fence known as the Commissioner, who had important political and underworld connections in six states and kept dozens of bootleggers supplied. He guaranteed to take all the whiskey we could heist at 40 percent of its value in the bootleg market.

We spent six months figuring out the logistics. I got a job in the warehouse, unloading barrels. The freight elevators to the basement storage vaults were electrically operated, and as a security measure the guards disconnected them at night.

There were two armed guards on duty at night, a watchman, a maintenance man and a checker. During a few beer-drinking sessions with the guards I learned enough about them, their family problems and so forth, to know they could be bought. They finally agreed to take a $75,000 cut each. The only people they were supposed to let into the warehouse outside of employees were cops. So to get them off the hook in case they were suspected, we decided to wear cops' uniforms and leave some phony evidence behind like a badge or a sergeant's cap. We would also gag and rope the guards.

The night watchman, the maintenance man and the checker we planned to handle differently. Smitty had arranged to bring in some mobsters from Chicago who would hold their guns on those three and walk the rounds with them, making sure they punched their clocks at the right times.

Dago Mike, meantime, made a deal with a racketeer trucker for a dozen trucks at $5,000 per plus $2,000 to every driver and loader. He also drew a plan of the warehouse, incorporating the inside details I gave him, the surrounding territory for nine blocks in every direction, and the truck routes.

For the actual heist we rehearsed almost fifty recruits. They included, besides the backfield—Mike, Smitty, Sauro and me—six Chicago hoods, twelve truck drivers, twelve loaders, the two bribed guards and a couple of extra lookouts.

Come eleven o'clock of the night we'd picked, we each took up a different position within fifteen minutes' driving time from the target and headed for it separately. That way we wouldn't draw attention. We posted our lookouts outside the main gate and on the roofs of buildings behind and in front of the warehouse. As the trucks rolled through the shipping yard and backed up to the loading platforms, the hoods, wearing cops' uniforms, moved into the warehouse quick and quiet, faked a few blows with their gun butts at the bribed guards, trussed them up and went looking for the other night employees. While they held them up, Mike and Sauro got the freight elevators going, and I dropped down to the basement, lugging my bag of tools. They were the most sophisticated boxman's tools obtainable and with them plus a little soup [nitroglycerine], when necessary, I could open the standard government steel vault door in under ten minutes. I did that and walked through to row after row of 50-gallon barrels of whiskey.

It took slightly over two hours to load the trucks to capacity. They delivered the stuff the same night to the Commissioner's warehouses. The final count was more than 2,000 barrels, top quality all of it. My share of the payoff came to nearly $100,000.

Because the amounts of liquor in bond appeared insufficient to meet all legitimate needs, the government allowed a few selected companies to resume limited production. Whiskey distilled for medicinal use between 1920 and 1923, when no more was authorized, totaled, in round numbers, 130,000,000 gallons. The distillation of rum (used in tobacco products) and brandy (medicaments and certain food products), which never stopped, amounted to 7,000,000 and 8,000,000 gallons respectively during the first nine years of prohibition. Almost 14,000,000 gallons of wine were distributed for therapeutic use to doctors and druggists or for sacramental rites to rabbis, priests and ministers. During the same period commercial brewers legally produced more than a billion gallons of beer with the understanding that they would convert it to near beer by reducing the alcoholic content. But only the brewer's conscience could oblige him to emasculate his product. Short of keeping a twenty-four-hour watch on each of hundreds of breweries, the government could not control the output. Even if the brewer chose to obey the law, it was a simple matter for the distributor or purchaser to restore the original strength by spiking the barrels with alcohol. Needle beer became a staple of the era.

Among the most coveted documents of the dry era was the "Permit for Withdrawal," the open sesame to stores of good liquor. President Harding named as Commissioner of Internal Revenue an abstemious Quaker from North Carolina, David Blair. While waiting for Congress to confirm the choice, he was persuaded by Representative John W. Langley, who had served continuously as a legislator for seventeen years, to appoint one Millard F. West Acting Commissioner. In 1921, within weeks of West's deputization, he gave Langley permits to withdraw 4,000 cases of whiskey. Langley then sold them at $24 a case, a total of $196,000, to various co-conspirators, who withdrew the whiskey for medicinal use from the Belle Anderson Distillery near Lawrenceburg, Kentucky, and diverted it into bootleg channels. After a two-year investigation by the Intelligence Unit of the IRS, all those involved were indicted. The case against West collapsed, the purchasers of the permits pleaded guilty and received light sentences, but Congressman Langley drew two years in the Atlanta penitentiary.

While Langley was appealing the verdict, the voters showed

what they thought of prohibition by reelecting him. But when the court of appeals confirmed the verdict, he resigned and departed for Atlanta.

For Washingtonians of modest resources there was a deluge of regionally distilled moonshine. "Hardly a day passes," Assistant U.S. Attorney Mabel Willebrandt disclosed, "that either police or prohibition agents do not make a sizable seizure of moonshine liquor flowing in from the stills in nearby Maryland and Virginia." As an example, she cited a single haul of 3,000 quarts of Maryland "corn" which had been temporarily stored in a garage. Since the number of Washington's incorruptible police and prohibition agents combined composed a force too small for the Augean cleanup demanded of it, the amounts they managed to intercept represented but a trifling fraction of what eluded them. Arrests for drunkenness in the District of Columbia totaled 3,565 at the outset of prohibition. Four years later the figure was 9,149.

Pittsburgh ale lovers prided themselves on the quality of the Canadian brands available locally and cheerfully paid 75 cents to $1 a bottle. But pride turned to dismay when prohibition agents traced the source to a wildcat brewery operating in an abandoned slaughterhouse. The brewers printed the Canadian labels on their own press. If the product had a distinctive flavor, as the Pittsburghers maintained, it was perhaps attributable to the receptacles used as ferment vats. These were the old wooden tubs in which the slaughterers dipped the carcasses of hogs before skinning them. Until raided, the brewery, along with seven others scattered around the Pittsburgh area, produced 10,000 gallons of ale and beer a day.

The standard Pittsburgh hard drink was "mooney," a corn sugar alcohol of low quality but high potency, manufactured by stills in the central and western regions of Pennsylvania. During one seven-month period, from September, 1925, to March, 1926, prohibition agents destroyed 208 stills, which together had been producing about 70,000 gallons a day, without seriously depleting the market. Until 1926 the price in Pittsburgh was $2 a gallon. Then "administration booze," so called because of the political protection its distillers and distributors enjoyed, entered the market, selling at $4 a gallon. It was still mooney, though of even lower quality. When left standing, a green scum would form on the surface. Speakeasy operators who yielded to their customers' complaints and switched back to the old stuff were promptly padlocked. If they wished to stay in business, they not only had to sell administration booze but buy a fixed weekly quantity.

To fake brand liquors, the Pittsburgh bootleggers would sometimes use genuine whiskey or highly diluted gin, sometimes wood alcohol and sometimes corn sugar alcohol. The district prohibition administrator, Frederick C. Baird, testifying before a Senate subcommittee in 1926, described the basic procedures as followed by two sham drugstores:

> . . . they will take . . . one pint bottle of good rye whiskey, and by the addition of so much alcohol, so much water, with caramel, and a few other ingredients, they will convert that one pint into two and a half quarts of synthetic whiskey. Then it is re-bottled, labels can be printed that are just as good as were ever printed, and counterfeit stamps are to be had that are a perfect duplicate of all the best that the government ever did print. So one pint is converted into five.

With wood alcohol, Baird explained:

> They can reduce the poison from five per cent to one per cent. When the one per cent is further reduced by the addition of an equal quantity of water to make synthetic whiskey, it is only then one-half of one per cent wood alcohol.
>
> You sent in an order for gin, and they would open a spigot on this big tank, run out so much alcohol, and so much water, and so much flavoring extract and coloring fluid and throw that into the gin. If you wanted a case of Scotch, open the same spigot, run the recovered denatured alcohol into a container in whatever quantity they wanted, the addition of water, a few drops of creosote or essence of Scotch, and a little caramel, and it would come to the bench for Scotch. The next man would come in for a famous old brand of rye. Open the same spigot, draw their alcohol, and that would come to the rye bench.

Senator James A. Reed of Missouri, an antiprohibitionist, asked the witness in mock horror: "They were even sacrilegious enough to undertake to imitate good old bourbon?"

"Exactly. And the only difference was in the coloring and the flavoring and the label."

In 1928 a federal grand jury returned indictments against 167 Pittsburghers for their involvement in a politico-criminal ring believed to control the city's entire liquor traffic. They included a county judge, two magistrates, the superintendent of police, three police inspectors, the chief county detective, a special county detective, eight constables, five Republican ward chairmen, a former deputy collector of Internal Revenue and numerous racketeers. All charges were dropped when the assistant U.S. attorney handling the case told the court he doubted that he could successfully prosecute it, by which he probably meant that the government's prospective witnesses no longer dared testify for fear of reprisals.

In southern Alabama, where sugarcane abounds, the intoxicant of choice was "shinney," distilled, like rum, from molasses and water. Householders in the area stopped buying zinc garbage cans because as fast as they set them out, the shinney distillers would steal them, having discovered that they made excellent stills. The Mobile press complained that they were also denuding the city's storm sewers of their iron grates on which to stand the stills over a fire.

One of San Francisco's largest speakeasies, the Blue Fox, operated unmolested on Merchant Street, directly opposite the building that housed both the Hall of Justice and the City Jail.

In Los Angeles, as in other cities with large Jewish communities, the diversion of sacramental wine from bonded wine storage seriously breached the prohibition dam. Neither the Protestant nor Catholic churches required much wine. Most Protestant denominations used unfermented grape juice. But in deference to Jewish ritual the Prohibition Bureau allowed each adult member of a Jewish family a gallon of wine a year, the total not to exceed five gallons. The rabbis obtained the withdrawal permits releasing amounts according to the size of their congregations. The great majority strictly observed the law, but a few reported congregations either larger than they actually had or nonexistent and bootlegged the wine thus procured. In some instances the celebrants themselves abetted the rabbi. At the outset of prohibition, for example, the congregation of Los Angeles' Talmud Torah Synagogue numbered 180. Within fourteen months almost 1,000 new members had joined, many of them impelled, it would seem, by a desire less than spiritual. In the spring of 1921 the majority voted to oust their Rabbi Gardner, not, according to him, for any violation of the Volstead Act, but quite the reverse. "They kept calling for wine, wine and more wine," said he as he took his leave, "and because I could not and would not supply it, they tried to break up the congregation."

In June, 1920, 200 Massachusetts Republicans left Boston aboard a special train bound for their national convention in Chicago. The train was routed through the Ontario peninsula, crossing the border back into the states at Windsor. There a sharp-nosed Customs inspector named Graham boarded it. In the first car he removed a dozen pints of whiskey and gin from the persons of festive Bay Staters. Putting down his haul, he proceeded to examine their baggage. When he turned around, the bottles had vanished. The remaining passengers, meanwhile, alerted by the cries of anguish from the first car, stowed their contraband so cunningly that though Graham held up the train for an hour, he could find no more than a small suitcase filled with miniature bottles and a few scattered quarts of whiskey. The voyagers included most of Massachusetts' thirty-five delegates to the convention, many of them political drys.

and in villages

". . . we found," Father Francis Kasaczun, pastor of Holy Family Church at Sugar Notch, Pennsylvania, told the Senate subcommittee, "that conditions have been very much corrupted amongst the mining families from previous times. Before prohibition the head of the family went to the saloon and drank, and at times got drunk, especially around pay day. Came home and had a little quarrel with his wife, and after a few strong remarks from one side or the other it blew over, settled their troubles, but at least the children were not the victims as they are today of prohibition.

"Saloons have been in some larger towns of the anthracite region closed, padlocked, but in the suburban towns I do not recollect of any of the saloons being closed. In my little town,

Sugar Notch, all the saloons are still open. In addition they have opened up pool rooms, cigar stores, lunch rooms, and candy stores where they sell hard liquors.

"And you can find stills in practically every other home. They make it, they drink it, they sell it. Anywhere from $1.50 a quart to $2.50 a quart. The private families that make it sell it. In some cases they sell it to the saloon keeper.

". . . [the stills] are copper kettles with a whole lot of coils, and the women folks take care of that. The men are at work, and the women folks take care of it. Drink it themselves, and in very many cases the children drink.

"Now, never in my occupation as a Catholic clergyman have I found children drinking hard liquors. I have never found the youth, anywhere from fourteen years old to eighteen or nineteen that drank hard liquors. And now you see children drink. You see them drunk. I have seen them drunk myself. There were a few children last year found drunk in the schools of the towns, public schools, and had bottles of it in their pockets. Last year there was a girl around fourteen in the town arrested drunk. . . . The school teachers have been complaining about children coming to school under the influence of liquor. . . .

"And, of course, the women are taking to it . . . and you can imagine the results. They are unfaithful to their husbands. I know of cases where women have run away with other men, especially with the star boarders, leaving the children behind without any care . . . and I have also seen cases . . . where one man went insane, and also one married woman went insane. . . .

"And we also find that young girls, anywheres from thirteen, fourteen years old, love to go out riding, and expect the boys that take them out to treat them with liquor. They do not think they are sports and they do not care to go with them unless they can take them somewhere where they can get it . . . and immorality amongst the youngsters in the anthracite region is on the increase very, very much . . . prohibition has made itself very attractive to the youngsters. They hear so much about it, they read so much about it, and they think there must be something in it, and they think, 'We have got to try it out for ourselves.' . . .

"The people make it usually around Christmas, around Easter, just before a christening, before a wedding, and in some cases before a funeral. . . . I asked one of my committee . . .

whether I could safely say that one out of five homes was making and drinking moonshine. 'Why,' he said, 'Father, you can safely say that one out of five homes are not making moonshine.' "

Senator Sheppard, who introduced the bill proposing the Eighteenth Amendment, owned a farm near the aptly named Jollyville, Texas. Barely eight months after the passage of the bill, he learned that the farm harbored a still with a daily capacity of 130 gallons.

nor hauled in anything on the face of the earth

From Canada chiefly, but also from Mexico, liquor flowed across the borders in a stanchless deluge. Under fake bills of lading, deceptively packaged and often with the connivance of Customs officials and shipping clerks, it entered the States by railroad, truck, passenger vehicle, speedboat. The smugglers plumed themselves on their ability to devise new tricks of concealment as fast as the old ones were exposed. Since long before prohibition, for example, there had been a brisk business in blocks of ice shipped for domestic refrigeration from Ontario to the American border communities. One gang of smugglers conceived the idea of forming such blocks around unlabeled bottles of gin and alcohol. They made several profitable trips until, partway across Lake Huron, the weather turned unseasonably warm, thawing the ice and sending the bottles rolling all over the cargo hold. Another gang would drive into Michigan wearing priests' habits and so were permitted by a reverent Customs service to proceed without examination. One day a tire blew out just as they were pulling away. An inspector offered to help, but the sweetly smiling driver assured him he could manage alone. As he struggled to pry off the flat tire, an unpriestly exasperation got the upper hand. "God damn this son of a bitch!" said he, causing the inspector to search the car. He found bottles under the seat, the hood and the chassis. Petty smugglers transported smaller quantities in the many, extra-deep pockets of specially tailored clothing, in lengths of rubber tubing stoppered at both ends and wound around their waists, in hot-water bottles, Christmas trees, barrels floated or towed shore to shore, bundles

of textiles and handicraft strapped to the backs of pack animals.
. . . At the Buffalo end of the International Bridge, spanning the
Niagara River, Customs officials once caught a returning citizen
with two dozen eggs which he had emptied through a small hole,
refilled with Canadian whiskey and sealed.

Canada interposed no obstacles. The profits it anticipated
through its neighbor's new law proved too tempting, and though
all nine provinces had enacted statutes between 1900 and 1917
prohibiting the sale of intoxicants within their borders, by 1921
only one, Prince Edward Island, had retained them. The
majority substituted some form of dispensary system whereby
their government bought liquor from the manufacturer and sold
it through approved stores. As for the dominion government,
except for two years during the World War, it had never
prohibited the manufacture, interprovincial transportation, export or import of liquor. Throughout most of the country, liquor
became a legal commodity. The smuggler committed no offense
until his purchase touched American soil, a problem of no
concern to Canadians.

Their expectations of vastly increased liquor revenue were not
dashed. According to their Customs records, whiskey exports to
the United States rose from 8,335 gallons (almost $11,000,000
worth) in 1921 to 1,169,002 (almost $19,000,000 worth) in 1928.
The value of all liquor cleared for the United States in 1928
exceeded $26,000,000. These figures were not comprehensive. An
enormous amount entered the States of which Canadian Customs had no record. The U.S. Department of Commerce put the
total for the years 1921–1923 at $90,000,000, an estimate U.S.
Customs considered too low. On the stock exchange the value of
shares in Canada's four biggest liquor companies showed a net
gain of $73,000,000 or about 315 percent, while the dominion
treasury took in millions of dollars from liquor export taxes.

As a good neighborly gesture, Canada and Mexico signed
conventions in 1925 obligating them to withhold clearances of
liquor cargoes unless export declarations were submitted and to
inform American officials of any such cargoes bound for the
United States. This did not curtail smuggling. Often the
information was received too late to intercept the contraband. To
avoid identification upon reaching the American side, the
smugglers would file false license and registry numbers of their
vehicles. In 1926 General Lincoln C. Andrews, whom Calvin

Coolidge had appointed Assistant Secretary of the Treasury in charge of prohibition enforcement, reckoned that of all the liquor smuggled into the United States since 1920 less than 5 percent had been seized.

When Washington accused Canada of bad faith, the dominion government suggested it look to its own Customs inspectors, whose frequent dereliction of duty was observable from the Canadian shore of the Detroit River. Here where the river ran only half a mile wide was the gateway through which passed most of the smuggled liquor. On May 21, 1929, the Minister of National Revenue, William D. Euler, told the House of Commons:

> I took the trouble last fall to go down to Windsor. . . . I could see the United States Customs office on the other shore, and I could also see that it was not difficult to detect any boats that left the Canadian shore to go to the American side. . . . I got into conversation with a man engaged in the business of exporting liquor. I asked him, "Do you cross in the daytime?" He answered, "Yes, quite often." I said, "How is it they do not get you?" He replied with a smile, "It just happens that they are not there when we go across." Our inspector went to Windsor not so very long ago. He observed the following vessels cross the river to Detroit in daylight with cargoes of liquor. [There followed a list, compiled from clearance records, of six boats, with cargoes totaling 15 quarter barrels and 5 half barrels of beer, 104 cases of whiskey, 6 cases of wine and 4 cases of brandy.] That was in one day.

The minister then read a report from the Canadian revenue collector at Ontario:

> There are about 12 boats plying between here and Buffalo. . . . The liquor and ale are brought from the distillery and brewery by truck, arriving here about two o'clock in the afternoon. The boats are all loaded and clearance granted about five P.M. and they are compelled to leave by six P.M. Some of these boats carry from eight hundred to one thousand cases, and on their arrival on the American side it takes from two to three hours to unload them. No effort as far as we can see is made by the United States authorities to seize any of these boats, as the United States Customs are always notified by us an hour or two before the boats leave. . . . Our officers who check these boats out were informed by one of the rum runners that they had no trouble in landing their cargo,

as they were assisted by the officers of the dry squad on the American side. . . . These boats are loaded directly opposite from the United States Customs office at Block Rock. You can stand by the window and see every case that is loaded on the Canadian side. I know that if conditions were reversed, we would have all these boats tied up in less than a week, and if the officers on the American side wished to put a stop to this business they could do it in about the same length of time.

Canada signed a new convention in 1930, calling for stricter controls, and U.S. Customs reinforced the northern border patrols. It made little difference. The smugglers still got through.

On a February morning in 1921 the *Henry L. Marshall*, a 90-foot black-hulled fishing schooner, glided out of Nassau Harbor before a steadily blasting trade wind. Her crew, recruited a few days earlier in the waterfront dives of Jacksonville, Florida, consisted of seven tough veteran seafarers, all of them drunk after a carousal ashore. Her skipper and owner, who never touched liquor, was William McCoy, a bronzed Floridian, standing six feet two, with the shoulders of a fullback. The schooner's hold carried a full-capacity cargo—1,500 cases of scotch.

At West End, on Grand Bahama Island, McCoy moored long enough to obtain a duplicate set of clearance papers from a complacent British Customs officer. He would produce them in the event the U.S. Coast Guard challenged the schooner. They certified her to be sailing for Savannah, Georgia, "in ballast"— that is, without any cargo.

Three days later the *Henry L. Marshall* stumbled through a howling gale into the mouth of St. Catherine's Sound, twenty miles below Savannah, and anchored at the edge of a bayou. By prearrangement with the owner of the cargo, a friend of McCoy's named William Hain, who had agreed to pay him $10 a case, lighters chuffed out to meet her under cover of night and before dawn had conveyed the liquor to shore. A week after leaving Nassau, McCoy was back, the richer by $15,000.

Such was McCoy's initial rum-running venture. During the next four years, averaging a delivery a month—a grand total of 175,000 cases, mainly scotch and rye, worth, after cutting, more than $70,000,000—he became a living legend. Though his claim to have founded the coastal Rum Row between Atlantic City

and New York may have been exaggerated, he was unquestiona-
bly its most audacious and successful navigator, a shining knight
to the drinking man and a bane to the coastguardsmen he
repeatedly outwitted. On his second voyage from the Bahamas,
McCoy landed the first big liquor cargo there, 1,500 cases of Old
Grand-Dad rye. He pioneered the New England area as well and
established the French possessions of St. Pierre and Miquelon
islands, off Newfoundland, as sources of supply rivaling Nassau.
"Mine was the first rumrunning ship ever to reach St. Pierre," he
boasted. "Since then it [the liquor trade] has brought the
inhabitants of that formerly poverty-stricken island millions of
dollars."

He developed new techniques for handling the contraband,
notably the packaging known as a ham, sack, or burlock. He
would arrange the bottles, protected by straw or corrugated
cardboard sheaths, in pyramids of six each—three on the bottom,
two in the middle, one on top—and wrapped in burlap sewn fast
with twine. By thus eliminating the bulky wooden cases, McCoy
found he could stow a third again as many bottles. According to
some etymologists, the expression "the real McCoy" commemo-
rates the high quality of the rum-runner's merchandise.* He
compared himself to the signer of the Declaration of Independence John Hancock, who, in McCoy's words, "smuggled liquor
and silk and other things, and grew richer at his nefarious trade
than I did. In the eyes of the law as it stood at the time he was a
bigger crook than I, for he resisted the government on other
counts as well."

What chiefly set McCoy apart from the majority of his fellow
contrabandists was his freedom from the control of gangsters.
While he had no reluctance to sell them liquor, he kept himself
independent, sailing Rum Row as much for adventure as profit.
He prided himself on never paying a cent for protection to any
racketeer, politician or law enforcement agent. "Dealings of that
sort would have killed the sport of the game for me," he said.
Deploring violence, he once saved a U.S. Treasury investigator

* The origin remains in dispute. Others say it derives from Kid McCoy, the world
welterweight champion (1898–1900). Supposedly, a drunkard, doubting the prizefighter's
identity, picked a quarrel with him and upon regaining consciousness exclaimed: "It's the
real McCoy!" In another version the phrase stems from a junkie's mispronunciation of
the notorious Far Eastern seaport Macao when appraising a supply of pure heroin—"It's
the real Macao."

who had come to Nassau to entrap him from annihilation by some Bahamian cutthroats.

McCoy was born in Seneca Falls, New York, and reared in Philadelphia, the second son of a bricklayer. Enamored of the sea from early boyhood, he enrolled as a cadet aboard the Pennsylvania training ship *Saratoga*, graduating first in his class and receiving a third mate's license. After a stretch with the merchant marine he rejoined his family, who had moved to Jacksonville, and with his brother Ben began building yachts for millionaires, among them the Vanderbilts, John Wanamaker and Andrew Carnegie. They also opened a motorboat transport service.

Not long after prohibition started, a Floridian whom McCoy had known as a down-at-heels fisherman drove into the boatyard behind the wheel of a new roadster, his necktie ablaze with a diamond stickpin. He owned a schooner, he explained, which was under contract to haul a cargo of rye from Nassau to Atlantic City and he would pay McCoy $100 a day to skipper her. McCoy declined, but the brothers' motorboat service had failed and the need to find a new means of livelihood drew him to Nassau. It was to be his headquarters for four years.

The capital of the British crown colony was entering its third great era of prosperity since the mid-eighteenth century. It had first served as a base for both slave traders and freebooters, then, during the American Civil War, for blockade runners to the Confederacy. Two young Scots named MacPherson inaugurated the third boom when they imported 1,000 cases of scotch to Nassau from their mother country for transshipment to the United States. At first the island authorities professed moral indignation. They even considered legal action against the MacPhersons until they stopped to think that for each case imported His Majesty's Customs collected $6. The MacPhersons were allowed to carry on. Such an infestation of outlaws followed as the island had not witnessed since the heyday of the pirate, Blackbeard.*

Returning to Jacksonville, McCoy sold the motorboats with his brother's consent and for $16,000 acquired the *Henry L. Marshall*, the first of five schooners which he placed under British

---

* The tycoons operating along Nassau's main thoroughfare, Bay Street, are still sometimes called "the Bay Street pirates."

BISHOP JAMES CANNON

". . . did not like many people."

(United Press International)

CONGRESSMAN ANDREW JOSEPH VOLSTEAD

"Law does regulate morality. . . ."

At President Coolidge's shoulder, Assistant U.S. Attorney Mabel
Willebrandt, scourge of bootleggers.

Seattle dry agents learn how to recognize a still.

(Underwood and Underwood)

In the Bronx dry raiders capture three stills.

Bill McCoy, founder of Rum Row,
aboard his schooner, *Tomoka*.

Crossing the Detroit River with a Coast Guard speedboat in pursuit,
a rumrunner jettisons his contraband.

In Brooklyn, dry agents destroy a million dollars' worth of liquor.

A "too-near" beer seizure in New York.

A Customs inspector jubilates over the seizure of a rumrunner's cargo.

WILLIAM EUGENE "PUSSYFOOT" JOHNSON
"Ethics be hanged. I have told enough lies for the cause to make
Ananias ashamed of himself."

PROHIBITION AGENT IZZIE EINSTEIN, MASTER OF DECEIT AND DISGUISE

Inspecting a seizure.

With his sidekick, Agent Moe Smith, uncovering another bootlegger's cache.

As a coal cart driver.

As a Texas rancher.

THE INSTANT MILLIONAIRES

EDWARD DONEGAN
"How about five grand to fix this thing up?"

ROY OLMSTEAD
"We'll have to go slow until the mayor gets back."

(Underwood and Underwood)
GEORGE REMUS
". . . there is not enough money in the world to buy up all the public officials."

(Underwood and Underw
RENÉ LA MONTAGNE
". . . ninety percent of the popul
would be with us."

MARY LOUISE CECILIA "TEXAS" GUINAN
"Hello, sucker."

Charles Berns (*left*) and John Carl "the Baron" Kriendler in front of their pre-21 Club speakeasy, The Iron Gate, at 42 West Forty-ninth Street. The year was 1929.

Wet Congressman Fiorello La Guardia and friends challenge the law by mixing malt extract, alcohol and near beer at a soda fountain.

MRS. CHARLES SABIN

singing "My Country 'tis of Thee" at a convention of the Women's Organization for National Prohibition Reform.

(Bettmann Archive)

The girls celebrate repeal.

registry and so circumvented U.S. jurisdiction. With the exception of his first two runs, he took care not to stray inside
American territorial waters. Three nautical miles offshore was
the limit of sovereignty accepted by most countries under a
late-eighteenth-century definition based on the maximum range
of a cannonball fired by a smooth-bored muzzle-loading cannon.
Through international conventions this was extended in 1924, as
far as rum-running went, to seven miles and ultimately to either
twelve miles or an hour's run from shore, which in the case of
ships with a speed of, say, fifteen knots meant fifteen miles.
McCoy would heave to beyond the limit, obliging his customers
to sail out to him. With liquor fetching twice as much ashore as
the price paid afloat, there was no dearth of buyers even in heavy
seas.

> They would come wabbling and bouncing out in their little
> open craft, one man steering, the other pumping for dear life, and
> swing in under my schooner's lee. Usually it was too rough to tie
> up. Four of us would hold the skiff away from our side with oars
> and boat hooks, and we would throw the hams of liquor out to the
> crew. The buyer would toss a roll of bills to me. "Twelve thousand
> dollars for two hundred cases, Bill," he would shout. . . . My
> reputation and the white form of the *Arethusa* [his best-loved
> schooner which could carry 5,700 cases or 7,600 if packed as
> hams] riding on the Row was all the advertisement I needed. I
> had an understanding with my customers that if the schooner was
> flying the British ensign, it was unsafe to come near her by
> daylight. For the guidance of shore boats at night . . . I put the
> bottom of a barrel beneath the lamp. It could be seen thus at a
> distance, but the disk of wood kept the deck and immediate
> vicinity of the *Arethusa* in deep shadow.

A seaman named Johnson captained the *Henry L. Marshall*
after McCoy chartered her to a Georgia bootlegger. He proved
less prudent. In August, 1923, he sailed her to the New Jersey
coast with 1,500 cases of the bootlegger's rye for Atlantic City.
Despite McCoy's written instructions warning him against
moving too close to the three-mile limit, he not only blundered
across it, but broached the cargo, got drunk with the crew and
went ashore in a motorboat, leaving the crew to drift about in
their besotted state. While he roistered up and down the
boardwalk, the Coast Guard cutter *Seneca* sighted the schooner.
The crew drunkenly attempted to jettison the cargo, but before

many cases had disappeared, the ship was forced under threat of gunfire to heave to. Seven coastguardsmen boarded the schooner, fastened a line to her bowsprit and towed her into New York Harbor. The written instructions found aboard, together with duplicate clearance papers and the drunken babbling of the crew, implicated McCoy. He was indicted *in absentia* by a federal grand jury and a warrant issued for his arrest.

It was the Coast Guard's first seizure of a large rum-runner, as well as the first of many to create an international incident. Since it actually occurred four miles from shore, not three, Britain, under whose flag the schooner sailed, protested. The United States justified the seizure by producing evidence of conspiracy to violate both its Customs regulations and the Volstead Act. After more than a year of legal skirmishes the U.S. district court of appeals upheld the verdict, and the Supreme Court denied a review.

Neither the indictment nor the loss of the *Henry L. Marshall* stopped McCoy. For the next three years, with Coast Guard craft hunting him up and down the Atlantic seaboard, he continued to deliver hams by the tens of thousands from Nassau, Halifax, St. Pierre and Miquelon. He bought two more schooners, the *J. B. Young* and the *M. M. Gardner*, and chartered a third, the *Mary Hurtel*. He was reindicted several times. Finally, on March 20, 1924, the *Arethusa*, with McCoy at the helm, was cornered by the *Seneca*, the same craft that had captured the *Henry L. Marshall*. Brought to trial the following year before a federal judge in Newark, New Jersey, McCoy pleaded guilty and was sent to the Essex County Jail for nine months.

He never returned to Rum Row but settled in Miami where he prospered as a real estate investor until he died of a heart attack at seventy-one on December 30, 1948, aboard his motor cruiser the *Blue Lagoon*. "This is not repentance," he had said, after his release from jail. "If the racket today promised half the fun I've had out of it in the past, I'd jump into it tomorrow. But the game has altered. . . . Modern efficiency does away with individual enterprise and the spirit of adventure. Big business wants safety and results, and present-day rumrunning is big business."

By big business McCoy meant organized crime. Rum Row had become the fief of New York gang bosses like the ex-steve-dore, William Vincent "Big Bill" Dwyer. The sobriquet referred not to Dwyer's physical size, but to the scope of his operations, for he was a nondescript figure of average height, bland, soft-spoken, his face round and ruddy. A conservative dresser, he allowed himself but a single distinctive adornment—a swastika-shaped ring framed in diamonds, with a ruby at the center.

From two Broadway office suites, one in the Loew's State Building on Times Square, the other in the East River National Bank building on Forty-first Street, where he kept large sums, he presided over a complex of different enterprises. In addition to heading a rum-running syndicate, he secured part or full ownership of two hotels, several nightclubs, the biggest brewery in Manhattan—the Phenix Cereal Beverage Company at Twenty-fifth Street and Tenth Avenue, which netted about $7,000,000 a year—two Miami Beach gambling casinos, racetracks in Florida, New Hampshire, Ohio and Quebec, the Brooklyn Dodgers football club and, after introducing professional ice hockey to the city, the New York and the American Hockey clubs. The latter acquired Mayor James J. Walker as one of its directors. Affluence gained the humbly born racketeer entry into elite society, especially the sporting, horsy set. He entertained regally at the suburban estate in Belle Harbor, Long Island, which he shared with his wife and five children.

Dwyer grew up on lower Tenth Avenue, the haunt of marauding gangs like the Hudson Dusters and the Gophers, specialists at pillaging the wharves and warehouses along the Hudson River. Though he never belonged to either gang, earning an honest living in his youth first as a vaudeville house usher, then as a dockwalloper, he recruited his own gang from both as he rose to the overlordship of Rum Row. He got his start through an older neighborhood friend, George Shevlin, who owned a chain of saloons. When prohibition came, Shevlin hired him as an assistant to handle bootleg supplies. Dwyer bought trucks and fast automobiles and leased garages as plants for storage, cutting and packaging liquor. Underneath the garages he built concealed chambers accessible by elevators which, when closed, showed only a blank brick wall. Each elevator could lower or raise a fully loaded ten-ton truck. To procure the first stocks, Dwyer turned to his boyhood acquaintances among the Gophers and the Hudson Dusters. For a share of the profits they were happy to break into liquor warehouses and to ride shotgun on the trucks transporting the loot to Dwyer.

By 1922 ships from practically every European and Latin

American country that had a coastline were steaming across the
seas with liquor for transshipment to the United States via the
West Indies or off-Canada islands. Some made direct contact
with rum-runners at sea. The later extension of the three-mile
limit to twelve caused no marked decrease in the quantities of
liquor reaching the coastal cities. It merely eliminated many of
the small-time rum-runners who could not afford the powerful
speedboats needed to cover the longer distance fast, and it left the
big syndicates to monopolize the traffic. Dwyer, who had cut
loose from Shevlin, established purchasing agents abroad and
assembled a fleet of oceangoing vessels to pick up the merchandise at the ports of embarkation. To meet them on the return
voyage and take delivery outside the territorial boundary, he
equipped eighteen speedboats with surplus Army Liberty airplane engines. Capable of making fifty knots, they could outrun
most of the Coast Guard craft.

Dwyer's supremacy rested on two fundamental achievements:
his alliance with the top dogs of New York gangdom and his
subversion of coastguardsmen. In 1923, ten months out of Sing
Sing, to which he had been confined for complicity in a gang
murder, Owney Madden, a former Gopher captain, joined Big
Frenchy De Mange, a Hudson Duster alumnus, in a series of
hijacking sorties. On December 2 they invaded Dwyer's Liberty
Storage warehouse and drove away a truck with a $16,000 load
of liquor. A less cool-headed chieftain than Dwyer might have
ordered the hijackers' execution. Instead, Dwyer, who valued
Madden as a persuader, offered him a partnership. The fortune
Madden subsequently made through rum-running and other
divisions of the Dwyer conglomerate enabled him to buy
controlling shares in breweries, nightclubs, industrial protection
rackets and the megalocephalic heavyweight fighter Primo
Carnera and to indulge a passion for breeding fancy pigeons.
Though his police record eventually numbered fifty-seven arrests
for felonies ranging from theft to murder, the Sing Sing sentence
was the only one Madden ever served, an immunity he owed
largely to the omnipotent Tammany sachem, James J. Hines.

Dwyer cemented at least five more valuable underworld
relationships. Larry Fay, another Hudson Duster and Hines
protégé (forty-six arrests, no jail terms), achieved success comparatively late in life. He was twenty-nine, driving a taxi around
New York, when he won a 100-to-1 shot at the Belmont Park

racetrack. With this windfall he bought his own taxi, the first of a large fleet. In the spring of 1920 a passenger got him to drive all the way to Montreal. Whiskey then sold there for $10 a case. Fay bought two cases, smuggled them into New York and turned a profit of $180. Subsequent smuggling expeditions produced the capital to buy more taxis and employ a squad of thugs who would beat up rival cabbies attempting to park at choice locations. In this way Fay maintained control of the Grand Central and Pennsylvania station stands, the two most lucrative in the city. By 1922 he had accumulated about half a million dollars and was developing additional sources of revenue like nightclubs and clip joints for which his taxi drivers served as steerers. When he cast a covetous eye upon the still-greater yields from Rum Row, Dwyer invited him to join forces with his growing outfit. That same year a Swedish-born Broadway impresario, Nils Thor Granlund, who produced some of the shows for the gangster-run nightclubs, including El Fey, founded radio station WHN. Presently, to his bemusement, he began to get requests from Fay's henchmen for poetry readings between musical numbers, specifically, selections from Kipling, Poe or Robert W. Service. Granlund obliged. Only months later did he learn the real reason behind the requests. WHN transmitted a strong eastward beam far out into the Atlantic. "If," "Gunga Din," "The Raven," "The Shooting of Dan McGrew," etc. each concealed a code signal to the Dwyer-Fay speedboats, telling them where and when to pick up cargoes.

Frank Costello, a power in the Unione Siciliane (an early synonym for the Mafia), acted for a time as Dwyer's payoff contact and frequently advised him on long-range operational planning. The homicidal Sicilian Frankie Uale, alias Yale—"the Undertaker," as he styled himself—who headed the Brooklyn chapter of the Unione Siciliane and dominated the borough's rackets, was nicely situated to assist rum-runners, having opened a Coney Island dime-a-dance dive, the Harvard Inn, almost at the water's edge. Al Capone got his first job there as a bouncer. Yale amassed his original stake through the laundry racket, collecting tribute from both management and labor. Laundry plants would pay him $150 a week to keep out union organizers; Yale would then force the workers to join his own union under threat of death or mutilation and charge them dues of $1 a week. Dwyer dealt with Yale to their mutual profit and through Yale with Capone in Chicago. In 1928 Capone had Yale liquidated to make way for a candidate he preferred as national president of the Unione Siciliane.

Dwyer sometimes augmented his seaborne stocks with liquor hijacked ashore. For such plunder he relied on Charles "Vannie" Higgins, an affiliate of Frankie Yale. Liquor unloaded on Long Island normally traveled in a truck convoy, led by a scout car, along Route 25, running 150 miles from the eastern tip of the island into New York. Higgins would set up an ambush with gunmen waiting by the roadside in parked cars, behind trees and buildings. Unless the convoy belonged to the Dwyer syndicate or had paid it for protection, two cars would shoot out from opposite sides of the highway, blocking the scout car. As the trucks ground to a halt behind it, the Higgins gang would enfilade them with tommy-gun fire, then, dumping the dead and wounded, drive the trucks to Dwyer's scattered New York drops.

The independent sea smuggler who neglected to buy safe passage from Dwyer risked a similar fate at the hands of his "go-through guys" (so called because supposedly no opposition could daunt them). As he made for some liquor ship outside the three-mile limit, one of Dwyer's souped-up speedboats would cut him off, its crew, holding tommy guns, would board his craft and take his bankroll, or, if he was heading back to shore, his liquor.

Vannie Higgins, whose hobby was aviation, once angered New York's Governor Franklin D. Roosevelt when he landed next to the state prison at Comstock on a field cleared for his plane by order of the warden, Joseph Wilson, with whom he then dined inside the prison. To Roosevelt's protest at this impropriety, Warden Wilson, a former brewer, blandly replied that Vannie was an old friend, and why shouldn't he entertain old friends?

The hijacker met his end in classic gangland style, cut down on a street corner by a passing carload of gunmen.

Dwyer's partners in the Phenix brewery also included Irving Wexler, alias Waxey Gordon (the nickname a tribute to the smoothness with which Gordon formerly picked pockets). Dwyer achieved almost total control of both the beer and hard liquor traffic on the West Side of Manhattan. His most important customer and an associate in various undertakings was Arthur Flegenheimer, alias Dutch Schultz, to whom the police ascribed 138 killings. Schultz occupies a special niche in the underworld pantheon by virtue of his last words. In his delirium, as he lay

dying of enemy bullets, he uttered an inexplicable but haunt-
ingly lovely iambic line—"A boy has never wept nor dashed a
thousand kim."

Late on the afternoon of December 27, 1924, the Coast Guard
Picket Boat No. *203*, Captain Edward Gallagher, sliced through
choppy waters toward one of Dwyer's oceangoing vessels, the
three-masted schooner *Elias B.*, anchored about thirty-five miles
southeast of New York Harbor. The *203* did not challenge her
but, on the contrary, exchanged friendly greetings with her and
put aboard two of Dwyer's supercargoes to help her crew
transship 700 cases of scotch and champagne. The *203* then
scurried back to harbor and tied up at a pier near Canal Street,
where, under the protective gaze of several policemen, the cases
were loaded onto Dwyer's trucks. Each coastguardsman received
$700 for his day's work. The policemen were on Dwyer's regular
payroll.

It was through a Mephistophelian petty officer named Olsen
that Dwyer found dozens of corruptible coastguardsmen. If Olsen
detected signs of moral frailty in a shipmate, he would bring him
to Broadway for a night of revelry. Dwyer provided a sumptuous
dinner, theater tickets, a girl and a hotel suite. The tender of a
bribe that followed next day usually met no resistance, neither
the pay nor the working conditions in the Coast Guard then
being very attractive. An enlisted man, first grade, earned $126 a
month; a warrant officer at sea, $153. Dwyer might offer ten
times those sums if the coastguardsman could suborn his fellow
crew members and still more for each assignment they carried
out.

The Coast Guard boats that Dwyer controlled, aided by the
police and prohibition enforcement officers in his pay, not only
landed an occasional cargo for him, but harassed any free-lance
rum-runner who failed to pay him his customary protection fee
of $2 a case. They developed a signal system. Three flashes of
their searchlights meant the way was clear for Dwyer's contact
boats to proceed to the mother ships. A steady beam warned
them to keep away. At the height of his operations Big Bill
Dwyer had four Coast Guard boats, with crews totaling almost
fifty men, under his orders.

In 1925 a New York attorney, A. Bruce Bielaski, whom the
Prohibition Bureau had retained as a special investigator,
managed to plant an undercover agent in Dwyer's gang and to

obtain evidence from several bribed coastguardsmen by promising them immunity. Of the ten defendants tried in July, 1926, all were acquitted except Dwyer and the manager of one of his garage drops. The convicted pair drew two years each in the Atlanta penitentiary.

When Dwyer was released thirteen months later with time off for good behavior, he found neither his business nor his social status greatly impaired. Under the supervision of Owney Madden and Waxey Gordon the Phenix brewery had continued to flourish. Thanks to an indulgent Atlanta warden, Frank Costello had been able to communicate regularly with Dwyer through an intermediary who visited the prison every month or so and had directed the rum-running syndicate in the boss' absence.

On March 11, 1936, the society page of the New York *Times* reported from Miami:

> Before the running of the Flamingo Polo Club Purse event, an innovation for gentlemen riders, at Tropical Park this afternoon, members of the club were guests of William Vincent Dwyer of New York, managing director of the Gables Racing Association, at a buffet luncheon.
>
> Those present were Sir Graeme Sinclair-Lockhart, Bart., and Lady Lockhart; Mr. and Mrs. Serge Mdivani, Count George du Manoir. . . .

or under the earth

The arrangement for dispelling the fumes eventually gave the game away: a pipe six inches around protruding from the top of a windmill. Federal agents spotted it and traced the rest of the pipeline to the side of a barn near the southern California town of Wilmington. Twenty feet below the barn a space had been excavated big enough to accommodate a maze of passages, pipes, electric wiring, machinery, mash, vats and stills. It was the most extensive moonshining setup discovered in the state up to that time—July, 1923.

Three years later, in northern California, outside Dyerville, the Prohibition Bureau padlocked a redwood tree twenty-four feet in diameter after its hollowed-out base was found to enclose a fifty-gallon still. The smoke rose through a flue concealed among the top branches. Over the entrance hung a curtain of canvas painted to look like bark. Following the raid, a government decree was nailed to the tree—CLOSED FOR ONE YEAR FOR VIOLATION OF THE NATIONAL PROHIBITION ACT.

In Iowa moonshiners dug out a cellar under an abandoned church and installed $50,000 worth of distilling apparatus. In Omaha they bored a sixty-foot tunnel beneath a barn. In Colorado they constructed a deep cave, covered the entrance with brush and buried dead animals in a shallow pit nearby so that the stench would disguise the odor of corn sugar mash.

In Detroit, on the night of April 4, 1929, Police Sergeant Clayton Williams, chancing to pass a garage half a mile from the center of town, saw a man dozing in the cab of a 2,000-gallon tank truck and decided to take a closer look. He noted three pipelines leading from somewhere outside the garage and a telephone, evidently part of an intercom system. One of the pipelines, feeding into the tank, was leaking beer. Williams roused the driver, John Moore, who neither then nor later at the stationhouse would answer any questions.

The case was referred to federal agents. They spent an entire day sounding and digging. Finally penetrating a ceiling eight inches thick, they lowered themselves into what they described as the most amazing brewery in that city of amazing breweries. A steel door, which they had to cut open with acetylene torches, opened into a passage several blocks long. At the far end they came to the main works and the terminal of the pipelines. There they found another telephone through which the brewery bosses issued loading instructions to the tank truck drivers in the garage. According to the theory of a knowledgeable police inspector, the trucks transported the beer to a plant for bottling under a Canadian label. But all the brewers had fled before the raiders broke into their hideaway, and with the exception of Moore nobody was ever directly implicated in the operation.

or in the air

When winter froze the lakes of Minnesota, fishing enthusiasts would chip holes in the ice and drop their lines through them. On a February morning in 1930 two fishermen were so engaged at Lake Osakis, 150 miles northwest of St. Paul, when they felt themselves bedewed with a moisture redolent of whiskey. Glancing up, they saw an astonishing spectacle. Two airplanes, streaking southward, one above the other, appeared to be linked by a long, flexible attachment. The baffled fishermen reported the anomaly to state troopers. The ensuing investigations on both sides of the Canadian border disclosed a novel form of rum-running.

It had doubtless been suggested by the U.S. Army's flight endurance tests the year before, when planes circling an airport were refueled in midair. Canadian smugglers, piloting planes fitted with extra 100-gallon tanks, would rendezvous with their confederates' aircraft over American soil and transfer liquor from tank to tank through fueling hoses, thus evading Customs. The replenished planes would then fly back to their base, landing with skids on some frozen lake in the Minnesota woods. There truckers waited to drain off the liquor into barrels and deliver it to Minneapolis and St. Paul.

Aerial rum-running of one kind or another was almost as old as the Volstead Act. The first plane reported to be cargoing liquor took off from Winnipeg in October, 1921. Soon scores of planes were flying liquor across the Canadian border. Like the land and sea smugglers, who violated no law when they exported liquor, the fliers did so with the knowledge and consent of the Canadian government. Under Canada's convention with Washington it had agreed to withhold clearance only if the fliers failed to file export declarations and to notify U.S. Customs when their cargo was known or suspected to be intended for American consumption. To avoid seizure of the planes in the States, the pilots would give the Canadian officials false registration numbers.

Intensified efforts to blockade the Detroit River was what chiefly stimulated the sky traffic. Its leading operators bragged about it. "Do you think we're going to quit this racket?" one of them asked a Detroit *Free Press* reporter. "The government can block the river. Let them. Airplanes cost less than a good speedboat. Fly loads right to Chicago. They'll have a tough time stopping us. We'll fly right over their heads and laugh at them."

During the spring of 1929 several Canadian-American combines obtained charters from the Canadian government, granting them the right to export liquor "by ship, truck or airplane" and to set up wireless stations. One combine improvised landing fields in three Michigan counties, never using the same one twice. Automobiles equipped with floodlights served the dual function of illuminating night landings and speeding the booze to its next destination. Wildcat pilots were hired at $5 for each case flown. Canadian Customs records showed that in a single month— April, 1930—at the Aero Club near Windsor, they had issued clearances for airplane cargoes totaling 953 cases. The manifests listed as destinations Saginaw, Michigan; South Bend, Indiana; Milwaukee, Wisconsin; Cincinnati and several smaller Ohio cities. This information reached the U.S. authorities too late for them to catch the smugglers.

According to federal agents, Al Capone's older brother, Ralph, directed a branch of the Chicago syndicate that owned twenty rum-running aircraft, including a trimotored cabin monoplane with a capacity of fifty cases. Between August, 1929 and May, 1930, the agents estimated, they transferred $1,400,000 worth of liquor from Ontario to Chicago. Ralph and eight associates were indicted for this offense, but an earlier indictment charging income-tax evasion took precedence, and he served a three-year sentence for that, the smuggling case being dropped meantime.

Two of the biggest aerial smuggling rings, operating thirty planes between them, came a cropper in the fall of 1930 after prohibition agents managed to infiltrate them, posing as bootleggers. One of the rings smuggled aliens, as well as liquor, into the States. Its leader was Clarence DeWallett, a fugitive from American justice living in Ontario since his indictment the year before for bribing Detroit Customs inspectors. The second ring was headed by Russell "Curly" Hosler, an ace pilot who had crashed his plane, injuring his spine, in the 1930 All-America Flying Derby.

At the outset the planes, each carrying up to forty cases a trip, took off openly from Canadian airports, then, as Canadian Customs officers began to cooperate with their American counterparts, from desolate, backcountry flats. They penetrated deep into Michigan, Ohio, Indiana and Illinois, having beforehand selected pastures and farm lots as landing fields without the owners' knowledge. If the latter proved compliant, they would pay them. If not, they would compel submission with threats of violence. Following exposure by the undercover agents, the rings collapsed in a flurry of seizures, fines and prison sentences.

Lightplanes were also used as aids to seafaring craft. There
was an amphibian that coastguardsmen cruising off Woods Hole,
Massachusetts, observed daily as it winged out to sea at dawn
and returned before dusk. Taking bearings, they traced its base
to a heavily turfed field, with landing markers up, near
Providence, Rhode Island. Shore police patrols prevented further
takeoffs.

11. *"Our little band of martyrs"*

It is the first instance in our history in which the effort has been made by Constitutional provision to extend the police control of the federal government to every individual and every home in the United States.

—The Wickersham Commission Report on the Enforcement of the Prohibition Laws, January 7, 1931

THE American shoreline, with its abundance of secluded coves, creeks, inlets and beaches, measures roughly 12,000 miles. The geography along the U.S.-Canada border embraces about 3,000 miles of lake and river frontage, much of it equally vulnerable to smuggling. The land boundaries separating the United States from Canada and from Mexico, traversed by hundreds of roads and trails, total close to 3,700 miles. The enforcement division of the Prohibition Bureau numbered 1,512 agents the first year (and at no time more than 3,000). It got some help from U.S. Customs, Immigration and the Coast Guard, but those services were undermanned, uncoordinated and burdened with many precedential responsibilities. Still less could the bureau count on state police, for though most states had adopted supplementary Volsteadean laws, they failed to appropriate enough money to administer them. In 1923 the combined expenditures on prohibition enforcement of all forty-eight states did not reach half a million dollars. The tendency throughout the country was to leave it to the federal government. Thus, even if charged with no other duty than to patrol the nation's borders, each prohibition agent would have had at least 12 miles to patrol.

Border patrol constituted a relatively small part of the Sisyphean task, of what the National Commission on Law Observance and Enforcement (popularly called the Wickersham

Commission after its chairman, former Attorney General George
W. Wickersham) described as "a police regulation over 3,500,000
square miles of territory, requiring total abstinence on the part of
122,000,000 people who had been accustomed to consume
2,000,000 gallons of alcoholic beverages per annum."

Such a regulation, demanding that in addition to guarding
more than 18,000 miles of national boundaries, the Prohibition
Bureau obstruct the diversion of the 170,000,000 gallons of
industrial alcohol produced yearly, check 11,000,000 doctors'
prescriptions, dam rivers of needle beer, search out and destroy
commercial stills without number and prevent home brewing in
22,000,000 homes—to list only the major sources of illegal
liquor—lay far beyond the available resources. The dimensions
of the task would have defeated the bureau even if every last
employee had been an exemplar of intelligence, courage and
honesty. This was hardly the case.

Few instruments of law enforcement ever aroused greater
contempt and loathing than the prohibition agents. "Swinish"—
so city editor Stanley Walker characterized them. "It was a
common sight in certain New York speakeasies," he recalled, "to
see a group of agents enter a place at noon, remain until almost
midnight, eating and drinking, and then leave without paying
the bill. The dry agent, not alone by the intrinsically unpopular
nature of his calling, but by his duplicity, his bad manners, his
cheapness and occasional brutality, made himself the symbol of
all that was wrong with the law." After Colonel Ira L. Reeves
resigned as prohibition administrator of New Jersey, convinced
that the Volstead Act was unenforceable, he wrote: "I do not
know of a single agent on my force who was accepted by the
community in which he lived as a welcome neighbor and citizen
in whom people could place confidence." So soiled did the
agents' public image become that a federal jury acquitted Helen
Morgan of serving liquor in her New York nightclub because, as
one of them later disclosed, "We couldn't take the word of two
prohibition agents against Miss Morgan."

Not every agent merited such obloquy, but the percentage was
high. Authoritative witnesses, testifying before the Wickersham
Commission, considered at least half the personnel of the
Prohibition Bureau to be composed of incompetents and crooks.
Assistant U.S. Attorney Willebrandt found, within the first
months of her appointment, that droves of agents were "as

devoid of honesty and integrity as the bootlegging fraternity . . .
no more to be trusted with a commission to enforce the laws of
the United States and to carry a gun than the notorious bandit
Jesse James."

Chicago produced the first reported instances of malfeasance
among dry agents. Barely ten days had elapsed since the
Volstead Act deadline when three of them attached to the
Chicago Internal Revenue Office were arraigned, two for
accepting a bootlegger's bribe, the third for selling confiscated
liquor. In March two Baltimore agents committed similar
offenses. Almost every month thereafter, for the next ten years,
there were Prohibition Bureau employees who erred. In December, 1921, the bureau fired 100 New York agents at a single clip,
following disclosures of fraudulently issued withdrawal permits.
Altogether, during the decade 1920–30, of the 17,816 persons
who worked for the bureau, 1,587—almost 12 percent—were
dismissed for cause. Their offenses included false statements in
their applications, concealment of criminal records, extortion,
bribery, fake expense accounts, collusion, conspiracy, illegal
disposal of liquor, embezzlement, failure to report violations,
theft, warehouse robbery, intoxication, immorality, assault, gambling, revealing confidential information, insubordination, contempt of court, perjury or subornation of perjury, political
activity, writing bad checks, failure to file tax returns, misuse of
firearms. "The figures do not, of course, represent the total
delinquencies," the Wickersham Commission noted. "They only
show those which are actually discovered and admitted or proved
to such an extent as to justify dismissal. What proportion of the
total they really represent it is impossible to say. Bribery and
similar offenses are from their nature extremely difficult of
discovery and proof."

Some prohibition administrators knowingly took on agents
with criminal records. E. L. Porterfield, who commanded the
Ohio-Michigan district in 1926, so admitted when the Cincinnati
Times-Star raised the question, following a shooting affray be-
tween Agent Sam Rosofsky, a former bootlegger, and his quarry,
Joe Comrad. Both men were wounded. "You can't use Sunday
School teachers to apprehend bootleggers," said Porterfield.
"There is no reason why a man with a criminal record, if he has
turned over a new leaf and has convinced us of his do-good
intentions should not be employed in this department. We feel

that a man of this type may be more able to obtain valuable information through the knowledge of how bootleggers operate."

Misconduct was not confined to the lower echelons. It prevailed at the summit. By courtesy of Roy Asa Haynes, an Ohio Republican who had replaced the Democrat John Kramer as Prohibition Commissioner, liquor for the Ohio gang's K Street jollifications was delivered to the front door in Wells, Fargo express wagons with armed dry agents on guard. Haynes owed his appointment to Wayne Wheeler, and through Haynes Wheeler controlled the Prohibition Bureau. A former mayor of Hillsboro, Ohio, cradle of the Woman's Crusade, active in the Methodist Episcopal Church, newspaper publisher, Republican Party wheelhorse, and a dry closely associated with the Anti-Saloon League, Haynes considered himself ideally qualified to head the bureau, an opinion shared by Wheeler, if not by every Leaguer. Soon after Harding entered the White House, Wheeler, "the legislative bully," as the New York *Evening World* described him, "before whom the Senate of the United States sits up and begs," urged Haynes upon him, and Harding, recognizing his political indebtedness, gave Haynes the job. Later, to appease Wheeler, the President went so far as to announce publicly his renunciation of liquor and thereafter restricted his tippling to his White House bedroom.

As Wheeler's puppet Prohibition Commissioner, a position he filled for six years, Haynes consistently issued glowing progress reports. "The Amendment is being enforced to an even greater extent than many of its devoted friends anticipated [January, 1922]. . . . [The] home brew fad is taking its last gasp [December, 1922]. . . . Bootleg patronage has fallen off fifty per cent [April, 1923]. . . . There is little open and above-board drinking anywhere [December, 1923]. . . ." Scandal, meanwhile, continued to erupt at every level of Haynes' command.

Among venal bureau officials caught redhanded were its administrator of Chicago and his chief agent in 1923; its director for Ohio in 1925; in 1927 its former administrator of Buffalo, his former assistant, and several agents active and retired, its deputy administrator of Fayetteville, North Carolina, and six agents, its former chief of the New York Druggist Permit Division. . . . "The prohibition service," said New Jersey's Administrator Reeves, "has proved to be a training ground for bootleggers. While in the service, the agents, inspectors and investigators naturally learn all the ropes of the underworld, as well as the government's methods in attempting to apprehend and convict violators. Naturally, when leaving the service of the prohibition forces, they are sought after by those engaged in illicit business."

The blame for this pervasive corruption lay partly with Wheeler and the Anti-Saloon League. It was an added price they paid for Congressional support of the Volstead Act, and they came to regret it. The act exempted prohibition agents from the civil service rules, leaving it to the party in power to dispense appointments as spoils. When William Dudley Foulke, president of the National Civil Service Reform League, delivered a speech denouncing the Anti-Saloon League for its failure to condemn the clause, the secretary of the latter organization, Samuel Edgar Nicholson, wrote to him: ". . . neither the Anti-Saloon League nor any other agency could have gotten into that law a civil service provision, and for the League to have forced the issue would have been to jeopardize the passage of the bill." Foulke wrote back: "The plain fact is that the Congressmen wanted the plunder and you let them have it . . . you are professionally engaged in a great moral reform and this cannot be done through immoral means."

As Foulke had feared, patronage loaded the personnel rolls of the Prohibition Bureau with illiterates, incompetents, misfits and criminals. In April, 1921, the federal grand jury for the Southern District of New York reported to the court: ". . . almost without exception the agents are not men of the type of intelligence and character qualified to be charged with this difficult and important duty and federal law." The jury had recommended the dismissal of three grossly delinquent agents, but political sponsors shielded all three. Even Wayne Wheeler, whose dictates, transmitted through Commissioner Haynes, were usually executed, often discovered that employees he objected to nevertheless retained their jobs thanks to some Congressman's favor. The chief of the prohibition agents, Edward C. Yellowley, indicated how matters stood in a letter addressed to all state directors: ". . . it is desired that you . . . suggest that he [the job applicant] secure congressional endorsement, endorsement of the Anti-Saloon League, and other endorsements."

In a grandstand play General Andrews, widely reputed as an incorruptible old ironsides, announced the termination of all appointments and the rehiring of those "selected for merit only."

At the same time he divided the country for the purposes of prohibition enforcement into twenty-seven districts, instructing their administrators to pursue duty without deference to any politician. But under political pressure Andrews soon modified that order.

As administrator of the Second District (New York City, Long Island and Westchester County) Andrews chose Major Chester P. Mills, an honest, if roughshod, fellow West Pointer. Before long the general was telling the major to consult the local Republican Party bosses about appointments. Mills complied at first and found himself saddled with a staff of 228 Republican spoilsmen and only 12 Democrats, many of them corrupt, stupid or both. He protested to Charles D. Hilles, a national committeeman of the Republican Party, who bluntly informed him that the patronage system existed everywhere, and the Second District would be no exception.

Regarding four of his most corrupt agents, Mills wrote later: "I can find relief only in army language when I think of their records." Agent Ike Friedenberg was protecting a West Side bootleg liquor depot. Bureau regulations required an applicant for the role of agent to swear under oath that he had never been associated with the wine or liquor business. Agent David Levy had bought a sacramental wine store and permit from an obliging rabbi and proceeded to divert deliveries into the bootleg market. Agent Emil Mazella, a Republican ward heeler, tried to extort $500 from a chemical laboratory with a threat to file a complaint charging illegal use of its alcohol allotments. Agent John J. Kerrigan, a thug formerly employed by Republican County Chairman Samuel Koenig as a bodyguard, was implicated in a murder committed during a drinking orgy. When Mills fired all four agents and stood fast under heavy pressure from Washington to take them back, the politicians demanded his head. Andrews set out for New York to investigate the situation personally. When he reached Mills' office, the four culprits were sitting in an antechamber, along with a dozen others the major had discharged for incompetence. "My God, Mills," were the general's first words, "what is that bunch waiting out there for?" and he implored him to reinstate them and make his peace with the politicians. He was too hard-nosed, the general warned; Hilles had complained to the President about him. In the end Mills was forced to rescind his order. Not long after, he resigned.

Andrew Volstead, interviewed in St. Paul, Minnesota, where, after losing his campaign for reelection to the House, he served as legal adviser to the Northwestern Prohibition District, suggested another reason for keeping the dry agents out of the civil service. ". . . because men were all wearing silk shirts and getting such high wages that we knew only lower-class men would ask for low-priced prohibition jobs. [During the first years the pay scale ranged from $1,200 to $2,300 a year, depending on length of service; later, from $2,300 to $2,800. A few agents received as much as $3,000; three a trifle more than that.] We didn't want to blanket a force of such men under civil service protection, so that they couldn't be easily removed."

However meager the salary, many an agent found compensation in the opportunities for graft. During a dispute with Agent Levy's political sponsor Major Mills asked somewhat ingenuously how anybody as valuable as the sponsor claimed Levy to be could content himself with such paltry pay. "We're all over twenty-one," Mills was told. "He wants the job to get his the same as the rest of them in this prohibition racket." Agent Kerrigan once had the temerity to estimate publicly that a dry agent's job was worth $40,000 to $50,000 a year.

Roy Haynes himself was dismissed in 1927. During the last years of his tenure, after President Coolidge invested General Andrews with superseding powers, the commissioner had done little besides reiterate his roseate assurances of progress and protect the political domain of his patron, Wayne Wheeler. General Andrews' appointment also ended under a cloud. The cause, according to what the chief of the Treasury Department's Intelligence Unit, Elmer Irey, revealed twenty years later, was an improper association.

I was somewhat upset to learn [Irey recalled] that political pressure had resulted in the appointment as an agent of one of the greatest bootleggers of our day. I was further perturbed to learn that the bootlegger-agent was a regular golfing partner of [Andrews]. I was aghast when an agent reported the following conversation between the bootlegger and the Assistant Secretary, which was overheard on the golf course:

Secretary: You know, all I want to do is get enough money to live well and retire.

Bootlegger: I'll help. I'll make investments for you and give you the profits.

The bootlegger did make the investments and I was forced to report the affair to the Secretary of the Treasury, Ogden Mills. Mills listened to me, then said: "Get Andrews in here and question him. This is a serious charge!"

When Andrews heard the charge, he denied it and said, "Mr. So-and-So is a fine man." I answered with, "Maybe. But he's a bootlegger." Ninety minutes later Andrews admitted I was right, and Mills said, "Mr. Andrews, please write out your resignation immediately." Poor General Andrews wrote it out and then watched the investments that had been made for him crumble away with the rest of the stock-market casualties in 1929.

In April, 1926, a subcommittee of the Senate Judiciary Committee held hearings on various proposals to amend the Volstead Act. They lasted for eighteen days, 212 witnesses testified, and the published proceedings filled 1,660 pages. As one result, every prohibition agent was required to pass a written civil service examination or face dismissal. The examination consisted of forty multiple choice questions that a not exceptionally bright schoolboy might be expected to answer correctly. For examples:

26. "Methods of smuggling vary with the geographical conditions under which the smuggler must operate in the different localities. On the Atlantic coast the crews of great liners coming across the ocean from England frequently engage in the traffic. On the Pacific the liquor is brought in small schooners, which are met by fishing boats and launches that land the liquor in coves and harbors. Across the Canadian border and Mexican border whiskey is sometimes smuggled by airplane or even behind horse teams."

   According to the statement, why do methods of smuggling liquor differ? (1) Funds available are different. (2) Different amounts are smuggled. (3) Methods of law enforcement differ. (4) Purposes of smuggling differ. (5) Places where liquor is smuggled are different.

29. "There is no place on the prohibition force for men who work from purely selfish motives. Prohibition officers must always work with an aim of benefitting the country, or contributing to the best interests of the public at large. They must be willing to cooperate with fellow officers of the prohibition forces."

According to the statement above, which one of the following is the chief purpose of the work of the Prohibition Bureau? (1) to insure impartial advancement of officers (2) to secure cooperation with other agencies (3) to promote general welfare (4) to reduce the taxes in this country (5) to create favorable public opinion

30. The word "fellow," as used in line 6 of question 29, means most nearly (1) subordinate (2) younger (3) inexperienced (4) superior (5) associate

Three-quarters of the examinees flunked. An agent named Gosnel, who had been on the prohibition payroll from the beginning, could neither read nor write. With 2,500 field jobs to fill, the bureau had no alternative but to draft still-easier questions. Oral tests and character investigations were also required. By the spring of 1929 the number of agents who had achieved civil service status totaled only 1,282; 604 others had been allowed to stay on without taking examinations as "temporary appointments," a special category for which they qualified by virtue of their political ties. In that year, too, the bureau was transferred from Internal Revenue to the Department of Justice, where it belonged in the first place.

The initial error had been largely Wayne Wheeler's doing. Internal Revenue lacked the experience, the machinery and the numbers to assume so vast a policing task. Wheeler, grabbing at the chance to manipulate the Prohibition Bureau, proffered his own unofficial assistance in selecting, organizing and guiding the enforcement branch. The overburdened service was glad to let him do it, and thus Wheeler functioned for a time as the *éminence grise* behind a commissioner of his own choosing. By the time the bureau finally became an arm of the Department of Justice the tradition of graft was so deeply ingrained as to resist reform.

Ex-Agent William Connors of Chicago remembers a big seizure
I'd been working for the stock exchange, a telephone man, marking the big board with chalk. We had an office ball team, and one fine day, sliding for home base, I broke my leg. By the time it mended the job was gone. I saw this ad in the papers for prohibition agents. So I took the exam, no problem, and in November, 1927, they made me an agent with a starting salary of $1,890.

They gave me a .45-caliber revolver from the Mexican War. It had a lanyard you tied around your leg, and it took two sets of three .45's on a clip that you shoved into the chamber. Nobody showed me how to handle the thing. It was up to me to find out. Luckily, I'd fired guns in the Navy during the World War. They put me on a case right away. No training, no nothing. You were supposed to learn by experience. They sent me with another rookie, name of Swanson, to search for a still in a certain house on the South Side. We took a street car. The people let us in without any fuss when we flashed our badges. We searched, and we searched, but we never found a drop. It was just a bum report.

But pretty soon we got a bona fide tip from one of our informers. He told us to expect a delivery that night by railway express of a shipment of liquor from Boston packed in wooden boxes marked FISH. We waited alongside the depot, me and Swanson, in a Model T Ford, until about 8 P.M., when a freight train pulled in and a lot of boxes marked like the informer said were dumped on the platform. (We found out later that each one contained three cases of pure, uncut whiskey, about $50,000 worth all told.) Meantime, a small panel truck had driven up. The driver picked up the cases and headed west. We rattled along after him.

As we hit Harrison Street, a blinding spotlight flashed on us from a car behind. We were caught in the beam. I knew instantly it was the gangsters' tail car, and I held up my badge in the beam and yelled as loud as I could, "Government agents!" It probably saved our lives. For all they knew we were hijackers. The truck turned left, and as I swung my wheel over to follow it, the car behind came on fast, trying to sideswipe me. I picked up speed. The truck had stopped for a red light at the far end of the street. In my rearview mirror I could see that the tail car had more power and was bound to catch up. I slammed down the accelerator, but it was no use. I braced myself with my hands against the wheel and my feet on the dashboard and warned Swanson to do the same. The car smacked us on the left. The impact stalled it momentarily; but it could still move, and I pulled up next to the panel truck.

By then I was fighting mad. I reached in and yanked the driver off his seat. I shoved him toward Swanson, who held him with his gun. Then I ran over to the stalled tail car with my revolver ready. The driver climbed out. He was about six feet four, a head taller than me, wearing a bright checked overcoat, the kind they used to call a niggerhead overcoat, and a black derby. He had his hands in his pockets, face calm as a picture. I finally recognized him from the mug shots we had at headquarters–Norm Silver, one of Bugs Moran's top lieutenants. I stuck my gun in his belly and told him to take his hands out of his pockets. He didn't move a muscle. "You big son of a bitch," I said, more scared than I like to admit. "You don't take your hands out of your pockets, I'll blow your guts out." I took a swing at him, but I couldn't even reach his jaw. Not a peep from him. He just stared at me, amused like. "You bastard," I yelled in his face. "The booze racket is one thing, but killing people is another." I cocked my gun, and Swanson called to me, "Bill, Bill, cut it out." Silver showed fear at last. "Beel, Beel," he echoed in a Jewish accent, "for Chris' sake, cut it out."

He tried to put his arm around me. "Look, let me go, let the truck go. I got five grand for you." I took another swing at him. He could probably have flattened me, but he said: "OK, take the truck and let me go. You still get the five grand." We took the pair of them in—Egan, the other hood was called—along with the $50,000 worth of booze.

A few days before they came to trial the assistant U.S. attorney, fellow named Anderson, sent for me. "Maybe you can't corroborate your statements," he said. It looked like Swanson was backing off, and I figured they might have gotten to him. "Maybe I can't," I said, "but I'm sticking to the truth as I know it." Outside the federal office a bunch of agents swarmed around me, fussing over me and patting me on the back. "You can't lick city hall," they said. "You're butting your head against a stone wall."

I realized how much protection Silver and Egan had, when they went to trial. Their boss was Bugs Moran. The courtroom was full of character witnesses, some of them bankers and former government attorneys. The place was crowded with big shots. I felt like a bum among them. There were two charges to be tried: attempted murder with a car and illegal transportation of liquor. After the judge read the first charge, the assistant U.S. attorney—the one who was supposed to prosecute Silver and Egan—get this—says, "Well, your honor, you know the crazy way people drive around this town." "Case dismissed," says the judge, and I figure everything has been fixed to get those two hoods off the hook.

The second charge is read, and the judge says, "Where's the arresting officer?" That's me. I am in the back of the courtroom, and I have to fight my way up to the bench through a mob that shoves and jostles me. I'm beginning to get scared. As I tell my story, I keep hearing, "He can't corroborate that. . . . Objection. . . . That's

*hearsay. . . ." Everybody is hollering at once. Then the judge pounds
the bench with his gavel, the hullabaloo stops, and I get the surprise of
my life. "Maybe this officer can't corroborate every statement," he says,
"but, gentlemen, I believe him." And he hands each defendant two
years in the pen.*

*I drank some before I got to be a dry agent—not whiskey, but beer; I
loved beer—and I didn't exactly deny myself afterwards. I was no
prohibitionist. I guess about 1 percent of us agents were prohibitionists.
We were never asked to take any kind of dry oath. Of course, you
weren't expected to drink. Unless you were a buy man. The buy men set
out specifically to trap saloonkeepers. They carried ear syringes and
little empty bottles in their pockets. If they could fool the bartender into
serving them, they would wait till his back was turned, suck up some of
the booze, squirt it into the little bottle, later mark it, seal it and turn it
over to the U.S. attorney's office as evidence. Some of the buy men liked
their jobs too much. I know a couple of them who became alcoholics. I
was never a buy man myself. I was too big. I weighed over two
hundred pounds. Big guys look like cops. The best buy men were kind
of small and mousey.*

*Like I say, my weakness was beer. One time we knocked over a
brewery out in Roger Touhy's territory.* [Touhy, in partnership
with Matt Kolb, a former Capone mobster, directed from
the Chicago suburb of Des Plaines both a beer and a
slot-machine business that together grossed about
$1,500,000 a year.] *Me and an old-timer, Dick Hammer, were left
to guard the place until the wreckers arrived. "Dick," I said, showing
him a big vat. "How do you get the beer out of this thing?" "Try this
valve," he said. "Only you better get something big to catch it in
because there's a lot of pressure on it. It'll be mostly foam." I found a
bucket and went to work. It took a long time for all that foam to settle,
but I gradually got a pretty fair bucket of beer. "Connors," said
Hammer, "you'll make a goddamn good agent."*

*I'm off in a corner by myself, full of beer and sweating when this
hard-looking character steps up out of nowhere and puts a pistol on me.
"What's going on here, kid?" he says. I recognized him all right.
"Look, Touhy," I said, with Dutchman's courage, "this outfit belongs
to you. So don't try to shit me." "I don't know what you're talking
about," says he. "You're a goddamn liar," I tell him. He turns red as a
beet, and I think he would have blown my head off. But there were too
many of us around.*

*I helped wreck the equipment. But Touhy's connections were good. I
don't think he even paid a fine.*

From 1920 to 1930 federal prohibition agents arrested, in
round numbers, 577,000 suspected offenders, of whom slightly
less than two-thirds were convicted. The agents seized 1,600,000
distilleries, stills, worms and fermenters, 9,000,000 gallons of
spirits, 1 billion gallons of malt liquor, 1 billion gallons of wine,
hard cider and mash, 45,000 automobiles and 1,300 boats
presumed to have transported liquor. The appraised value of
confiscated property totaled $49,000,000. The figures on state
and municipal enforcement were never computed but during the
early years probably surpassed the federal totals.

In a country where, as General Andrews reported, bootlegging
was coextensive with its entire territory, these arrests and seizures
represented only a small fraction of all violations, perhaps 5 to 10
percent. Yet they sufficed to overwhelm prosecutors, judges and
prison wardens. In New York City, in 1926, for example,
according to the calculations of Charles Merz, if all the violators
of the Volstead Act arrested during a single month (400 to 500 of
them) demanded a jury trial, every federal judge available for
prohibition cases would be occupied for a year. The backlog
accumulated during the other eleven months would then keep
them busy for eleven years, and at the end of the second year,
they would have twenty-two years of work. To avoid paralysis of
the whole legal machinery, the courts began to set aside "bargain
days" on which pending cases were disposed of without a jury by
promising the defendants light sentences if they would plead
guilty.

In the fall of 1925 an attractive new Manhattan speakeasy, the
Bridge Whist Club, opened at 14 East Forty-fourth Street, a step
from Fifth Avenue. With its nostalgic turn-of-the-century am-
biance, soft-lit booths, palatable liquor and copious free lunch, it
was an immediate success. Six months elapsed before the true
character of the Bridge Whist Club burst upon its outraged
clientele. It was a trap baited by an undercover dry agent, one
Ralph Bickle. With money from a special Prohibition Bureau
fund he had sublet the premises and converted it into a blind pig

for the sole purpose of snaring bootleggers. The operating cost during the six months came to $45,000 over and above the profits from the liquor Bickle sold. In a rear booth he had concealed a dictograph connected by wires to an adjoining room where a stenographer transcribed every word uttered within range of the machine. He thus hoped to inveigle his provisioners into betraying themselves.

But Bickle bagged only a single quarry of any importance, a wholesaler named Samuel Senate, whose blandishments the dictograph recorded as he offered $5,000 for help in landing a cargo of alcohol from a Belgian schooner. The other bootleggers Bickle dealt with remained securely anonymous, accepting orders only through middle men. One of them grew suspicious when a truck that had delivered whiskey to the Bridge Whist Club was seized almost immediately afterward. When policemen stopped by for a free nip, the bootlegger learned further, headquarters somehow always heard of it and disciplined them. A rogue with a puckish sense of humor, the bootlegger confided to Bickle shocking tales of hard-drinking, loose-living Anti-Saloon Leaguers, dry legislators and other whited sepulchers—all of them pure invention.

When Bickle's operations came to light, Mayor La Guardia demanded his indictment for breaking the liquor laws, as well as that of his superiors, Bruce Bielaski and Major Mills, for abetting him. If U.S. Attorney Buckner failed to take action against all three, the mayor added, he should be impeached. (Bickle, meanwhile, had abandoned his clumsy little man-trap and sold the sublease. Incredibly, it continued under its new management to function as a speakeasy for several more months.)

The Bridge Whist Club was no unique instance of the Prohibition Bureau's extralegal tactics. For weeks it maintained in a suite at Washington's Mayflower Hotel an undercover agent whose assignment was to entertain bootleggers. His expense account for one dinner party ran to $279. A Maryland agent wormed his way into the affections of a young woman bootlegger and proposed marriage in order to induce her to sell him liquor. At the instigation of the Virginia Anti-Saloon League the bureau dispatched agents to Norfolk to establish a black speakeasy. Directed by the state League secretary, who provided the agents with cash to buy liquor and stored it in his office temporarily while they sought a likely location for their speakeasy, they finally chose a remodeled stable on Chapel Street, hired a black bartender and a black ex-convict as manager. Their intention was to entrap suspect policemen by bribing them not to raid the place. In the words of the agent in charge, Leighton Blood, they aimed "to jam the cops for conspiracy."

A report to the bureau by Blood's assistant, Agent D. D. Mayne, read:

> I visited the premises operated by Investigator Blood. . . . I found everything operating—pool tables, bar and lunch counter—and several colored patrons were at the bar where the bartender and Investigator Blood were dispensing "white mule," or, as they call it here, corn liquor.

The gross illegality of the stratagem so troubled the bureau's counsel in Washington that Blood received a cautionary memorandum:

> . . . It will be no justification in case you are called as a witness, for you to say you did not sell . . . you can hardly escape acknowledging that you knew all about it.
>
> Of course, if you are getting evidence for the police board or expect pleas of guilty, all O.K.; but if you are to testify, the juries may want to convict you instead of the defendant.

Casting their net farther, Blood and Mayne set up stills in both Virginia and North Carolina, hiring blacks to run them. Wholesale convictions of police, county sheriffs and constables resulted. In a mixed mood of self-disgust and race hatred, Blood asked one of his Washington superiors: "Does the Treasury Department have any appropriation for fumigating its representatives? You know our colored brethren have a smell all their own and I'm much among them and am to cater to them with a swell pool hall. I'll need delousing more than any bird you ever saw."

Ira Reeves, a teetotaling Methodist, who had quit the bureau in revolt against its ethical standards, wrote:

> The most damnable and un-American methods of deceiving the incautious by Federal agents have been practiced in every enforcement district in the United States since the day attempted prohibition enforcement went into effect. The most despicable of all, to my mind, is carried on in the entrapment of bell-boys in

many of the leading hotels. The scheme usually pursued is for a
prohibition agent to take a room in the hotel, go to bed feigning to
be recovering from a spree, and plead with the bell-boy to get him
a drink. He frequently succeeds in inducing the bell-hop to do so.
Then a raid follows, the hotel is "pinched" and the bell-hop is
arrested—a most glorious achievement by the officials of the great
United States.

Besides instigating entrapment, the Anti-Saloon League took it
upon itself to pursue offenders. Thomas Jarvis, superintendent of
the League's Cincinnati district, urged members of the Women's
Christian Temperance Union to mingle with non-Union neighbors, lead them into a discussion of prohibition and discover who
might be drinking in the privacy of their homes. "We need
women of the type that are called nosey," he told them, "and the
nosier they are the better results they will get. If positive evidence
of liquor violations is found you may rest assured information
will be welcomed by the Anti-Saloon League and such homes
will be visited."

One of the League's most ruthless *agents provocateurs* was an
itinerant evangelist from Illinois, the Reverend W. C. Gant. In
1923 he traveled under League auspices to Knoxville, Tennessee,
where he preached the Gospel while secretly reporting to the
federal authorities any followers whom he could spy out as liquor
law violators. His first victim was a boy he persuaded to procure
some white mule, then had arrested. Deciding to take prohibition
enforcement into his own hands, Gant adopted the ominous
pseudonym "Mr. Shoot" and hired himself out to a Jefferson
County farmer as a field hand. When cutting corn one morning,
he faked sudden sickness, dropped to the ground and whimpered
for a restorative. A fellow corn cutter administered a slug of
moonshine. Restored to his labors, Gant so ingratiated himself
with the other field hands that they confided to him the existence
of a still not far away operated by three villagers, Anderson
Green, his son Claude and Sam Bailey. Gant sought them out. If
they needed a buyer, he assured them, he knew a Knoxville
bootlegger who would pay top prices for all the booze they could
distill, and he offered to act as go-between. The trio agreed. Gant
arranged to handle the first delivery on the night of September
29, 1923. He said he would wait on a road near the still, blinking
his lights to identify himself.

Gant arrived at the appointed time and spot after depositing a prohibition agent named Hill in a hiding place a few hundred feet away. When the moonshiners appeared on foot, he insisted they load the liquor into his car before he paid for it. They balked, and a dispute erupted. Though without police powers of any sort, Mr. Shoot pulled a gun and shouted: "You're under arrest!" upon which the moonshiners started back down the road with their liquor. Gant fired a burst. Anderson Green fell, shot in the back. He died three days later in a Knoxville hospital, after naming Mr. Shoot as his murderer.

A Knoxville jury indicted the evangelist, but the Prohibition Bureau, no doubt at the behest of the Anti-Saloon League, had the case transferred to federal jurisdiction. It was able to do this under a law, dating from 1833, which authorized the removal to a federal court of the trial of a government officer for an offense committed in his official capacity. The trial got under way ten months later. Both the dead man's son and Sam Bailey testified against Gant. The latter had, meanwhile, become a candidate for sheriff of Knox County and, according to witnesses from the local prohibition force, had suggested that "we keep this little Jefferson County shooting affair quiet" lest it spoil his chances for election. Agent Hill swore that he, not Gant, fired the fatal shot. It was, he explained, an accident. The jury acquitted Mr. Shoot.

"The putting of the fear of God in the minds of those who fear neither God nor man is the chief function of good government," said the Reverend Clarence True Wilson, general secretary of the Methodist Board of Temperance, Prohibition and Public Morals and a pillar of the Anti-Saloon League, and he proposed calling out the marines to enforce the Volstead Act. The League spirit, as exemplified by Wilson, gradually gained ground among some of the law's top administrators. Commissioner of Internal Revenue David Blair issued a leaflet urging all citizens to spy on their neighbors and to use telephones outside their neighborhood to report offenders anonymously. Every bootlegger, Blair said in a speech at Philadelphia's Point Breeze Presbyterian Church, should be stood up against a wall and shot. The U.S. Attorney for the Western District of Pennsylvania, John D. Meyer, appealed to students at the Carnegie Institute of Technology and at the University of Pittsburgh to inform on fellow students who drank liquor. When attacked for his fanaticism, Meyer retorted:

"If necessary, I will put a spy on every doorstep in Pittsburgh."

Few officials of the Prohibition Bureau itself more perfectly reflected the League mentality than Charles Williams, custodian of captured liquors for the District of Columbia. "You think that a man ought to have the penal servitude fixed on him for selling a glass of beer?" Senator Reed asked him during the 1926 Senate hearings.

"Yes, that is my private opinion," Williams replied.

"Do you not think it would be a worse crime to take a man away from his family and lock him up in a penitentiary for a year or two and put prison stripes on him—that that would be an infinitely worse crime against nature than the act of selling a man a glass of beer. . . . ?"

"No, sir, I do not think so," said Williams.

In Lorraine, Ohio, Mrs. Julia Nazure, almost nine months pregnant, incurred a jail sentence for a minor infraction of the liquor law. She gave birth the next day. As soon as she could leave the hospital, she was committed with her baby to the Marysville Reformatory.

Charles Gundlacht, born in Germany seventy years before his adopted country went dry, never lost his native love of beer. Since the early days of the Noble Experiment he had been brewing it himself on the meager little farm he worked with his wife near Leonardtown, Maryland, about forty miles south of Washington. A convivial soul, Gundlacht let no visitor, whether friend or stranger, leave his house without offering him some home brew. In September, 1927, a stranger named, oddly enough, Rudolph Brewer, stopped by ostensibly to ask directions, and Gundlacht pressed a foaming mug into his hands. Later that day, in Gundlacht's absence, Brewer returned, showed Mrs. Gundlacht his Prohibition Bureau credentials and proceeded to break every bottle he could find. On September 16 he came again accompanied by three fellow agents. This time the old farmer confronted them with a shotgun. "I know who you are," he said when they flashed their badges, "and I don't give a goddamn." He warned them not to move any closer. They advanced, and he fired a blast, wounding one agent in the knee. An answering volley felled him with a bullet through the foot. Then, before his wife's eyes, as he lay on the ground begging for mercy, Brewer stood over him and put a bullet through his head.

A federal jury accepted Brewer's plea of self-defense. The indictments of his three companions were nol-prossed.

Gundlacht was one of hundreds of suspected or proven liquor law violators killed by prohibition agents. Hundreds more died at the hands of coastguardsmen, Customs officers, state and municipal police.

New York City, March 11, 1920. Four agents enter a flat on East Seventy-sixth Street, where a chauffeur, Harry Carlton, occasionally sells liquor. After buying a bottle, they show their badges. Carlton draws a knife (or so they later testify) whereupon Agent Stewart McMullen shoots him dead. "A cold-blooded murder without justification," says the assistant district attorney assigned to prosecute him. The case is transferred to a federal court. McMullen fails to produce any knife to support his plea of self-defense. He is nevertheless acquitted.

Havre de Grace, Maryland, August 1, 1925. John Buongore, a war veteran, sells two quarts of liquor to two undercover agents. They arrest him. Buongore bolts. One of the agents, Fubershaw by name, shoots him twice as he runs, a third time fatally after he falls. Case transferred to a federal court. Fubershaw pleads self-defense. Buongore, he claims, was reaching for a gun. Acquitted.

Niagara Falls, New York, May 28, 1928. Jacob Hanson, secretary of the Elks' Lodge, is driving home early in the morning. Two coastguardsmen, Glenn Jennings and Frank Beck, signal him to halt by waving flashlights. Since they wear overalls and sheepskin coats instead of their uniforms, Hanson takes them for bandits and speeds up. Now certain they have intercepted a liquor smuggler, they open fire. A bullet, crashing through the windshield, gouges out Hanson's right eye and lodges in his skull. For four months he lingers in agony in a hospital. The Niagara County grand jury indicts Jennings and Beck for second-degree assault. Seymour Lowman, who succeeded General Andrews as Assistant Secretary of the Treasury in charge of prohibition enforcement, summarizes the shooting in his report to Undersecretary Mills thus: "Refused to submit to search and tried to run down officers." He neglects to mention that the car carried no liquor.

Hanson finally dies, and the coastguardsmen are reindicted for manslaughter, second degree. "Thereupon," the New York *World* editorializes, "United States District Attorney Templeton began a series of legal maneuvers on behalf of the defendants. No shyster lawyer skating on the edge of disbarment has gone farther to defeat justice. . . ." The outcome: trial and acquittal in a federal court.

Next to self-defense the commonest alibi offered by trigger-quick agents was accident, a plausible one since they received scant training in marksmanship before the Prohibition Bureau entrusted them with weapons. There were the tireshooters who only meant to put the suspect's car out of commission and the stumblers who lost their footing at the crucial instant and misdirected the bullet.

On June 8, 1929, Henry Virkula, a Minnesota confectioner, was driving near the Canadian border with his wife and two children when a pair of Customs inspectors ordered him to stop. Before he could obey, the car moved about another ten feet. A fusillade of twenty-six bullets pierced it, killing Virkula. No liquor was found in the car. "I fired into the ground," one of the agents explained, "and then fired two shots at the wheels, hoping to flatten the tires."

Agent Crumpton typefied the stumblers. Having shot to death Jesse Coffee, a moonshiner, at his still near Muscadine, Alabama, Crumpton deposed that he had aimed to the right of Coffee, but slipped, causing his pistol to swerve.

Now and then an agent's stray bullet killed or wounded the innocent. In February, 1924, the victim was a United States Senator. Strolling along Pennsylvania Avenue with his wife, Senator Frank L. Greene of Vermont heard gunfire from an alley, started toward it and stepped between a fleeing bootlegger and a prohibition agent. A bullet caught him above the right eye. He recovered after surgery and a month in the hospital.

Almost invariably the federal authorities tried to remove an agent indicted by a local grand jury from the jurisdiction of the local courts which were likelier to convict him and so intensify public opposition to the Volstead Act. When possible, they also kept the shooting secret. The Prohibition Bureau admitted its agents had killed 137 persons during the twenties, while the Customs Service and the Coast Guard conceded responsibility for 36 deaths, but these figures fell far short of the actual totals. Senator Millard E. Tydings of Maryland uncovered 51 killings omitted from the official reports, and he estimated that if the people slain by state and municipal officers were included, the

total would exceed 1,000. In a national survey the New York
American counted 1,550 dead. How many hundreds had been
injured nobody even attempted to compute. Newspaper cartoons
depicted the dry agent as a hulking brute with a smoking pistol
in each hand and a badge inscribed LICENSED TO KILL.

The reaction of prohibition fanatics to violent and bloody
enforcement revolted rational drys, as well as wets. On the
Senate floor Senator Smith Brookhart of Iowa dismissed the
protests against the slaughter as "gush stuff about murder by
men who make mistakes once in a while." Kindred spirits in the
House broke into applause at the news that a Washington
policeman had shot down the young driver of a liquor truck. In
Aurora, Illinois, on March 25, 1929, six state enforcement agents
invaded the home of Peter DeKing, a suspected bootlegger. One
of them clubbed him over the head with the butt of a shotgun. As
he dropped senseless, his wife, Lillian, sprang to his side. A blast
from the shotgun killed her. When told of the atrocity, Ella Boole
of the WCTU, remarked: "Well, she was evading the law, wasn't
she?"

Many of the shootings were no doubt justifiable on the grounds
of self-defense. During the same ten-year period fifty-five prohibition agents lost their lives in the line of duty, not to mention
fifteen Customs and Immigration officers and five enlisted
coastguardsmen who clashed with liquor smugglers. "Our little
band of martyrs," Commissioner Haynes called them.

"What the prohibition situation needs first of all," said the
humanitarian and temperance leader Jane Addams, "is disarma-
ment."

*Former Special Agent Clarence Pickering remembers the people he
killed*

    *The very day it started is when I became a prohibition agent. I was
an absolute dry. Still am.*

    *I'd been knocking around the world for thirteen years, ever since I
left home at the age of fifteen. Bummed my way back and forth across
the States any number of times. Sailed in the merchant marine for
almost six years. Just before the World War I operated a locomotive.
In 1917 I joined the Navy and saw plenty of action as a deckhand,
then quartermaster's mate.*

K

*A U.S. Senator—Senator Porter J. McCumber of North Dakota—
happened to be visiting Detroit, where I was living at the time,
somehow heard about me and recommended me to the Prohibition
Bureau. I got no specific orders. They didn't know a thing about
enforcement, and I didn't either. They simply told me that an
overwhelming quantity of liquor was crossing the Canadian border at
North Dakota and for me to report to the federal office in Bismarck. I
picked up my badge there, a .45 Colt, 300 rounds of ammunition and a
nice long blackjack. Later they gave me "Aunt Symanthia," which is
what I called my machine gun.*

*I started out on my own in a big old government Cadillac touring
car with half the top gone. I drove into Canada. My idea was to hang
around the big distilleries, see what U.S. cars were loading liquor and
follow them back to where they stored it in the States. After several
days I finally got a tail on four loads moving south toward the North
Dakota border. I crossed over behind them and kept them in sight until
they came to a spot about seven miles from Minot. It was night then.
They suddenly cut their lights and turned down a side road. I didn't
dare follow too close. I decided to wait till morning before taking the
side road. It led to the tipple of a worked-out coal mine, and I knew
they were down inside.*

*I left the Cad behind a bunch of trees and entered the mine,
swtiching on my flashlight, went down along a shaft and into an open
space. There were a couple of hundred cases piled up in there. But I
had no time to count them. One of the men started shooting at me. I
returned the salutation and sent him to his reward. The others took off.
I left the body and drove back to Minot to get the sheriff. Him and his
deputies helped me impound the liquor—332 cases, it turned out—and
round up the fugitives. We caught them all.*

*I had one of them beside me in the Cad on the way to the marshal's
office, and I made a bad mistake. I let him have too much freedom, as I
disliked to abuse anyone as long as he behaved. That guy really thought
he had it made and took a fairly healthy swing at me. The only thing
he hadn't counted on was my long blackjack. He found it in a hurry as
I stopped the car and let him have it on the side of the head. It laid him
out cold.*

*That posed a problem. I had one very dead man already to account
for, and if this one didn't survive the impact of my blackjack, I was in
a way of having to explain to my bureau. I could hear the sob sisters
say loud and clear, "Why, all this man did was to use his fist to keep
the officer from jailing him." Anyway the thug survived and went to*

trial with the rest of them. They each got two years in Leavenworth.

The man in the coal mine was the first I killed. (I'm not talking about the war, of course.) I never liked the idea of killing anybody, but if he was going to kill me and I got a chance to kill him first, I was going to do it, and I still would. I followed that practice all the way through. I think I killed forty-two people.

One killing was accidental. They teamed me up with an agent named Dean, told us to get off our dead asses and find out who was bringing all the booze into upper Michigan from Canada. We hired ourselves a motor launch, stocked it with a week's supply of grub and went out on the lake. The second night we spotted a lugger running without lights. We sailed up to her to ask what she might be hauling. A rifle shot answered us, hitting our stern, and she ran away. We had a couple of pineapples aboard and I tossed one after her. It tore holes in her side, but she kept on going. So I opened fire with good old Symanthia. That stopped her. When we finally boarded her, we found a woman's body lying on top of the cargo with a machine bullet in her and two live men. They were all aliens. It seems she'd been on the tramp, got acquainted with those two and gone along with them for a joyride. It was a hell of a mess to explain; but we were exonerated, and the two foreigners went to jail.

About the hottest shoot-up I ever got into happened outside the town of Deering, North Dakota. I had a new partner then, Thomas McClean, a redheaded, freckle-faced giant—"Big Red"—the greatest guy I was ever privileged to work with. We'd trailed these six carloads of liquor from Canada to an empty corral near Deering. We watched for a while through field glasses. There were a dozen men, half of them carrying .30-.30 Springfields. I'd packed one myself during the war, and I knew they could tear your head off a mile away. The cars were parked in a circle, each one facing out for a quick getaway. It was getting dark, and we decided to spend the night under the stars. We bedded down for a few hours in a field near the corral. At dawn we moved in from different directions, Red with a .45 Colt and me with old Symanthia.

They'd all been sleeping in the ranch house. The first to appear and see us let out a yell. I spoke a few well-chosen words to the effect that they were all under arrest. Only one of them chose to argue enough to chance death. He grabbed for a rifle and was swinging it toward me when a bullet from Red's Colt entered his head just below his right eye.

We had no more trouble after that. Red took the first car with one of

the monkeys as driver and led the parade to Minot. . . . The sentence
for the eleven defendants was two years apiece.
   I worked with Red off and on for four more years until we were
ambushed by some gangsters in Cicero. I came to in the hospital with
slugs in my shoulder and side. Red was dead.
   With Red gone I lost my taste for the game and a few months later I
quit.
   I still believe in prohibition. I feel it should be revived if only they
could get somebody to enforce the law. But what are you going to do
when you have crooked sheriffs, crooked federal officers . . . you can't
weed those people out.

Early on the morning of November 22, 1922, Jerry Costello
the owner of a Manhattan livery on East 107th Street, opene
his door to two strangers, the one squat, round and pursy, th
other ponderous but considerably taller. They were, said th
shorter man, speaking in a rich Italian accent, fruit an
vegetable venders. Their street cart had met with an acciden
and they wanted to rent a horse and wagon for the day. Whil
Costello busied himself hitching up a dray horse, the stranger
wandered around the stable, eyes peeled and nostrils flared. A
length they detected a winy aroma that drew them to a flight c
steep, narrow stairs. With their bulk the descent was not easy
but they managed to squeeze themselves down into a basemen
storage room. There they counted fifty-three barrels of wine
"This is enough," whispered the shorter man, resuming th
accents of their Lower East Side neighborhood. "You drive th
wagon out a ways while I get a search warrant."
   Izzy and Moe had triumphed again—to the huge amusemer
of millions. It was an irony that the most effective, honest agen
in the history of the Prohibition Bureau should have been th
only ones to charm and tickle the public. They were the comi
relief of enforcement. Hiding their cunning behind the mask c
buffoonery, they had the appeal of funny paper characters, an
the press never wearied of reporting their antics. By an incredibl
diversity of dodges and disguises they arrested, in the course c
five years, almost 5,000 lawbreakers, the great majority of whor
were convicted, and confiscated more than 5,000,000 bottles c
booze worth about $15,000,000. Of all the prohibition cas

prosecuted in New York City up to 1926 fully a fifth resulted from the wiles of Izzy and Moe.

Isidor Einstein was a forty-year-old $40-a-week postal clerk when the Volstead Act took effect. With a wife, four children and his father to support, he immediately applied for the slightly better paid job of dry agent. He brought to it an unusual combination of talents. Of Austrian origin, he spoke fluently not only German, but also Hungarian, Polish and Yiddish, knew a little Russian, Spanish, French and Italian and even a few words of Chinese. In English he could mimic any foreign accent. A self-taught musician, he played the harmonica, the trombone and the violin. "I ain't no Heifetz," he said, "but I could earn a living." He could probably have earned a living as an actor, too.

Izzy's first target was a Brooklyn workingman's saloon. Wearing grease-stained overalls, he followed one of the habitués into the place, waddled up to the bar and ordered a near beer. Standing five feet five and weighing almost a quarter of a ton, bald, double-chinned and globular, he looked as harmless as a panda. "Wouldn't you like a lollipop on the side?" asked the barkeep acidly, causing merriment among the whiskey-drinking regulars. He was newly employed in New York, Izzy hastened to explain, and unfamiliar with its customs, but lest he appear a piker, he would buy a pint of whiskey, if not too costly. The bartender sold him one, whereupon Izzy, in gentle melancholy tones, pronounced the words that became his standard refrain: "There's sad news here. You're under arrest."

After a succession of coups Izzy persuaded his old friend, Moe Smith, to join him in the service. Moe ran a cigar store on the Lower East Side and also managed a small boxing club, having himself fought professionally in his youth. A taciturn, introverted man, he was the perfect foil for the ebullient Izzy. Together they developed a repertoire of more than a hundred masquerades, not one of which, they claimed, their quarry ever penetrated.

To collect evidence, each sewed into his breast pocket a funnel connected by a rubber tube to a concealed flask. He would hand the bartender a bill to change and, as he went to the cash register, toss the drink down the funnel. Izzy never packed a gun. Moe always did, but fired it only twice in his entire career as a dry agent, the first time to scare off a vicious dog, the second to shoot open a locked door.

A winter night. The partners stand outside a speakeasy, Izzy in the guise of an ailing derelict, coatless, teeth chattering. Moe, playing the good Samaritan, hammers on the door, when it opens, cries: "Give this poor man a drink. He's frostbitten." As Izzy slumps fainting against his rescuer, the owner lets them in, fetches a hooker of whiskey and lifts it to Izzy's lips. Izzy gazes up at him dolefully. "There's sad news here. . . ."

The Bronx. A soft-drink parlor frequented by a sporting crowd, where, according to rumor, beverages stronger than pop are dispensed to those the management knows. Across the way, Van Cortlandt Park with its various athletic fields. From the park come bounding Izzy and Moe, mammoth in football togs, their faces muddied, leading nine other agents similarly camouflaged. Uttering boyish whoops, they announce their victory in the last game of the season. They can now break training. How about a drink to celebrate? Not to dampen such joyous spirits, the proprietor yields and, as Izzy puts it later, "*his* season was ended."

The Fern Club, a theatrical water hole, admission by membership only. Introducing himself as "Ethelbert Santerre," an actor at liberty for lack of a suitable role, Izzy qualifies. He then sponsors Moe and a third agent posing as actors. The denouement: summonses for the manager and the waiter who served them drinks.

On St. Patrick's Day of 1923 Izzy and Moe festooned themselves with shamrocks and scattering "Begorras!" right and left, knocked over a couple of shebeens. They invaded Harlem in blackface to get the goods on a bootlegging delicatessen. In Sheepshead Bay they averted suspicion by entering their victim's establishment, a fishermen's haunt, with a string of fresh-caught fish. They impersonated hayseed tourists, farmers, cattle ranchers, society swells twirling gold-headed canes, dairymen, coal heavers, hod carriers, longshoremen, street cleaners, gas meter inspectors, streetcar conductors, shipyard workers, firemen, gravediggers, department-store truck drivers ("I delivered a little C.O.D.—," Izzy recalled. " 'Come on Down' to the federal building."). Working alone, Izzy cast himself as a Polish count, a long-haired violinist, a cosmopolitan gourmet who ordered his dinner in French ("And gave the head waiter and the proprietor some bad news in plain English"), a beauty contest judge and, to get into the exclusive Assembly, where jurists could drink

discreetly, a magistrate ("The Assembly was adjourned"). Izzy
found he could sometimes fool a bartender by telling the simple
truth. "Care to sell a pint to a deserving prohibition agent?" he
would ask with a roguish wink and dropping his voice to a mock
conspiratorial whisper, "I'm Izzy Einstein." "He says he's Izzy
Einstein," the bartender would tell the other customers and amid
the general laughter slip the agent a pint.

Moe tended to shun publicity, as a prudent snooper should,
but the ham in Izzy craved the limelight. He often notified the
press of an impending raid. For the edification of the Reverend
John Roach Straton's Calvary Baptist congregation at 123 West
Fifty-seventh Street Izzy timed a raid on a neighboring speakeasy to coincide with the recessional of a Sunday morning
service. The communicants were thus afforded the gratifying
spectacle of Satan's brew streaming down the sewer as dry
wreckers with axes staved in barrels of beer and smashed cases of
whiskey. That same Sunday Izzy and Moe surpassed themselves
with a record-breaking seventy-one arrests.

"Einstein," wrote O. O. McIntyre in his syndicated column,
"New York Day by Day," "has become as famous in New York
as the Woolworth Building. No morning paper is complete
without some account of his exploits." The *Tribune* described Izzy
as "the master mind of the Federal rum-ferrets." The Brooklyn
Eagle reported:

> Izzy does not sleep. He's on the job night and day, and
> accomplishes more for the drys than half a dozen Anti-Saloon
> Leagues.
> It's getting so now that a saloon-keeper hesitates in serving the
> wants of his oldest and best-known customer, for fear that he may
> suddenly develop into Izzy.
> A few more Izzies scattered over the country and the U.S.
> would be bone dry, parched, and withered.

Speakeasy owners who could obtain a photograph of Izzy—
which was not hard since he cheerfully posed for press photogra-
phers—would hang it behind the bar inscribed with the warning,
LOOK OUT FOR THIS MAN or THIS MAN IS POISON.

Occasionally the Prohibition Bureau dispatched Izzy and
Moe, singly or together, to other sinful cities. In Ithaca, New
York, the seat of Cornell University, masquerading as alumni,

they nosed out the undergraduates' favorite drinking spots. In Hollywood, wearing armor, they mingled with extras on the set of a medieval spectacular. A halberdier and a troubadour led them to a notorious movie actors' gin mill and shortly, to use a classic Einsteinian phrase, "what it was out of was business."

During his travels Izzy kept track of how long it took him to find a drink in each city. New Orleans set the speed record. Between the station and his hotel he asked the taxi driver where he could slake his thirst. The taxi driver offered to sell him a pint then and there. Elapsed time: thirty-five seconds. In Pittsburgh, where he disguised himself as a Polish mill worker, it was eleven minutes; in Atlanta, seventeen minutes. Chicago and St. Louis tied at twenty-one minutes. In Cleveland Izzy had to wait twenty-nine minutes before a vaudeville theater usher could leave long enough to steer him to a speakeasy. Washington required the longest search—one hour. Izzy finally got an address from a policeman.

Detroit was the scene of Izzy's proudest ploy. In a Woodward Avenue dive the bartender refused to serve him because, he apologized, pointing to a picture of Izzy himself draped in black crepe, "Izzy Epstein's in town." Izzy corrected him. "You mean Einstein, don't you?" The bartender insisted it was "Epstein." "I'll bet you," Izzy ventured. "What'll you bet?" said the bartender. Izzy suggested the price of a drink. The bartender poured him a shot. After emptying it into his funnel, Izzy arrested him.

The enforcement careers of Izzy and Moe ended abruptly. Professional jealousy was largely responsible. "You get your name in the newspapers all the time," one of Izzy's superiors complained, "whereas mine hardly ever gets mentioned. I must ask you to remember that you are merely a subordinate—not the whole show." On November 13, 1925, the two agents were dismissed "for the good of the service." Wayne Wheeler had once written admiringly to them: "The bootlegger who gets away from you has to get up early in the morning." He interceded in vain. A bureau spokesman solemnly declared: "The service must be dignified. Izzy and Moe belong on the vaudeville stage."

They both became insurance salesmen. Izzy died in 1938 of an infection following the amputation of his right leg. Moe survived him by twenty-two years, dying in 1960 at the age of seventy-three.

Albie Einstein remembers his father, Izzy

Every summer Pop used to take us up to Saratoga Springs, Mom, and me and my three older brothers. We stayed at this same old farmhouse outside the city. I was seven the first summer in 1922, and it wasn't for a couple of years that I understood the reason. Pop had been assigned to the area because of the racing season with all the socialites and gangsters gathering there and the nighbclub activity.

It must have been in 1924 when I was surprised one morning to see Pop and Joe—he was fifteen then, my oldest brother—dressed up in old rags with their faces black from coal dust, mounting a horse and wagon full of coal. They said they were going to Albany. I'd seen Pop dressed up so many different ways I figured he was going on another raid. Albany is almost thirty miles from Saratoga Springs, but they were back the same day. They'd raided a coalyard that sold liquor on the side. But that was nothing. In his coal man's outfit Pop once made twenty raids in a single day.

Another time Pop used me as a kind of decoy, though I didn't realize it at the time. We were driving home on Sunday from visiting some relatives in New Jersey. Pop never learned to drive. He either got a friend to drive him, or he hired a car and chauffeur for the day. On this trip back he suddenly told the driver to pull over and he says to me, "Albie, come with me." I was about nine years old. "Where are you going?" Mom wants to know. "We'll be right back," Pop says and tells her to stay in the car.

We walk into this saloon. Pop goes up to the bar, holding me by the hand and says to the bartender, "Give the kid a glass of milk, and I'll have a fast one." I was flabbergasted, but I knew enough to keep my mouth shut. Out comes the milk and a shot of booze. "You're under arrest," says Pop.

Pop rarely drank himself. I never saw the stuff in the house during prohibition. Wine, we had wine for the high holidays. But never booze. He wasn't against drinking. Not at all. He was no temperance man. But this was his job. He felt that as long as prohibition was the law of the land, it had to be enforced. I think it got to be a game with him.

There wasn't much profit in it. All through prohibition we lived in a tenement on Ridge Street, a four-story walk-up. We had the first floor, two parents and four kids jammed into three rooms.

I saw Moe Smith there often. He and Pop would make their plans at our house and start out from there. Moe always gave me a quarter.

Some nights three or four agents would come to the house. Before *they left, they would all check out their guns. Except Pop. I knew he kept one in his roll-top desk, but I never saw him take it out. After they left, I would look in the desk. The gun was always there.*

I waited up for him all one night, watching by the window. He finally came in around 6 A.M., dog tired. I was so relieved to see him. I asked him what happened, and he told me he'd made one of the biggest raids of his career—a tremendous haul, about half a million dollars' worth.

I cried when Pop told us he'd been fired. I just couldn't believe it. I asked him, "Could this really happen to you? Say it isn't so." He patted me on the shoulder and said, "Never mind. I'm still with them." He thought they were going to keep him on in some undercover role. But it didn't work out that way.

The day they fired him he got a telegram from some theatrical big shot, Charles Dillingham, I think it was. It said, "We're ready to offer you six figures for a vaudeville tour." I was there. I saw it. I read it. My brother Joe explained to me what six figures meant—at least $100,000. "Oh, Pop's going into vaudeville!" I said. He just laughed and tossed the telegram aside.

12. *The Poison Cup*

YOU could hear them before you saw them. They made a percussive sound on the pavement—the thump of the crutches, the toes tap-tapping, the slap of the heel. It was the way the "jake-jazzed" walked, when they could still walk at all. Thump-tap-slap, thump-tap-slap. . . .

The earliest reported cases of jake foot occurred in Wichita, Kansas, where thirty years earlier Carry Nation had wielded her hatchet against the saloons of James Burnes and John Herrig. The jake trotters, as they were also known, dragged their useless feet past the monument raised to Carry at the railroad station. By March, 1930, 500 Wichitans—1 percent of the adult population—had been afflicted. Day after day scores of them made their painful way to the office of the city health commissioner, all telling the same story. They had been drinking Jamaica ginger. Though legally available through medical prescription only, it was bootlegged by nearly every drugstore in the city at 30 to 50 cents a two-ounce bottle. Wichitans too poor to afford the whiskey distilled in this supposedly driest of the forty-eight states, drank Jamaica ginger, sitting at the soda fountain and blunting its fiery bite by mixing it with a milk shake.

The fluid extract of Jamaica ginger, a few drops of it tempered with a little warm water and sugar, had long been a household remedy for stomachache. It contained water, oil of sugar, ash and 82 percent ethyl alcohol, an intoxicating preparation, but no deadlier than whiskey. Because of its alcoholic content, the Prohibition Bureau had restricted it to medical use.

The first symptoms produced by bootleg jake appeared within three or four days. The calf muscles hurt. Then the fingers began to tingle and grow numb. Soon the victim could no longer manipulate them, could not strike a match, wind a watch, tie a shoelace, hold a knife and fork. By the end of the second or third week paralysis attacked his feet. They drooped forward uselessly, the toes pointing down, all control lost. Manual workers—carpenters, painters, masons—became totally unemployable. They crowded the county poor farms beyond capacity.

Jake foot was not confined to Kansas. During the spring of 1930 it broke out among the blacks and poor whites of Mississippi, 8,000 of them; it spread through Texas, Oklahoma, Tennessee, Georgia, Louisiana. Several hundred cases were reported in New England. All together, between March and June, U.S. Public Health officers counted about 15,000 cases. Among the principal wholesalers of jake was a Kansas ring that numbered four Sedgwick County deputies and the county attorney of nearby Ford County.

There was no cure for jake foot. Quack doctors swindled victims who had any savings left to pay them. A Wichita veterinarian charged $5 for massaging the afflicted with liniment while they held the electrodes of an old galvanic battery. Under the delusion that crude oil would help them, droves of sufferers hobbled to oil pools to dangle their feet in the muck.

For months the exact ingredient of jake that caused paralysis remained a mystery. Then a government chemist, analyzing a confiscated batch, found the compound tricresyl phosphate. Through ignorance or indifference the bootleggers' chemists, unable to obtain pure ethyl alcohol, had combined gingerroot and alcohol denatured with tricresyl phosphate. Its effect on the human organism, the investigators concluded still later, was to inhibit the mechanism of nerve transmission. This observation led to the development by German chemical warfare researchers, during World War II, of a Pandora's box of horrors—the nerve gases Tabun, Sarin and Soman.

Methyl alcohol, also called carbinol, methanol, wood spirit and wood alcohol, is a colorless, faintly aromatic liquor obtained naturally by the destructive distillation of wood and synthetically by combining carbon monoxide and hydrogen. Industry uses it chiefly as a base for varnishes, a fuel, an intermediate in the manufacture of formaldehyde and an automobile antifreeze. It is a virulent poison that attacks the brain and spinal chord. Thirty to sixty milligrams—a droplet not easy to see with the naked eye—can kill. Depending on many variables, the symptoms of methyl alcohol poisoning may appear within half an hour to a day or more. They include general debility, nausea, vomiting, severe headache, abdominal pain, labored breath and a bluish discoloration of the skin, a sign that the blood is not receiving enough oxygen. The victim's temperature drops below normal; his skin grows cold and clammy; he becomes delirious, goes into convulsions, then into coma. Finally, the respiratory system is paralyzed, and death quickly follows. Methyl alcohol damages the nerve cells of the retina so that even if the victim survives, he is apt to be partly or totally blind for life.

The action of phenol or carbolic acid, a drug used extensively as a disinfectant, is corrosive. Half an ounce taken internally will usually prove fatal in two to twelve hours. Introduced through a wound or body cavity, a much smaller amount can cause death. Though it has a characteristic pungent odor, a man already drunk or with a defective sense of smell might easily mistake it for a harmless beverage.

Mercuric chloride or corrosive sublimate, which serves mainly as an antiseptic, is one of the deadliest substances known to toxicologists. Minutes after ingestion, it tears at the intestines. The victim vomits blood-stained matter. He is seized by a sudden, violent diarrhea and passes bloody stools. As the poison progresses through his system, he feels an intense need to empty his bowels and bladder, but can no longer do so. He may die in an hour or linger for two or three weeks. . . .

Lest it wreck a major segment of American industry, the Prohibition Bureau had to release enormous quantities of alcohol. Dyes, paints and varnishes, explosives, photographic film, synthetic textiles, anesthetics, insecticides, vacuum tubes—to list at random a few products among thousands—required alcohol to manufacture. To confine this alcohol to legitimate, nonbeverage uses, the bureau devised a complex system. First, pure ethyl alcohol was distilled under government license. Most of it was then denatured according to various formulas by the addition of poisons, including, besides those described above, sulfuric acid, hydrochloric acid, pyridine, benzol, aniline, iodine. By 1928 there were fifty-five alcohol distilleries scattered around the country, seventy-two bonded warehouses and eighty-two denaturing plants. Many distilleries maintained their own denaturing plants. In either case government inspectors were ever present to prevent diversion and to ensure that the denaturers observed the prescribed formulas.

Of the approximately 650,000,000 gallons of ethyl alcohol distilled during the first eight years of prohibition, about 115,000,000 were allocated in the pure state mainly to food products, pharmaceuticals and scientific research. The rest underwent denaturation, rendering it unfit to drink. There were seventy-five denaturing formulas, each designed to meet the requirements of different manufacturing processes. Six of them, applicable to products like antifreeze solutions, varnishes and canned heat, called for complete denaturing with wood alcohol predominant. Such evil-smelling poisons as pyridine and benzene were added to discourage anybody reckless enough to imbibe the stuff. Completely denatured alcohol defied detoxification by redistilling or any other method. Under the regulations every container had to be labeled with a skull-and-crossbones, the word "POISON," and the warning: "Completely denatured alcohol is a violent poison. It cannot be applied externally to human or animal tissues without serious injurious results. It cannot be taken internally without inducing blindness and general physical decay, ultimately resulting in death."

The remaining sixty-nine special denaturing formulas applied to commodities that could not be manufactured at all with wood alcohol or whose use precluded malodorous compounds, such as barbers' supplies, liniment and surgical thread. Formula No. 5, for example, authorized for use in the manufacture of photographic collodion, specified 65 pounds of sulfuric ether, 3 pounds of cadmium iodide and 3 pounds of ammonium iodide—all toxic—to 100 gallons of ethyl alcohol. A skilled chemist, however, could "clean" most varieties of specially denatured alcohol and recover ethyl alcohol.

To obtain a withdrawal permit, the manufacturer had first to submit a technical description of the commodity he wished to wholesale and a justification of the amount of alcohol requested. For denatured alcohol he paid no tax. Ethyl alcohol carried none either if intended for hospitals or scientific research. Otherwise, the tax was $1.10 a gallon.

The system failed spectacularly. General Andrews once called the industrial alcohol plants "nothing more or less than bootlegging organizations." As the alcohol traveled its circuitous route from distiller to market, it became increasingly difficult to control. Even at the initial stage, the distillation, a substantial amount of pure ethyl alcohol reached bootleggers. This was the kind most sought after since it could be flavored and sold within a few hours. Bribable storekeeper-gaugers were glad to augment their wretched wages of $4 a day, paid only by the day, with the $1,000 or more the lawbreakers could afford to offer them. They would let distillers secretly distill more alcohol than their permits allowed. The surplus went to bootleggers, who split the profits with the distillers. Some bootlegging gang lords had their own underlings trained in the technique of gauging so that they could qualify for distillery inspection jobs.

At the second stage, denaturation, a wealth of possible chicanery presented itself, all of it requiring the connivance of both gaugers and manufacturers. If the denaturer held a permit for, say, 300 fifty-gallon barrels of ethyl alcohol a week, he might denature only 200 and sell the others to a bootlegger. Or he might falsely label the extra barrels DENATURED. On his books the transaction would appear perfectly legal, thanks to a few manufacturers who allowed him to list their names as consignees. They might receive part, all or none of the consignment, or the bootlegger himself might maintain a factory entitling him to a specified amount of alcohol for industrial use. Whatever the arrangement, the diverted gallons would end up in the bootlegger's cutting plant.

The hardest dodge to detect was diversion by reconsignment. Here the denaturer would address his shipment to a bona fide consignee, but in the freight yard or en route an employee accompanying the shipment would reconsign it to the bootlegger under a spurious label as paint or varnish. What made reconsignment almost foolproof was the fact that from the moment the railroad issued a bill of lading the shipment belonged to the consignee, not to the shipper. The bill of lading thus became as negotiable as a bank draft, and the railroads had to honor the routing orders of the last consignee. In this way alcohol consigned to Manufacturer John Doe in Boston might pass through a dozen hands before it reached Bootlegger Richard Roe in Miami.

During Major Mills' tenure as prohibition administrator of the Second District a New Jersey outfit calling itself the Percheron

Products Company was challenged to show bills of sale of the toilet articles for which it had purchased 900,000 gallons of alcohol. It could show none. At about the same time two trucks carrying between them fifty barrels of alcohol, dispatched by the Brooklyn Alcohol Company, one of the country's largest denaturers, parked in an alley en route to a consignee while "scrapers" removed the identifying marks on the barrel heads preparatory to reconsigning them. Federal agents caught them at it. The following day a squad from Mills' office paid the Brooklyn company a surprise visit and demanded to see the consignee's receipts. A clerk promptly produced them. His mouth fell open when the visitors then asked him how the consignee could possibly have received the barrels when they were at that moment in government custody.

A somewhat more sophisticated practice was to change the barrels' markings inside the delivery truck as it moved along. Hidden from public view, two scrapers, having obliterated the original markings, would stencil on new ones and label the barrels PAINT.

Frequently, the manufacturers listed by a lawless denaturer were merely cover houses existing on paper only or perhaps with a one-room office and a single employee to sign alcohol receipts and otherwise counterfeit legal clearance. The Whyte Company, one of 130 New York cover houses traced by Mills' investigators, admitted receipts of 14,500 gallons of products lightly denatured and therefore readily cleaned alcohol, but failed to prove the disposition of a single pint through legal retail channels.

The amount of ethyl alcohol diverted at the first stage was paltry by comparison to the amount diverted at the third, the manufacturing stage. Of the end products those containing specially denatured odorless alcohol were the most highly prized by the bootleggers since they required far less manipulation.

George Bieber, Chicago criminal lawyer, remembers Cosmo Hair Tonic

I was fifteen when the Volstead Act went into effect, working in the Division Flower Shop on the corner of Western and Division streets. The owners weren't interested in selling flowers. They kept half a dozen bunches in the window, but if some stranger came in and placed a big order, they'd fill it through a genuine florist nearby and send it out under the Division label. That was my job, standing around in the front of the shop and handling people who actually wanted to buy flowers.

The boss was Vincent "Schemer" Drucci. They nicknamed him Schemer because of the wild schemes he was always thinking up to defeat the law. The real business of the Division Flower Shop was converting denatured alcohol into drinkable liquor. Drucci and his partners had first set up a hair tonic plant. This entitled them to buy No. 39B alcohol [½ gallons of diethyl phthalate—nauseating but not deadly—to 100 gallons of ethyl alcohol].

Up to a point the Cosmo Hair Tonic Company was legitimate. They advertised widely. They even paid celebrities to endorse the product. I recall seeing on billboards: PAUL ASCH—he was a well-known bandleader—USES COSMO HAIR TONIC. And they sold quite a number of bottles. Not nearly as many as their books showed, though. To deceive the government inspectors, they would sell a few hundred cases to a friendly wholesale distributor and throw in a few hundred more free as a bribe. The books would then show sales of thousands, and on the basis of such a big volume the government would allot the company corresponding amounts of 39B alcohol.

The conversion to drinkable liquor took place in the basement of the flower shop under the direction of a chemist we all called Karl the Dutchman, who was formerly employed by a toothpaste manufacturer. (Years later I represented Karl when the manufacturer sued him for counterfeiting the toothpaste and underselling the original name brand. The case was settled out of court.) To fake scotch, bourbon, rye or whatever, Karl would let the rectified alcohol stand for a few weeks in charred barrels in which authentic whiskey had been aged. I would pick up these barrels from a cooperage on Lake Street. They brought enormous prices—as high as $50 or $60 a barrel. The owner's son would help me load them onto a truck, and I remember he wore a diamond ring the shape of a barrel. Sometimes Karl used ordinary barrels in which he mixed the alcohol with shavings from charred barrels. Either way the alcohol would absorb the flavor of whiskey.

Some of Drucci's customers came from out of town, and if he figured a man was a shnook, he would sell him the liquor in a trick 5-gallon can. This can had a tube soldered inside to the top and bottom. Only the tube contained whiskey. The rest of the can was filled with water to give it weight, as the shnook would discover when he got it home.

*There was another unusual feature of the flower shop basement—a
life-size picture of a cop. The boys used it for target practice.*

*While working for Drucci, I studied at night to get my high school
credits, and after I passed my exams, I went straight to law school. In
those days the Illinois law didn't require prelegal training. I started
practicing the day after I got my license. My first clients were people
I'd met as a kid through the flower shop operation. They would be
charged with violating Section 3—the state liquor law. I represented
fifty or sixty of them all together, including Vince Drucci, Bugs Moran,
who was Al Capone's chief competitor until the St. Valentine's Day
massacre removed Bugs' top men, and Sam "Golf Bag" Hunt, who
allegedly went around with a tommy gun concealed in a golf bag. In
most cases the court would sustain my motion to exclude evidence on the
grounds that it had been illegally obtained and discharge the defendant.
In order to obtain evidence of bootlegging, the police would usually have
to make an illegal entry—they couldn't get a search warrant on the
mere suspicion that liquor was present—and, of course, evidence so
obtained was inadmissible. But often the police were less concerned
with establishing admissible evidence than with putting the bootlegger
out of business. They would wreck the premises and destroy all the
equipment. They would, that is to say, if he didn't have the right
connections. Otherwise, they would leave him alone and raid his
competitor across the street.*

*Drucci had the right connections. The Division Flower Shop kept
going right up to the end of prohibition, but not under Drucci's
ownership. He lost his cool one day while being taken to police
headquarters in a squad car and made a grab for the arresting officer's
gun—or so the official version ran. The officer killed him.*

Not all bootleggers commanded the services of technicians like
Karl the Dutchman or cared to install the costly, complicated
and time-consuming fractionating stills needed to thoroughly
clean denatured alcohol. A hasty partial cleaning might be
attempted in some noisome secret cellar, loft or barn by mobsters
with a knowledge of distillation limited to stoking a fire under an
iron boiler. But many bootleggers, untroubled by the danger to
the consumer, were satisfied to market an alcohol that didn't
smell or taste too dreadful, however deleterious the denaturants,
after coloring and flavoring it to simulate whiskey or gin.

In 1923 the Surgeon General of the U.S. Public Health

Service, Hugh S. Cumming, reviewed the analyses made by government chemists of samples collected from confiscated bootleg liquor. Most of it showed traces of one or more poisons, including wood alcohol, phenol, mercuric chloride, sulfuric acid, hydrochloric acid, pyridine, benzol, aniline, iodine. According to Cumming, denatured alcohol had come to constitute the bulk of the ingredients used by bootleggers. "America's new national beverage," Major Mills called it.

At the time of these analyses reports of deaths by alcohol poisoning were pouring into the Prohibition Bureau—from Philadelphia in January alone, 307; from Chicago since the preceding October, 163, among them several children whose mothers had fed them a spoonful of whiskey to cure a cold. During the next four years the chemists analyzed samples from hundreds of thousands of contraband gallons. Almost 99 percent contained denaturants. In 1927 the deaths totaled 11,700.

Industrial alcohol was, of course, no novelty. The demand for it had been increasing since the turn of the century as the chemical industry expanded and developed innumerable new products. To encourage this growth, the government, in 1906, exempted industrial alcohol from the excise tax on distilled liquor, provided denaturants were added to make it unpotable. Before prohibition no temptation existed to rectify and market this denatured alcohol as a beverage. But after 1920 poison liquor abounded, especially in regions far from the coast and land frontiers where the real stuff was harder to get. The bureau knew this not only from the samples its chemists analyzed, but, statistically, from the withdrawal permits it issued. Its records showed that in 1925 about 87,000,000 gallons of ethyl alcohol were legally distilled. Six million went to hospitals, doctors, pharmacists and research scientists. The remaining 81,000,000 gallons were supposedly denatured and distributed to about 1,000 industrial companies. But nothing like 81,000,000 gallons appeared in the finished products. The Prohibition Bureau could not account for at least 10,000,000 gallons. Where did they go? Almost certainly to bootleggers' cutting plants and thence into the stomachs of unsuspecting customers. At a conservative estimate 10,000,000 gallons would make up into 100,000,000 quarts or nearly a bottle for every man, woman and child in the country.

When, in 1926, the bureau, having utterly failed to stem the diversion, proposed to double the amount of wood alcohol in its formulas for complete denaturation, it provoked howls of indignation among wet legislators and the antiprohibition press. The government, they charged, was trying to enforce the law by deliberately poisoning its violators. Senator William Cabell Bruce, Democrat, of Maryland said: "The Volstead Act has converted the federal government with its denaturing outfit of poisons and filth into a more monstrous Caesar Borgia than any that medieval Italy ever knew." The New York *World* echoed the analogy. The Borgias, it declared, poisoned only individuals, but the United States government planned collective slaughter. "A skull and cross-bones becomes the badge of the enforcement service. . . . [The Borgias] never could be accused of preparing venomous doses for purposes of reform." The New Haven *Journal-Courier* protested: "To meet the frailties of human nature by processes that do not prevail in the enforcement of any other law, save that of capital punishment, is a perversion of sound government and public morals."

But the fatalities drew no sigh of regret from Wayne Wheeler. "The government is under no obligation to furnish people with alcohol that is drinkable when the Constitution prohibits it," he argued, adding, "the person who drinks this industrial alcohol is a deliberate suicide."

John Arthur Henricks, electrochemist and member of Alcoholics Anonymous, remembers jake and chock beer

It blistered my lips. It burned worse than Tabasco. It was liquid fire, the wildest, most horrible drink you can imagine. I tried some once, just to show off, in Texas where the mark of a man was not to cut your jake with water but toss it down straight. It stoned you into a weird type of intoxication, a violent, brawling, broad-chasing insanity. Matter of fact, jake got to be a police blotter nuisance. In Oklahoma respectable people rose up in arms, the church ladies screamed and the legislature finally passed a law making Jamaica ginger elixir illegal. Only the powdered gingerroot could still be used for medical purposes, but I don't think a pound of it was sold in the whole state. The bootleggers went right on supplying the same old jake. You could walk into any drugstore and with a wink get a bottle.

Another time with some Texans in Big Spring, showing off again, I *was drinking lousy white corn out of a fruit jar, and I started to be derogatory about the quality of their local beverages. I told them what a civilized community we had in Chicago, where I came from, and how you could get beer, delicious beer for hot-weather drinking. "Son," said one of the Texans, "can you drink beer?" "That's my drink, boy," I said. "I was raised on beer." "Well," says he, "we reckon we can show you a little Southern hospitality and get you some beer." We drove for miles out into the brush country to a Tobacco Road character who brewed this chock beer. The name comes from the Choctaw Indians. They were kind of low man on the Five Nations totem pole as far as bootlegging went, but they did evolve a distinctive home brew which, after yeast fermentation of malt, molasses and hops, they laced with shelled corn and raisins. I don't believe I drank more than two or three bottles. It was the damnedest stuff—practically explosive. I passed out cold.*

I became a problem drinker at about fifteen, an instant boozer. Prohibition was probably a determining factor, but by no means the only one. When the old church ladies say you're not to drink anything, it's a worthy challenge. It lighted my fuse. In high school I had as my peer group a number of buddies, all of them rebellious and openly defiant like most of the public at that time, and they drank with me. None of them became alcoholics, though, as I did.

My father drank a lot, a common thing in his line of business. He managed the Knickerbocker Ice Company in Chicago, where I was born. It was essentially a restaurant and saloon business, and he was a very gregarious type—looked like Jackie Gleason, hale and hearty, and he fitted right into that scene. I think the change in the quality of booze after prohibition, the horrible stuff you got, brought out the worst in him, made him a problem drinker. That and his getting older. The aging drinker loses his tolerance. My father would have qualified very well for my present fellowship. But nobody realized it then. His only admonition to me was that you should always drink like a gentleman. The old tradition. People who fell on their face were not socially acceptable.

I was still very young when my father went into a new business—freight car manufacturer and maintenance repair. It took us to New York City, where he superintended the Interboro Rapid Transit yards. We attended the Cathedral of St. John the Divine, and I was imbued with the spiritual approach, awed by the whole thing. The conflict in me between good and evil came when I was torn loose from that atmosphere—adolescence is always upsetting anyway—and transplanted to the wide open city of West Hammond, Illinois, my father's next assignment. West Hammond was so notorious that the citizenry changed the name to Calumet City, but it remained just as notorious. It vied with Cicero in ignominy.

In the church I went to there (this was well into prohibition) we had a little phenomenon common enough in churches, we had the sanctimonious closet drinker—in this instance, the choirmaster. He was a real heavy drinker, and he tried to cover it up by dousing himself with French cologne, which smelled worse to me than whiskey. We kids sneaked a drink from him now and then. There was also plenty of liquor around my house, and I dipped into that. As I say, I wasn't sixteen yet. At first it was strictly showoff, like smoking cigarettes, to impress your peers, and I made rapid headway. The DeMolay, the junior auxiliary of the Masons, a kind of Cub Scout approach to Masonry, blackballed me because of my drinking. Drinking got me into trouble at school, too. The mark of manhood in my group, as you went from knickerbockers to long pants, was to walk up one side of State Street and drink a beer in every joint—there were dozens of them—then down the other side the same way. None of us ever quite made it.

I went to Indiana University. Those were my golden years. Hoagy Carmichael was a junior then at Indiana. He wrote some of his best music there. Bix Beiderbecke and the original Wolverines played at all our big dances. During holidays, back home in Chicago, I'd go to the Friar's Inn to drink and listen to Leon Rappolo, who invented that fantastic clarinet style whereby Benny Goodman rose to glory. . . . It was the peak of the bathtub gin era, the real white hot.

At Indiana they picked me to find some good liquor for a visitor from Wabash College, a Phi Gamma Delta man no less and a millionaire, coming to a weekend football game. This was Ed Ball, later chairman of the board of his family's Ball-Mason jar company in Muncie. We aimed to wine and dine him royally, impress him, so he'd remember us after he got to head the company. I went down to a pool hall to see my favorite bootlegger, but damned if he hadn't been knocked off in a gang shoot. So I had to pinch around and bring back what I could. It turned out to be the vilest gin ever made. I was amazed. We damn near killed Ed Ball. He laid around for hours, green and groaning. We all got deathly sick.

I couldn't graduate from Indiana because my father came down with a terminal cancer and I had to go to work. My first job was with a refinery construction company, and I traveled all over the Southwest with a bunch of wild Cal City polack and Irish bricklayers and riveters, heavy drinkers all. We had no trouble getting a drink anywhere, not even in Oklahoma, which entered the Union as a dry state.

In Big Spring, Texas, we found a special situation. There was no budget to speak of for law enforcement officers' salaries. They had to make it themselves. The old sheriff, Jess Robbins, and his deputies worked on a fee basis. The penalty for being drunk and disorderly was a fine of $17.80. The county got $2.80, the deputy who brought you in got $5, and Jess got $10. They only locked me up once. The reason for this immunity was because my co-workers needed somebody to bail them out, and I was in the payoff end as the materials clerk. The one time they arrested me I asked Jess, after I sobered up, how he classified offenders. "Well, you're a pretty good boy," he said. "You get your boys out, you help me. You notice I don't throw you into the cooler, though I think sometimes you've had more to drink when you come here to get them out than they had when they went in. As a general approach to the matter, if it's one of our own boys and if he can move any of his ten fingers, he really ain't drunk, but one of you damn mouthy Yankees, by God, if I can smell liquor on your breath, you're drunk and disorderly."

Oklahoma had the worst epidemic of jake foot I ever ran into. There were small towns where practically every drunk dragged one foot or the other—hundreds of cases, many of them on the way to total paralysis.

For twenty years I went on drinking practically anything alcoholic I could lay my hands on. Then in 1945 I joined AA and haven't lapsed from sobriety since.

The poor man's thirst gave rise to a plethora of cheap, plentiful regional concoctions varying in potency and toxicity according to the ingredients at hand and the skill of the moonshiner. In the Deep South a relatively safe beverage was black-strap alky or pack, distilled from New Orleans molasses. The term "pack" may have derived from a British general named Packenham who died in the Battle of New Orleans in 1815 and was supposedly shipped home preserved in a cask of rum. Rugged Southwestern topers of meager means, who found the fulminating chock beer insufficiently stimulating, would add snuff to the bottles and bury them in the hot sand for further fermentation. In the Midwest they would scoop out a hole in a block of ice, fill it with lemon extract and pour off the liquid, which, being alcohol, didn't freeze. Midwestern farmers favored pumpkin wine, prepared by emptying a pumpkin, introducing cider, alcohol or fruit, sealing the opening with wax and letting the mixture ferment for a month or so. In Kansas, another poor man's drink was white line, alcohol diluted with water; in Washington and the contiguous sections of Maryland and Virginia, panther whiskey, which had a perilously high percentage of fusel oil; in the Virginia hinterlands, jackass brandy, reputedly distilled from peaches, but likely to erode the intestines; in Philadelphia, happy Sally, jump steady, and soda pop moon, all loaded with violently toxic industrial alcohols; in Chicago, yack yack bourbon, flavored and colored with burned sugar and iodine. Skid row bums everywhere drank rub-a-dub (rubbing alcohol) and other potions containing wood alcohol, thereby courting blindness or death. Some of them would recover a few mouthfuls by squeezing Sterno through a sock.

13. *The Instant Millionaires*

FROM Cincinnati's Queen City Avenue, paralleling the Ohio River, an unmarked road shot off toward farm country. Drivers could easily miss it unless they knew to look for a tar line curving into the side road. It had been painted there for the guidance of whiskey truckers, leading them to a hideaway, part depot, part arsenal, known as Death Valley Farm—the nerve center of a five-state bootleg network created through a brilliantly simple scheme by a former Chicago criminal lawyer.

George Remus handled medicinal whiskey exclusively. Early in 1920 he had abandoned his law practice, which was bringing in about $45,000 a year, to buy a distillery licensed to produce such whiskey. It was the first of several he bought in Ohio, Kentucky, Indiana, Illinois and Missouri. Soon after, he took title to both a bonded warehouse and a drug company authorized to withdraw whiskey. This triple ownership violated no law, and the law placed no limit on the quantity of whiskey he could distill, store or dispense for medical use, given the proper permits. It was en route to the drug company that the violations occurred. The whiskey never got there. Remus' trucks transported it instead to Death Valley Farm. The consignee named on the withdrawal permit never complained because the consignee was Remus. He simply robbed himself to pay himself.

The whiskey remained briefly in storage at the farm pending purchase orders from retail bootleggers scattered through the five states. Then the trucks would take to the road again with gunmen aboard to repel hijackers. Though the retailers invariably cut the contraband, it left Remus' custody in simon-pure state. "I never poisoned anybody," he boasted. "That's something they can say for Remus."

By 1924 he owned fourteen distilleries, employed 3,000 truckers, salesmen and guards and controlled approximately one-seventh of all the medicinal liquor distilled in the United States. From $2,000,000 the first year his gross income soared to

$25,000,000 the third. His capital together with the value of his regal estate exceeded $40,000,000. "I love the fine and beautiful things of life," he said, speaking of his treasure-stuffed mansion on Cincinnati's Price Hill.

Remus was a short, stout, bald man of Napoleonic aspirations. A fringe of iron-gray hair sprouted above his ears. His shiny pate distressed him, and in the presence of strangers he preferred to wear a hat. He dressed with sober elegance, favoring gray or black suits. His manicured fingernails glistened with pink polish. His speech retained some of the floridity of his courtroom days. He liked to dip into the literary classics. Despite his corpulence, he had developed powerful arms and legs as a swimmer and boxer. He exercised daily in a Cincinnati athletic club. He neither smoked nor drank. Hot-tempered and fearless, he had been known, upon warning that rival bootleggers planned to attack Death Valley Farm, to leap out of bed in the dead of night, grab a rifle and swear to shoot any intruder who dared show his face.

Remus' German parents brought him to Chicago in 1873 at the age of four. At nineteen he wangled a pharmacist's license by adding two years to his age on his application and went to work behind a drugstore prescription counter for $8 a week. At the same time he attended night law school, graduating in his late twenties. During his first year of practice he represented eighteen defendants charged with murder, most of them successfully. On several occasions he defended himself. In 1914 a client accused him of extracting $300 by fraud and won a judgment of $200. The Chicago Bar Association then summoned Remus before its ethics committee, but he managed to avoid disbarment. He next argued in his own behalf in a divorce suit filed by his wife, Lillian. The stated grounds were cruelty; the actual grounds, intimacy with a divorcée, the mother of two daughters, whom he employed in his law office, Mrs. Augusta Imogene Holmes of Evanston. The decree was granted with alimony of $25 a week, $50,000 outright to Mrs. Remus and $30,000 to her daughter, Romola. All in all it was a trying year for Remus. Immediately following the divorce he was charged with suppressing evidence to win a client's divorce suit, but once again he exculpated himself.

With prohibition Remus' clientele began to number some bootleggers. "I was impressed by the rapidity with which those men, without any brains, piled up fortunes in the liquor business," he recalled later. "I saw a chance to make a clean-up." Further reflection, buttressed by a countryside survey, led him to choose Cincinnati as the base of his operations "because eighty per cent of the bonded whiskey in the country was within three hundred miles of that city."

He left Chicago accompanied by Mrs. Holmes, who became both his wife and business associate. In his law practice he had accumulated cash assets of $100,000, but a down payment of $10,000 sufficed to secure his first distillery. He took on several partners, among them one Ernest "Buck" Brady, who also served as his "superintendent of transportation"—that is, antihijacker. Brady received a commission of $2 for every case that reached its destination. Deliveries were not accomplished without occasional bloodshed. Pitched battles on the highways left numerous fatalities. No guilt was ever assigned. The coroner's verdict invariably read: "Killed at the hands of persons unknown." Buck Brady earned altogether $208,000.

Remus' heaviest item of overhead expense, more than a fourth of his gross profit, was the payoff to local enforcement agents, storekeeper-gaugers and federal officials. Through the Ohio Gang's chief fixer, Jess Smith, who pocketed $1.50 to $2.50 per case, he obtained withdrawal permits galore. Altogether he paid Smith $250,000. His total bribery costs worked out to between $19 and $21 a case, but the price at which he sold it, $75 to $90, left ample margin for profit. The first year he sold 700,000 gallons.

Remus' methods of diversion varied imaginatively. When he bought the famous Jack Daniels distillery in St. Louis, he devised an intricate system of troughs and rubber hoses through which the whiskey was pumped directly from the barrels to barrels on the waiting trucks—37,500 gallons, or almost $4,000,000 worth one year. To conceal withdrawals from an incorruptible gauger, his distillers might fill some of the barrels with water and just enough alcohol to impart the odor or station a few barrels of unadulterated whiskey at the start of the gauger's customary inspection route. Remus controlled so many officials that he was once able to send eighteen freight cars of whiskey to the Cincinnati yards, whence his trucks whisked them to Death Valley Farm.

After occupying a Cincinnati hotel suite, Remus, his new wife and two daughters by her former marriage, moved in 1922 to the Price Hill mansion, a mammoth gray-stone fantasia standing in an arboretum of exotic specimens and ringed by a wrought-iron fence. Inside Remus installed a marble Greco-Roman swimming pool costing $125,000, a gold piano and a collection of rare paintings, books and manuscripts, including an autograph of George Washington. At a New Year's Eve housewarming 200 guests, lolling around the pool among a dazzle of flowers and foliage, were served vintage champagne by chorines in white tights while musicians, dancers and aquatic performers entertained them. Mrs. Remus herself, clad in a daring one-piece bathing suit, executed a series of fancy dives, and Remus, carried away by the Bacchic spirit, plunged into the pool wearing his dinner jacket. He then retired briefly to his library to eat ice cream in solitude and peruse a biography of Abraham Lincoln. At the climax of the evening he distributed gifts—$25,000 worth of jewelry to the men and to each woman, an automobile.

As Remus' business expanded, he took over an entire office building in the heart of Cincinnati, renaming it the Remus Building. But his operations had become so far-flung that he could no longer maintain sufficient secrecy. As early as October, 1920, in fact, the Internal Revenue Service had assigned an agent, William Mellin, to bug his office. "One day alone," Mellin later disclosed, "Remus had forty-four people in, and some of them were federal prohibition agents or federal marshals. He paid them an average of $1000 apiece." When Mellin reported his findings to a federal official stationed in Cincinnati, the latter told him: "Son, there's times when a man has to be practical in this business. It's only a few weeks to election and the information you've dug up is political dynamite. The men you spied on—the agents and marshals—are political appointees. Go back to New York [Mellin's home office] and forget it." Mellin went to Washington instead and submitted his report to the prohibition authorities there. No action followed.

For two years Remus continued to prosper under Jess Smith's protection. Then Smith failed him. Either he did not know or, if he did, could not prevent, what was happening in the investigative branch of the Department of Justice. No longer able to ignore Remus' blatant activities, it assigned a special agent to the case. As Remus later observed, "A few men have tried to corner the wheat market only to find out that there is too much wheat in the world. I tried to corner the graft market only to find out that there is not enough money in the world to buy up all the public officials who demand a share in the graft."

The special agent, Franklin L. Dodge, Jr., led a squad of raiders against Death Valley Farm on April 15, 1922, and seized enough contraband to obtain indictments of Remus and twelve associations for conspiracy to violate the prohibition laws. The blow fell just as the bootleg king was completing negotiations to purchase for $5,500,000 twenty-three more distilleries and warehouses, which would have extended his ownership of bonded whiskey to a third of the nation's total supply. A second indictment charged the defendants with "maintaining a common nuisance" at Death Valley Farm.

Jess Smith assured Remus that he would never be convicted. But despite additional payments to the great fixer, despite Remus' own eloquent courtroom performance and that of three crack defense lawyers from as many different cities, the U.S. district court at Cincinnati imposed a $10,000 fine and a two-year term in the Atlanta penitentiary, plus a $1,000 fine and a year in a county jail on the nuisance charge. The other defendants received slightly lighter sentences. Jess Smith then extracted a final payment of $30,000 from Remus by promising him that the court would suspend sentence. It did no such thing.

On January 24, 1924, Remus and his co-conspirators departed for Atlanta. A sizable crowd gathered at the Cincinnati station and cheered them as they boarded the train. Remus' largesse enabled them to travel in style. They rode a private car. A staff of waiters served them epicurean fare. Remus himself spent most of the journey reading Dante's *Divine Comedy*. On arrival he gave the porter his monogrammed silk shirt, and he gave Mrs. Remus, who accompanied him to the prison gates, a king's ransom in diamond jewelry.

In prison, Remus' standard of living underwent no very great alteration, thanks to a cooperative warden. A maid tidied his cell every day and brightened it with fresh flowers. He ate all his meals in the chaplain's home. Such light work as he cared to perform was confined to the prison library. Rumors of these privileges brought the warden, A. E. Sartain, under investigation. During a grand jury hearing Remus denied offering him any bribe, then in the same breath added: "What did it matter if I did give Sartain a little money for the few comforts I was

allowed? Anything that makes the awful grind of the penitentiary a little easier is all right, it seems to me. You know the
government doesn't lash your back with rawhide—it breaks you
mentally. . . . If I'm allowed a handful of comfort, the other
prisoners get a finger. It lets down the bars at least a little bit for
all." Warden Sartain ended up an inmate of his own prison.

A third indictment, meanwhile, was returned against Remus
for the diversion of whiskey from the Jack Daniels distillery. It
named twenty-five other defendants among them Mrs. Remus, a
Missouri state senator, a former federal tax collector, a former
circuit court judge, a member of the St. Louis Democratic city
committee and a member of the Republican city committee.
"Everything I did was by direction of my husband," said Mrs.
Remus. The charges were dropped probably because Remus had
agreed to testify in the long-overdue Senate investigation of the
Ohio Gang. He disclosed his payments to Jess Smith only to
retract his testimony a few months later.

While Remus was finishing his term in Atlanta, his marriage
collapsed. According to his account, Mrs. Remus, to whom he
had given power of attorney, not only stripped him of a
substantial part of his fortune—almost $2,000,000 by his reckon-
ing—but took a lover. To compound the offense, she chose as the
object of her affections none other than Franklin Dodge, the
special agent who had brought about her husband's downfall.
On the eve of his release Remus received copies of her petition
for divorce. He had barely time to file an answer, accusing his
wife of infidelity, before he was removed to the county jail at
Troy, Ohio, to serve his one-year sentence for maintaining a
nuisance at Death Valley Farm. It was late 1927 when he finally
returned to Cincinnati a free man, raging for vengeance. The
divorce hearing had been scheduled for October 6. It never took
place.

That morning Remus and a bodyguard-chauffeur, George
Klug, waited in a car outside the hotel where Mrs. Remus was
staying with one of her daughters, Ruth. As the two women got
into a taxi to go to Domestic Relations Court, Remus ordered
Klug to follow. Driving through Eden Park, the car cut in front
of the taxi, forcing it to a halt. Remus, shouting obscenities,
reached into the taxi, seized his wife by the wrists and pulled her
out. As her daughter and the cabdriver watched helplessly,
Remus clasped her tightly against his body and, drawing a

revolver, pressed it to her breast. "Oh, Daddy," she cried, "you know I love you. Don't do it." He fired once.

An hour later Remus wandered into police headquarters. "I want to give myself up," he said. "I've shot my wife."

"Where's the gun?" a police lieutenant asked him.

"I don't know."

"How many times did you fire?"

"I don't know."

"Did you hit her?"

"I hope so."

He had. She died in the hospital.

Remus betrayed no remorse. "I did a duty to society," he said. "The unwritten law will free me." He referred to the dead woman as "that decomposed mass of clay."

While awaiting trial in the Hamilton County jail, he resumed his flamboyant life-style. James Kilgallen, a crime reporter for Hearst's International News Service, recalled years later:

> I went to the jail on the chance I might be able to see Remus. It was no trouble at all. "Come right up," said Remus through a speaking tube. He had private quarters on the top floor. Unlike the other prisoners, he was not confined to a cell. He greeted me warmly and showed me his books and his wardrobe of about twenty suits of clothes. He had liquor available, although he never drank. Whenever he wanted, he could go up to the roof and exercise to keep himself fit.

At the trial, a national sensation which began on November 14 and lasted a month, Remus pleaded not guilty by reason of "temporary maniacal insanity." His attorney of record was Charles H. Elston, a distinguished figure later elected to Congress, but Remus conducted most of the defense himself. It was a spectacular performance. "Ladies and gentlemen," he declaimed, "before you stands Remus, the lawyer, and there"—arm outflung, pointing to the witness chair—"sits Remus, the lawyer." He desired neither sympathy nor compassion, he insisted. "I defended the sanctity of the home." But if the jury felt he deserved death, he would not have them flinch from their duty.

To demonstrate his tendency to momentary aberration, Remus threw a fit in the courtroom. With an ear-shattering scream he bolted from his chair, waving his arms wildly, then fell back, limp. After a court physician examined him, he was carried back to his comfortable jail quarters, an ice pack on his head, and put to bed with orders to remain absolutely quiet. When reporter Kilgallen looked in on him, Remus asked: "How did I do?"

The jury pronounced him not guilty "on the sole grounds of insanity," and the judge committed him to the Lima State Hospital for the criminally insane. Six months later he won his freedom by satisfying a three-judge panel that he had fully recovered his sanity.

Remus stayed in Cincinnati, where, he said, "the people have been good to me," followed criminal trials as a hobby, married again and lived to the age of seventy-nine. Regarding the killing of his second wife, he remarked after his release from the state hospital: "It's always a pleasant thought of contentment." Mention of prohibition drew tears to his eyes. "This infamous piece of legislation was put on the statute books by paid reformers, by men and women who make their living at the expense of thousands of unfortunates."

Few New Yorkers ever pursued a humbler trade than the Gowanus Canal "woodchuck." It consisted of scrounging logs washed ashore from the fetid little waterway skirting South Brooklyn and peddling them for firewood. In 1919 Edward Donegan was a Gowanus Canal woodchuck with a wife and three children to support. In 1920 he was a Croesus, maintaining two establishments—one for his family and another for his mistress—and banking as much as $500,000 a month.

Donegan, who loftily described his former occupation as that of a "contractor," achieved his rapid change of fortune with the aid of a bevy of women employed in the office of the New York State prohibition director, Charles R. O'Connor. As a precaution against fraudulent withdrawal permits the Prohibition Bureau had instituted a new rule requiring every bonded liquor warehouse and distillery, upon receipt of a permittee's order, to wire the state director for confirmation of its authenticity. The telegrams addressed to O'Connor passed through the hands of a twenty-one-year-old clerk named Regina Sassone, and it was her responsibility to check the permits and reply to the telegrams. How Donegan in his lowly station learned of this system and saw a way to exploit it, how he raised the initial capital and made his first contacts inside O'Connor's office are not known, but early in 1920 he managed to meet and charm Regina Sassone. He lavished gifts and money upon her, set her up in a room at the Hotel McAlpin and, in the words of a federal court judge, "debauched her." When, thereafter, Regina received a distiller's query, she would notify her lover and delay the reply.

Thus armed, Donegan would adopt one of two courses. If the permit proved genuine, he would approach the permittee, posing as a prohibition official, deplore the bureaucratic red tape that was holding up the answering wire to the distillery and promise to expedite matters for a fee. Most of the time he got it. In the case of spurious permits, he would first berate the offender for attempting to swindle the government and threaten to arrest him, then propose a payment of perhaps $20 a case as the only way to ensure authentication of the permit. If he agreed, Regina would type the confirming telegram, affix Director O'Connor's rubber-stamp signature and let Donegan take it to a Western Union office for transmission to the distiller. He paid her $100 a telegram, no munificent recompense considering that such messages released thousands of cases of liquor worth millions of dollars.

The second clerk whom Donegan subverted was a Mrs. Mary Parkins, age thirty-eight. She, in turn, recruited other clerks, as well as a dry agent or two. Donegan established her in a room adjoining Regina's, and with the door open between the two rooms they became his headquarters and the scene of festivities staged to allure potential accomplices from the Prohibition Bureau.

Donegan presently altered his *modus operandi*. He began dealing directly with bootleggers, selling them forged or stolen permits obtained through his bureau friends and, when they placed their order, seeing to it that Regina returned a favorable answer to the inquiry from the distillery.

What eventually aroused the suspicions of Chief Elmer Irey's Intelligence Unit were the sumptuous parties Mary Parkins gave at the McAlpin. Among the guests there appeared one day Agent Harold Stephenson from Washington. Secure in his conviction that every man had a price, Donegan offered him $10,000 if he could produce a permit to withdraw 100 barrels of whiskey. Stephenson promised to consider the proposition. Instead, he

L

reported the offer to Irey. A few days later an Intelligence Unit agent, Walter P. Murphy, accompanied by three other agents, arrested Donegan in the Hotel McAlpin suite. Searching him, they found a revolver, a deputy sheriff's badge, $45,000 in cash and a sheaf of distillers' telegrams querying O'Connor about permits which, if honored, would have unfrozen more than $4,000,000 worth of whiskey.

Donegan was not perturbed. As the agents later deposed, when Murphy handed back the $45,000, Donegan asked him, "How about five grand to fix this thing up?"

Murphy feigned innocence. "We're from Washington. We're not on to your New York slang. We don't know what you mean."

Donegan showed them. He peeled off five $1,000 bills and added $1,500 more for good measure. He then turned his back, coyly assuring the agents, "I'm not seeing anything." They marked the bills as evidence and charged Donegan with attempted bribery.

Donegan raised his offer to $25,000 and began stuffing bills into Murphy's overcoat. When this failed to move the agents, he called to a man waiting in the other room, a recently acquired member of his ring. Samuel Bien, alias Sigmund "Beansie" Rosenfeld—"the Honorable Rosenfeld," he liked to be called—card shark and gambling house operator, had been serving a prison term a few months earlier when he was pardoned because of failing health. He promptly joined the Donegan ring. Beansie's pockets, too, bulged with distillers' telegrams as he entered the suite. Assessing the situation at a glance, he held up a reassuring hand. "You don't know how to handle a thing like this, Eddie," he told Donegan (according to Murphy's report). "Let me handle this." He stepped up confidently to the agents. "I am placed in a very embarrassing position. I've dealt with all sorts of officials, city, state and federal and I want to fix this thing up. I'll give you fellows twenty-five grand and two bucks on every case we move. This is too sweet a racket to break up. And you won't be in any danger. I'll pay it through a third party. Anybody you say. A lawyer, politician, anybody." The agents made no sound or motion other than to jot down Beansie's remarks. "Look, fellows," he went on, "don't be silly. If I don't keep my word, do you know what you can do? You can arrest me."

They didn't wait. They delivered Beansie to justice along with Donegan, Regina Sassone and Mary Parkins. Their combined bail was set at $250,000, which Donegan produced within a few minutes. A federal grand jury indicted the foursome for stealing government documents and conspiring to violate the Volstead Act. In addition, the Internal Revenue Service filed a claim of $1,635,797 against Donegan for taxes due on his 1920 income, plus penalties. It was a historic tax claim—the first ever brought against a bootlegger.

Beansie Rosenfeld died in February, 1922, three weeks before the trial. The charges against Mary Parkins were dropped when she turned state's witness. William Fallon, the flashiest trial lawyer of his day— "the Great Mouthpiece"—defended Donegan. Regina made a full confession on the witness stand, and the jury, sympathetically viewing her as a victim of seduction, acquitted her. Donegan they speedily convicted. The judge fined him $65,000 and sentenced him to ten years in the Atlanta penitentiary. Mrs. Donegan was present, and she went into hysterics. "I paid them lawyers two hundred thousand bucks and got ten years," Donegan said after the appellate court confirmed the verdict. "A hundred-buck Brooklyn lawyer would have gotten me half that and been glad to wait for his money."

At the extreme opposite end of the New York social scale from the ex-Gowanus woodchuck were the four dashing La Montagne brothers. Scions of old-line French vintners with affiliates on both sides of the Atlantic, they had achieved distinction as businessmen, sportsmen and Social Registerites. They held memberships in a dozen elite Manhattan and Long Island clubs, including the Racquet and Tennis, the Piping Rock, the Knickerbocker and the Brook. Through the marriage of a cousin they were related to the illustrious president of Columbia University, Nicholas Murray Butler. Montaigu, the eldest La Montagne brother, an accomplished horseman, maintained his legal residence in France—the Château de Grandbourg at Evry Petit Bourg near Paris. Morgan, named after an uncle who owned a fleet of cargo vessels, occupied a suite at the Hotel Weylin near Park Avenue, while René, a seven-goal polo player, who headed the United States team during the 1914 series against England, shared his apartment a block away with the youngest La Montagne, William, a Yale graduate.

From their father, René, Sr., the brothers had inherited the international liquor concern of E. La Montagne's Sons, Inc.,

which controlled both the Green River Distilling Company and
the Eminence Distilling Company. When prohibition came, they
saw no reason to abandon the traditional family pursuit. Had not
their celebrated in-law, Dr. Butler, declared that the Volstead
Act contravened the will of the people and so to violate it could
constitute no offense against society?

The La Montagnes became the only bootleggers of impeccable
social status in the annals of prohibition. "If all the dry-law
violators were caught," René La Montagne later observed
"ninety per cent of the population would be with us." Permits
obtained through their connections in government circles enabled them to withdraw the liquor from the distilleries they
controlled and supply scores of New York's fashionable hotels
cabarets and private clubs. Already prosperous before 1920, they
amassed a fortune during the first three years of the decade at the
rate of more than $2,000,000 a year.

What finally brought the brothers to grief was a bachelor
dinner given in late 1922 at the Racquet and Tennis Club by a
fellow member named Bartow. They provided the champagne. A
disgruntled employee of E. La Montagne's Sons, Inc. reported
the affair to an assistant U.S. district attorney, Major John
Holley Clark, Jr., claiming, though unable to name them, that
several federal officials were accomplices. Summoning the brothers, Clark offered them immunity if they would identify the
officials. They haughtily declined and were indicted.

At first the brothers pleaded guilty, but when they realized
that many Racquet and Tennis Club confreres would have to
testify, to spare them embarrassment, they did the gentlemanly
thing and changed their plea. "According to several commenta-
tors," reported the New York *Times*, "high society has been
shocked." But if shocked, it was not so much by the brothers
bootlegging as by their undoing and the consequent stoppage of
excellent liquor. Luminaries of high society in New York and
Washington flocked to their aid. "Every conceivable political
and personal appeal, including an appeal by a Cabinet officer
was made to quash the case," Assistant Attorney General
Willebrandt revealed. "A part of the appeal included statements
that eighteen thousand dollars had been voluntarily contributed
to the Republican national campaign by politicians who had
secured permits for distilleries releasing the liquor in question
Attorney General Daugherty . . . told me of the pressure that

had been brought on him to 'call off any further investigation in this matter.' . . . I . . . advised the Attorney General that no prosecutor could in good conscience be requested to withdraw from the case without himself becoming an accomplice in suppressing a crime. . . ."

The federal court meted out relatively light sentences—a $2,000 fine for each brother, four months in the Essex County jail for René, Morgan and William and two months for Montaigu. In view of the influence exerted on behalf of the defendants the county prison committee formally cautioned Warden Richard McGuiness against any special treatment. After the prison gates closed behind them, the warden announced: "We haven't had such a group of good fellows here for a long time."

The *Social Register* continued to list the La Montagne brothers until 1929, then dropped them forever. President Coolidge, on the other hand, personally restored the citizenship rights they had forfeited as convicts.

One of Seattle's first radio stations, KFOX, was founded in 1924 by a former police lieutenant named Roy Olmstead and operated from his home. To the delight of mothers with small restless children, the early broadcasts included readings of bedtime stories by Olmstead's vivacious wife, Elsie. A persistent rumor held that the adventures of Flopsy, Mopsy, Cottontail and Peter, of the Brownies and Winnie the Pooh, as Elsie Olmstead transmitted them, concealed coded messages to vessels lying offshore with cargoes of Canadian liquor. Whether this was fact or fancy, nobody questioned Roy Olmstead's supremacy among regional rum-runners. According to the Seattle *Times*, he "was said to have corrupted more public officials than any other man in the Northwest while operating the biggest rumrunning venture in Puget Sound history."

For years the Olmstead liquor deliveries, made in trucks variously marked ORIENTAL BREAD, FRESH MEATS, DAIRY PRODUCTS, PASTRY GOODS AND COOKIES, averaged 200 cases a day and grossed monthly profits of almost $200,000. In addition to a radio station and a fleet of high-powered motorboats, Olmstead acquired an ocean freighter, land transport of every description, warehouses and a huge work force of scouts, dispatchers, loaders, truckers, checkers, salesmen, collectors, telephone operators, office clerks, bookkeepers and attorneys. Olmstead's crews, ninety men strong, bearing sobriquets like "The Plum," "Captain Hat," "Eddie the Pup," "Short Card," "Scrap Iron," referred to him with respect and affection as the Major or the Commander.

Many reputable Seattle inhabitants shared the sentiments of Olmstead's employees, for he was a sympathetic figure. Tall and trim, his quick, flashing smile like a beacon light, he operated with a bravura, a gaiety, that tickled the unredeemed. He scarcely troubled to conceal his exploits, sometimes unloading his boats onto the Seattle piers in broad daylight and twitting the dry agents for failing to trap him. The liquor he smuggled from British Columbia he sold uncut at only $2 a bottle more than the government stores there charged. No sum of money, he emphasized to his crews, could justify taking a human life, and he forbade them to carry weapons. To those myriad Seattleites who regarded the Eighteenth Amendment as an abomination calling for defiance, Roy Olmstead was a modern Scarlet Pimpernel. The city's exclusive Arctic Club welcomed him. William Boeing, the airplane manufacturer, was his friend, as well as his customer. "Public officials, professional men, merchants and bankers waved cheery greetings to him," a contemporary recalled. "Twenty men would speak to him in one block on Second Avenue. He had the power that goes with good liquor, easy to get, and good money, easy to give. He was the toast of parties where popping corks warmed the gregarious spirit. It made a man feel important to casually remark, 'As Roy Olmstead was telling me today.' . . ."

Like every state that anticipated the Eighteenth Amendment with its own noble experiment, Washington was accustomed to illicit booze by the time the national enactment took effect. In Seattle, within a few months of January 1, 1916, when state legislation closed the saloons, two gangs were competing to dominate the local liquor traffic. The brothers Logan and Fred Billingsley, fugitive bootleggers from their native Oklahoma, which had gone bone-dry four years earlier, opened the Stewart Street Pharmacy mainly to˙ sell whiskey "for medicinal purposes." The large quantities not covered by legitimate medical prescriptions they accounted for as "leakage and spillage." To investigators they would say, "Can we help it if we're the clumsy type?" The rival gang was headed by an ex-police officer, Jack Marquett. He had been dispensing liquor even before the Billingsleys, almost from the first day of state prohibition, and the encroachments of these aliens from Oklahoma enraged him, the more so when they expanded their operations and began importing liquor from California, Canada and Cuba. The ensuing warfare rapidly thinned the ranks of both gangs. In 1917 their leaders wound up behind bars, leaving a power vacuum. A horde of petty operators now fought savagely over the vacated territories—to the benefit of none. There were frequent hijackings and shootings.

Roy Olmstead, at age thirty the youngest lieutenant on the Seattle police force, followed the hostilities with more than professional interest and from it learned a great deal about methods of rum-running and bootlegging. As an officer universally liked and trusted, the friend of important politicians, including the mayor, he already wielded considerable influence behind the scenes of officialdom. With the Volstead Act and the accompanying steep increase in bootlegging profits, he determined to combine his knowledge and prestige to create an orderly, businesslike wholesale liquor organization. No moral qualms deterred him. In a society where practically everybody drank, where the available liquor ran to raw, if not impure, moonshine, was he not rendering a public service?

Olmstead's first major foray, undertaken three months after national prohibition began, while still a member of the police force, met defeat. In the small hours of a March morning he and a contingent of smugglers under his command were offloading a cargo of Canadian whiskey on a beach at Meadowdale near Seattle. Federal dry agents, who had somehow got wind of the shipment and were waiting in hiding behind a clump of trees, burst out, firing their pistols. The rum-runners escaped unhurt, but not before the attackers recognized Olmstead. They arrested him at home later that day. The police department discharged him, and he was indicted by a federal grand jury. On his plea of guilty the court fined him $500.

The setback failed to curb Olmstead's exuberant self-assurance. He next assembled a group of eleven silent partners, each of whom invested $1,000 while he put up $10,000, giving him 49 percent of the prospective profits, and with this capitalization he proceeded to develop an international enterprise. Bribed Customs inspectors in both Canada and the United States enabled him to establish a rum-running route between the two countries. The first intermediate point was a sparsely populated little island

off the coast of British Columbia. Here Olmstead's freighters
would deposit Canadian liquor which had been falsely cleared
for Mexico in order to avoid the exploitative duty of $20 a case
levied by Canada on consignments to the United States.
Speedboats from Seattle would then pick up the contraband and
transfer it to landings along Puget Sound.

Ever since the Meadowdale fiasco William Whitney, the chief
assistant to the district prohibition administrator, had kept
Olmstead under surveillance. The two men knew each other
from the days when Olmstead worked on the side of the law, and
now when they met, they would exchange banter in a games-
manly spirit. Whitney frequently dropped around at the dry
dock where Olmstead had his boats repaired to chaff the crews
and promise to catch them next time out, while they greeted him
with cheerful derision. What Whitney never mentioned were the
wiretaps on Olmstead's office phones which intercepted conversations with his associates, with conniving police and with
members of Whitney's own staff. For examples:

"Hello. Say, this is George Christy of the dry squad. Is the
Commander there?"

"No, Roy isn't here."

"Well, have you got the place at 2014 Third Avenue cleaned
up? We'll have to go up there."

"All right, Christy, Comstock called up a while ago and told me
about it and I told him to go up there."

OLMSTEAD (to an employee): ". . . We'll have to go slow until
the mayor gets back. I know about our Third Avenue joint. They
said a complaint had been made and they would have to get out a
paper on it, and I told them to go ahead. We'll just take things
easy and look after the best customers until Doc gets back."

A rum-runner named Green: "Hello, there, you old jailbird.
How are you?"

OLMSTEAD: "Hello, there, how are you? They came pretty near
getting you, didn't they?"

GREEN: "No. Any old time I can't get away from that damn fool
Whitney I want someone to shoot me."

Olmstead found out that his phone was tapped when the wiretapper hired by Whitney offered him the transcript of the conversations for $10,000. The rum-runner threw him out of the office. A subsequent search of the building uncovered one of the taps in the ladies' room. The discovery did not trouble Olmstead, for he clung to the belief, encouraged by his attorneys, that no court would admit evidence so obtained. Gleefully, Olmstead began phoning false landing instructions to his crews, then correcting them on an untapped outside phone. One night while Whitney, thus misdirected, kept cold, lonely vigil on a desolate beach a playful crew member slipped a lighted lantern into his car.

In November, 1924, the long-suffering prohibition official, having accumulated hundreds of hours of tapped dialogue, decided to strike. He led a raid against the Olmstead mansion in Seattle's gilded Mount Baker district. At the time Elsie Olmstead and a covey of guests were taking turns broadcasting bedtime stories over station KFOX. Whitney arrested them all. Then, impersonating Olmstead on the telephone, he tricked several of the city's leading bootleggers into making deliveries and arrested them as they came through the door. The following night he triumphantly hoisted the lantern that had been left in his car up a flagpole atop the federal building.

The indictment of Roy Olmstead and of ninety employees and associates, including his wife, occasioned no suspension of his illicit activities. Serenely trusting his attorneys to keep him at liberty, he continued, while free on bail, to run Canadian liquor into Seattle. Two years elapsed before he stood trial. A fourth of his co-defendants had meanwhile fled the country, and several others turned state's evidence. But no peril could ruffle Olmstead's composure. He laughed out loud in court when Whitney described the hoax that lured him to the wrong beach. He winked at one of the assistant U.S. attorneys whom he had regularly provided with liquor right up to the trial. Though the judge admitted the tapped conversations in evidence, Olmstead and his attorneys remained confident that the High Court would reject them.

The "Whispering Wires Case," as it was known, aroused grave concern among jurists throughout the country. Even that implacable hunter of Volstead violators, Mabel Willebrandt, deplored wiretapping. "I thoroughly disapprove of the practise," she wrote. "Irrespective of its legality, I believe it to be a dangerous and unwarranted practise in enforcing the law. Many of the states have laws against such interceptions of communications [though not the state of Washington]. The point involved in the Olmstead case was whether, in the absence of a state law, the Federal Constitution alone prevented obtaining evidence by tapping wires."

The jury convicted Olmstead and twenty-three co-defendants, but acquitted his wife. The court fined him $8,000 and sentenced him to four years at hard labor in the federal penitentiary on McNeil Island. The others got one year. "I am satisfied with the verdict," said Olmstead. "Twelve good, loyal Americans did their duty as they saw it. It was not the way I saw it. But they did their best."

His attorneys carried the appeal to the Supreme Court, which, to his incredulous dismay, upheld the admissibility of the evidence by a vote of 5 to 4, Justices Oliver Wendell Holmes, Louis Brandeis, Pierce Butler and Harlan Stone dissenting. It was cold comfort to Olmstead that Congress shortly passed an act invalidating such evidence.

After serving his sentence, the great rum-runner announced: "The old Roy Olmstead is dead." So it seemed. He became a Christian Science evangelist and a foe of alcohol.

George Remus, lawyer; Edward Donegan, scavenger; the La Montagne brothers, pre-Volstead wine merchants, sportsmen and ornaments of international society; Roy Olmstead, police lieutenant. . . . They exemplified a large, new class of offender created by prohibition. It was a class distinct from the professional mobsters, the Al Capones, the Jack Diamonds, the Dutch Schultzes, for whom prohibition offered only an additional source of easy money, though by far the most productive. Before prohibition the mobsters' chief ventures consisted of robbery, extortion, whoremongering, and after it they would also go heavily into labor-industrial rackets and gambling. But bootleggers of Olmstead's stripe had no general felonious proclivity. Without the Volstead Act their names might never have appeared on a police blotter. They eschewed terrorism as a business practice, sold drinkable liquor and saw no basic moral difference between themselves and their clientele. "Prohibition is not accepted by the great majority of people," said Remus, "and therefore bootlegging is not criminal." When convicted, René La Montagne remarked that most Americans shared his guilt. In support of these rationalizations the instant millionaires could cite commanding figures like Nicholas Murray Butler and Clarence Darrow. "The Eighteenth Amendment is an unenforceable law and a bad law," the latter contended. "It should be treated with contempt."

"Barefoot" Rafer Dooley remembers the gangs of St. Louis, Los Angeles and Chicago

I come from Tennessee. I run away from home with my older brother Ben. My folks were ignorant, illiterate hillbillies, but they tried to push me through school. I quit when I was fourteen, and Ben and me we come to St. Louis. I took whatever menial jobs I could find there and elsewhere around the country. I had the wanderlust in me, and I put it into effect. Most kids of that age can't. I was a dishwasher at a lumber camp. I started boxing and so forth until I articulated back to St. Louis.

I got to know a lot of the boys in St. Louis. I knew Dinty Colfax, who headed up what later come to be called the Egan Rats. He had a saloon, a hangout for the boys. The names that come from that are too numerous to mention. You could go on into the night—Fred "Killer" Burke,* Gus Winkler, Johnny Moore, Buddy Eppensheimer—on and on. I'd deliver messages for Dinty when he didn't want to use the phone. I would also deliver liquor for him to selected customers. I became known as trustworthy. I am working wherever I can work, and I am stealing whenever I have to steal.

I'd already been in Mexico—Tijuana—and I began running whiskey across the border into California. It wasn't as complicated then as it later turned out to be. For a small stipend the guard would look the other way, and you just drove your pickup truck past him.

I organized a bunch of constituents in Los Angeles. I made contact there again with my brother Ben. He's going much stronger than I am, so he fit me in with some of his operations which consisted of hijacking whiskey. We had some bad scrapes, and it looked as though we were going to get killed in California because we interfered with stronger mobs than us.

---

* One of the gunmen hired by Al Capone for the St. Valentine's Day massacre.

There never was a hijacking without a tipoff, you understand. I mean it would be impossible. Well, the gambling czar of Los Angeles at this time I'm telling about, in 1922 or '23, was Farmer Page, and he was in liquor too. One of his drivers told his girlfriend where he was going to collect a load of whiskey off a boat—in a little town that sits right on the ocean, adjacent to Long Beach. She happened to be a better girlfriend of my brother than she was of the driver. She revealed the information, so naturally we went in force with sawed-off shotguns, eight or ten of us. Numbers would be the thing that would dissuade you from resistance. We waited till they loaded the truck. Then we merely told them to get out of the truck, that we were taking over. No harsh words. We didn't harm them. We just drove off and left them as is.

We had a drop for the whiskey with another competitor of Page's. We had the whiskey sold before we stole it. He paid us $5,000, a lot of money at the time when eggs cost a dime a dozen and you could buy a new Ford for $350—a different monetary system than you have today. My cut was 10 percent.

It became known that it was us that did it. There was a confrontation, and quite a few of my brother's constituents fell and became deceased on the spot.

Ben branched out from hijacking into the heist. He was unsuccessful, and they sent him to San Quentin for ten years. I articulated back to Chicago. Having performed with the Egan Rats, some of whom had moved there from St. Louis, I arrived with good credentials, extremely good credentials, though I was only a neofate of eighteen. Nowadays a guy eighteen, with his long hair, you wouldn't pay him no more mind than a billygoat.

At this time, if I'm not exaggerating, there were about ten mobs in Chicago. There was the Irish North Side mob under Deanie O'Banion, the O'Connell mob on the West Side, Joe Saltis and Frankie McErlane on the South Side—oh, dear God, never has there been such tough guys. The North Side mob gave me and my constituents, about twenty-five of them, a district, an allocation, five blocks square. This was our reward for faithful service in the past. With it went the right to distribute beer and whiskey. Of course, you had to protect your territory. You couldn't call for help. If you couldn't handle it yourself, you lost it. That was the law. So when you were infringed upon, you had to retaliate immediately, or you didn't have nothing left.

It was a nightclub district, full of bars, handbooks, crap games, gambling joints. It seemed as though every wise-guy heist artist, mechanic, con man and burglar gaviated to our district. We worked hard for their patronage, and we reached some affluence, but easy come, easy go and all that.

I met muscle with muscle trying to defend my equity, and I got hurt. I was shot several times. In fact, I was cut all to pieces. The worst fight was with some characters who figured that if they eliminated me, they could take over the territory easy. That was unavailing. They didn't fare well at all.

I had a close immediate contact with Al Capone in about 1926. He urinated on my shoes. It happened in the men's room of the Croydon Hotel. He was drunk, and I was drunk. He didn't know who I was, but I knew him. I had the reputation of being the most vicious left-hook puncher in Chicago, that's the God's truth. We were on the verge of slugging it out when Al thought better of it. He didn't exactly apologize, but he admitted to a social error. I decided to overlook the indiscretion. We had a drink and whenever he saw me around town after that, it was "Hello, kid, how you doing."

Capone was cunning as a fox, but he didn't have the balls of the Irish gangsters like Deanie O'Banion, not the kind it takes to walk into a bank and make an unsecured loan at the end of a .38 pistol.

I was pinched at least a hundred times, but they made the charge stick only once. That was when I paid a return visit to California in 1927. They accused me of robbery. There was this rodeo, and it's alleged that me and some associates heisted the cash box. I laid in jail for a year. The experience showed me I was just a neofate, after all, and it taught me to improve my modus operandi.

As soon as I got out, I articulated back to Chicago. I never again fell into the toils of the law. Nevertheless, I became discouraged. The rewards were getting less and less. Too many of my constituents were being killed or landing in jail. Maybe I was luckier or maybe more sagacious. I decided to quit the rackets.

They say crime don't pay. You tell that to the real higherarchery of crime and they'll laugh theirselves into nervous hysteria. It don't pay only if you're apprehended. The saying is a misnomer used to dissuade youthful offenders from progressing into criminology. If the venture succeeds, like when me and my constituents were distributing liquor on the North Side, it pays fine, very fine indeed.

14. Nabobs and Bacchantes

UNTIL 1918 there had been hardly any organized resistance to the drys except for the brewers and distillers. In that year Captain William H. Stayton founded the Association Against the Prohibition Amendment with financial aid from both groups, incorporating it under the laws of the District of Columbia shortly after the Eighteenth Amendment had been ratified. As set forth in its charter, its two primary aims were "to prevent the country from going on a bone-dry basis" and "to make the Eighteenth Amendment forever inoperative." During the next eight years a number of related organizations sprang up, most of them backed by the liquor interests. The Crusaders consisted of young businessmen with the slogan "Join the Crusaders and substitute real temperance for prohibition temperance." The National Association Opposed to Prohibition, subsidized by hotel and real estate interests, chose the daisy as its emblem of protest, reminding members that Chaucer called it "the eye of the day." June 30, when the flower had reached full bloom, was named "Daisy Day," and on that day they wore daisy boutonnieres. The Moderation League demanded "a reasonable and working definition of intoxicating liquors." The Voluntary Committee of Lawyers repudiated the Eighteenth Amendment on the grounds that it was "inconsistent with the spirit and purpose of the Constitution of the United States and in derogation of the liberties of the citizens and the rights of the states as guaranteed by the first ten amendments thereto." Both the American Legion and the American Federation of Labor added their weight to the wet cause, the former objecting to "a condition endangering respect for the law," the latter crying, "No beer, no work!" Without going so far as to approve of hard liquor, Samuel Gompers, president of the AFL, said in hearings before the Senate Judiciary Committee: ". . . depriving the American workingman of his glass of beer tends to promote industrial unrest and discontent." Already in Detroit, dry since the spring of 1918, Gompers pointed out, the radical "Wobblies" (Industrial Workers of the World) were gaining ground in the factories. "Such things as this arbitrary legislation breeds Bolshevism."

Considering how deeply the Anti-Saloon League was entrenched, these countermoves appeared at first blush feeble and quixotic. Yet a tremor of apprehension agitated it when Captain Stayton's little sodality began to attract some redoubtable adherents. Foremost among them were the munitions makers, Pierre Samuel Du Pont and his brothers, Irénée and Lammot. Until 1926 the Du Ponts had been uncompromising prohibitionists, who long before the Volstead Act forced the saloons in the vicinity of their factories to close and threatened with instant dismissal any workman drinking on or off duty. Now, professing concern for the freedoms guaranteed by the Constitution, the Du Ponts assumed leadership of the AAPA. With them came such a concentration of wealth and power as the Anti-Saloon League had not known in its palmiest days. At full strength the association's directors totaled 227, nearly every one a titan of industry, commerce or politics. There was John J. Raskob, vice-president of E. I. du Pont de Nemours Company and chairman of the Democratic National Committee; Elihu Root, corporation lawyer, Secretary of War under William McKinley and Theodore Roosevelt, Secretary of State under Roosevelt and a Republican Party policy adviser; Herbert L. Pratt of Standard Oil; Charles H. Sabin, president of the Guaranty Safe Deposit Company and chairman of the board of the International Rubber Company; Percy S. Straus, president of R. H. Macy Company; Newcomb Carlton, president of Western Union. . . .

The defense of the Constitution did not solely motivate the association's tycoons. Between 1916 and 1921 the taxes collected by the federal government had increased sixfold. It occurred to the Du Ponts—how mistakenly seems fantastic in hindsight— that a restoration of legal liquor with the accompanying excise would eliminate the burden. In a circular distributed to the nation's heaviest taxpayers, Pierre Du Pont argued: ". . . the British liquor policy applied in the United States would permit the total abolition of the income tax both personal and corporate. Or this liquor tax would be sufficient to pay off the entire debt of

the United States, interest and principal, in a little less than
fifteen years." Irénée Du Pont believed that a tax on beer alone
would save just one of the family companies $10,000,000.

The association bemoaned the millions spent on prohibition
enforcement without appreciably curtailing the liquor traffic. As
the Prince of Wales quipped when asked during his visit to
America in 1925 what he thought of prohibition, "Great! When
does it begin?" Lulled into complacency by the assurances of
Wayne Wheeler that enforcement should require no vast sums,
Congress initially appropriated a mere $2,200,000. The 1921
appropriation was three times as much. In 1926 it came to
almost $10,000,000, and so it went until 1929 when a new
Prohibition Commissioner, James M. Doran, informed Congress
that any serious attempt to enforce the law would cost at least
$300,000,000. Congress gave him $12,000,000. Additional
amounts allocated to the Coast Guard and Customs to prevent
smuggling of liquor, plus the expense of criminal prosecutions,
brought the annual totals to more than $30,000,000, not
counting state and local expenditures for enforcement.

The AAPA modeled its tactics on those of the Anti-Saloon
League, backing wet candidates for office, pressuring newspapers
and magazines through their advertising departments and vilify-
ing the League's leaders. An Authors and Artists Committee,
constituting the association's propaganda arm, enlisted almost
600 members, among them the humorist Irvin S. Cobb; the
playwright Channing Pollock; the journalist Wallace Irwin; and
the writer of college boy stories (*Stover at Yale*) Owen Johnson.
Just as the Anti-Saloon League's American Issue Publishing
Company had inundated the country with literature depicting
the horrors of drink, so the committee produced tons of
pamphlets, books and cartoons ascribing to prohibition practically every evil that afflicted mankind. Disease, insanity, poverty,
unemployment, crime—all were on the rise or in decline
according to which organization's facts and figures were accepted
and how interpreted.

Whatever the association's motives and methods, it undeniably
reflected a growing disillusionment with the Noble Experiment
among people of all classes, as numerous referendums indicated.
Of 922,383 readers polled by the *Literary Digest* in 1922, 40
percent favored modification of the Volstead Act, and 20 percent
repeal of the Eighteenth Amendment. Four years later the

Newspaper Enterprise Association conducted a poll through the 326 newspapers it represented in forty-eight states and the District of Columbia. Of 1,747,630 votes cast, 81 percent were for either modification or repeal. During the same year the Hearst press ran a referendum showing a 75 percent majority for repeal.

Thoughtful drys, as well as wets, deplored the debasement of social intercourse resulting from prohibition. Ceaseless chatter about liquor monopolized attention at dinner tables, clubs, business and professional gatherings, where to get it, how to make it, whose bootlegger sold the best stuff. It was among the reasons that Henry Luce espoused the AAPA cause, one of the rare instances when he differed on a major issue from his Presbyterian missionary father. "All the drinking," the co-founder of *Time* recalled in later years, "and all the talk about drinking absorbed too much intellectual energy."

"According to the wets, I am dangerously ill," Wayne Wheeler felt obliged to announce publicly in the spring of 1927. "This is unmitigated bunk. I have been thirty-three years in this fight and will never quit as long as God gives me breath to fight the lawless contraband. My health is better than the wets wish it and it is getting better every week."

In reality he had been sick for months. Overwork had weakened the muscles of his heart, and he had also developed kidney trouble so that between his appearances before the Senate to press for more effective enforcement measures he was obliged to keep to his bed. The onslaughts of the wet legislators further depressed his spirits. One of them stigmatized him as "this hireling of the Anti-Saloon League." Another charged: "It has been again the tactics and trickery of the dry forces in this body to railroad a bill through the chamber without adequate debate, simply because Wayne B. Wheeler cracked his whip. . . . [He] had the temerity and audacity to tell Secretary Mellon that 'poison must remain in alcohol.' . . ."

Hoping to recover his health, Wheeler retreated during the summer with his wife and father-in-law to a cottage he owned at Little Point Sable, Michigan. On the evening of August 13 Mrs. Wheeler was preparing supper over a gasoline stove while Wheeler worked in his study upstairs. The stove exploded, setting fire to her apron. Wreathed in flames, she ran screaming into the living room, where her father, who had recently undergone a coronary, was sitting. The shock caused another attack, and he dropped dead. The explosion and the screams brought Wheeler rushing down the stairs. He wrapped a rug around his wife and smothered the flames, but she was too deeply burned. She died in the hospital.

The double tragedy hastened Wheeler's end. On September 2 he was taken to the Battle Creek Sanitarium, where he died three days later.

The supreme command of the dry forces now passed to James Cannon. The first major objective to which the bishop, a lifelong Democrat, applied his heightened powers was to dissuade his party from nominating Alfred Emanuel Smith for President in 1928. The jaunty, cigar-chomping governor of New York, then serving his fourth term, with his brown derby and sidewalk wit, epitomized everything Cannon and his Southern Methodist cohorts detested. He was a wet and a Catholic. The bishop attended the Democratic National Convention at Houston, Texas, in June, 1928, as a representative of the Anti-Saloon League and thirty other dry organizations, only to realize he could not stop Smith. Still faithful to the party, he endorsed a platform that included a pledge to enforce the Eighteenth Amendment, but when Smith, in his first campaign speeches, spoke out more forcefully in favor of modifying the Volstead Act, Cannon called it "political double-dealing . . . an act of brazen, political effrontery," bolted, threw his support to the Republicans' Herbert Hoover and launched against Smith one of the most vicious assaults in the annals of election campaigns. He made Smith's religion a central issue, arousing the fear among millions of Southerners that the Vatican would dictate White House policy. Anti-Catholicism was no new theme for the bishop, who years earlier, in his Baltimore and Richmond *Christian Advocate*, had characterized the Catholic Church as the "Mother of ignorance, superstition, intolerance and sin." Nor was his exploitation of anti-Semitism and xenophobia new. "Governor Smith wants the Italians, the Sicilians, the Poles and the Russian Jews," he told the Baltimore *Sun*. "That kind gives us a stomachache. We have been unable to assimilate such people in our national life, so we shut the door to them. But Smith says, 'Give me that kind of people.' He wants the kind of dirty people that you find today on the sidewalks of New York."

The League's tub-thumpers echoed the bishop. In Birmingham, Alabama, the Reverend Arthur James Barton warned native-born Anglo-Saxon Protestants: "Elect Al Smith to the presidency and it means that the floodgates of immigration will be opened. . . . Elect Al Smith and you will turn the country over to the domination of a foreign religious sect. . . ." On the same podium the Reverend Bob Jones ranted: "I'll tell you, brother, that the big issue we've got to face ain't the liquor question. I'd rather see a saloon on every corner in the South than see the foreigners elect Al Smith President!"

Had liquor alone been the issue, Smith would probably have made a far better showing at the polls, because support for modification or repeal was gaining. Smith had the moneyed AAPA behind him. His campaign manager was John J. Raskob ("this wet Roman Catholic Knight of Columbus and chamberlain of the Pope of Rome," Cannon termed him). But the appeals to bigotry found too wide a mark. The Solid South, for generations a Democratic bulwark, disintegrated politically. Eight Southern states voted for Hoover and, with the Republican ballots cast elsewhere, gave him a plurality of 6,378,747. In the new Senate the drys outnumbered the wets 80 to 16 and in the House, 329 to 106.

But it was the drys' last great victory. From that pinnacle their power steadily waned. Among the decisive factors was the emergence of an unexpected foe.

When the Nineteenth Amendment, which followed the Eighteenth by a year, granted women nationwide suffrage, the permanence of prohibition seemed assured. Even without the vote women had exercised a political influence through the WCTU second only to the Anti-Saloon League's. Not a single feminine voice had ever been heard to oppose prohibition. What chance did the wets stand now that women could take direct action at the polls? "Prohibition is here to stay," Izzy Einstein was convinced at the end of his career as the country's most successful dry raider. "The Amendment will not be repealed in our lifetime at least." Clarence Darrow reached the same conclusion. Much as he deplored prohibition, talk of repeal struck him as nonsensical. "Thirteen dry states with a population less than that of New York State alone can prevent repeal until Halley's Comet returns," he reasoned. "One might as well talk about taking his summer vacation on Mars." They failed to consider a rising phenomenon of the twenties—the New Woman.

On April 3, 1929, the Women's National Republican Club, which supported prohibition, gave a lunch in honor of its founder and president, Pauline Sabin, the wife of Charles H. Sabin, treasurer of the AAPA. Mrs. Sabin was also the first woman ever to have served on the Republican National Committee. Blond and diaphanous, an *arbiter elegantiae* of the Manhattan smart set, she had moved one Senator to exclaim when she first appeared in Washington: "Thank God, a pretty woman in politics at last!"

At their national convention the Republicans, like the Democrats, had pledged themselves to enforce prohibition, while Herbert Hoover promised, if elected, to appoint a commission to assess the efficacy of the Eighteenth Amendment. Soon after he took office, he appointed the Wickersham Commission but vitiated its efforts by saddling it with an inquiry into the entire question of law observance and enforcement. Mrs. Sabin startled her luncheon companions by announcing her resignation from the National Republican Committee in order to promote modified liquor laws. "I had thought . . . Mr. Hoover meant [a commission] to concentrate on the results of the Prohibition law alone," she told them. "I had worked for him in that belief. When I heard his inaugural address, I realized the commission was to investigate the whole federal system of jurisprudence. I made up my mind I was fooled."

To the dismay of the WCTU votaries, who could scarcely imagine such depravity in one of their sex, Mrs. Sabin reaffirmed her defection during the following days. "When I said . . . I was going to fight prohibition," she said, "the letters began pouring in from all over the country. . . . I found I had spoken for thousands of other women. There was a large group ready to be organized, wanting to be organized. . . . I could not turn back from it."

She rallied twenty-four sister dissenters, and in May 28 in Chicago, once the headquarters of the White Ribboners, they launched the Woman's Organization for National Prohibition Reform. Chapters were established in forty-three states and the District of Columbia. Within a year 300,000 women had joined, and by 1932 the membership had passed the 1,000,000 mark.

The preponderance of the leaders were, like Pauline Sabin, related by blood or marriage to bigwigs of the AAPA. Mrs. Pierre Du Pont headed the Delaware committee. The New York

State vice-chairmen included Mrs. Herbert L. Pratt and Mrs. Edward W. Root, daughter-in-law of Elihu Root and later the official historian of the movement. Rich, urbane, leisured and socially elite, they provided a striking contrast to the stolid, dowdy officers of the WCTU. In her history Grace Root mischievously juxtaposed photographs of the cool, svelte Mrs. Sabin and the heavyset president of the New York State WCTU, with her pince-nez and toothy grin, Mrs. Ella Alexander Boole—to devastating effect.

The "Sabine women," as they inevitably came to be called, did not flinch from a glass of wine or even an occasional martini. When entertaining, some served their guests from portable home bars, an innovation that appalled the journalist Ida Minerva Tarbell, who wrote in *Liberty* magazine: ". . . tea parties have become cocktail parties. . . . Where fashion points, women follow . . . these insidious and sinister ladies at the bar are too sinister a fact to deny. . . . They are spreading a fatal poison."

As they fought alongside their brothers-in-arms of the AAPA, gradually winning support among local, state and federal politicians, the attacks grew harsher. According to the *American Independent*, an organ of the Kentucky drys, "you cannot find two dozen women in the State who openly advocate the Repeal of the Eighteenth Amendment, who is not either a drunkard, or whose home life is not immoral, or who does not expect to get in the liquor business when and if it is again legalized." As for the WONPR, which was dispatching speakers to Kentucky, "most of them are no more than the scum of the earth, parading around in skirts, and possibly late at night flirting with other women's husbands at drunken and fashionable resorts." The chairman of the National Prohibition Committee, David Leigh Colvin, described them as "Bacchantian maidens, parching for wine—wet women who, like the drunkards whom their program will produce, would take the pennies off the eyes of the dead for the sake of legalizing booze."

Grace Root, at eighty-two, remembers the Bacchantian maidens
    It was my father-in-law, Elihu Root, who got me interested. That was the basis of the whole thing. He didn't suggest the work to me, but I was very fond of him, and I saw he had strong feelings about

prohibition, and once I see strong feelings in someone I care about, well, I just move along. Mr. Root didn't believe in women voting, though. That was a subject I would never discuss with him because he was too smart for me. Some of his ideas were old-fashioned. Of course, he was glad we could vote when the issue was prohibition.

We lived in upstate New York, my husband, Edward, and I, in Clinton where the Roots had lived for three generations. My father-in-law's summer home was next door, and we were constantly visiting back and forth. He had his whiskey at night, and he always wanted to give me some; but I drank only wine. I was very interested in wine. We always served it to our dinner guests. My husband had an excellent cellar. There was an Aloxe-Corton—1909, I think it was. . . .

I became involved in working for repeal because, as Mr. Root said, prohibition was an invasion of property rights, private rights. I used to take notes of things he said—I still have them here—and once I went with him to Washington when he argued before the Supreme Court against the validity of the Eighteenth Amendment. That was in March, 1920. [Reading from her notes]:

"Chief Justice White—Would you hold, Mr. Root, that if the people of the United States want to have prohibition, they cannot have it?

"E. R.—No, your Honor, there are two ways in which they can have it; they can make a new Constitution on new principles and put prohibition in it, or they can amend Article One, Section Eight [which defines Congressional powers], *and give Congress the power to deal with the liquor question in this way; but they cannot amend this Constitution fundamentally, and in a revolutionary spirit, as is now proposed."*

At the end of the argument Mr. Root said: "If your Honors find a way to uphold the validity of this amendment, the government of the United States as we know it will have ceased to exist. Your Honors will have found a legislative authority hitherto unknown to the Constitution and untrammeled by any of its limitations. Your Honors will have decided that two-thirds of a quorum in each house of the legislatures of three-fourths of the states may enact any law relating to the life, the liberty or the property of the citizen, to the form and fabric of this government or to the Bill of Rights itself, without recourse and without appeal. In that case, your Honors, John Marshall need never have sat on your bench."

When Mrs. Sabin started her group, I went to New York City and joined it. I had never met her before. I found a very beautiful woman, very interesting, with a deep, vibrant voice. Never said a dull thing. I went to many of the New York meetings after that, and every year I went to the national convention in Washington.

My assignment as a vice-chairman was to organize support for repeal in my part of the state. I worked with Mrs. Herbert Pratt. We'd move around from county to county, trying to stir up local feelings. We had charts with the counties marked in different colors, and if one of them came over to our side, we'd color it red. It was devilish hard work. Upstate New York was pretty dry. It was a milk shed. People took milk there. In the beginning the only people we could get on our side were the hop growers. Nobody else would listen to us. The first real support we had was from a German family of hop growers in Rome, the Kessengers. My son John, who was six then, took part in our work, too. He stole antirepeal signs off churches. The Methodist minister in Clinton preached a sermon against me, not by name, but everybody knew who he meant. He called me a scarlet woman. Before that I'd been in garden clubs and all those soft, gentle things, you know. And now, a scarlet woman! Some people would cross the street so as not to pass me.

Our national headquarters sent up a troop of professional speakers, and I was told I had to introduce them at meetings. I'd had very little experience at that sort of thing. I got up on the platform, and for the first time in my life I faced a microphone. I intended to say something about how glad I was to find an instrument that made speaking easier. What came out was, "This is the first time I've ever stood in front of a speakeasy." It brought down the house.

Incidentally, I never did go into a speakeasy. Some of the others may have, but I didn't even know where a single speakeasy was located in New York City. I believe there was a place called 21, but only from hearsay.

I was asked to debate in a church near Utica against a man—I don't recall his name—a famous dry. He was also violently opposed to smoking. If he saw a boy smoking, he'd knock the cigarette out of his mouth. "Don't you go, Grace," Mr. Root told me, and when I asked him why not, he said, "You can't make any sense with that man." Well, I did go, one of the only times I disagreed with Mr. Root. The question for debate was total abstinence or moderation. We didn't get very far. We couldn't reach any exact conclusion. The minister then suggested we all sing hymns. I happened to know most of the hymns by heart, so I stood up and sang brightly and that brought the house down, this tainted woman, so to speak, who could sing hymns. The congregation applauded me and booed my opponent off the platform. Mr. Root was amused and delighted.

The whole area wasn't absolutely bone-dry, mind you. There were moonshiners and home brew and all that sort of stuff. One night just before Christmas our house was hijacked. Yes, cars drove across the lawn, and there was a lot of running to and fro and shouting. My husband and I were in the bedroom on the top floor. He wanted to get out his revolver, but I made him stay quiet. All the lights went out. They'd cut the wires. They broke into the house with flashlights and went down to the cellar and took away most of the wine bottles. The Aloxe-Corton 1909. . . . Terrible thing. . . .

I worked with the WONPR right up to the end, always greatly influenced by my father-in-law. "The WCTU," he said to me one evening in his house [reading from her notes], *"have the inquisitorial type of mind. They want to coerce you into believing in their god. . . . Temperance means moderation through self-control. When one is grown-up, compulsion through the law creates revulsion. You cannot make man just through the law, you cannot make man merciful through the law, you cannot make a man affectionate through the law."*

The repeal movement was immeasurably advanced by the exposure of clay feet on some of the prohibitionist idols. In the hour when liquor became illegal, the New York State superintendent of the Anti-Saloon League, William Hamilton Anderson, had revolted millions of drinkers with his scoutmasterish exhortations. "Be a good sport about it," he had said. "No more falling off the water wagon. Uncle Sam will help you keep your pledge." They could scarcely repress a cheer when, five years later, he was convicted of third-degree forgery in a complicated piece of skulduggery involving League funds and sentenced to a term of one to two years at hard labor in Sing Sing.

Anderson's transgression was a mild blow to the drys compared to the seismic shock when Mabel Willebrandt resigned from the U.S. attorney's office in 1929 to become counsel for Fruit Industries, Inc., a merger of California wine grape growers. After narrowly interpreting the Volstead Act for nine years, "that Prohibition Portia" (in Al Smith's phrase) now exhibited the utmost liberality on behalf of her new employers. When they proposed to market the grape concentrate Vine-Glo, which fermented into wine with an alcoholic content of 12 percent, Mrs. Willebrandt convinced Washington that this would entail no violation of the law. As the corporation's literature reminded its prospective customers, "Section 29 of the National Prohibition Act specifically permits you to have Vine-Glo in your home provided simply that you do not transport it or sell it"—an exemption originally designed to keep the farm voters happy. In a subsequent political move the Federal Farm Board had lent the California grape growers $20,000,000 and so fostered home winemaking. Washington heeded Mrs. Willebrandt. Fruit Industries, Inc., was not molested. At the same time wine bricks manufactured by a competitor, Vino-Sano, Inc., were seized and the retailers arrested. Both wets and drys saw in this favoritism an expression of gratitude by the Hoover administration for Mrs. Willebrandt's services as an anti-Smith campaigner.

The drys were still shaking their heads over the former prosecutor's apostasy when their minister plenipotentiary, Bishop Cannon, "the most powerful ecclesiastic ever heard of in America" (as H. L. Mencken described him), fell with a resounding crash. Among the Wall Street bucket shops abounding during the twenties was Kable & Company, which offered speculators, through widely circulated ads, securities purchasable on the installment plan—in effect, on margin. Bucketing consisted of holding the customer's money pending a rise or fall in the securities he ordered, instead of investing it immediately. If the customer wanted to buy a stock selling at $100 and the bucketeers foresaw a drop, they would wait until it touched, say, $90, then buy for the customer's account and pocket the $10 difference. Conversely, if they figured a stock would rise, they might wait to sell at $110 and again keep $10 a share.

Eventually Kable & Company ventured a disastrously wrong guess. Having counted on a drop, it could not pay off its customers when the stock rose more than 100 percent. In June, 1929, the company was adjudged bankrupt, and the partners were convicted the following October of using the mails to defraud. Before the debacle one of the partners, Charles Kable, disclosed to the dripping wet New York *World*, for $4000, the transactions of their most distinguished speculator. The ensuing headlines screamed: BISHOP CANNON REVEALED AS A BIG CLIENT OF STOCK HOUSE ACCUSED OF FRAUD.

No evidence ever confirmed the suggestion of the state-appointed receiver that Bishop Cannon was a silent partner of Kable & Company. Actually, he had sustained considerable losses. An ordinary layman would have incurred no opprobrium in that day of frantic speculation, but the famed cleric had repeatedly denounced gambling. It was largely at his insistence that in 1922 the General Conference of the Methodist Episcopal Church, South unanimously adopted a resolution condemning it. "Instead of reading stock market reports," the New York *Times* commented, "it would be better if Bishop Cannon carried with him the injunction of the Apostle that a Bishop should not be 'greedy of filthy lucre,'" and the Reverend John Thompson, pastor of Chicago's largest Methodist Church, said in his Sunday sermon: "Bishop Cannon has brought reproach on the church of Christ and the cause so dear to Him and to all lovers of temperance and prohibition."

Hard on the heels of the bucket shop scandal, both the New York *World* and the equally wet Chicago *Tribune* exploded another. Rooting around in the bishop's past, they discovered that within weeks of America's entry into the World War he had bought 650 barrels of flour ostensibly to make sure the students at his Blackstone Female Institute would have enough bread to eat, but in reality to hold for sale at a black-market profit. He escaped prosecution only because the purchase preceded the effective date of the Food and Control Act by a few days. On the floor of the Senate, in late 1929, wet Senator Bruce unleashed the most blistering attack yet against the bishop:

> God forbid, that any clergyman of this kind should ever come near me for the purpose of exercising any office that appertains to his profession. If he were to sprinkle baptismal water upon the head of a child, I should expect its scalp to be scalded rather than hallowed. If he solemnized the marriage of a maid, I should not be surprised to see the orange blossoms that encircled her brow immediately wither and die under the scorching effect of his abusive breath. So far as I am concerned, just as soon would I have a raven perched upon the head of my bed as to have such a clergyman approach me in my last agony. If he were to preach a funeral sermon over my corpse, I believe that like Lazarus, I would throw aside the cerements of the grave and come back to life in indignant resurrection.

Going before a ninety-man Committee on Episcopacy, the bishop entered a feeble defense of his Wall Street maneuvers: He had been "buying stocks for investment," not gambling. If true, the *Wall Street Journal* observed, "then drawing one card to an inside straight is conservative investment." The committee nevertheless chose to accept the bishop's picture of himself as a blameless victim of slander jointly contrived by the wets and the Roman Catholics and decided not to try him. "See where the church freed Bishop Cannon for plunging in Wall Street," Will Rogers noted. "They figured that a man's losses were punishment enough. Imagine a preacher having to wait till the deacons come in with the collection box to see if he could buy United States Steel or just Blue Jay Corn Plasters. The church has asked him and any others to stop it. You can't save souls and margins too. During the crisis last fall the Bishop might have had one eye on the text, but I bet the other was on a ticker." (Fortunately for the bishop, what nobody suspected until Virginius Dabney, the editor of the Richmond *Times-Dispatch*, published it twenty years later in his biography, was that he had juggled his tax return to conceal his stock purchases.) Still direr accusations were to come.

In the summer of 1930 the bishop, aged sixty-five and widowed for two years, traveled abroad with his middle-aged secretary, Mrs. Helen Hawley McCallum, and married her in London. Before they returned to the States, the Philadelphia *Record*, followed by the Hearst press, published a story alleging that the bishop first introduced himself to Mrs. McCallum under a fictitious identity in the lobby of a New York hotel while his wife was still alive and ailing; that, finding her in financial straits, he gave her $20 the same night and not long after, settled on her a monthly allowance of $200 for the upkeep of an apartment; that he visited the apartment whenever he came to New York, including the day before his wife died. . . .

Once again the bishop faced an ecclesiastical investigating committee, charged this time not only with gambling, but hoarding, lying, immorality and adultery. Precisely what took place behind the closed doors of the hearing room none of the participants disclosed, but after five days the presiding Bishop William N. Ainsworth of Georgia announced: "The committee found no trial necessary." The exoneration, if such it was, did not bolster the bishop's fading prestige. The *Christian Herald* succinctly summarized his situation: "Bishop Cannon is a lost leader."

The Wickersham Commission submitted its final report in 1931 after two years of study. It proved a disappointment to the drys. While only one of the eleven commissioners, former Secretary of War Newton D. Baker, argued for repeal, seven recommended modifications or revisions. Instead of unconditionally prohibiting "the manufacture, sale or transportation of intoxicating liquors," as stipulated in Section 1 of the Eighteenth Amendment, the majority proposed to empower Congress to "remit the matter in whole or in part to the States, or to adopt any system of effective control," thus reopening the door to some legal liquor. Among the specific changes contemplated was the lifting of limitations on the amount of spirits available for scientific and medicinal purposes. As far back as 1921 Wayne Wheeler had antagonized the entire medical profession when he told the House in reply to the physicians' objections: "If it comes to the point where it must be a choice between medicaments for medicinal preparation and enforcement of the law, I think we must choose law enforcement."

The long economic depression ushered in by the stock market crash of October, 1929, further weakened the dry cause. With millions thrown out of work the repeal forces could plead compellingly that the money spent for enforcement would be more humanely applied to unemployment relief. The rebirth of the legitimate liquor industry, they also pointed out, would create hundreds of thousands of desperately needed jobs.

On June 6, 1932, a week before the Republican National Convention in Chicago, the Anti-Saloon League reeled under the blow dealt by a notable defector. Dr. Nicholas Murray Butler had proposed as a plank in the party platform a resolution calling on Congress to submit repeal to a national referendum. He received the following letter:

> With this resolution I am in complete sympathy. . . .
> My position may surprise you, as it will many of my friends. I was born a teetotaler; all my life I have been a teetotaler on principle. Neither my father nor his father ever tasted a drop of intoxicating liquor, nor have I. My mother and her mother were among the dauntless women of their day, who, hating the horrors

of drunkenness, were often found with bands of women of like mind, praying on their knees in the saloons. . . .

When the Eighteenth Amendment was passed I earnestly hoped . . . that it would be generally supported by public opinion and thus the day be hastened when the value to society of men with minds and bodies free from the undermining effects of alcohol would be generally realized. That this has not been the result, but rather that drinking has generally increased; that the speakeasy has replaced the saloon . . . that a vast army of lawbreakers has been recruited and financed on a colossal scale; that many of our best citizens . . . have openly and unabashed disregarded the Eighteenth Amendment; that as an inevitable result respect for all law has been greatly lessened; that crime has increased to an unprecedented degree—I have slowly and reluctantly come to believe. . . .

In my judgment it will be so difficult for our people as a whole to agree in advance on what the substitute [for the Eighteenth Amendment] should be, and so unlikely that any one method will fit the entire nation, that repeal will be far less possible if coupled with an alternative measure. For that reason I the more strongly approve the simple, clear-cut position you are proposing to recommend and which I shall count it not only a duty but a privilege to support. . . .

The letter was signed John D. Rockefeller, Jr.

In the 1932 Presidential race between Hoover and Franklin Delano Roosevelt prohibition no longer figured as a real issue. It was foredoomed whichever candidate won. Both had doubtless read the latest nationwide *Literary Digest* poll, which showed a prorepeal majority. After two decades of wobbling on the question, Roosevelt declared for repeal in his acceptance speech. So did Hoover, the first and only President to have assigned top priority to enforcement of the Volstead Act. In a complete turnabout that cost him almost all his dry support he advocated the restoration of controls to the states as each saw fit to impose them. The anguished drys turned away from both Presidential contenders, pinning their hopes on Congressional candidates. The archconservative Republican capitalists of the AAPA could not bring themselves to endorse the maverick Roosevelt, but as far as repeal was concerned, their efforts had already ensured it. The "parching Bacchantians" of the WONPR, who did endorse Roosevelt, could congratulate themselves on having helped to annihilate in less than three years what their sisters of the WCTU had taken sixty to achieve.

On December 6, 1932, the month following Roosevelt's landslide victory, Republican Senator John J. Blaine of Wisconsin drafted a joint resolution calling for submission to the states of the Twenty-first Amendment, which would void the Eighteenth. Two months later both houses adopted it and on February 21, 1933, Washington forwarded the proposed amendment to the state governors. Each state was to hold a referendum and, if repeal won, to summon a convention whose delegates would cast the final ballots in favor of the amendment—the first use of such a procedure for ratification in preference to legislative action. Ratification by the required two-thirds of the states was expected to take years. No sooner inaugurated than Roosevelt asked Congress to modify the Volstead Act to the extent of legalizing 3.2 percent beer. The diehard dry leaders girded for a last stand. In an appeal calculated to touch the stoniest heart, Mamie Colvin, wife of the prohibitionist elder and herself vice-president of the New York WCTU, held aloft a loaf of bread, a bottle of milk and some children's toys as she tearfully predicted: "If the man gets his glass of beer, the children will have to give these up for Christmas." Out West Billy Sunday thundered: "Somebody should smash the noses of our Congressmen! It's an insult to America! We don't want beer!" But Congress took no more than nine days to comply with the President's request.

Sudsy joy swept the nation. In the bar of Baltimore's Old Rennert Hotel admirers of H. L. Mencken gathered around while he sampled the first glass of the newly legalized brew. Lest it impair the sensitivity of his famous palate, he had declined a terrapin dinner offered him by the hotel manager. As the thirsty witnesses waited anxiously for his opinion, the "Sage of Baltimore" downed the brew, gullet wide open in the German manner, wiped the foam from his lips, paused reflectively and at length smiled. "Pretty good," said he, "not bad at all." The Great Austrian violinist Fritz Kreisler, homeward bound aboard the *Europa*, entered a mild dissent. He found the beer a trifle light, "but after all it's the sentiment of the thing." The president of the U.S. Brewers' Association counseled against "untoward celebration." Nobody heeded him. At the Anheuser-Busch Brewery in St. Louis, "beer capital of the nation," it was like a Hollywood premiere. Floodlights played upon the beer sheds as the first barrels were trundled forth, and 30,000 beer lovers surged toward the company trucks that formed a motorcade twenty blocks long. In Milwaukee lederhosen-clad celebrants sang *"Ach du lieber Augustin"* to the accompaniment of brass bands. A New York barbershop tenor was so infuriated by a fellow singer who muffed the words to "Down Where the Wurzburger Flows" that he seized him by the collar, shook him hard, and bellowed the correct words into his face: " 'The Rhine by the moonlight's a beautiful sight'—imbecile! 'When the wind whispers low through the trees'—*trees, trees*, not vines, idiot!" To show their contempt for near beer, a band of waiters drove a hearse full of it up to Manhattan's Brass Rail Restaurant, broached the kegs and poured the stuff down the sewer. Amid the frenzied bustle at the Kreuger Brewery in Newark, New Jersey, a worker was brained by a falling barrel. Crosse & Blackwell, the food specialty company, advertised "Pickles that come in 11-ounce beer mugs. This is the economical age—buy your pickles and get your beer mugs, too! Or buy your mugs and get the pickles thrown in!" A glass of beer generally cost a nickel, with free lunch and, in some places, entertainment included. A million and a half barrels were consumed within the first twenty-four hours, resulting in a nationwide shortage the following day.

Even the most sanguine wets were astounded by the speed with which the states acted on the Twenty-first Amendment. By early December, 1933, thirty-five of them had ratified it—one short of the needed three-quarters. The Utah convention shilly-shallied, though it had a mandate to ratify since November, because it wanted to make sure it would be the deciding thirty-sixth. "No other state shall take away this glory from Utah," proclaimed the president of the Utah League for Prohibition Repeal. Finally, on December 5 at 5:32 P.M., Washington time, delegate S. R. Thurman, having satisfied himself that the thirty-fifth state (Pennsylvania) had ratified, cast the last ballot for Utah. At seven o'clock, thirteen years, ten months and eighteen days after the Noble Experiment began, President Roosevelt signed the proclamation ending it.

Compared to the beery revels of the preceding spring, repeal came as something of an anticlimax. Because it came so late in the day, liquor trucks could not make many deliveries to hotels and nightclubs before closing time. The English liner *Majestic*, delayed at sea by a storm, with 6,200 cases in her hold, did not

dock until morning. Most speakeasies, having survived a decade
of illegality, declined to risk a penalty now by operating without
a license, but the licensing officials could not handle all the paper
work. The chairman of the New York State Alcohol Control
Board, Edward P. Mulrooney, stayed at his desk all night,
managing to validate barely 1,000 licenses. In Manhattan's
Merry-Go-Round the clientele groaned as the owner, Omar
Champion, pressed a button, stopping the bar's rotation, had
chicken netting thrown over it and a sign posted, NO DRINKS
SERVED. "Not a drop till we're legal," he said, and the frustrated
celebrants wandered off in search of a licensed water hole. The
average price of cocktails, where available, was 30 cents, down 50
percent. At the Waldorf-Astoria bar, the literary critic Benjamin
de Casseres waited, glass in hand, by a news ticker. The instant
Utah ratified, he put through a transatlantic call to a colleague
on the London *Sketch*. "Listen," he said, as he poured a finger of
scotch into his glass. "I could plainly hear the gurgle," the
Englishman attested later. The marquee of Minsky's Burlesque
in Forty-second Street spelled out in lights WE'LL TAKE GIN, but
the crowd in Times Square was far less boisterous than on any
New Year's Eve. New Jersey's Governor A. Harry Moore vetoed
a state liquor control measure as unconstitutional, thereby
postponing a legal drink for Jerseyites, but at the same time he
remarked: "Liquor has been sold illegally for thirteen years in
New Jersey and it will not hurt if this is done for a few days
more." Throughout the nation effigies personifying prohibition
were variously shot, hanged, drowned and electrocuted. New
Orleans greeted repeal with cannon salvos lasting twenty minutes. In Baltimore Mencken had his say, as usual: "It isn't often
that anything to the public good issues out of American
politicians. This time they have been forced to be decent." He
then perversely tossed down a glass of water. "My first in thirteen
years," he said. To the fuming Anti-Saloon League, the drinkers
were all "moral cowards," and it prophesied: "The people will
render their verdict when they see the difference between
prohibition and legalized liquor sales."

Epilogue 1973

Prohibition did not fail. On the contrary, it was a tremendous success. . . .
[It] brought significant gains to society as a whole and made life more livable
for many American families. . . . America prospered economically during the
Prohibition period . . . it actually brought about a marked decrease in crime of
all kinds. . . .

—A Methodist editor in *The American Issue*, January, 1970

THE death of prohibition was not the death of
prohibitionism. The body still twitches. Fifteen surviving dry
organizations coordinate their activities through the National
Temperance and Prohibition Council, and not by a hair have
they modified the dogma of their founding fathers. Although per
capita alcohol consumption has more than doubled since repeal
and the estimated number of alcohol abusers and alcoholics has
soared to about 9,000,000 or 5 percent of the population, they
will brook no approach to the problem that does not include the
total abolition of all alcoholic beverages. The idea of moderation,
of temperance in its original meaning, of exempting light wines
and beer, remains anathema. "We regret," says the WCTU,
"that the National Institute on Alcohol Abuse and Alcoholism
was set up with an appropriation of many millions of dollars to
promote 'responsible drinking' which is moderation and rehabilitation rather than prevention."

Wherever and whenever an opportunity presents itself to
restrict the freedom of drinkers or of liquor dealers the council's
member groups marshal their scanty forces behind it. They were.
heard from loudly, for example, by the Senate Committee on
Interstate and Foreign Commerce when it considered, during the
late fifties, a bill to prevent drinking aboard airliners. (The bill
was tabled, but the airlines voluntarily agreed to limit drinks to

M

two per passenger.) Many of the countless state liquor regulations
reflect little prohibitionist victories, such as Washington's no sale
by the drink between two o'clock in the morning and two in the
afternoon or after ten at night; Texas' ban against outdoor liquor
advertising within 300 feet of a church, school playground or
park; New York's ban against a saloon calling itself a saloon
. . . At last reports the dry groups were urging the inclusion of
alcohol in the Uniform Narcotics Act, which could make the sale
of liquor a prison offense.

The Prohibition Party, now headquartered in Denver, Colorado, continues to put forward candidates for political office. Its
perennial choice for President since 1964 has been Earle Harold
Munn of Hillsdale, Michigan, a Free Methodist and former
academic dean of Hillsdale College. His running mate in 1972
was a water pump salesman from Hutchinson, Kansas, Marshal
Uncapher. In the only four states where they could qualify on the
ballot they polled 13,444 votes.

The Anti-Saloon League, which renamed itself the American
Council on Alcohol Problems, has been reduced to a modest
office in Washington, D.C., and a staff of three—Mrs. Claribel
Snodgrass, the office manager; Clayton Williams, treasurer and
editor of the old *American Issue*; and the Reverend John L. Smith,
a Baptist from Birmingham, Alabama, the unsalaried executive
director who travels around the country striving to keep the torch
of prohibitionism aflame. According to treasurer Wallace, the
organization is financially dependent on "church persons."

Of the surviving dry militants the WCTU retains the greatest
vitality. It boasts 250,000 members scattered through fifty states
and affiliates in seventy-two foreign countries, maintains a
Washington lobbyist, still publishes its monthly organ, *The Union
Signal*, and holds annual conventions. It is not likely, however, to
attract many followers from the ranks of the Women's Liberation
Movement. "We feel the good Lord intended the wife to be in
subjection to her husband," says its president, Ms. Fred J. Tooze
(whose name rhymes with booze).

During the 1972 convention at Miami Beach President
Tooze's account, in her keynote address, of a particularly galling
recent defeat cast momentary gloom over the normally ebullient
assembly. Three months earlier the city council of Evanston,
Illinois, headquarters of the Union, home of its founder, Frances
Willard, and bone-dry by charter since 1855, voted to let

estaurants serve liquor. President Tooze vowed to fight the
uling in court. The convention went on to pass resolutions
upporting a Senate bill to require health warnings on liquor
ottles and another to prohibit television liquor ads during hours
when the young were apt to see them, opposing a third bill that
would allow confectioners to put cordials in candy, "inevitably
eading many children and youths to acquire a taste for alcoholic
everages at an age when they cannot realize the dangers
nvolved," urging newspaper and magazine food editors not to
rint recipes calling for liquor and the Small Business Adminis-
ration not to lend money to businesses which derive half or more
of their revenue from the sale of liquor. . . .

Narcotics have come to concern the White Ribboners almost
s much as liquor. "History repeats itself," wrote President Tooze
n the *Union Signal*, "except the culprit today is marijuana and
ubsequently, other hallucinogenic drugs, to replace or add to the
lcoholic beverage traffic." She compared the proposals to
egalize marijuana to the movement that killed the Eighteenth
Amendment. But there is a closer analogy. The old-time
emperance preachers held that beer led to rum and rum led to
lcoholism. According to a similar fallacy propounded by
atter-day extremists, who would impose Draconian penalties on
he country's millions of grass smokers, marijuana leads to heroin
ddiction.

Sources and Acknowledgments

ALL those survivors of the prohibition era who share with me their recollections are too numerous to mentio individually, and I hereby thank them collectively.

For a good deal of my documentation I am grateful to th Internal Revenue Service, the Distilled Spirits Institute, th American Council on Alcohol Problems (formerly the Anti-Sa loon League) and the National Woman's Christian Temperanc Union.

The following individuals were magnanimous with their tim and expertise: Herman Kogan of the Chicago *Sun-Times*; Stuc Terkel; King Solomon; Mrs. Jeannette Rattray, publisher of th East Hampton *Star*; Louis Sobol, the former Broadway colum nist; and Patterson Smith, the country's leading dealer i criminological literature.

To my requests for material from their files *True Detecti* Corporation (Albert P. Govoni, president), the Detroit *News* an the Cincinnati *Enquirer* responded handsomely. The newspape files most frequently drawn upon were those of the New Yor *Times* and the defunct New York *Herald Tribune* (now in th possession of New York University).

My task was immeasurably facilitated by the librarians of th New York Public Library, the Society Library of New York, th New-York Historical Society and the Ohio State Universit Library.

I am deeply indebted to William Targ of G. P. Putnam's Sor for his patient and sensitive editorial guidance and to my wif Evelyn, for her tireless help in research and the preparation the final typescript.

Books and Pamphlets

ANONYMOUS, *A Condensed History of the Prohibition Party*. Chicago, The National Prohibitionist, 1944.

————, *The Anti-Prohibition Manual*. Cincinnati, Ohio, 1916.

————, *Origin of the Maine Law . . . with a Brief Memoir of James Appleton*. New York, 1886.

————, *Permanent Temperance Documents of the American Temperance Society*. Boston, 1835.

————, *Program Material for Temperance Day or Frances E. Willard Day*. Evanston, Ill., National W.C.T.U. Publishing House, n.d.

————, *This Fabulous Century*, Vol. III 1920–30. New York, Time-Life Books, 1969.

ADE, GEORGE, *The Old-Time Saloon*. New York, Ray Long & Richard Smith, 1931.

ALLSOP, KENNETH, *The Bootleggers*. London, Hutchinson, 1961.

ANDERSON, WILLIAM H., *The Church in Action Against the Saloon*. Westerville, Ohio, 1906.

ANDREAE, PERCY, *The Prohibition Movement Addresses and Writings of Percy Andreae*. Chicago, Felix Mendelsohn, 1915.

ANGLE, PAUL M., and MIERS, EARL SCHENCK, eds., *The Living Lincoln*. New Brunswick, N.J., Rutgers University Press, 1955.

ANTI-SALOON LEAGUE OF AMERICA, *Proceedings of the Conventions*.

ARMSTRONG, LEBBEUS, *The Temperance Reformation*. New York, Fowler & Wells, 1883.

ARTHUR, T. S., *Grappling with the Monster or the Curse and the Cure of Strong Drink*. Edgewood Publishing Company, 1877.

ASBURY, HERBERT, *Carry Nation*. New York, Alfred A. Knopf, 1919.

————, *The Great Illusion*. New York, Doubleday & Co., Garden City, 1950.

ASSOCIATION AGAINST THE PROHIBITION AMENDMENT, *Scandals of Prohibition Enforcement*. March 1, 1929.

BANKS, THE REVEREND LOUIS ALBERT, *The Lincoln Legion, the Story of Its Founder and Forerunners*. New York, The Mershon Company, 1903.

BARBICAN, JAMES, *The Confessions of a Rum Runner.* New York, Ives Washburn, 1928.

BEECHER, LYMAN, *Autobiography, Correspondence, Etc.* New York, Harper & Bros., 1865. 2 vols.

———, *Six Sermons on the Nature, Occasions, Signs, Evils, and Remedy of Intemperance.* New York, The American Tract Society, 1827.

BENSON, LUTHER, *15 Years in Hell.* Indianapolis, 1885.

BLACK, JAMES, *Brief History of Prohibition and the Prohibition Reform Party.* New York, 1880.

———, *The Cider Question.* Chicago, 1862.

BROUN, HEYWOOD, and LEECH, MARGARET, *Anthony Comstock, Roundsman of the Lord.* New York, A. & C. Bony, 1927.

BYRNE, FRANK L., *Prophet of Prohibition: Neal Dow and His Crusade.* State Historical Society of Wisconsin, 1961.

CARSE, ROBERT, *Rum Row.* New York, Rinehart & Co., 1959.

CARTER, JACOB, *My Drunken Life from 1825 to 1847.* Boston, printed for the author, 1849.

CHERRINGTON, ERNEST HURST, *The Evolution of Prohibition in the United States of America.* Westerville, Ohio, The American Issue Press, 1920.

———, *History of the Anti-Saloon League.* Westerville, Ohio, 1913.

———, ed., *Standard Encyclopedia of the Alcohol Problem.* Westerville, Ohio, 1924. 6 vols.

CHURCHILL, ALLEN, *The Year the World Went Mad.* New York, Thomas Y. Crowell Co., 1961.

CLARK, NORMAN H., *The Dry Years of Prohibition and Social Change in Washington.* Seattle, University of Washington Press, 1965.

COLVIN, D. LEIGH, *Prohibition in the United States.* New York, George H. Doran Co., 1926.

COMMISSIONER OF PROHIBITION, *Annual Reports.*

CONDON, EDDIE (narration by THOMAS SUGRUE), *We Called It Music.* London, Peter Davies, 1948.

CRANFILL, JAMES B., *From Memory.* Nashville, Tenn., Boardman Press, 1931.

CUYLER, THEODORE Ledyard, *Recollections of a Long Life.* New York, American Tract Society, 1902.

Cyclopaedia of Temperance and Prohibition, The. New York, Funk & Wagnalls, 1891.

DABNEY, VIRGINIUS, *Dry Messiah: The Life of Bishop Cannon.* New York, Alfred A. Knopf, 1949.

DANIELS, THE REVEREND W. H., *The Temperance Reform and Its Great Reformers.* New York, Nelson & Phillips, 1879.

DARROW, CLARENCE, *The Story of My Life*. New York, Grosset & Dunlap, 1932.

DICKENS, CHARLES, *American Notes for General Circulation*. London, Chapman & Hall, 1842.

DISTILLED SPIRITS INSTITUTE, *Annual Statistical Review*, 1969.

———, *The Local Option Fallacy*. Revised. Washington, D.C., 1942.

———, *Summary of State Laws and Regulations Relating to Distilled Spirits*. Washington, D.C., June, 1969.

DOBYNS, FLETCHER, *The Amazing Story of Repeal*. Chicago, Willett, Clark & Co., 1940.

DORCHESTER, THE REVEREND DANIEL, *The Liquor Problem in All Ages*. New York, Phillips & Hunt, 1884.

DOUGLASS, EARL L., *Prohibition and Commonsense*. New York, Alcohol Information Committee, 1931.

DOW, NEAL, *The Reminiscences of Neal Dow*. Portland, Maine, The Evening Express Publishing Co., 1898.

DRAKE, SAMUEL GARDNER, *Biography and History of the Indians of North America*. Philadelphia, Charles de Silver, 1860.

DU BOIS, W. E. BURGHARDT, *John Brown*. New York, International Publishers, 1962.

DUTCHER, GEORGE M., *Disenthralled: A Story of My Life*. Hartford, Conn., 1874.

EARHART, MARY, *Frances Willard: From Prayers to Politics*. University of Chicago Press, 1944.

EASTMAN, MARY F., *The Biography of Dio Lewis*. New York, Fowler & Wells, 1891.

EDDY, DANIEL CLARKE, *The Sovereignty of Saloons in Cities*. N.p., n.d.

EINSTEIN, IZZY, *Prohibition Agent No. 1*. New York, Frederick A. Stokes Co., 1932.

FINNEY, BEN, *Feet First*. New York, Crown Publishers, Inc., 1971.

FORD, PAUL LEICESTER, *The Many-Sided Franklin*. New York, The Century Company, 1921.

FRANKLIN, FABIAN, *What Prohibition Has Done to America*. New York, Harcourt, Brace & Co., 1922.

FROTHINGHAM, OCTAVIUS BROOKS, *Gerrit Smith*. New York, G. P. Putnam's Sons, 1878.

FURNAS, J. C., *The Late Demon Rum*. New York, G. P. Putnam's Sons, 1965.

———, *The Road to Harpers Ferry*. New York, William Sloane Associates, 1959.

GOLDEN, HARRY, *The Right Time: An Autobiography.* New York, G. P. Putnam's Sons, 1969.

GORDON, ANNA A., *The Beautiful Life of Frances Willard.* Chicago, Woman's Temperance Publishing Association, 1898.

GOUGH, JOHN B., *An Autobiography.* Boston, 1845.

——, *Platform Echoes,* Hartford, Conn., 1886.

——, *Sunlight and Shadow or, Gleanings from My Life.* Hartford, Conn., 1881.

GRANLUND, NILS T., *Blondes, Brunettes, and Bullets.* New York, David McKay Company, Inc., 1957.

GREEN, ABEL, and LAURIE, JOE, *Show Biz from Vaude to Video.* Garden City, N.Y., Garden City Books Reprint Edition, 1952.

GRINDROD, RALPH BARNES, *Bacchus—An Essay on the Nature, Causes, Effects, and Cure of Intemperance.* New York, 1843.

HAWLEY, LOWELL S., and BUSHNELL, RALPH POTTS, *Counsel for the Damned.* Philadelphia, J. B. Lippincott Co., 1953.

HARLOW, RALPH VOLNEY, *Gerrit Smith.* New York, Henry Holt & Co., 1939.

HAWKINS, JOHN HENRY WILLIS, A public address recorded by the Reverend John Marsh in *Hannah Hawkins, the Reformed Drunkard's Daughter.* New York, American Temperance Union, 1846.

HAY, JOHN, *Lincoln and the Civil War in the Diaries and Letters of John Hay.* New York, Dodd, Mead & Co., 1939.

HAYNES, ROY ASA, *Prohibition Inside and Out.* New York, Doubleday, Page & Co., 1923.

Hearings Before the Subcommittee of the House Committee on Appropriations. Treasury Appropriation Bill for 1929.

Hearings Before the Committee on the Civil Service on H.R. 6147. February 28, 1924.

Hearings Before the Subcommittee of the Committee on the Judiciary, United States Senate, 69th Congress. First Session on Bills to Amend the National Prohibition Act, April 5 to 24, 1926. Washington, 1926, 2 vols.

HECKEWELDER, THE REVEREND JOHN, *Account of the History, Manners, and Customs of the Indian Nations, Who Once Inhabited Pennsylvania and the Neighboring States.* Philadelphia, The Transactions of the Historical and Literary Committee of the American Philosophical Society, Vol. 1, 1819.

HOBSON, RICHMOND P., *Alcohol and the Human Race.* New York, Fleming H. Revell, 1919.

HORAN, JAMES D., *The Desperate Years: A Pictorial History of the Thirties.* New York, Crown Publishers, Inc., 1962.

Hunt, The Reverend Thomas P., *The Cold Water Army*. Boston, 1840.

——, *The Life and Thoughts of Rev. Thomas P. Hunt*. Wilkes-Barre, Pa., 1901.

Hunter, Francis T., ed., *The Iron Gate of Jack & Charlie's "21."* New York, 1950.

Irey, Elmer L., as told to William J. Slocum, *The Tax Dodgers*. Garden City, N.Y., Garden City Publishing Co., 1948.

Isaac, Paul E., *Prohibition and Politics: Turbulent Decades in Tennessee 1885–1920*. University of Tennessee Press, 1965.

Kilpatrick, George, *Prohibition and the Bible*. Norristown, Pa., 1928.

Kitman, Marvin, *George Washington's Expense Account*. New York, Simon and Schuster, 1970.

Kobler, John, *Capone*. New York, G. P. Putnam's Sons, 1971.

Lee, Henry, *How Dry We Were*. Englewood Cliffs, N.J., Prentice-Hall, Inc., 1963.

Leonard, The Reverend Delavan L., *The Story of Oberlin*. Boston, The Pilgrim Press, 1898.

Lewis, Dioclesian, *The New Gymnastics for Men, Women and Children*. New York, Clarke Bros., 1867.

——, *Our Girls*. Harper & Brothers, 1871.

——, *Prohibition a Failure*. Boston, James R. Osgood & Co., 1875.

Livingstone, Belle, *Belle Out of Order*. London, Heinemann, 1960.

Lynch, Denis Tilden, *Criminals and Politicians*. New York, Macmillan Co., 1932.

Martyn, Carlos, *John B. Gough: The Apostle of Cold Water*. New York, Funk & Wagnalls Company, 1894.

McKenzie, Frederick Arthur, *"Pussyfoot" Johnson*. New York, Fleming H. Revell Co., 1920.

Mencken, H. L., *The American Language*, Supplement I. New York, Alfred A. Knopf, 1945.

Merz, Charles, *The Dry Decade*. Garden City, N.Y., Doubleday, Doran & Co., 1931.

Mezzrow, Milton "Mezz," and Wolfe, Bernard, *Really the Blues*. New York, Random House, 1946.

Monhan, M., ed., *A Text-Book of True Temperance*. New York, 1909.

Moray, Alastair, *The Diary of a Rum Runner*. London, Philip Allan & Co., 1929.

Morris, Charles, *Broken Fetters*. Philadelphia, 1888.

Morris, Joe Alex, *What a Year!* New York, Harper & Brothers, 1956.

Morris, Lloyd, *Incredible New York*. New York, Random House, 1951.

MORROW, HONORE W., *Tiger! Tiger! The Life Story of John B. Gough.* New York, William Morrow & Co., 1930.

NATION, CARRY A., *The Use and Need of the Life of Carry A. Nation.* Topeka, Kansas, F. M. Steves & Sons, 1905.

NATIONAL COMMISSION ON LAW OBSERVANCE AND ENFORCEMENT, *Report of the Enforcement of the Prohibition Laws of the United States.* January 7, 1931.

NATIONAL TEMPERANCE SOCIETY AND PUBLICATION HOUSE, THE, *Moderations Vs. Abstinence, or Dr. Crosby and His Reviewers.* New York, 1881.

NEW YORK SOCIETY FOR THE SUPPRESSION OF VICE, *Annual Reports,* 1874–1896.

NICOLAY, JOHN G., and HAY, JOHN, *Abraham Lincoln.* New York, The Century Co., 1890. 10 vols.

OBERLIN COLLEGE, *General Catalogue,* 1833–1908.

ODEGARD, PETER, *Pressure Politics, The Story of the Anti-Saloon League.* New York, Columbia University Press, 1928.

PALFREY, JOHN G., *Discourses on Intemperance.* Boston, 1827.

PALMER, A. B., *The Temperance Teachings of Science Intended for the General Public and Especially for Young People.* Boston, 1886.

PEEKE, HEWSON L., *Americana Ebrietatis.* New York, privately printed, 1917.

PHILLIPS, CABELL, *From the Crash to the Blitz 1929–1939: The New York Times Chronicle of American Life.* New York, The Macmillan Co., 1969.

PHILLIPS, THOMAS, JR., *The Bible Versus Prohibition.* Butler, Pa., 1930.

PICKERING, CLARENCE R., *The Early Days of Prohibition.* New York, Vantage Press, 1964.

PICKETT, ELBERT DEETS, ed., *The Cyclopedia of Temperance, Prohibition and Public Morals.* New York, Methodist Book Concern, 1917.

PILAT, OLIVER, and RABSON, JO, *Sodom by the Sea.* Garden City, N.Y., Garden City Publishing Co., 1943.

POTTS, RALPH BUSHNELL, *Seattle Heritage.* Seattle, Washington, 1955.

RANDELL, CAPTAIN JACK, as told to MEIGS O. FROST, *I'm Alone.* Indianapolis, Bobbs-Merrill, 1930.

RICHARDSON, BENJAMIN WARD, *Total Abstinence: A Course of Five Addresses.* New York, National Temperance Society and Publication House, 1882.

RICHMOND, A. B., *Leaves from the Diary of an Old Lawyer.* New York, American Book Exchange, 1880.

ROGERS, THE REVEREND PATRICK, *Father Theobald Mathew.* New York, Longmans, Green & Co., 1945.

ROGERS, WILL, *Rogers-Isms.* New York, Harper & Bros., 1919.

ROOT, GRACE C., *Women and Repeal.* New York, Harper & Bros., 1934.

ROURKE, CONSTANCE MAYFIELD, *Trumpets of Jubilee.* New York, Harcourt, Brace & Co., 1927.

RUDENSKY, MORRIS "RED", and RILEY, DON, *The Gonif.* Blue Earth, Minn., The Piper Co., 1970.

RUSH, BENJAMIN, *An Inquiry into the Effects of Ardent Spirits upon the Human Body and Mind.* Boston, 1790.

RUSSELL, FRANCIS, *The Shadow of Blooming Grove—Warren G. Harding in His Times.* New York, McGraw-Hill Book Co., 1968.

SALERNO, RALPH, and TOMPKINS, JOHN S., *The Crime Confederation.* Garden City, N.Y., Doubleday & Co., 1969.

SANDBURG, CARL, *Abraham Lincoln—The Prairie Years.* New York, Harcourt, Brace & Co., 1926. 2 vols.

———, *Abraham Lincoln—The War Years.* New York, Harcourt, Brace & Co., 1929. 4 vols.

SANN, PAUL, *The Lawless Decade.* New York, Crown Publishers, 1967.

SCHMECKEBIER, LAURENCE E., *The Bureau of Prohibition.* Washington, The Brookings Institute, 1929.

SCOTT, ANNE FIROR, *The Southern Lady from Pedestal to Politics 1830–1930.* The University of Chicago Press, 1970.

SHAW, ARNOLD, *The Street That Never Slept.* New York, Coward, McCann & Geoghegan, Inc., 1971.

SHAW, S.B., *Touching Incidents and Remarkable Answers to Prayer.* Grand Rapids, Mich., n.d.

SHAY, FRANK, and HELD, JOHN, JR., *My Pious Friends and Drunken Companions.* New York, The Macaulay Co., 1927.

———, *More Pious Friends and Drunken Companions.* New York, The Macaulay Co., 1928.

SHUMWAY, AL, and BROWER, C. DeW., *Oberliniana.* Cleveland, 1883.

SIEBERT, WILBUR H., *The Underground Railroad from Slavery to Freedom.* New York. The Macmillan Co., 1898.

SINCLAIR, ANDREW, *Prohibition: The Era of Excess.* Boston, Little, Brown & Co., 1962.

SINCLAIR, UPTON, *The Cup of Fury.* Great Neck, N.Y., Channel Press, Inc., 1956.

SMITH, ARTHUR D. HOWDEN, *John Jacob Astor, Landlord of New York.* Philadelphia, J. B. Lippincott Co., 1929.

SOBIESKI, JOHN, *The Life-Story and Personal Reminiscences of Col. John Sobieski.* Shelbyville, Ill., J. L. Douthit & Son, 1900.

SOBOL, LOUIS, *Along the Broadway Beat.* New York, Avon Publishing Co., 1951.

————, *The Longest Street*. New York, Crown Publishers, Inc., 1968.

SPRINGWATER, DOCTOR (pseud.), *The Cold-Water-Man; or a Pocket Companion for the Temperate*. Albany, 1832.

STEWART, ELIZA "MOTHER STEWART," *Memories of the Crusade*. Chicago, 1890.

STOUT, CHARLES TABER, *The Eighteenth Amendment and the Part Played by Organized Medicine*. New York, Mitchell Kennerley, 1921.

STOWE, LYMAN BEECHER, *Saints, Sinners and Beechers*. Indianapolis, Bobbs-Merrill, 1934.

SYLVESTER, NATHANIEL BARTLETT, *The History of Saratoga County, New York*. 1878.

THOMPSON, CRAIG, and RAYMOND, ALLEN, *Gang Rule in New York*. New York, Dial Press, 1940.

THOMPSON, ELIZA JANE TRIMBLE and others, *Hillsboro Crusade Sketches*, Cincinnati, 1906.

THRASHER, FREDERIC M., *The Gang*. Chicago, The University of Chicago Press, 1927.

TIETSORT, FRANCIS J., ed., *Temperance or Prohibition?* New York, The Hearst Temperance Contest Committee, 1929.

UNGER, SAMUEL, *A History of the National Woman's Christian Temperance Union*. (A PhD thesis.) Ohio State University, 1933.

VAN DE WATER, FREDERIC F., *The Real McCoy*. Garden City, N.Y., Doubleday, Doran, 1931.

VAN DOREN, CARL, *Benjamin Franklin*. New York, The Viking Press, 1938.

VILLARD, OSWALD GARRISON, *John Brown*. Garden City, N.Y., Doubleday, Doran, 1925.

WALKER, STANLEY, *The Night Club Era*. New York, Frederick A. Stokes Co., 1933.

WARBURTON, CLARK, *The Economic Results of Prohibition*. New York, Columbia University Press, 1932.

WHIPPLE, SIDNEY B., *Noble Experiment*. London, Methuen & Co., 1934.

WHITE, CHARLES T., *Lincoln and Prohibition*. New York, The Abingdon Press, 1921.

WILLARD, FRANCES E., *Glimpses of Forty Years*. Woman's Temperance Publication Association, 1889.

————, *Woman and Temperance*. Hartford, Conn., 1883.

WILLEBRANDT, MABEL WALKER, *The Inside of Prohibition*. Indianapolis, Bobbs-Merrill, 1929.

WILLOUGHBY, MALCOLM F., *Rum War at Sea*. Washington, D.C., Treasury Dept., United States Coast Guard, 1964.

WITTENMYER, ANNIE, *History of the Woman's Temperance Crusade*. Philadelphia, 1878.

WOODMAN, CHARLES T., *Narrative of Charles T. Woodman . . . A Reformed Inebriate*. Boston, 1825.

Fiction, Plays and Poetry

CLARK, MRS. D. O., *Slaying the Dragon*. New York, National Temperance Society and Publication House, 1888.

FOSTER, CONANT S., *The Temperance Telescope*, a poem. New York, National Temperance Society and Publication House, 1883.

PAULL, MARY ANNA, *Packington Parish, and What Happened in It*. New York, National Temperance Society and Publication House, 1886.

PENNY, LIZZIE, ed., *The Juvenile Temperance Reciter*. New York, National Temperance Society and Publication House, 1892.

ROUSE, LYDIA L., *Catharine Grafton's Mistake, or, Light at Eventide*. New York, National Temperance Society and Publication House, 1877.

WILCOX, ELLA WHEELER, *Drops of Water*. New York, National Temperance Society and Publication House, 1886.

WINSLOW, MARGARET E., *Saved by Sympathetic Kindness*. New York, National Temperance Society and Publication House, 1877.

WRIGHT, JULIA, *Jug-or-not*. New York, National Temperance Society and Publication House, 1870.

Periodicals

ANONYMOUS, "The Experience and Observations of a New York Saloon-Keeper." *McClure's Magazine*, January, 1909.

———, "Ups and Downs of the Flying Bootleggers." *Literary Digest*, April 4, 1925.

———, "What Lincoln Really Said," *Pictorial Review*, February, 1927.

ADAMS, SAMUEL HOPKINS, "My Bootlegger." *Collier's*, September 17, 1921.

BARTLETT, ARTHUR C., "Father of Prohibition." *The Mentor*, February, 1930.

BLYTHE, SAMUEL G., "The Booze Complex." *Saturday Evening Post*, March 4, 1922.

CAHALAN, JOHN C., JR., "Rum-Running at Detroit." *The Commonweal*, August 21, 1929.

CARPOZI, GEORGE, JR., "The Incredible Sheltons." *True Detective*, January, 1961.

———, "The Nine Lives of Legs Diamond." *Master Detective*, May, 1969.

———, "The Waxey Gordon Story." *True Detective*, April, 1961.

COOK, FRED, J., "The Dutch Schultz Story." *True Detective*, April, 1960.

CUNNINGHAM, BILL, "Liquor Floods the Campus." *North American*, June, 1930.

DAVENPORT, WALTER, "Bartenders' Guide to Washington." *Collier's*, February 16, 1929.

FLYNN, JOHN T., "Home, Sweet Home-Brew." *Collier's*, September 1, 1928.

FORD, COREY, "The Anti-Speakeasy League." *Vanity Fair*, May, 1930.

GEBHART, JOHN C., ed., "Reforming America with a Shotgun." *Washington, D.C. Survey Graphic*, November, 1929.

———, "Scandals of Prohibition Enforcement." *Washington, D.C. Survey Graphic*, March, 1929.

GRAHAM, STEPHEN, "The Bowery Under Prohibition." *Harper's*, February, 1927.

GREEN, WALTON, "Denatured Alcohol Our National Drink." *Saturday Evening Post*, January 28, 1926.

———, "The Twilight Zone of Prohibition." *Saturday Evening Post*, May 8, 1926.

HARDIN, ACHSAH, "Volstead English." *American Speech*, December, 1931.

HARLOW, RALPH VOLNEY, "Gerrit Smith and John Brown." *The American Historical Review*, October, 1932.

HARMON, WENDELL E., "The Bootlegger Era in Southern California." *The Historical Society of Southern California Quarterly*, December, 1935.

HARRIS, GARRARD, "The Rising Tide of Prohibition Law Violators." *The Outlook*, September 10, 1924.

HUTCHINSON, WOODS, "The Long Wake of John Barleycorn." *Saturday Evening Post*, March 20, 1920.

JOHNSON, WILLIAM "PUSSYFOOT," "I Had to Lie, Bribe and Drink to Put Over Prohibition in America." *Hearst's International-Cosmopolitan*, May, 1926.

KENNEDY, ALBERT J., "Saloons Retrospect-Prospect." *Survey Graphics*, April, 1933.

KENNEDY, JOHN B., "Under Cover. An Interview with A. Bruce Bielaski." *Collier's*, August 13, 1927.

LANDMAN, DAVID, "A Day to Remember." *Argosy*, May, 1960.

LAWRENCE, David, "The First Hundred Years of Prohibition." *Saturday Evening Post*, May 31, and June 14 and June 28, 1930.

Literary Digest, "Bootlegging and Murder in Detroit." September 29, 1923.

———, "Rich Bootleggers Sent to Prison." February 24, 1923.

———, "The Battle over 'Bricks of Bacchus.' " August 22, 1931.

———, "Introducing the Man Who Will Enforce Prohibition [John F. Kramer]." December 20, 1919.

———, "Killing Rum-runners—'Murder' or 'Justice'?" January 18, 1930.

———, "The Man Who Made America Dry [William H. Anderson] Tells Why, and How." August 16, 1919.

———, "New York's Poison-Liquor Epidemic." October 27, 1928.

———, "A Soldier to Fight Bootleggers." April 18, 1925.

———, "The Tiger Claws of 'Pussyfoot' Johnson." May 1, 1926.

———, "Washington's Prohibition Tragedy." March 1, 1924.

———, "Why the Nation Went Dry." January 25, 1919.

———, "Zero Hour in the Rum War." November 2, 1929.

LUNT, CAMMETT, "Intricacies of the Dry Law." *World's Work*, August, 1929.

MacDonald, A. B., and Cumming, Hugh S., "Bootleg Liquor—and How It Kills." *The Ladies' Home Journal*, May, 1923.

McNutt, William Slavens, "Wet Washington." *Collier's*, January 27, 1923.

Mills, Chester P., "Dry Rot." *Collier's*, September 17, 1927.

———, "Where the Booze Begins." *Collier's*, October 15, 1927.

Niebuhr, Reinhold, "Protestantism and Prohibition." *The New Republic*, October 24, 1928.

O'Donnell, Jack, "The Camels and the Wise Men of the East." *Collier's*, January 10, 1923.

———, "Can This Woman Make America Dry?" *Collier's*, August 9, 1924.

———, "They're Drinking More Than Ever." *Collier's*, June 21, 1924.

Pritchard, R. E., "The Failure of Prohibition in the South." *Harper's Weekly*, March 18, 1911.

Randolph, Vance, "Wet Words in Kansas." *American Speech*, June, 1929.

Rattray, Jeannette Edwards, "Rum-Running Tales from the East End." *New York Folklore Quarterly*, March, 1963.

Rodann, Curtis (Charles Remsberg), "Big Bill Dwyer—King of the Rum Runners." *True Detective*, February, 1961.

Ruhl, Arthur, "From the Jury Box." *Collier's*, May 26, 1923.

Shepherd, William G., "A Big Catch on Rum Row." *Collier's*, June 6, 1925.

———, "At the Rum Row War." *Collier's*, May 30, 1925.

———, "Kansas, by Ginger!" *Collier's*, July 26, 1930.

———, "The Price of Liquor." *Collier's*, December 1, 1928.

———, "Rotten to the Core." *Collier's*, September 19, 1925.

———, "The Rum Runner's New Enemy." *Collier's*, May 25, 1925.

———, "What Can a Wet Town Do?" *Collier's*, September 7, 1929.

———, "Who Laughs Last." *Collier's*, September 21, 1929.

Shepherd, William G., and Saunders, W. O., "Who Is Drinking in America—and What." *Collier's*, May 2, 1925.

Smith, Edward H., and Grey, John W., "The Sober Crook." *Collier's*, September 10, 1921.

A Symposium, "Prohibition After Eight Years." *Current History*, April, 1928.

Sobol, Louis, "Dear Old Golden Saloon Days." *Town & Country*, March, 1962.

———, "Speakeasy." *Hearst International-Cosmopolitan*, March, April and May, 1934.

TARBELL, IDA M., "Ladies at the Bar." *Liberty*, July 26, 1930.

TYDINGS, MILLARD E., "Suppressed Prohibition Killings." *Plain Talk*, November, 1929.

WHEELER, WAYNE B., "The Inside Story of Prohibition's Adoption." The New York *Times*, March 28–April 1, 1926.

WHITE, OWEN P., "Anti-Saloon Drinkers." *Collier's*, September 6, 1930.

———, "Dripping Dry Dallas." *Collier's*, July 20, 1929.

———, "Lips That Touch Liquor." *Collier's*, March 6, 1926.

WHITE, WILLIAM ALLEN, "As Kansas Sees Prohibition." *Collier's*, July 6, 1926.

WILSON, CLARENCE TRUE, "Call Out the Marines." *Collier's*, July 13, 1929.

WINKLER, JOHN, "Izzy and Moe Stop the Show." *Collier's*, February 6, 1926.

Unpublished Material

ANONYMOUS, Life of the Hon. James Black. N.p., n.d.

ANDERSON, WILLIAM H., Excerpts from a series of wire-recorded interviews, Columbia University's Oral History Project, 1950.

BOOLE, ELLA A., Excerpts from a series of wire-recorded interviews, Columbia University's Oral History Project, 1950.

CAMPBELL, MAURICE, The daily diary of Maurice Campbell, Federal Prohibition Administrator for the Eastern District of New York from July, 1927 to June, 1930. Typescript, the New York Public Library manuscript collection.

GROSS, M. LOUISE, Correspondence. The New York Public Library manuscript collection.

——, History of the Women's Anti-Prohibition Movement. The New York Public Library manuscript collection.

——, Papers, the greater part covering 1926–1939, relating to her officeship in the Women's Committee for Repeal of the 18th Amendment. The New York Public Library manuscript collection.

PICKERING, CLARENCE R., Typescript, relating his experiences as a special agent of the Prohibition Bureau.

RUDENSKY, MORRIS "RED," Typescript, recounting his adventures as a safecracker, and letters to the author.

Index